CAD Systems Development

Springer-Verlag Berlin Heidelberg GmbH

D. Roller   P. Brunet (Eds.)

CAD Systems Development

Tools and Methods

With 159 Figures and 6 Tables

Springer

Dieter Roller
Universität Stuttgart
Institut für Informatik
Breitwiesenstrasse 20–22
D- 70565 Stuttgart
Germany

Pere Brunet
Universitat Politècnica de Catalunya
Dep. de Llenguatges i Sistemes Informàtics
Av. Diagonal 647, 8a
E-08028 Barcelona
Spain

Cataloging-in-Publication Data applied for

Die Deutsche Bibliothek - CIP-Einheitsaufnahme

CAD systems development : tools and methods / D. Roller ; P. Brunet (ed.). - Berlin ; Heidelberg ; New York ; Barcelona ; Budapest ; Hong Kong ; London ; Milan ; Paris ; Santa Clara ; Singapore ; Tokyo : Springer, 1997
  ISBN 978-3-642-64523-5   ISBN 978-3-642-60718-9 (eBook)
  DOI 10.1007/978-3-642-60718-9

NE: Roller, Dieter [Hrsg.]

Typesetting: Camera-ready copy by authors
Cover design: *design & production* GmbH, Heidelberg

SPIN 10529763   33/3142 – 5 4 3 2 1 0 – Printed on acid-free paper

Preface

This book is based on lectures presented at the first seminar on CAD Tools for Products at the Schloß Dagstuhl International Conference and Research Center for Computer Science. Experts from academia and industry were invited, and reported on selected and relevant topics in the area. The resulting papers, published in this volume, give a state-of-the-art survey of the relevant problems and issues.

This volume is divided into six chapters, focusing on the most significant aspects in future CAD architectures, product modeling, feature based design, design of complex surfaces, parametric and constraint modeling, and algorithmic aspects.

The first chapter includes new advances in future CAD architectures, with contributions from Abeln, Dankwort, Hoffmann, Mink & Roller, and Krause, Jansen & Kiesewetter. In his section, Abeln presents the CAD-Reference Model join project, supported by the German minister for research. Proposals for an improved, feasible configuration for CAD systems are being generated. In the second section, Dankwort presents a common long-term strategy for the CAD-CAM R&D departments of the German automotive industry. It has lead to the concept of a new CAx system architecture which is described. Hoffmann presents an overview of the EREP project, offering a neutral CAD product representation able for exchanging design data that incorporates features and constraints. The fourth section is devoted to electrical engineering CAD systems. Mink and Roller make proposals for the development of the architecture of the new generation electrical engineering CAD systems, requirements for ECAD and differences with respect to mechanical CAD systems being emphasized. Eventually, Krause, Jansen and Kiesewetter propose a multimedia based working environment, allowing the integration of commercial CAD systems with distributed product data management into a system environment for distributed cooperative work.

Chapter two, on product modeling, includes three sections on product modeling tools. Jared discusses the main problems and trends associated with Design for Manufacture and Design for Assembly, and how to provide product model support for them. Mantyla's section deals with extracting reusable product data, presenting the process planning system MCOES++. MCOES facilitates the reuse of production data at various time scales on the basis of feature-oriented product and production process models. Finally, Rix and Kress discuss the integration of existing technologies in CAD modeling, design, analysis, simulation, networked cooperation and virtual reality, in order to use virtual prototypes to support the integrated product development process.

The third chapter presents new advances in feature-based design. Dealing with feature validation and conversion, Jan de Kraker, Dohmen and Bronsvoort present a new approach supporting multiple feature views of the product. A central cellular model links the feature models from the different views and performs feature conversion when needed. De Martino, Falcidieno and Petta present the feature recognition subsystem in an integrated system using design-by-features and feature recognition; it is based on a feature classification strategy. On the other hand, extending feature concepts to free form surface models is the goal of Hagen and Hahmann's section: they present feature stability as an analysis tool for complex surfaces, by detecting regions that are likely to bend or deform. Finally, a new representation scheme for feature based parametric design is proposed in Brunetti and Vieira's section: a parametric feature representation is introduced including geometry, topology, parameters and constraints, such that it can be used in feature-based parametric design integrating design by features and parametric design.

Chapter four, on complex surface design, includes three sections on novel techniques for surfaces. The transfinite B-Spline interpolation problem with derivatives is discussed by Gschwind and Hagen. They propose an scheme for the transfinite interpolation of a grid of B-Spline curves, G1 or G2 continuity being required. The problem is transformed into an equivalent point interpolation problem. Heinz's section describes an application of variational design algorithms to surface reconstruction with variable offsets. After this, Sapidis presents an algorithm for variable-order surface reconstruction through region growing, transforming a dense point cloud from range image sensors into a CAD polynomial surface model. Finally, the conversion of Dupin Cyclides into Principal Patches is studied by Zhou and Roller: the relationship between the two rational parametric representations of cyclides is studied and conversion algorithms are proposed.

Chapter five deals with parametric modeling and includes three sections. Pratt discusses several considerations which have arisen in the enhancement of STEP in order to support parametric and constrained geometry and feature-based representations. Rosendahl, Berling and Du propose a new kind of segments that encapsulate objects with possible geometric and numerical relationships among each other. Relationships are possible also between objects belonging to different segments. Eventually, a hybrid constraint solver using exact and iterative geometric constructions is presented by Hsu and Brüderlin: they propose a hybrid constraint solver on a graph, based on degrees of freedom and valencies which combines a direct geometric approach with an iterative algorithm based on the multivariate secant method.

Finally, several algorithmic tools for novel CAD architectures are presented in chapter six. Joan-Arinyo, Perez-Vidal and Gargallo introduce an adaptive algorithm to compute the medial axis transform of 2D polygonal domains. The algorithm is based on the refinement of a coarse medial axis transform by an adaptive subdivision of the polygonal domain. Garcia-Alonso and Matey's section is dedicated to tools for mechanical analysis and simulation: two network-based facilities for CAD-CAE of multibody systems are described, namely a computer supported cooperative work environment and a distributed simulation prototype. The section from Klein proposes an improved divide-and-conquer algorithm for the construction of the constrained Delaunay triangulation of a polygonal domain. After this, tools for handling very complex environments and assemblies are presented in the two final sections: Navazo and Vila propose an algorithm to compute a weak visibility graph for a large data set based on its discretization by means of a regular uniform grid, being useful as a preprocess step in walk-through navigations. On the other hand, Ayala, Brunet, Joan-Arinyo and Navazo discuss several simplification algorithms for the automatic generation of multiresolution models of polyhedral solids, presenting and discussing octree-based simplification algorithms.

Many people have contributed to the success of the seminar and to the preparation of this book. Particularly, we would like to thank the authors who submitted papers and prepared them for this edition, and we also want to thank the reviewers for their efforts in setting the standard for the quality of contributions in this volume.

Stuttgart / Barcelona   Dieter Roller
Autumn 1996   Pere Brunet

Contents

Chapter 1

Future CAD Architectures

Overview

The "CAD-Reference-Model" An Architectural Approach to Future CAD - Systems

Olaf Abeln*

This section describes a joint project being carried out by eight research centers in Germany, together with industry and CAD vendor participants. The objective is the development of a new-generation CAD system which builds on past experience but meets the requirements of users much more satisfactorily than is the case with existing systems. The paper concentrates on the "CAD-Reference-Model" which has been created during the initial stage of the project.

Introduction

The German industry has been using CAD-systems for more than twenty years. Most of the companies have installed some kind of CAD-workstation and software-packages for special tasks of the design process. But in the course of fulfilment of a business commission the penetration of using CAD-systems is lower than 20%. The rather complicated handling, the unmoveable structure of the systems, the overload number and variety of commands of the CAD-systems, the absence of any integration tools and the lack of a common product data model are the main reasons for this discrepancy and for the missing acceptance of the users. The future

*The Computer Science Research Center at the
 University of Karlsruhe, Karlsruhe FRG

CAD-systems have to bebased on a new concept, which is easily structured, can be configured and is able to support the whole design process, dealing with the special claims of a company and its products. The individual demands of a design engineer or a design group and the easy handling of the system have to be supported.

The joint project supported by the German Minister for Research and Development has been developed by eight research centers of Germany, accompanied by a group of different industry partners, vendors und users, to make proposals for a new system generation. It respects the long time experiences of different CAD-packages of the past and it makes a lot of proposals for an improved, but realizable CAD-system configuration. This paper presents the results of the existing works and the concept for further activities as a contribution to an international cooperation of standardisation.

The structure of the project

The whole project has been developed in the last two years and is divided in eight working packages. In the first step the main problems and demands from the application engineers point of view and the requirements for system improvements are described for dedicated fields. An answer is given in detail for a better solution to every package, described by network of single so called "data structure machines (DMS)"(figure 1), which is a new short and more abstract description for the following software engineering process and in a first approach is independent of any hardware and software. The working packages are described in the following :

I. Management of the Design Process
There is a need to initialize, supervise and control several aspects of the design process, in particular for the early phases.

These aspects include:

* Acceptance, analysis and management of design orders
* Supervision and control of all results of the engineering
  process

which means:

- the management of individual and company oriented design rules,
- the time and cost management of the design work inside the company and for the data transfer to the manufacturing unit,
- the management of corporate design work between the concurrent working of the designers and engineers of the main contractors und suppliers.

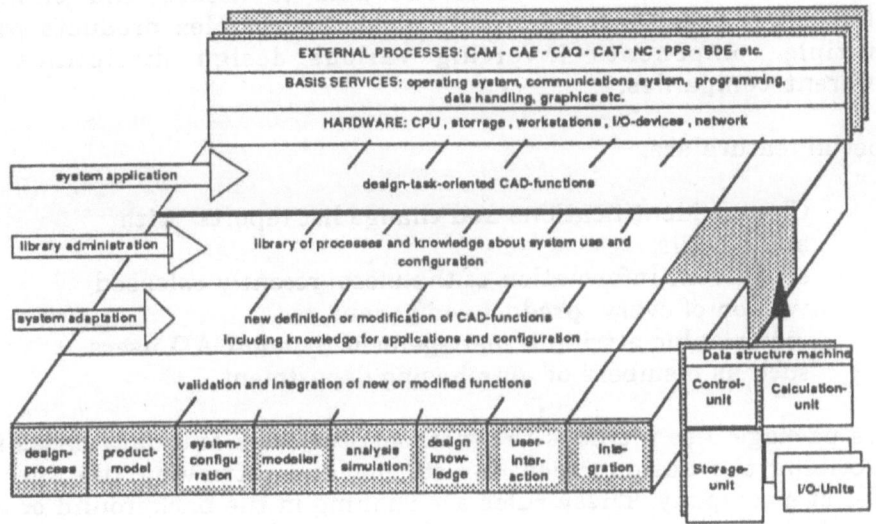

Figure 1: The data structure machines

As the use of computerized processes increases throughout design and manufacturing organisations, a new set of problems relating to data management is revealed, because

- the amount of data to be stored and managed is very large, and differing requirements make it difficult to store all the data in one system,
- storing large amounts of nongraphic data in a graphics data base increases the size of the data base to unacceptable levels and reduces system performance
- each system to be integrated requires different types of data and produces different output

- duplicated data exists on various systems, the data is frequently unsynchronisized, leading to errors in the different areas of the commission.

Engineering data management sytems can be the right solution, if this system is realy integrated into the CAD envirement and supports the most important features of a concurrent engineering teams in conjunction with one another. This requires that many users with different tasks and skill sets are able to access and change information simultaneously, particularly for complex products with multiple components involving various design disciplines of different companies.

Special feature are:

- Change identifications and change list reports with audit trails,
- concurrent information of the most recently released version of every product component,
- nongraphic attribute management by non-CAD users such as members of purchasing department.

This package also includes the methods, the tools and data bases for describing the design rules, for storing and retrieving the special rules of a company. These rules are running in the background of the CAD-design process, to control and to restrict the individual ideas of the engineering process to keep the standards for the dedicated commision.

II. Product Definition Data Bases - Product Model
Engineering data based systems will play a much more important role in the whole order and product definition and manufacturing process in a company in future. The product model defines the structure und should include all data, which supports the individual order, to be able to reconstruct the existing order at every stage inside the process of its fulfilment; but only these data are really necessary.

The structure of the data base is based on the often used identification methods of the "bill of material" inside a company, which is extended to the form elements and features for design and manufacturing including NC- and processing-programs. The CAD graphics are only related to this data base and are used only for simulation and documentation. This package describes the range and the size of all data which are necessary, including tools and system support for implementation. The bill-of-materials based product model will be the main integration element for the whole CIM-process.

The product model maximizes the benefits of integrated modeling for component design inside a multiuser, multi product and complex assembly environment. This assembly data base includes hierarchical relationships among the various elements and their graphical representation, or product structure, of the assembly's subassemblies and components and their interrelationships.

III. Application Oriented System Configuration
There are many critical views that the existing CAD-systems will not be accepted by the engineers in the future because of their rather complicated handling and the fairly unlimited combination of commands and modes of user interaction. A normal engineer can handle only 100 to 150 commands in average at one time. The result is, that only a small part of the power of the CAD systems today is really used in practice. So we can imagine the death of the " CAD-software-dinosaur" of the design-systems today if nothing will change.

The only solution is a new structuring and application oriented configuration technique of CAD working places. There should be a "starting configuration" on the design work which is described by a number of rules inside a decision table, depending on the individual demands of the design work. This configuration reduces the number of programs and simplifies the structure of commands.

The next step is a "dynamical configuration" during the running design process which manages the foreground/background distribution of the CAD software and reduces the volume to an absolute necessary number of commands which have to be used in practice.

Application oriented configuration needs a strongly structured software architecture und a powerful "linkage editor" with legal combinations of all resources. Specific configurations are stored in local resource files and can be tailored to the different applications.

This package describes the technique and the design model for production oriented configuration.

IV. Modeller

This working package will not define a new graphic modeller in addition to the existing programs. We have to concentrate and to standardize the number of different modellers for an unlimited use within different CAD systems. All geometric forms, using wireframe, surface, and solid model geometry should be integrated and interchangeable.

For example, a designer can create a preliminary profile using standard wireframe techniques, then sweep the profile to create a surface or solid model easily. Additional operations provided for explicit modeling include nodal construction, the creation and manipulation of figures for instancing, the assignment of nongraphic properties to entities, and the placement of text for detailing operations. A common modeller reduces the variety of internal representation of design models, it helps to have a better data exchange between CAD-systems, it supports the integration and it reduces the efforts for interfacing today.

Users in an engineering design department require various degrees of sophistication from their design automation systems. The range can extend from project managers who only require viewing and redlining capabilities up to design specialists with detailed know how of surface design by NURBS analyzing complex product models.

These high-end users require a comprehensive assortment of geometric modeling tools. Those using more advanced engineering will use an unified parametric modeler combining dimension-driven modeling technologies with all types of geometry (wireframes, surfaces, solids). This allows selection of the best geometry approach. Regardless as to whether a designer creates an explicit or parametric model, all geometric informations should be stored in the same format in the same file.

The modeling system should include:

* integrated parametric wireframe, surface, and solid modeling
* constraint modeling with symbolic equation solver to solve sets of
       simultaneous linear or nonlinear equations with variable
       names that tie directly to parameters within the model,
* two-dimensional sketching as a first design and user-defined
       dimensions in a later approach,

  * feature-based modeling by using of predefined libaries in
        PDES/STEP standards to add details to a model using
        engineering or manufacturing terms instead of geometric
        terms.

The working package describes the necessary functions and the
system integration tools inside the reference model for neutral
modeller like ACIS.

V. Analysing and Simulation
The electrical, thermal, and mechanical structure analysis and
calculation are necessary components of the enterprise engineering
process. Many of these applications have much more of a controlling
feature and can usually run in the background of the graphic design
process. The design features are controlled by an accompanied
calculation for crash analysis or electrical relationship e.g.. This
feature oriented background calculation often needs a reduced and
simplified geometric model, which can be derived directly and as far
as automatically from the extended design model. These methods
have to be defined in order to reduce the geometric data amount.

Special integrated analysis tools allows users to calculate the
geometric and initial property of any two- or three-dimensional
component or assembly of components for example:

  * **Mass properties and interference detection** to identify interfering
        objects that obstruct the function of others
  * **Stress Analysis** as an integrated finite element modeling,
        calculation, and results display tool
  * **Heat transfer** analysis on mechanical, electrical, and
        electromechanical components and assemblies
  * **Process analysis** of injection-molding plastic parts to optimize
        critical cost parameters, such as type and amount of
        material used, plastic injection rates, and machine throughput
  * **Kinematic and dynamic motion** analysis to realize all gains that
        can be achieved in different areas such as preventing
        interference between a product's moving parts. This can be
        done most easily at the beginning of the design cycle, before
        resources are committed to the creation of physical models.

Parallel running simulation for functional kinematics of the
product, for manufacturing simulation and assembly are important
system tools during the design process. In this case the details of the

design model have to be reduced to a substituted model for keeping with the relevant parts of the simulation process.

VI. Application Oriented Knowledge Processing and Documentation

There are two broad categories of knowledge that a knowledge based engineering product could utilize to aid design. The first category are the design rules like codes and standards from a professional organisation, company policies, or local engineering group policies on valid designs. When a violation is detected, the system should propose a resolution that is in conjunction with the design rules.

The second category of design knowledge covers goals being to capture and reuse existing process models to solve whole classes of similar design problems. To use these design rules effectively, there must be some set of objects or actions that the knowledge base can reason with. The best form of objects in CAD to assume this role are features. The knowledge engineer would use the creation, modification and deletion of features as the triggering actions to the rule set.

There is no CAD-system available today which really includes a knowledge based engineering program or expert system. Normally these programs have to run separately using a complicated data transfer from and into the CAD-system. The aim of the package is to integrate these programs as a part of a feature based product model and to manage design rules during the graphic modelling process. Its not easy to integrate expert system programs, because of the different program and system structures and because of the quite different user interfaces. CAD-systems have to be restructured to combine the tools of these application fields.

There are different approaches to solve this problem:

a) You can switch between the different engineering programs by solving the data transfer and by the process of interfacing.

b) You can organize foreground/background technique between graphic modelling und expert systems. You may start the graphic process and select an dedicated size in the model and than switch to the expert system. The result of the knowledge based experimentation can modify the feature of the product model. After that, you can continue the current process.

c) You can use the expert system as an knowledge based monitor for combining different CAD-packages and to build up the product model.

It depends on the application field for the best solution of the engineering process. It depends on the configuration tools which concept is useful, but the different models should be available.

VII. User Interface and Customer Support

The different techniques in common structure for user interface are really welcome for the design process. The aim is to have an individual configuration for the common interface and the graphics presentation. Otherwise more standards for a common presentation should be reached; we have to find out a compromise of a common based level of commands, which are a real support inside the whole CIM-process. The rest of the necessary commands should be individually configured and simultaneously installed during the design process.

This dynamic configuration of user interface reduces the great amount of training and learning how to use the different engineering programs, because there is no designation what kind of user interface tools will succeed in reaching the acceptance of the users. Many different methods and tools should be available to allow a company oriented, free defined user interface technique.

Special software utilities enable a user to "customize" existing menus and/or create new icons and menus. For the direct manipulation by the user a depress- and drag-technique is proposed to

* create completely new menus to perform unique sets of application and customers oriented operations
* create and to edit special icons by combining simple graphic elements with different colors and shaded manipulations.

VIII. Integration

This package separates different kinds of integration:

a) Internal integration inside the CAD-system links and to manage different programs under an individual and common user command language.

b) Integration between different CAD-systems inside one company, between different companies and between different application software packages like electronical, schematic und mechanical design. The solution is a product definition data base which supports different programs in common.

c) Integration inside a company oriented CIM-process to include process engineering, manufacturing engineering and assembly engineering like robotics.

The effort which all industrial companies have to spend today has reached a critical size, it is really unsatisfied and meanwhile exceeds the costs of the whole CAD-system. The CAD reference model supports the activities in the "STEP" standardisation. But the main aspects and goals are to build up a common data base which is the crossing line for all kinds of different programs and common data use.

An unique set of CAD/CAM software components should be proposed and standardized in the future. These components can be used for development of in-house applications and independently offered poducts, as well as customized applications accessing others enineering software modules with direct link to core geometric modeling, data base technology, and framework.

Conclusion

The aim of the CAD-reference model is to break up the eight packages into details of system- and programming parts, in respect to the available programs as far as possible and to build up a common product definition data base. The methods of defining data structure machines as the higher level of system description and documentation are used. Modern and well known software engineering tools like SADT for process structure und "EXPRESS" programs for the data structure definition, will help to understand the system elements through an international acceptance.

The new architecture

Beside the work organizing aspects for the improvement of the construction work a first proposal for a new system architecture has been developed, that meets the aims of human oriented work figuration, effectuates a qualitative and quantitative improvement of work results, and supports the whole design process adapted to the users and the tasks.

Hence the aim of the reference architecture is the conception and the design of an architecture of CAD systems on a logical level, that meets the requirements from the view of work science, user and information technology. To achieve this, an open, modular, flexible, and adaptable architecture is necessary.

Particularly the architecture meets the following requirements:

- pointing out solutions for the recognized common weak points of CAD systems in the terms of openness, user's requirements, modularity, flexibility, and the abilities to configure, to integrate, to communicate, to migrate.
- consideration of international standards (STEP, ISO/OSI), industrial standards (OSF/DCE, OSF/Motif and ACIS) and current research work (for example CFI and CORBA) as far as possible.
- use of current technologies of information technology (object-oriented methodology, network technologies, client-server-architecture, data base technologies, telecooperation technologies/ CSCW).

The first level of such a architecture can be devided into four main components (figure 2).

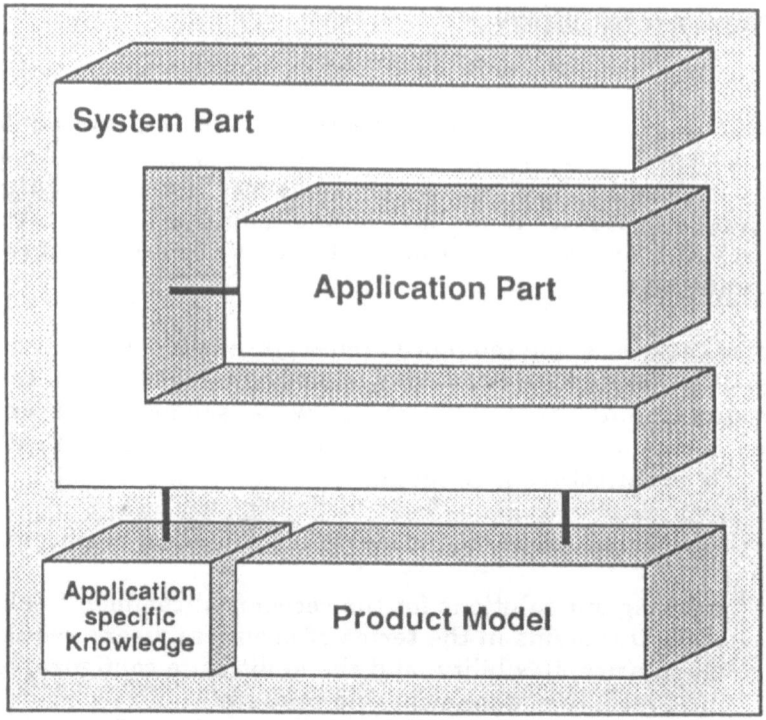

Figure 2: Basic Architecture

Application Part - quantum of all application-oriented components available in a CAD system for the realisation of design specific functionality, including the specific modeller.

System Part - quantum of application-free service components available in a CAD system, that are necessary for preparation, configuration, work out, and integration of components of all specific applications.

Product Model - unit of all product dates for the description of a class of products during the whole product life cycle.

Application specific Knowledge - quantum of application-specific knowledge for the solution of construction tasks and for the support of the engineers.

The explicit separation of application and system components in the reference architecture is supposed to supply the exchange and the expansion as well of the application-oriented as of the application-free components.

To achieve a configuration of the application and the system components, that means as efficient as possible and adapted to the application requirements, different stages are introduced in the frame of reference architecture. These achievement stages supply the specification of a requirement profile for each of the application and system components with regard to their functionality, performance, and availability in the network and together with an optimal adaptation of the main system to the application requirements.

Thereby the main components of the reference architecture are described in further detailed levels in each case by four characteristic attributes: their ability to communicate (interface), the structure of the components (statics), the sequence logic (dynamics), and their component parameters (data). Figure 3 shows the specification of the architecture on the second level [Ab95].

By this structure and its description a firm modularized system and application architecture can be achieved, that allows as well to use the latest computer system services as to reach an adaptation to the user's requirements.

These activities are supposed to achieve the needs of the German industry, but these needs are similar in the international market, especially of the middle class, which does not have its own system and development teams, can be articulated more intensive and can be brought into the international CAD development scene. Therewith the project fulfils a contribution for the transparency in the area of CAD and allows a more intensive co-determination in international standardizations, too.The discussion with several vendors confirms this contribution. This requires an agreement of the concerned user and vendor even going over the project frame, that is supposed to be animated by this project. The results of this first phase of the integrated project have been summarized in a final report [Ab95].

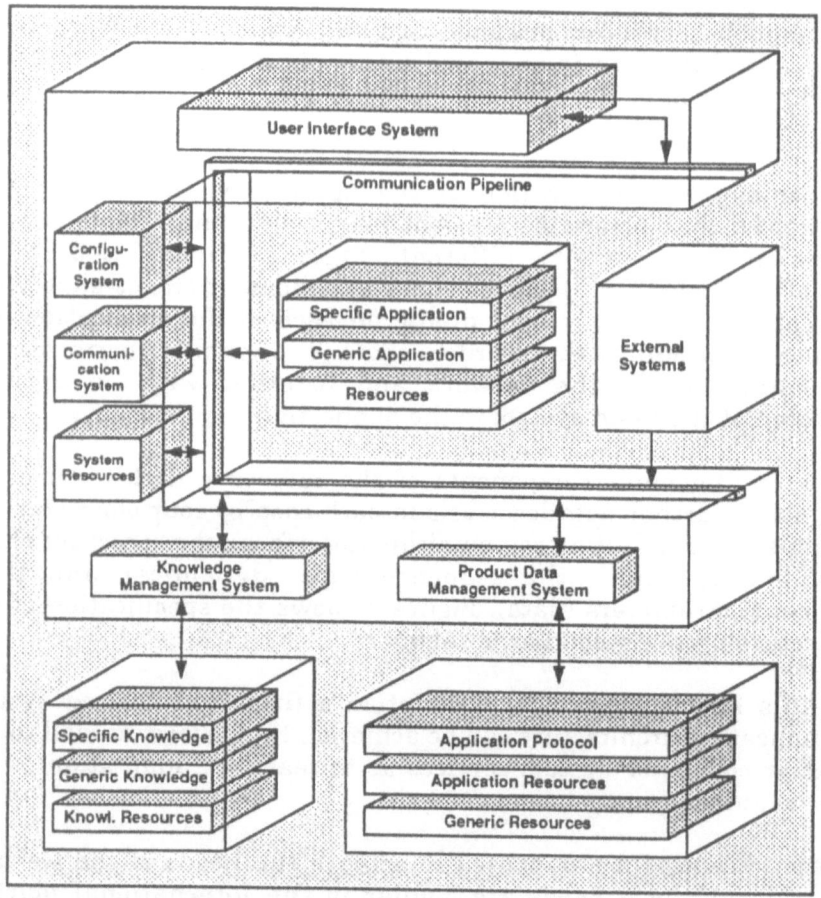

Figure 3: General Architecture level 2

Meanwhile a second phase of this joint project has been started. The motivation of this phase is the operational conversion of the model for practical use in small and medium size engineering companies. The first step is a detailed analysis and reorganisation of the design process in the different enterprises. The aim of this analysis is to find out the best reengineering concept for more parallel and simultaneous processes in the area of design, which future CAD-systems must support and to show how far the interest of the industrial partner covers the problem area already mentioned.

Then an expansion of the reference architecture to the regard of the specific problem of the company has to be done. The aim of the joint project is not to define a brand new CAD-software product. The joint CAD vendors derive from the current requirements the development steps for their own new generation of CAD-systems. The realization of the demands inside the CAD vendor product depends on the concept in hardware and software and how these concepts can easily be integrated in their current product or their future development.

The task of the scientific institutes is the realization of several prototypes to show the validation of the reference architecture. This realization takes place in two steps: first an application-independent and operating-neutral prototype in consideration of present hardware and software (good things shall remain) is going to be developed, that means to be evaluated and enhanced under operating-specific aspects. Hereby shall be shown, that the concept underlying organisation and technology structures are qualified very well. They are supposed to fulfil the cooperator-oriented as well as the company-oriented requirements to an innovative, flexible, and above all human oriented figuration of work.

Several demonstrators for the prototype realization are scheduled (figure 4), e.g.:

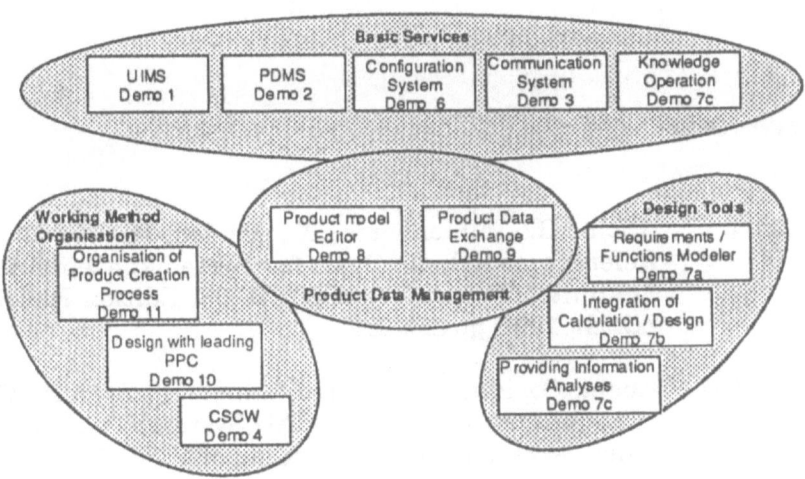

Figure 4: The demonstrators of the architecture

- basis services demonstrators
- application independent demonstrators in the area of user interface management system, product data management system and communication system.
- application specific demonstrators like CSCW, knowledge management, configuration and support of early design processes.

The use of the new generation of CAD-systems respectively the prototype demonstrators will be evaluated in the daily practise by the scientific institutes in cooperation with the joint enterprises. They have the task to show the economic advantages and the improved acceptance of this new generation of CAD-systems inside their company.

This aim requires a good cooperation between workers in the fields of computer science, and design, that is possible through the composition of the 8 research establishments coming from different purviews. The interdisciplinary character of the project team promises different points of view on the problems, that shall be solved. By the inclusion of two German vendors and several CAD user companies of different product and business structure the feedback from industrial practice is amplified and shows a realisation into a commercial product and an improved application.

References

[AFJ91]   Abeln, O., Finkenwirth, K., Jansen, H.: "CAD-Referenzmodell, die Basis für Systemkonzepte der Zukunft?", Proceeding of ICED '93, Edition Heurista, Zürich, 1991, pp 890-895.

[AKMS95]   Abeln, O., Krause, D., Meerkamm, H., Storath, E., "The Reference Model for CAD Systems - on the way to a new Architecture", Proceeding of ICED '95, Edition Heurista, Zürich, 1995.

[Ab95]   Abeln,O., Aktueller Stand der CAD-Technik und der
              rechnergestützten Konstruktionsarbeit - eine kritische
              Beurteilung der Problemfelder, Verbundprojekt:
              "CAD-Referenzmodell - Gestaltung zukünftiger
              computergestützterKonstruktionsarbeit",
              Forschungszentrum Informatik (FZI), Karlsruhe,
              1995.

[Ab95]   Abeln, O. (Hrsg.), Das CAD-Referenzmodell, Teubner
              Verlag, Stuttgart, 1995.

CAx Systems Architecture of the Future

C. Werner Dankwort [1]

Introduction

Significant changes have been underway in the development and roduction processes of many companies in the past few years. This has also led to new demands on information and CAx technology. Parallel to these developments, recent revolutionary innovations in these areas have shown the need to replace the old systems, for economic reasons. The R&D departments of the German automotive industry have founded a working group [2] whose aim is to develop a common CAD/CAM long-term strategy. A preliminary result is the concept of a CAx system architecture that not only influences the applications within automobile companies but also the products of the system suppliers. The following takes a look at the possibilities for these two groups to gain common advantages from this concept.

The present situation, revolution in CAD applications

In the past ten years, the use of CAD/CAM technology in German industry has made immense strides forward, as regards both penetration of the market (i.e the number of CA users in relation to conventional working engineers), as well as complexity of CA technological possibilities. Most recently, there have been substantial changes in all the relevant

---

1 Institute for Computer Applications in Engineering Design, University of Kaiserslautern, F.R.G.

2 AUDI, BMW, MB, PORSCHE, VW, Univ. Kaiserslautern: the Working Group "CAD/CAM Strategies of the German Automotive Industry", Dr. J. Peterson, H. Ederer, Dr. W Renz, D. Leu, Dr. P. Kellner, Prof. W. Dankwort

areas, i.e. information processing, CAx technology and especially CAx applications.

Information processing technology

- Those central computer installations which up to now have survived in the CAD world must give way to modern workstations, which continue to increase in performance while decreasing in price.
- Client/Server architectures with large networks, including those extending over more than one location, will be used for CAx systems.
- New software standards, in particular with respect to graphic and object-oriented techniques, have left their mark in the field of CAx systems.

CAx technology

- The classical large program systems, often still written on the basis of Fortran, are hardly maintainable. They must be fundamentally overhauled or completely rewritten using new software techniques.
- Based on the possibilities of new work stations, high demands will now be made on interaction and will have to be realized.
- New functionalities are being developed with increased requirements on computer performance, such as parametric or interactive free form modelling.
- In the area of CAD data, besides the unresolved demands on data exchange, the following main points must be considered:
  - expanded data structures, with corresponding standardization efforts
  - product information systems or engineering data bases

Because of the increasingly more difficult economic situation, market activities have become more aggressive. Some system suppliers have disappeared completely or merged, so that the number of products is decreasing. An overview of the life span of CAx components is shown in Figure 1.

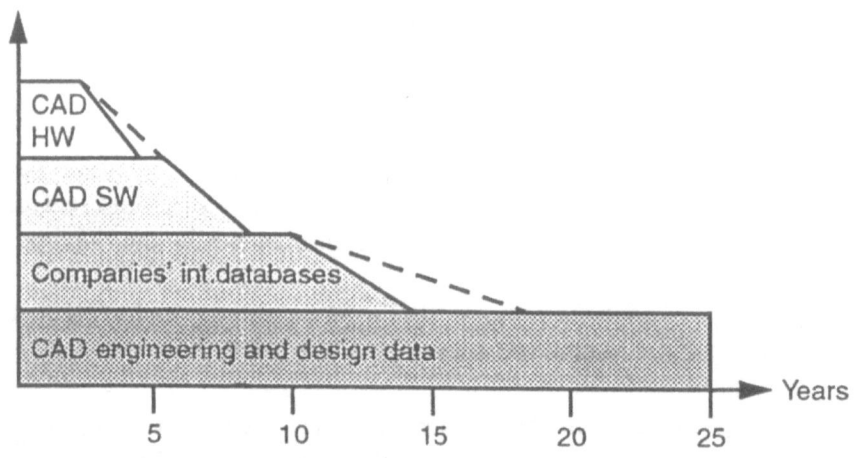

Fig. 1: Life span of CAx components

CAx applications

*   The demand for increased efficiency in engineering work and at the same time reduced training time requires substantial improvements in systems appropriate to engineers' thinking (handling, operations, management, application, administration).

*   Besides the wish for expansion and improvement of functionalities, it is becoming clearer, that it is not so much the functions but far more the control of data and information flows that is of decisive importance.

*   In contrast to earlier local optimization of individual work steps, CA support for process chains, and the integration of CAD, CAM, CAE and further CA technology will be promoted.

*   CAx applications are becoming more complex so that special branch specific modules will be needed.

The considerably harder conditions on the world market are also a driving force in the optimization of development and production processes in this field.

Conditions, aims, and the need for decisions

All companies in a particular branch (here a special look at the automotive industry) show a common background for a long-term CAD/CAM
strategy.

- The companies concentrate on core automotive processes. This
  means:

  Reduction of in-house production depth
  and of in-house development depth

- The companies are networked, i.e. world-wide cooperation even
  between competing companies in certain areas which do not
  directly affect product competition. Realization of the concepts
  "simultaneous engineering" and "concurrent engineering" will
  lead to a new way of thinking and to new demands on

  Personnel   Organization   Communication   Information
  Processing

The quick change of processes will necessitate new and more flexible CA
techniques. The objectives of a common CAD/CAM strategy can be
developed from this:

- Integration of dynamic processes / process steps; simplification of
  workflow processes
- Control of product information flows in the global process
  (CAx and administrative data, company internal and between
  cooperating enterprises)
- Economical and flexible CAx technology:
  - Use of the optimal CAx tools for each application and workflow
    problem by making use of the possibilities of various software
    products parallel to one another
  - Availability of each necessary CAx functionality; in principal
    every necessary function can be bought or developed by a third
    party
  - Stronger use of standards (It is essential for industry to have
    an impact on these standards and through management put
    them into use.)
- Fulfillment of demands on communication:

  Communication of all data that describes products and processes;
  availability of the right data whenever needed and at each
  relevant step in the process, in defined quality according to needs

- Openness of the systems as regards data structures, interfaces, internal modularity and connection to external program building blocks

- Cooperation between users and system suppliers.

In many companies today, the internal CAx system landscape is being re-examined in view of possible changes. There are several reasons for this:

- Optimization of the complete process, new demands on technical communication with other companies; large companies as customers require special CAx techniques

- Data management has become difficult to control, a global overview of all the product data has become necessary (a common database for technical and administrative data)

- The necessity to use newly available functionalities

- Existing hardware must be replaced, whereby a change in the existing CAx software would also be made possible

- Decentralization / Parallelization of technology: company internal and between companies

- Reduction of costs and other expenses in technology and application.

Alternative procedures

There are several possible approaches as to the way in which the CAD/CAM world of the application industries could be restructured.

In general, several possibilities can be theoretically developed:

(A) All companies involved in one industrial branch will use the exact same CAD/CAM system

(B) The various companies of a branch use different systems, however, these are all linked through bilateral coupling software

(C) The various companies of a branch use different systems, however, these all use a (certified) STEP interface

(D) A reference system can be developed, that can be used as criteria for other systems and/or which can be used as a plan for the development of a new system which would solve problems already known and fulfill the requirements of the applications industry. ("from scratch" approach).

A discussion of alternatives (A) and (B) has been sufficiently carried out in the past. There is, for example, a well-grounded conviction that there is no "universal system" which fulfills all application needs (besides further serious disadvantages of such a concept from the view of company politics). Use of the STEP standard (C) is necessary but cannot alone fulfill the existing requirements, not even when taking into cnsideration short-term plans for extensions.

These approaches show different sides of CAD/CAM information processing. When proceeding pragmatically with priority on application, further alternatives can be developed or assessed:

(E) The current CAx situation will be accepted and industrial applications and processes adjusted to the proposals of the systems suppliers.

(F) By concentrating on the objectives of a CAD/CAM strategy, methods can be developed by which these aims can be reached; however, at the same time taking into account the existing system landscape and also, not ignoring any unsolvable economic or technical conditions or neglecting any clear strategic interests of the user companies. Cooperation between the user companies and the system suppliers is necessary. Especially for the latter, these changes will necessitate a shift in aims and company strategy.

The approach using CAD reference system is being pursued by O. Abeln, 1995 [Ab95]. Another more general project approach is being made by the European Initiative AIT, 1994 [AIT94]. The suggestion that user companies just accept the circumstances and conform to the CAx landscape is comfortable, however, it is inconsistent with the vision of the auto-motive industry, whose interests can hardly be taken into consideration in such a suggestion.

Other alternatives are certainly possible. Suggestion (F), given in more detail below, concentrates on developing objectives and tasks from the strategic goals of the car industry, which can then be carried out in cooperation with system partners.

Future initiatives of the German automotive industry

Since the 1980's, the automotive industry has been a pioneer in CAD/CAM applications. Therefore, it is not surprising that this branch is trying to develop and promote concepts for the future.

Many important activities have their roots in the CAD/CAM working group of the VDA (German Automotive Industry Association) in cooperation with the VDMA (German Mechanical Engineering Association).

Since the beginning of the 1980's, this working group has tackled the task of improving CAD/CAM applications and in particular data exchange by car manufacturers and car parts suppliers. In 1994 the working group put together strategic guidelines for user companies and system suppliers, the "VDA-CAD/CAM-Policy" 1994 [He94]. A few priorities are summarized in the following points:

- The introduction and use of a heterogeneous system landscape is necessary in order to take into account the demands of the complete process

- The product data must be available throughout all steps of the development, manufacturing and lifecycle of the product, even in the case of parallel use

- CAD/CAM system independence: the economic and functional competition in a heterogeneous system landscape is a central condition, in order to ensure the various system capabilities demanded by the different processes, for both the short and long-term.

For the members of the VDA-CAD/CAM working group and for the entire automotive industry, this means:

- The interests and demands of the companies must be collected and presented to the system suppliers.

The VDA-CAD/CAM working group places special priority on pushing for the application and the stabilization of STEP (ISO STandard for the Exchange of Product model data):

- Product model data for the automotive industry based on STEP will be defined (STEP - Application Protocol 214 Automotive Design) and internationally standardized (through the ProSTEP organizations)

- The productive use of (the provisory) STEP AP 214 building blocks for data exchange and for archiving will be pushed through (together with user companies, system suppliers and the ProSTEP organizations).

In addition to the CAD/CAM activities of the VDA, which concentrate on data exchange between car manufacturers and their parts suppliers, the working group "CAD/CAM Strategies of the German Automotive Industry" has the concrete task of developing strategic goals and corresponding procedures for a future, company internal CAD/CAM world.

A "CAx Checklist" has been proposed to evaluate decisions in the CAD/ CAM branch so as to avoid problems in the close cooperation between the car industry and car parts suppliers; problems which in the past have lead to and even today still lead to increased expenses. Following is a list of priorities used to evaluate decisions in the CAD/CAM branch:

- System architecture (see paragraph 5)
- System implementation

   (Independent of hardware and operating systems, network capability)
- System maintenance and usage
   (Functionality lists are no longer strategic decision making points)
- General strategic demands

   (Willingness of the system suppliers to cooperate; participation in the STEP organizations).

These requirements will be coordinated by the user companies and discussed with the various system suppliers. It is vital that these concepts be worked out jointly by the participants. Progress will not be possible under confrontation. The above-listed priorities have been kept general and therefore, are not only of importance for the automobile companies. Car parts suppliers, in particular, can find support for their decisions here. The cooperation in the industrial process between car manufacturers and car parts suppliers was especially kept in mind while composing this checklist.

An important result of the working group is the concept of a CAx system architecture, which can be used as a base for the fulfillment of the strategic requirements. This concept will be discussed in detail in the following paragraph.

Description of the CAx system architecture

The structure of the CAx system architecture is shown in Figure 2. The fundamental ideas can be summarized in a few points:

- Replacement of conventional concepts, i.e. each user works with one system, or respectively in the case of (sequential) usage of more systems, with special data communications between these systems

   >>> From the user point of view, in future, there will no longer be **the** CAD/CAM system

• The user works with a "tool box" and uses tools from different suppliers. A combining of tools will be ensured through standards, that is through coordinated interfaces (industrial standards). In principal, all the components of a computer supportive system from product development to manufacturing can be integrated into such a structure.

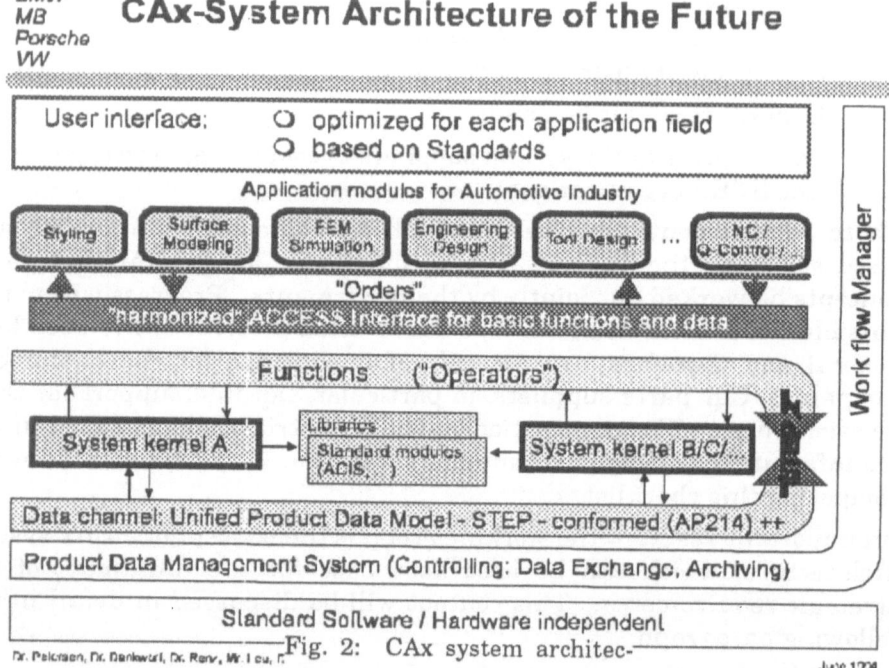

Fig. 2:   CAx system architec-

• The product description is based on STEP AP 214, as far as it meets requirements. In the case of more demanding requirements, especially in regard to operations and workflow, a STEP-compliant expansion is needed and must be brought into the standardization process by system suppliers, and later adjusted to the actual standards.

On the technical side, the following points are of importance: a CAD/ CAM application environment is structured as a model with various layers; the system "building" is made up of building blocks that stem

from different system suppliers and can be interchanged. This calls for
the following prerequisites:

- Independence of these building blocks from each other
    - the user interface
    - user module / application function blocks
    - kernels with system basic functions
    - data channels (based on STEP AP 214)
    - data management systems (Engineering DB, Workflow)
- Opening and coordination of the interfaces by the system
  suppliers
- Hardware independence

(Static) data and functions must be handled as a whole within the
structure of the product information (i.e. object-oriented approach). This
also means a common handling of CAD data, documentation of design
paths, structural and process data and additional administrative data.

Procedures / Projects to reach the goal

The draft of such a general architecture of strategic importance has little
value, if the partners concerned do not find a common objective. For this
reasons, discussions with system suppliers were already held in
advance. Many basic questions, which have been discussed by the
system users in this paper, are also found in the developments of the
system suppliers.

In order to put the proposed architecture into practice, the feasibility of
the concept has to be proven, and additionally the willingness of all the
parties involved is necessary. On the technical side, one can differentiate between several tasks, whereby two have a key function:

- Product data models / Data management systems
- Access to the system kernels / Basic functionalities

The CAx working group has, therefore, started two projects:

Product Data Management System (PDVS)

This should show proof of the feasibility of the concept in
industrial practice. In order to achieve this, a software prototype
will be developed which uses a simplified product model based on

STEP AP 214 to manage CAD and structural data. This model will be integrated into one or more CAD/CAM systems and tested by pilot users in the participating companies. (Project of the German automotive manufacturers under the direction of ProSTEP GmbH.)

Analysis of the Access Interfaces of various CAD/CAM Systems (ANICA)

The access to currently (or in the near future) available system kernels of the different system suppliers is being analyzed and a common access structure is being developed. A software prototype will be developed to prove the possibility of concurrent CAD design in real time with several CAD systems on different hardware platforms (Project of the German automotive industry together with five system suppliers, under the direction of the University of Kaiserslautern, with financial support from the Rhineland Palatinate Foundation for Innovation).

Further activities that affect the application software packages and the user interfaces are in the planning stage. The fundamental information processing aspects, such as hardware, operating systems, graphic standards, etc., have not yet been discussed but do play a role in the background.

Effects on system users and suppliers

The realization of the proposed concept has substantial consequences for CA users. A few significant advantages are:

- The present dependency of a company on a CAD/CAM system supplier will be eliminated
- For each application, the optimal tools available on the market can be used
- The product data description „belongs" to the company, the data flow can be controlled, the long-term availability of production information is assured.

However, there are also some disadvantages: the company internal CA support will need additional time and effort during the transition period. This will lead to an important new orientation on the part of the current system suppliers. Instead of just selling software, these companies can concentrate on CA services by supporting the CA process in the user companies. These CA service companies would then use the market software that is optimal for the customer. The companies' own software development will be out-sourced to subcontractors. A similar process to that which took place in the automotive industry could develop here, whereby, following a decrease in the in-house production depth, a decrease in the in-house development depth has also been targeted.

References

[Ab95]   Abeln, O. (Hrsg.), Das CAD-Referenzsystem, Teubner 1995

[AIT94]   AIT - Advanced Information Technology, IT-Reference model, ESPRIT 7704

[He94]   Heggmair, L.: "The VDA CAD/CAM Policy", VDA 1994

EREP Project Overview

Christoph M. Hoffmann[1]

The EREP project develops a neutral CAD representation that supports feature-based, constraint-based design and permits a high level of abstraction. We sketch the architecture that has been adopted to accomplish this objective and explain a number of technical issues that arose. These issues derive from the requirements to support variational constraints, to support feature-based design and editing, and to keep the representation independent of a CAD system that might be used to support implementing the system.

Introduction

A common problem in CAD-based product design is the inability to exchange design data that incorporates features and constraints. A number of standardization efforts have recently been initiated, for instance the Parametrics interest group organized within the conceptual landscape of the emerging STEP product data standard. These efforts are destined not to achieve complete CAD system interoperability because of intrinsic problems that originate from variational constraint-based design.

The EREP[2] project, begun about three years ago in collaboration with Professor Robert Joan-Arinyo of the Polytechnic University of Barcelona, has developed such a representation and has implemented a prototype system that demonstrates the viability of the representation.

To devise a neutral design representation that supports features and constraints requires solving certain technical problems that arise from the interaction of the design schema, devised by the user, with the constraint schema and the feature mechanism. These problems go well beyond choosing information models of the data that is to be communicated, and require an algorithmic

---

[1] Computer Science Department, Purdue University, West Lafayette, Indiana, USA.
[2] EREP stands for *editable representation*.

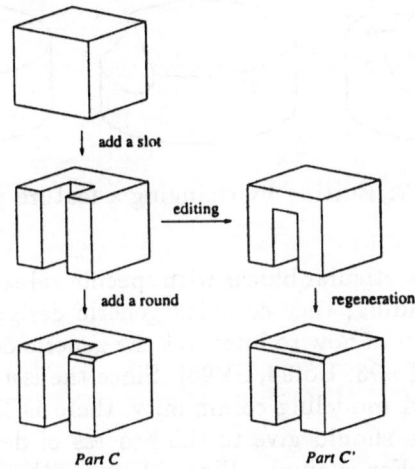

Figure 1: Example of editing semantics

semantics that has eluded many researchers and CAD vendors to date. This synopsis briefly summarizes the technical problems and guides the reader to publications that detail ways of addressing them.

The adoption of a neutral representation carries many benefits, among them CAD system interoperability, a well-understood semantics of design operations that presently may differ significantly between CAD systems, and the promise of functional interoperability between major functional tasks involved in effective product design by computer. These benefits have been characterized in [HJ93]. When the neutral representation departs from the tradition to include a full boundary description of the current design instance, moreover, a great economy of storage can be achieved that is orders of magnitude smaller than conventional representations.

Semantics of Editing Designs

Commercially available CAD systems support design paradigms deeply influenced by allowing the user to define features. A user-defined feature is elaborated based on a constraint schema. The constraint schema does not necessarily prescribe procedurally how to solve the constraints given specific values for dimensions and angles. This style of *variational constraint solving*[3] requires us to distinguish a generic design from design instances.

For example, if a block is defined with constraints on length, width and depth, then the generic design is the block with this constraint schema. Its

---

[3] The term appears to originate in industrial CAD circles.

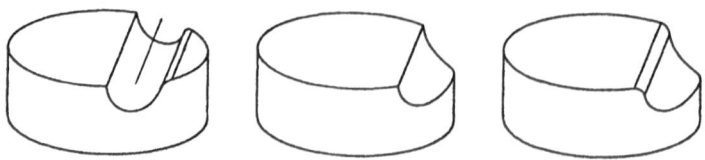

Figure 2: Editing by changing a feature position.

design instances are particular blocks with specific values for length, width and height. By compounding, very complex generic designs can be constructed that raise the question of how to interpret the generic design for specific value constellations; e.g, [Hof93, Hof94, SV95]. Since the issue has not been deeply discussed in the solid modeling community, there is little consensus on the precise semantics one should give to the process of deriving instance design from generic design. For example, Figure 1 shows the design of a block with a through-slot and one rounded edge. Subsequent editing changes the slot to a blind slot. Here, the blend was kept and extended to include the edge segment formerly unblended on the other side of the slot. Now edit again, making the slot once more a through-slot: Should there be two rounded top edges on either side of the slot? Or should we return to the original design?

Persistent Naming

Consider Figure 2. In the leftmost panel, one edge of a round slot has been blended. By changing some dimensions, it is easy to reposition the slot, and one would expect in such a case that the blend travels with the edge. But what should happen if the edge no longer exists? Should we preserve the round, attaching it to the other edge, as shown in the rightmost panel, or should we drop the blend altogether, as in the middle panel?

A key concept needed to clarify such questions is an identification of what elements, of the instance boundary, a generic design refers to. This problem has been called the *persistent naming problem* and several papers address it; [Kri93, CCH94, CH94a]. The persistent naming problem arises as follows: The user is permitted to select, on the visual instance, specific shape elements for dimensioning or feature attachment. This selection is intended to be paradigmatic, and to be valid under a wide range of different design parameters. Consequently, the system is obligated to generalize the selection and devise a scheme that permits reusing the identification for deriving a different design instance. Since different instances could differ significantly in their topology, the problem is interesting.

Feature Attachment

Without taking a position in the ongoing debate over what constitutes an appropriate notion of feature, we note that commercial systems already implement particular notions. Therefore, if we wish to devise a design representation schema that minimally supports current practice, we need to explain operations such as *make a hole from A to B*, where *A* and *B* could be faces the user has identified, or could be derived from a constraint schema that stipulates the hole's extent with the help of reference geometry. In [CH94b] this issue has been explored in the context of the EREP system. In view of the many possible ambiguities, the semantics defined there is based on a conceptual sequence of appropriate CSG operations for which there does exist an unambiguous semantics [Req77].

Even without addressing features and constraints, issues that compound semantic difficulties, many accepted operations in solid modeling remain without adequate semantic foundations. For example, consider *fillets* and *rounds*. although everyone understands the concept in a qualitative sense, there is clearly no precision in the concept.

Suppose we wish to round an edge. We would need to know, what surface would it be exactly? Should it be a *rolling ball blend*, the shape that bounds a ball rolling along the edge in contact with the adjacent faces? If so, and if the ball is allowed to vary in diameter, how exactly can this variation be defined? Moreover, where the edge ends, a transitional surface is required that caps the blend. Depending on the topology of the surface and on the geometry of the adjacent faces, many different surfaces could be interpolated. For examples demonstrating the numerous situations in need of explanation and algorithmic treatment see, e.g., [Bra96] or texts on solid modeling.

Constraints

It is a well-known fact that a constraint schema involving distance dimensions corresponds to a nonlinear system of equations, and that such systems have multiple solutions. Examples are easily constructed that demonstrate the possibility of an exponential explosion in the number of solutions; e.g., [BFH+95, FH94]. Using n points in the plane, $2n - 3$ constraints are needed to make a well-constrained configuration of them. Here we can expect $O(2^n)$ distinct solutions. For a simple example of multiple solutions to a *well-constrained* schema see Figure 3.

The multiplicity of solutions has significant consequences: Since it is not efficient to enumerate all solutions — there are too many — and since different constraint solvers use different strategies to construct a solution, we cannot expect that two different constraint solvers construct congruent solutions for the same constraint problem. Therefore, if we are to devise a neutral represen-

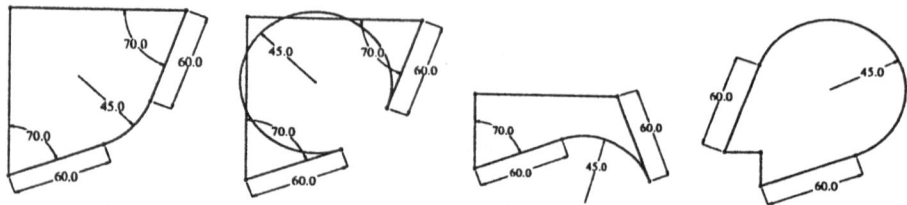

Figure 3: Multiple solutions of a well-constrained problem

tation that supports the current practice of variational constraints, we must exchange more than the problem specification itself. Different possibilities come to mind.

1. We exchange the constraint schema plus a solution instance. This results in a *translation semantics* for CAD system interoperability: We can reconstruct one instance, but there is no guarantee that a design change that alters the constraint parameters will give identical results on different CAD systems.

2. We exchange the constraint schema and the constraint solver. This sounds extraordinary, but since only one instance of the solver would be needed for exchanging every design prepared on a particular CAD system, the suggestion is not a priori impractical. In fact, if the solver algorithm is public, one could simply exchange the problem plus an identification of the algorithm. For an analogy, consider exchanging a matrix to be inverted along with the stipulation to use LU decomposition.

3. We exchange the constraint schema plus a canonical enumeration of the solution space. Since the solution space is exponential, this strategy requires giving a procedure that does the enumeration. In essence, the procedure could be a precompiled solver that solves only one particular constraint schema.

The name *translation semantics* for Approach 1 is explained by the fact that in Approach 1 the receiving CAD system simply translates the solution instance while mapping the constraint schema to its own representation. Approaches 2 and 3 could then be termed *editing semantics* since they preserve the behavior of the constraint schema when editing dimension values.

The EREP Architecture

Following the conceptualization of the original paper [HJ93], the system architecture we have implemented is as shown in Figure 4. The main components we implemented are the graphical user interface (GUI), the constraint solver

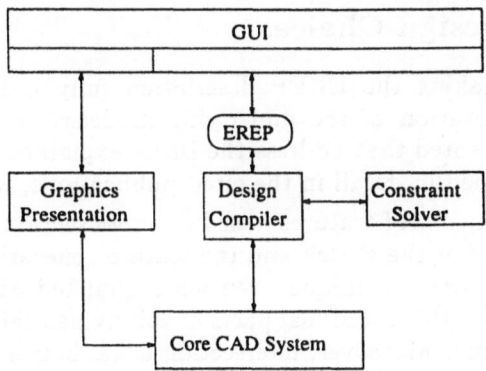

Figure 4: Architecture of the EREP prototype

described in [BFH+95], and the design compiler featured in [CH95]. The core CAD system is ACIS, a C++ solid modeling library commercially available.

The GUI not only prepares a visual representation of the design in progress but also puts together a textual description of the design, the EREP, that is interpreted by the design compiler and translated into a sequence of operations carried out by ACIS, with assistance of the constraint solver. All communication is by text files to maintain a strict separation of the components. As such, the prototype could serve as blue print for a feature-based, constraint-based design data exchange schema. Here, parts of the GUI would constitute the translation from the CAD system's internal representation into a neutral exchange representation. Conversely, the design compiler and constraint solver would constitute the bulk of the translation from the neutral data representation to the CAD system internal representation. At the time of writing, such a set of translators is under consideration by a consortium of CAD vendors and end users.

Early on, we decided not to reference any boundary details in the textual design description. The representation therefore is fully independent from the representational structures used by ACIS. Moreover, since the design operations of the system are explained independently, the operational architecture of ACIS is not reflected in the EREP.

One could include a partial or full boundary representation that describes a particular design instance, and it is common to do so in commercial systems and in STEP extensions currently under development. There is an efficiency advantage when including a boundary representation of the current design instance. No re-evaluation is needed when retrieving it. The disadvantage is that the boundary information gives many opportunities to become CAD system dependent, and that it is bulky. An EREP design description is much more concise.

The EREP Design Choices

In addition to making the EREP description fully independent from the boundary representation of the underlying modeler, certain design choices have been implemented that address the issues explained before. Since these choices are explained in detail in the cited publications, we are brief.

The shape elements of features based on cross sections are named by the geometric elements of the sketch and the feature generation rules. By themselves, such names are not unique, even when qualified with a unique feature name. For example, the individual parts of subdivided faces and edges would have the same name. Moreover, intersection edges between different features are not uniquely named in this way. To disambiguate further, we use a mix of topological adjacency information and geometric use by adjacent uniquely named elements. Special rules are applied to resolve incomplete name matches when evaluating the EREP; see also [CCH94, CH94a]. The sequence in which features have been defined does enter into the naming scheme and thus feature reordering is complicated. A more modular scheme would simplify feature reordering.

The constraint solver uses graph decomposition. Roughly speaking, the solution of a constraint problem is constructed by a sequence of construction steps derived by analyzing the constraint graph. Each step has a known number of different solutions, and which solution is chosen is a matter of applying the heuristics described in [BFH+95]. Thus, the solution sequence is a path in the tree of all possible choices. Such a path can be described succinctly by a canonical enumeration of the choice made at each step without having to explore the entire solution space. Thus, we can record a solution instance without coordinatization of the geometric elements, and we can enumerate the solution space without having to explore it. It is easy to explore alternative solutions by traversing the solution tree, and our implementation can do this interactively.

An EREP is evaluated feature-by-feature. When editing a feature, the design is unwound to that point and is re-evaluated beginning with the edited feature. All subsequent features are also re-evaluated.

Acknowledgements

The support of the Office of Naval Research under contract N00014-90-J-1599, and of the National Science Foundation under grants CDA 92-23502 and CCR 95-05745 is gratefully acknowledged. The EREP project is the result of contributions made by many collaborators over the recent years. I thank in particular Robert Joan-Arinyo, William Bouma, Jiazhen Cai, Xiangping Chen, Ioannis Fudos, Robert Paige, and Pamela Vermeer who contributed to the ideas and the implementation.

References

[BFH+95] W. Bouma, I. Fudos, C. Hoffmann, J. Cai, and R. Paige. A Geometric Constraint Solver. Computer Aided Design, 27:487–501, 1995.

[Bra96] Ian Braid. Nonlocal Blending of Boundary Models. Computer-Aided Design, 1996. to appear.

[CCH94] V. Capoyleas, X. Chen, and C. M. Hoffmann. Generic Naming in Generative, Constraint-Based Design. Computer Aided Design, 28:17–26, 1996.

[CH94a] X. Chen and C. Hoffmann. On Editability of Feature Based Design. Computer Aided Design, 27:905–914, 1995.

[CH94b] X. Chen and C. Hoffmann. Towards Feature Attachment. Computer Aided Design, 27:695–702, 1995.

[CH95] X. Chen and C. Hoffmann. Design Compilation for Feature-Based and Constraint-Based CAD. In Proceedings 3rd ACM Symposium on Solid Modeling, 1995.

[FH94] I. Fudos and C. M. Hoffmann. Correctness Proof of a Geometric Constraint Solver. International Journal of Computational Geometry and Applications, to appear, 1994.

[HJ93] C. M. Hoffmann and R. Juan. Erep, an Editable, High-Level Representation for Geometric Design and Analysis. In P. Wilson, M. Wozny, and M. Pratt, editors, Geometric and Product Modeling, pages 129–164. North Holland, 1993.

[Hof93] C. M. Hoffmann. On the Semantics of Generative Geometry Representations. In Proceedings 19th ASME Design Automation Conference, pages 411–420, 1993. Vol. 2.

[Hof94] C. M. Hoffmann. Semantic Problems in Generative, Constraint-Based Design. In Parametric and Variational Design, pages 37–46. Teubner Verlag, 1994.

[Kri93] J. Kripac. Topological ID System – A Mechanism for Persistently Naming Topological Entities in History-based Parametric Solid Models. PhD thesis, Czech Technical University, Prague, 1993.

[Req77] A. Requicha. Mathematical Models of Rigid Solids. Technical Report Memo 28, University of Rochester, Production Automation Project, 1977.

[SV95] V. Shapiro and D. Vossler. What is a Parametric Family of Solids? In Proceeding 3rd ACM Symposium on Solid Modeling, 1995.

New ECAD System Technology

Ulrich Mink[1] and Dieter Roller[2]

In terms of computer support within the design phase of product development, requirements for electrical design are discussed in this section. The field of electrical engineering CAD (ECAD) bears some major differences to CAD for mechanical applications (MCAD): the main task is to describe the functional design of an electrical control unit and/or electrical connections of technical systems. This is accomplished via schematic drawings, representing the appropriate logical information. Typically, these schematics are organised as a set of sheets. Within a schematic, components (e.g. relais) might be represented by a distributed set of symbols on different sheets of the design. Then typically cross references to the other parts of the component are being made. In subsequent development steps, different production documents need to be derived from the schematics. Examples of such documents are parts lists, terminal lists and connection lists.

Another kind of drawings relate to control cabinet design. They show how components are to be placed within the cabinet. This is performed in a scaleable manner using a geometric view of the components. Support of 3D-Graphics, automatic routing of cables, interference checking and design rules are useful approaches to this problem. Besides these, there are some further highly sophisticated requirements for ECAD systems to be foreseen. Examples will be given in this section.

Knowing that contemporary ECAD systems are founded on software packages that have been designed simply for drawing schematics, it is understandable that they cannot be a solid basis for the fulfilment of the advanced future requirements. In a co-operation project, TCS

[1]Technische Computersysteme Süssen GmbH, Süssen, F.R.G.

[2]Institut für Informatik, Universität Stuttgart, F.R.G.

GmbH and the Universität Stuttgart have started the development of a next generation ECAD system. In the following part, some analysis results and the architectural approach developed in this project are described.

Differences between MCAD and ECAD

ECAD systems, i.e. systems for electrical computer aided design have to be distinguished carefully from systems dealing with electronics, such as printed circuit board (PCB) design, integrated circuit (IC) design and logic design. The type of systems that are considered in this text are those that help an engineer to design conventional and/or programmable logic control systems (PLC). Examples of application fields for these control systems are machinery equipment, power plants and power distribution.

The control designs are based on conventional components, such as relais, connectors, switches, fuses, motors, lamps etc. Some parts of the control may be implemented by use of PLC's and this way doing the control flow in software.

The basis for ECAD systems is the generation and modification of schematic drawings, which describe the functional design of an electrical construction. This is done by placing electrical symbols on a sheet (geometrically speaking a plane). The resulting schematics is called a ladder diagram. As the symbols represent components, they need to be annotated with an unique identifier. They can be shaped quite differently, but usually contain a letter identifying the type of component (e.g. lamp, relais, switch) and either a counter or references to the sheet and part of the sheet the symbol is placed on. In ladder diagrams, the electrical connections between the components are represented by lines between special connection points of the concerned symbols. Fig. 1 shows a small section of a typical ladder diagram as an example.

Generation of these schematics bears only small geometric problems, compared to those that need to be handled in modern MCAD systems. However, in ECAD there is the need to trace and evaluate the designed logic scheme. First of all, unique identifiers for the symbols need to be generated and managed in a way to support the fact that physical components used in the design may have to be spread on different sheets of a schematics. If we consider e.g. a relais, it is common practice that the main circuit of a control is in one set of schematics - so we find the main circuit switches here - and the control circuit is in another set - which means that we find the coil and control switches there. In this case, a unique naming denotation of such components is the minimum need.

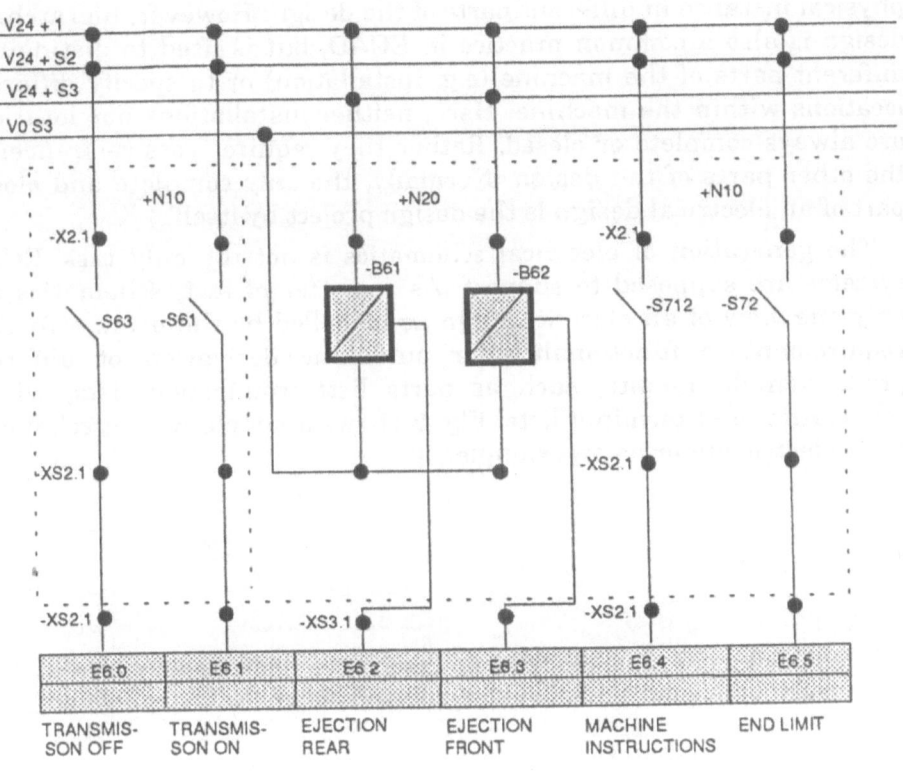

Fig. 1: Example of an electrical ladder diagram

Moreover, it is common practice to show the cross references of those distributed parts to make the design understandable. In the example of the relais, each switch would generate a cross reference to the coil, and close to the coil there would be a complete schematic of all parts of this component, showing where each individual contact of this component can be found in the design schematics. Similar cross referencing has to take place in other parts of the design - e.g. for voltage potentials or designated signals.

This consideration brings up another significant difference between MCAD and ECAD: one sheet (or model) of a mechanical construction represents a closed part of the design - probably referencing a more detailed view of the same part in a hierarchical design, whereas one sheet of an electrical design references other sheets, identifying one physical instance in different parts of the design. However, hierarchical design is also a common practice in ECAD, but is used to distinguish different parts of the machine (e.g. installation) or to specify different locations within the machine. Here, neither installations nor locations are always complete or closed. Rather they require cross references to the other parts of the design. Normally, the only complete and closed part of an electrical design is the design project by itself.

The generation of electrical schematics is not the only task ECAD systems are supposed to support. As a matter of fact, schematics are only one view of an electric design as modelled by the user. A further requirement is functionality for automatic derivation of different production documents, such as parts lists, connection lists, wiring schematics, and terminal lists. Fig. 2 shows a simple wiring schematic of an electric motor as an example.

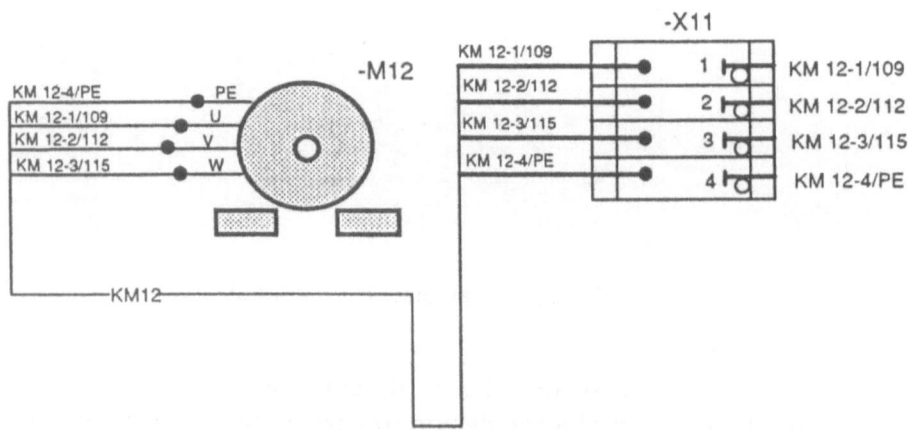

Fig. 2: Wiring schematic for an electric motor

Another important part of electrical design is the layout of control cabinets. This cannot be accomplished by schematics and has to be to scale. It is required that the ECAD system 'knows' the geometry of the used components and helps the designer to place the components into the control cabinet according to rules given by the component's manufacturer.

It is interesting to note that many of the major ECAD system vendors are German companies, distributing their systems on a world-wide basis. This implies that their systems have to be adopted to different national standards what in return results in a tremendous demand of flexibility within the CAD products. For instance, the flow direction in European schematics is vertical, whereas in the USA, according to JIC, it is oriented horizontally. Thus, national standards do not only imply different symbol sets, but also place a requirement for different modes of internal logic handling within the ECAD system.

Requirements for ECAD

Up to this point, we essentially considered ECAD Systems as they are used in industry as of today. Let us now see how the market requirements will evolve within the next couple of years. This consideration is split into two parts: one showing the view of users, the other the information technology (IT) point of view.

From the users viewpoint, efficiency is the most important challenge [RoRi95]. Electrical design departments commonly had to cut their design budges down to 60 to 80 % within the last two years, and this tendency still lasts.

Nowadays ECAD systems support the design process in a rather narrow sense. What will be needed in future is a support of the complete life cycle of a new product - starting from sales process (pre-calculation) through analysis, design, production, maintenance, modifications and finally ending in support of the disposal process in order to improve the overall productivity.

Another way of improving efficiency is simultaneous / concurrent engineering. Here again, the distribution of one physical component to different parts of the design creates new challenges to ECAD systems.

Electrical component manufacturers typically are innovative companies developing new components in continuously shorter time frames. ECAD system users on the other hand expect their system to support these new components as soon as they become available on the market. This implies that ECAD systems have to be easily extensible to new parts libraries.

Another functionality that potentially can boost the users efficiency is the support of design rules. If in a design there is for instance a motor circuit and the user wants to add a fuse to this circuit, the system should automatically check if the fuse is correctly dimensioned for the selected motor.

In the design of control cabinet layout, a three-dimensional model [ToCh93] holds the potential for a higher level support. Users could have sophisticated assistance of the ECAD-System in the fields of components placement and consideration of component's specific physical properties, like minimal distances to other parts or their weight. As the system knows about the connections between the components gathered in the control cabinet, it should be able to route the wires and cables and to calculate the various lengths needed. Also, there should be interference checking, not only geometrically [SoTu94], but also electrically, taking into consideration physical effects as electromagnetic, thermal and electro-static interference.

Simulation is a very helpful approach to figure out, if the design leads to the correct behaviour of the control. This way time consuming error correction at the almost finished machinery could be reduced.

Another important topic is connectivity to other applications, e.g. workflow management, production planning systems and PLC systems.

From the IT point of view, the following topics can be summarised to fulfil these user requirements:

- Easy possibilities for integration of external systems to be able to create connectivity to other applications.

- Support of heterogeneous computing environment. Companies want to use different hardware and software platforms for different applications. Thus to achieve connectivity, this is a must.

- Consistent and configurable user interface. This is needed for easy usage and reduction of learning costs for new users.

- Conformance to international standards.

- Modularity. To allow users to choose - and pay - only those parts of the system they are going to use.
- Extendibility and maintainability. This is important to be able to fulfil market requirements in a timely manner.

The development of most ECAD systems started in the early eighties with a schematic editor. In the past, extensive work has been done to extent the functionality in order to fulfil at least partially the needs of the users. Today, typically maintenance of these complex structured systems is extremely cost intensive. Therefore, the development a new ECAD system from scratch has been started. Throughout this project, object oriented technologies have been used, including an analysis model according to the Booch method [BoG95]. In the next paragraphs, the underlying architectural concept is described.

Architecture for a next generation ECAD System

For the new system, the software architecture is based on the CAD reference model [Abe95], which has been developed by a group of scientists in close co-operation with industrial companies. The CAD reference model project still is under further development and financially supported by the Bundesministerium für Forschung und Technologie. The main goal is now to proof its application for new CAD systems.

As a matter of fact, the CAD reference model has been developed mainly with mechanical applications in mind. However, with little adoptions and modifications, it can be applied to an electrical CAD system as shown below. As the Reference Model itself is discussed in another section of this book, here we focus on the differences for ECAD and the implementation aspects of this model.

The basic architecture of the CAD reference model is split into the following major components (c.f. Fig. 3):

- The *application components* contain the set of application dependent software parts used to build design-specific functionality.
- The *system components* contain all parts within the CAD system, that are application-independent.

- The *product model* contains all relevant product specific data and secures the logical and physical integrity of all these data. By doing so, it enables an integrated co-operation of all CAD applications using the same product model.
- The *knowledge component* delivers formal and informal application specific knowledge for the solution of a given design job.

These architectural components are now being considered at a more detailled level.

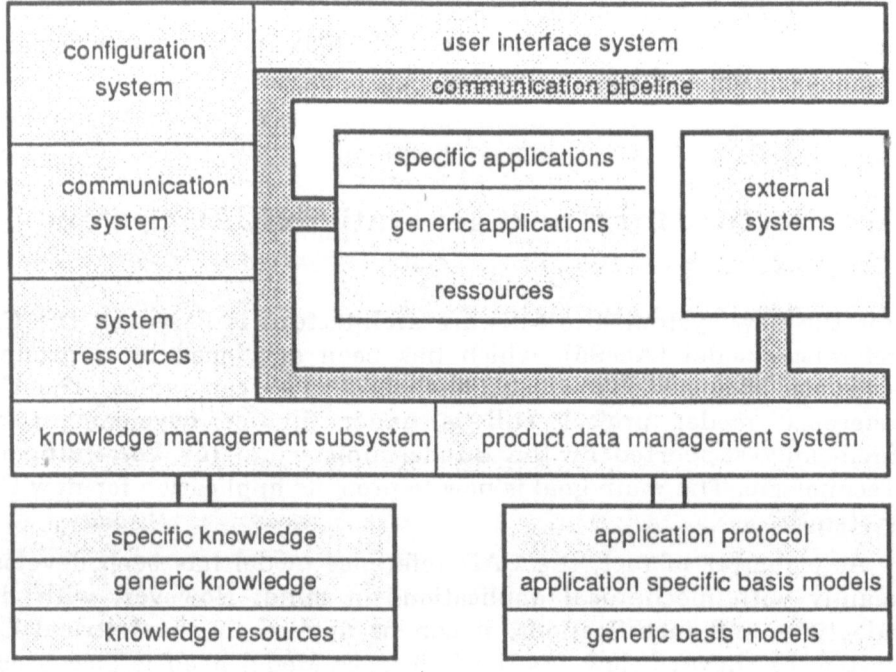

Fig. 3: Architectural overview of the CAD reference model

Application components

The CAD reference model divides the application components into three hierarchical layers: specific applications, generic applications and resources.

Resources contain the common application independent basis of CAD functionality. This does not include rudimentary functions for drawing a line or circle on the screen - as this is platform dependant, it is handled within the system component. Resources mean functionality on top of basis functions, like dimensioning, cross-hatching, symbol or group handling, scaling, etc.

Generic applications contain problem oriented functionality for generic CAD tasks. Within the new ECAD system, this part will hold functionality for component designation, connection points, and on top of this designated objects for motors, fuses, relais, terminals, connections etc.

Specific applications hold product, user or company specific application components. Within ECAD, this will be used to model for instance special assemblies, PLC programming and so on.

Within our new system, there are three major applications internally: a project manager module, which helps users to navigate through different projects and locate parts of the design they want to work on. This is supported by the second application, the design editor. The third application is an item editor, which allows to create and/or modify basic objects like symbols, electrical items, list layouts etc..

System components

The services needed to execute an application are delivered by the system components. The CAD reference model splits the system components into six different modular subsystems:

The *user interface system* delivers a standardised, consistent and ergonomic handling of user initiated actions, throughout all components integrated in the overall system. A commercially available interface builder is used in our project to implement this subsystem. This interface builder allows to run a defined user interface on different hardware and software platforms without any adaptations.

The *configuration system* delivers the functionality for a task and user dependent system configuration. It manages the components within the system and the knowledge needed for the configuration. It performs influence to the user interface (the user should not see functionality which he or she is not allowed to use), as well as the loading of additional modules or functionality when required.

The *communication system* and the *communication pipeline* deliver the services for communication and co-operation of the subsystems and the system environment like operating system services and networking. The different components of the architecture do not communicate directly, but use the pipeline and the communication system instead. This enables to exchange any subsystem without harm to the overall system, as long as the new subsystem delivers at least the same functionality. This makes the architecture portable and distributable. This subsystem is based on a CORBA (Common Object Request Broker Architecture) implementation, which provides an object oriented heterogeneous common access to any objects within the system.

The *resources* within the system component represent all application independent tools. They include all basic services and resources, such as OSF/Motif, graphical system (PEX), compiler etc.. This is the place for error handling and recovery, too.

The *product data management system (PDMS)* organises and implements the data access to the product model. It is responsible for the generation of product model schemas, for consistency checks and access possibilities to different views of the product model. It takes care of the users access privileges and is responsible for locking.

The *knowledge management subsystem* gives access to the application specific knowledge. The CAD reference model advises to use the knowledge management to automatically perform design functions within an application. Our implementation initially will only provide services for processing and extension application specific knowledge, and can be later on extended to perform advisor functionality.

The modularity of the CAD reference model - particularly within the system components - allows an open, configurable and modular implementation of a new ECAD-System.

Product model

The product model usually holds different partial models, which form different views of the product. One view could be the mechanical design, another the electrical design, and a third view a three-dimensional view of the control cabinet layout. According to the STEP approach [ISO93], the CAD reference model is layered in three hierarchical structures: the application protocol, the application dependent basic models, and the generic basis models.

The generic basis model contains data common to all applications, whereas the application dependent basic models covers the application specific structures. In ECAD, the application specific model will include the logical information. The application protocol provides the interface for the PDMS to the underlying structures.

Application specific knowledge

In the CAD reference model, the application specific model is split into three hierarchical layers, dependent on commonality and specificity. The layers defined are knowledge resources, generic knowledge and specific knowledge.

Within ECAD, knowledge resources will contain common knowledge about electrical problems, typically taken from books or articles. Generic knowledge includes information about special components and information of component manufacturers. The specific knowledge has to be build up by the users of the system It contains the specific know how of the user's company and products.

The knowledge base captures formal knowledge as well as informal knowledge. Formal knowledge is formulated syntactically, and as such allows automatic checking of design decisions. Informal knowledge needs context-sensitive retrieval and visual inspection of its contents by the user.

Variational design within ECAD

In general, variational design denotes the reuse of an existing design by more modifications and/or variations in order to fit the design fitting to a similar problem. Within MCAD, this usually relates to geometrical variations.

Within ECAD, variational design is a completely new area and covers different problems that have not been treated much in research yet. The following requirements examples from the users point of view shall demonstrate the scope of this problem domain:

- *Different voltage*

  There exists a machine, which works well in Germany and now has to be redesigned for an US customer. This implies a variation in voltage and frequency from 220V/50 Hz to 110V/60Hz.

- *Different power consumption*

  There exists a machine, which almost does the job of the new design. However, the parts which need to be moved by the machine now are heavier, thus the used motors need to be exchanged by more powerful ones. Of course, this influences other parts of the main circuit, such as circuit breakers and fuses.

- *Different number of entities*

  Typically designs depend on certain numbers of entities. Examples of such entities are the number of floors within an elevator design, or the number of printing stations in the design of printing machines.

- *Different manufacturer of components*

  In practice, many companies demand the use of components of a specific manufacturer. In the re-use of a machine design, the components may have to be exchanged by components of another manufacturer. As long as there are equivalent components from both manufacturers, this might be performed just as a change in the parts list. However, if the dimensions differ, it could influence many other parts of the design, even the control cabinet layout. If there is no direct equivalent of the second manufacturer, there will be the need to redesign parts of the schematics.

- *Different security standards*

  Depending on the country a machine is to be operated, the particular country's security standards have to be met. This obviously can affect a design in a rather complex way.

- *Different documentation type*

  As mentioned earlier, there exist local differences in the documentation of electrical designs (horizontal control flow vs. vertical control flow). Therefore, one design can lead to completely different sets of documentation.

- *Different naming*

There exist a number of different ways to designate components. Often, users demand one particular way of item designation. This implies a completely different name set for components, which has to be consistent within the overall design.

This enumeration just gives a glance, how variational design needs to be viewed within the ECAD environment. In practice, there is even the need of arbitrary combinations of the mentioned variations. As an example, the variation of an elevator design from Germany for use in a building in the USA would imply the application of virtually all of these variational design aspects.

Conclusion and prospect

Next generation electrical CAD systems will relieve the user significantly from contemporary routine work. Furthermore, ECAD will be embedded in the overall development process via a common product data model. In order to accomplish this progress, a new system architecture is needed. Future ECAD systems will not substitute electrical design engineers but rather support them by a more intelligent behaviour and system internal knowledge resources.

References

[Abe95]   Abeln,   O.:   CAD-Referenzmodell,   Teubner-Verlag, Stuttgart, 1995

[BoG95]   Booch, Grady: Object-Oriented Analysis and Design with Applications, 2nd Edition, Benjamin/Cummings Publishing Company, Inc., 1995

[ISO93]   ISO-10303, Product Data Representation and Exchange-Part 1: Overview and Functional Principles, ISO/ICE Schweiz, 1993.

[RoRi95]   Roller, D., Richert, U.: "Requirements analysis for next
            generation CAD user interfaces", in: J. Soliman, D. Roller
            (eds): Mechatronics- Efficient Computer Support for
            Engineering, Manufacturing, Testing&Reliability, ISATA
            Proceedings, Automotive Automation Ltd., Craydon,
            England, 1995, pp. 359-366.

[SoTu94]   Sodhi, R.; Turner, J.U.: Relative positioning of variational
            part models for design analyses, *Computer-Aided Design*,
            Vol. 26, No. 5, May 1994, S. 366-378.

[ToCh93]   Toriya, H.; Chiyokura, H.: 3D CAD Principles and
            Applications, Springer-Verlag, 1993.

Cooperative Product Development with heterogeneous CAD systems via EDM and Broadband Communication Technique

Frank-Lothar Krause[1], Helmut Jansen[1] and Thomas Kiesewetter[2]

The following exposition introduces a proposal for a multimedia based working environment which has been developed within a compound research project SEBID (*S*imultaneous *E*ngineering *B*roadband *I*ntegrated *D*evelopment). The concept developed in SEBID covers manyfold facilities of broadband communication technology, delivering new and powerful capabilities of information processing for the product development process. Video conferencing, distributed cooperative modelling and hypermedia techniques are noval tools for the designer enabling him to understand his product development task as a group task which can be concurrently performed in terms of distributed subtasks. Different aspects of the proposed working environment are discussed. The exposition concludes with an outlook on further development work within the project SEBID2 which also is currently running in Berlin. Main task of this project is the integration of commercial CAD systems CADDS5, CATIA V4 and ProEngineer with distributed product data management and hypermedia systems into a mutual system environment for distributed cooperative work.

---

[1] Fraunhofer Institute for Production Systems and Design Technology (IPK), Berlin, Germany
[2] Institute for Machine Tools and Factory Management (IWF), TU Berlin, Germany

Introduction

Due to current demands for the improvement of „time to market", companies are forced to follow new strategies organizing and performing their product development process in terms of distributed single subtasks. In consequence the increasing distribution of product development tasks onto different locations requires a fast and comfortable cooperation between designers involved for adjusting their development activities. Todays CAD systems do not support simultaneous engineering work sufficiently, since they have not been made for those requirements [KrJK95]. CAD systems used to design and develop todays products of rapidly growing complexity must therefore address more needs than before [VHou92]. Noval techniques are suited to support the designer in a very intuitive way developing new products. The number of products which are not only manufactured but also developed by supplier industries is increasing permanently. Many companies use this method of 'outsourcing development tasks' to accelerate the product development process and hence shorten lead time. Closer collaboration between supplier and customer is emerging due to the need to coordinate the interfaces among designers. Distribution of design tasks follows the target of allowing different phases of the design process to run in parallel. Engineers are to be abled to perform development tasks in their specific areas of responsibility simultaneously with those of their colleagues, without regard to the local distance separating them [KrKK94].

Broadband communication networks on the basis of B-ISDN/ATM (Broadband-ISDN/Asynchronous Transfer Mode) allow interactive cooperation without delay. They also support dynamical processes with very high data transmission rates such as exchange of video data or simulation processes.

Integration of video conferencing and CAD

Due to high speed data transmission new services such as video conferencing and hypermedia technique will be tapped as noval tools for the product developer. In this way there is a fine possibility for the designer to organize his problem solving process independent from spatial distances via teamwork and simultaneously performed distributed subtasks. Broadband communication techniques like B-ISDN/ATM allow higher data transmission rates, as often used in LAN-networks

[RiKa91]. So it is possible to establish CSCW techniques (*Computer Supported Cooperative Work*) in the WAN area too. Different users can work jointly and simultaneously on the same design object and can interactively follow up the work of their collegues on the screen. Based on suitable hardware the simultaneous exchange of real-time video- and audio-data will be possible. During design conferences virtual working sessions can be performed in this way (Fig. 1).

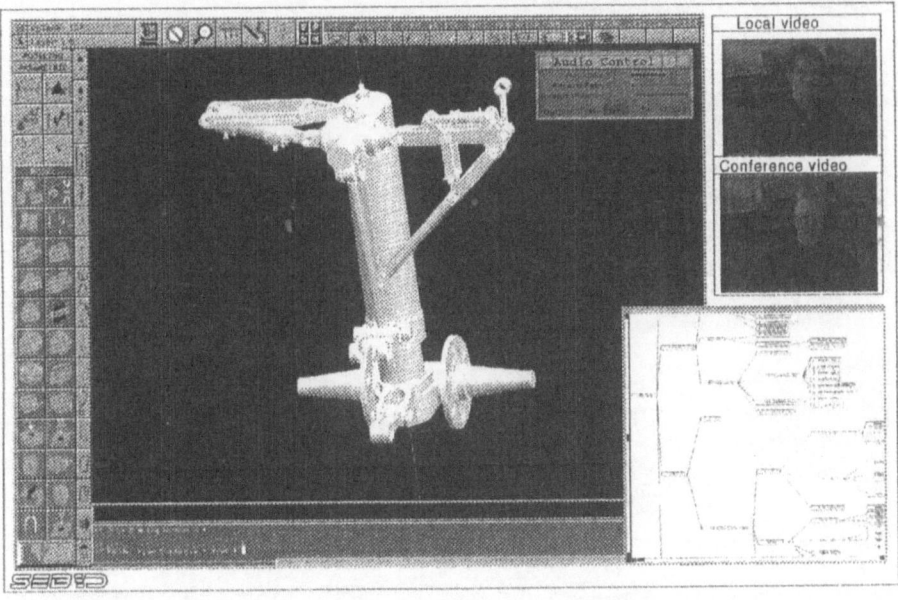

Fig. 1: Snapshot of a typical video conference session for distributed product development

Within the bounds of the project SEBID2 a broadband based working environment for distributed product development purposes will be planned and realized by the Institute for Machine Tools and Factory Management (IWF) in cooperation with the Institute for Machine Design - Design Technology (IMK-KT) both are institutes of the Technical University of Berlin, and some further industrial partners. As distinguished from traditional CAD working environments the essential components of a workstation of that new kind are:

- hardware and software modules for broadband communication,
- product data management system for distributed work,
- Hypermedia product information system (Fig. 2),

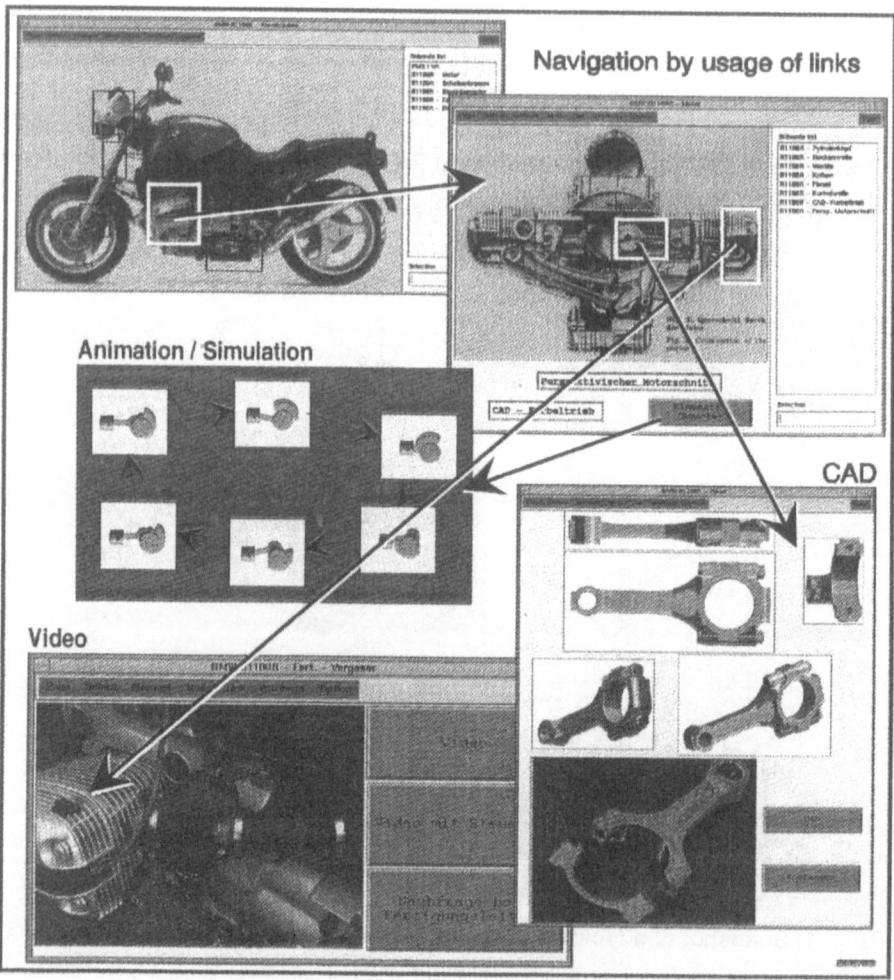

Fig. 2: Intuitive navigation through product data by sensitive regions and links

- integrated commercial CAx systems as well as
- tools for CSCW.

The realized product development environment includes a hypermedia system which has been enhanced by special functionalities to make it feasible for a multimedia product description. Sensitive regions above views of three-dimensional CAD models can be used to realize an intuitive and fast navigation through complex product data. Video descriptions of manufacturing processes or simulation results can be placed and invoked at any 'point of interest'.

Product data management for distributed appli-cations

There are two main reasons for the development of an own product data management system for distributed applications:

- a product data management system for distributed applications (PMS/DA) should include specific functions which cannot be found sufficiently realized in commercial CAD systems.
- a PMS/DA should be completely open to be adjustable to any further technical demands.

In the first step of realization of the planned client-server-architecture of the PMS/DA network software has been selected according to the existing demands for distributed work. Within most of the commercial systems 'Remote Procedure Call' (RPC) has been succeeded on this level of realization. A standardized format for the exchange of data, the 'External Data Representation' (XDR), has been used for this. Benefits for implementation of distributed applications by using RPC's are as follows:

- ability for running on heterogeneous platforms,
- support of UDP and TCP/IP,
- configurability of RPC's, such as 'timeout behaviour',
- as-it-were-standard of client server implementations.

Fig. 3 shows the client server architecture of the PMS/DA.

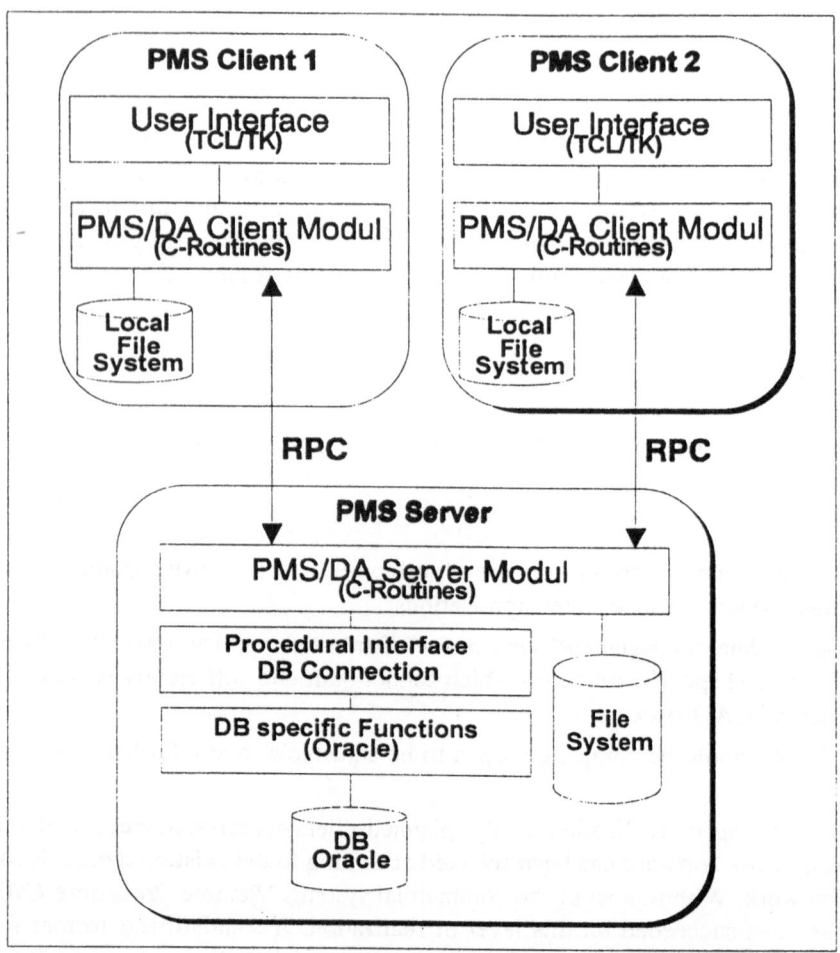

Fig. 3: Client Server Architecture of the PMS/DA

Client Server Interface

For the definition of the interface between client and server the following criteria have been especially considered:

- due to the way of realization the server should become independent from the user shell,

- the clients should provide a minimal amount of status information as far as possible,
- the interface should be open for later functional extensions.

Since the PMS/DA server should also be addressable by further applications the server functions have been realized independently from user interface technology of the client. This is unalterable for the connection of the PMS/DA server to new generation of clients for specific demands. For further development needs of the whole system no effort has been spared to guaranty open system qualification of the implementation.

Session management

Since the PMS/VA is to offer specific support for the distributed product development process the demands of the user regarding network transparent working has been of concrete concern during implementation steps. Therefore, a session management function has been integrated in the client server system. Contrary to the procedure often practised within commercial systems that the user is poorly informed about the current system status, as there is for example display of a message about the fact that a user is not allowed to have access to specific product data since somebody different is currently accessing these data, the PMS/DA provides the user with further important information concerning his current working situation. So in such a situation the user will be informed by the PMS/DA, who currently is using the product data of common interest and is therefore locking them against further access, for which reason he is doing that and which system he just is using. In this way the session management offers the possibility to control the distributed design process and in case make necessary agreements with colleagues.

In order to offer error-redundant system capabilities reference information about used clients as well as about handled product data is stored in a session list within the data base. In case of power failure or other system disturbances leading to an interrupt of the server activity, this information will be saved. It is used for regeneration of working conditions as it has been before system break-down concerning client-server connections and the status of handled product data as well.

Integration concept for heterogeneous CAD and EDM systems

Main task is the development of a supporting tool for distributed cooperative work on complex products on the basis of different heterogeneous CAD systems. The functionality of todays EDM systems is partially ripe already. EDM system vendors frequently offer interfaces for the integration of heterogeneous CAD systems into their data management environment [ABFJ91]. But during realization it often can be stated that these solutions allow the integration of just one specific single CAD system platform. Aim of the described solution in this project however is the development of capabilities to manage the administration of a product structure in the target system which combines CAD data of heterogeneous systems such as CADDS5, CATIA V4 and ProEngineer as well as especially given multimedia product data.

The described approach has been started to be realized with the following three CAD systems:

- CADDS5,
- ProEngineer and
- CATIA V4.

Working at distributed locations using different product modelling tools forces the decomposition of the complex product into single subparts according to criterions depending both on the company structure and the kind of the product. A typical example for this can be found in those subparts of a product which can form a specific compound part of the product structure, for they are developed and manufactured by the same supplier company. In the same way manufacturing technology- or department-oriented criterions can lead to specific product structures.

In case of distribution of product development tasks between different cooperating product developers, data management must guarantee observance of basic conditions, overall consistancy of the product model and actuality of used data for everybody involved in the distributed development process.

Presently, it seems to be clear that there is a concrete need for CSCW technology for distributed product development tasks, since professional discussions by video conferencing represent extremely high comfort for problem solving procedures. If available and easy to handle for every designer, this technology strengthened will support exchange of ideas and design discussions which could lead to higher product quality.

Competed against the overall working time of a designer video conferencing generally will be used just in a small part of the whole product development process. In contrary a product data management system which cannot be missed for distributed cooperation has to be disposable reliable and network-wide over 24 hours a day. It is fundamental for successful and fast product development distributed over different locations. This is the reason for the generation of a multilevel concept for the integration of heterogeneous CAD systems using EDM software.

Integration level 1

The first step to be taken in order to integrate heterogeneous CAD systems into a central EDM system is to integrate the model data correlating with the CAD systems. Therefore programming interfaces of EDM or script languages can be used to make the model data of each used CAD system manageable by the EDM system. The client-site will have to be enriched by functionalities to check-in, store, check-out and archive the data given by each specific CAD system. In a first realization stage the user is able to define and work with a product structure consisting of heterogeneous CAD data. If he asks for a part to be checked-out for visualization or modification the CAD model will be transferred to the system currently running the client. If an executable of the CAD system exists on that client system it can automatically be invoked with the choosen model data. If not the user will be informed about this fact and consequently has a chance for an adequate reaction (Fig. 4).

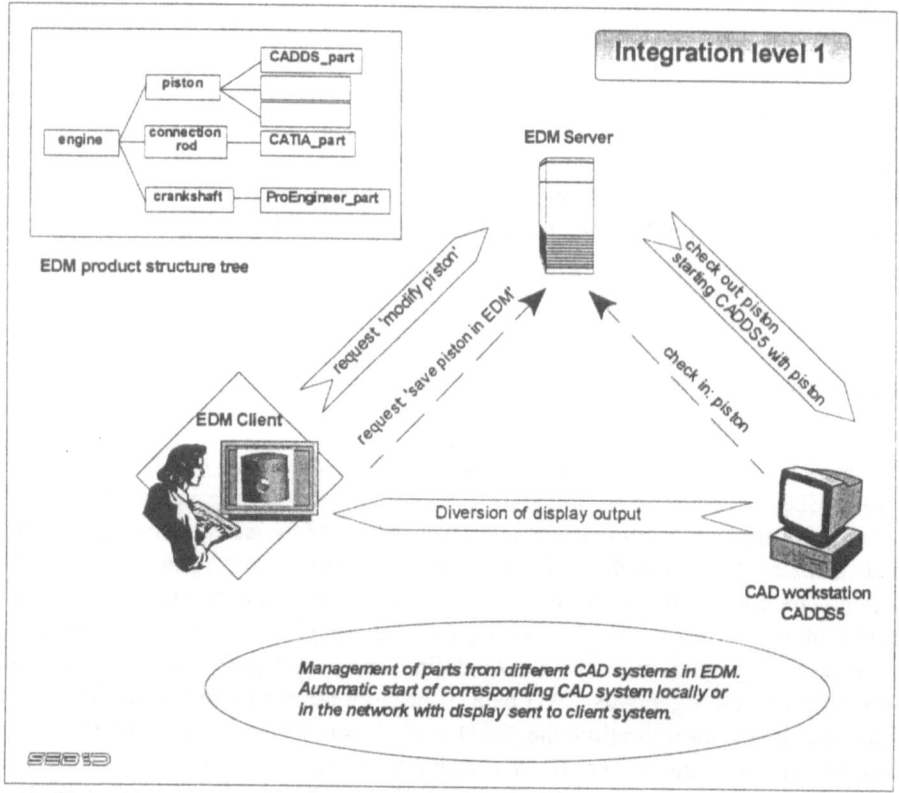

Fig. 4: Integration of heterogeneous CAD systems using EDM system

In a more advanced implementation of the first integration level the model data will be checked-out to another system in case of local nonexistence of the CAD system on the client-site. In this case the user should be able to define each workstation in the broadband network that will be used for a specific CAD system. Therefore the client has to inform the server about the location of the 'CAD server' to be used. The product data then will be checked-out to this server in order to be invoked with the CAD system, sending its output display to the EDM client. To use this functionality the performance of the network should be very high. The advantage of the described realiziation is that each user does not need to have licences for each CAD system used during the product development process what means saving of money this way. The priciple of this technique is shown in figure 4.

Integration level 2

The second integrational level defined within the procject SEBID2 is based on the first level. In addition to the functionality of level 1 the next implementation will integrate CAD data in neutral formats such as IGES or VDA/FS into the EDM system additionally to the original CAD model data. After each modelling process the system automatically runs a converter towards one of the mentioned neutral formats and stores the resulting file in the same folder the CAD model is stored. Another user running another CAD system on a remote site is now able to preconvert the neutral file into its target format and afterwards loads the resulting CAD model into its model structure. For digital mock-up or control of assembly manufacturing this functionality can be used sufficiently. This architecture comes along with another facility. After a selection of a specific node in the heterogeneous product structure tree the user finds another menue, called 'VIEW ONLY' which will run a CAD viewer to easily view the model. Users working with a specific CAD system over years will therefore not have to run another CAD system just for viewing a part. The implementation described here will be based on a command trigger functionality which enables system developers to define trigger points inside EDM when a specific own application will have to be started up. On the CAD system's side some requirements are necessary for the realization of this implementation. The convertion from or towards neutral data formats must be available in form of a script or an executable running without the CAD system. If this conversion can only be done inside the CAD system the system is not open enough for this architecture. The concept is described in figure 5.

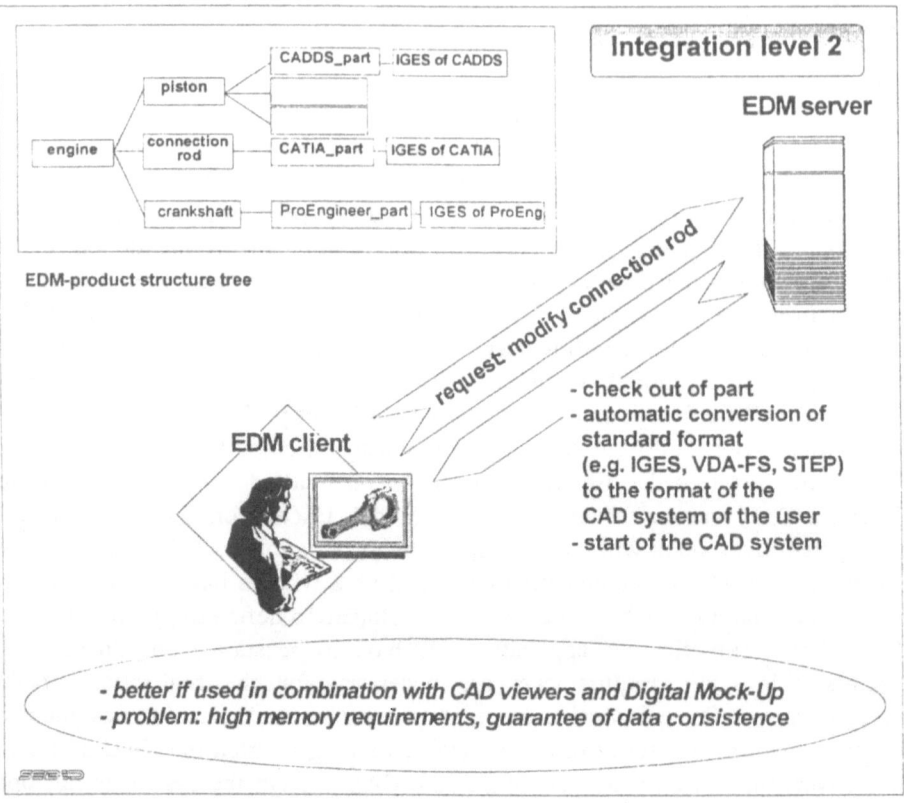

Fig. 5: Integration of heterogeneous CAD systems using EDM systems and standard format data

Integration level 3

The next integration level again consists of two stages. The first stage follows a similar procedure as described in level 2 with the integration of STEP as the neutral file format. Because of lacks in describing parametric information at the current state of definition and implementation it is not sufficient to handle only physical STEP files of CAD models. Currently they have to be used in addition to the original CAD data format. By integrating pre- and post-processors towards STEP API 203 and 214 which will be invoked automatically, if the user is not working with the CAD system corresponding to the choosen part or sub-assembly part, the integration of heterogeneous CAD systems into an EDM system can be performed (Fig. 6).

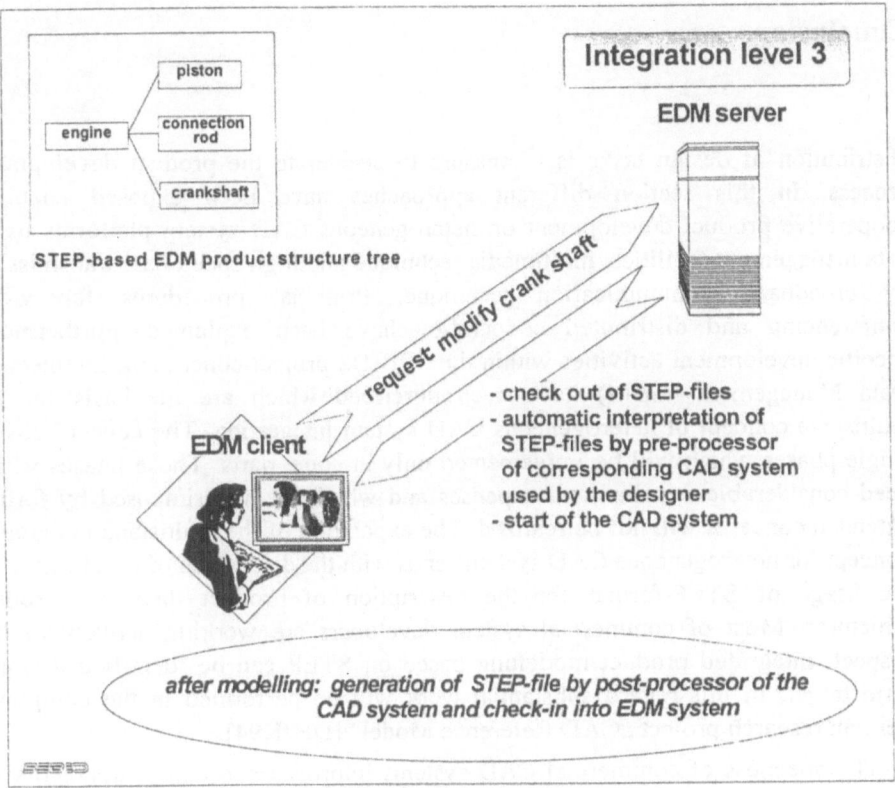

Fig 6: Integration of heterogeneous CAD systems by management of product structures defined with STEP in EDM system

The final aim of integration will be the internal management of product structures inside EDM by STEP conform data management procedures instead of lists in a relational database such as ORACLE. This step towards product modelling can only be taken in cooperation with the vendors of EDM systems because of the necessity to change internal system structures. The architecture of such a target system is described in figure 6.

Conclusion

Distribution of design tasks is a measure to accelerate the product development process. In this section different approaches have been exposed enabling cooperative product development on heterogeneous CAD system platforms using data management facilities, multimedia technique and high speed data transmission by broadband communication technique. Principal procedures for video conferencing and distributed cooperation have been explained. Furthermore, specific development activities within the SEBID2 project concerning Engineering Data Management (EDM) have been described which are the basis for the multistage concept of heterogeneous CAD system integration. The concept covers single phases which will be implemented only in some parts. Those phases which need considerable development expenses and which are superimposed by further extended concepts will not be realized. The exposition of the multistage integration concept for heterogeneous CAD systems ends with the discussion of capabilities for the usage of STEP-format for the description of product data and product structures. Most of commercial system developers are working actively in this respect. Integrated product modelling based on STEP can be identified as long-term target. In this regard substantial work will be performed in the compound german research project „CAD Reference Model" [DHJK94].

The openness of commercial CAD systems improves constantly. Indicators for that are standards such as CORBA and DCE which are supported more and more by those systems. Due to this fact integration of heterogeneous CAD and EDM systems will be possible easier. Beside that, this technology will obtain a further push by reinforced succeeding object orientation of the developed software which includes easy adaptation and data encapsulation.

Just so in the area of network technology which is indispensable for realisation of that kind of systems as described in the section, very fast development of this advanced technology can be stated. So the glass-fiber network concentrates permanently and its availability grows continually, so that described direct and interactive possibilities for distributed cooperation via high-speed networks as well as centralized administration and control of most complex product data will not remain just a vision for the product developer. Only integrative usage of the described systems in total will lead to considerable support of product developers for their daily team-work [KJK96a].

Acknowledgement

The results described in this section have been achieved within the research projects SEBID and SEBID2, both sponsered by DeTeBerkom GmbH Berlin.

Special thanks to Uwe Böttge and Heiko Dierking for their fine support.

References

[ABFJ91]   Abramovici, M.; Bickelmann, S.; Friedmann, T.; Jungfermann, W.: Engineering Data Management Systeme, Technologiereport Ploenzke Informatik, Wiesbaden, 1991.

[DHJK94]   Dietrich, U.; Hayka, H.; Jansen, H.; Kehrer, B.: Systemarchitektur des CAD-Referenzmodells unter den Aspekten Kommunikation, Produktdatenmanagement und Integration, in: J. Gausemeier (Hrsg.), CAD'94 - Produktmodellierung und Prozeßmodellierung als Grundlage neuer CAD-Systeme, Carl Hanser Verlag München, 1994, 353-374.

[KJK96a]   Krause, F.-L.; Jansen, H.; Kiesewetter, T.: Integration von CAD-Systemen in eine multimediale Breitband-kommunikationsumgebung zur kooperativen Produkt-entwicklung, in: D. Ruland (Hrsg.), CAD'96 - Verteilte und intelligente CAD-Systeme, PRODUserv Springer Produktions-Gesellschaft Berlin, 1996, 296-310.

[KJK96b]   Krause, F.-L.; Jansen, H.; Kiesewetter, T.: Verteilte kooperative Produktentwicklung - durch Integration heterogener CAD-Systeme in eine multimediale Breit-bandkommunikationsumgebung, ZwF 91 (1996) 4.

[KrJK95]   Krause, F.-L.; Jansen, H.; Kiesewetter, T.: Breitband-kommunikation in CAD-Prozessen zur Optimierung der Produktentwicklung, in: U. Dietrich; B. Kehrer; G. Vatterrott (Hrsg.), CA-Integration in Theorie und Praxis, Springer-Verlag, Berlin, Heidelberg, New York, 1995, 223-240.

[KrKK94]   Krause, F.-L.; Kiesewetter, T.: Kramer, S.: Distributed Product
             Design, in: Annals of the CIRP, Vol. 43/1, 1994, pp. 149-152.

[RiKa91]   Ricke, H.; Kanzow, J. (Hrsg.): BERKOM Breitband-
             kommunikation im Glasfasernetz, R.v.Decker's Verlag, G.
             Schenck, Heidelberg, 1991.

[VHou92]   Van Houten, F. M.: Manufacturing Interfaces, in: Annals of the
             CIRP, Vol. 41/2, 1992, pp. 699-710.

Chapter 2

Product Data and Development Process

Overview

Product Modelling for Design for Manufacture and Design for Assembly

Graham Jared[1]

Design for Manufacture and Design for Assembly are now established as important tools in implementation of Concurrent Engineering. Their integration into the CAD environment is desirable for several reasons which are discussed. However, there are difficulties in getting accurate information from the designer. An alternative scenario is therefore examined in which data required by such design evaluation tools is extracted from a geometric / CAD / product model. The tools and their product data requirements are described together with an assessment of the relevant capabilities of 'state of the art CAD systems'. An outline is given of the progress and present status of a research response to the resulting challenges to product modelling and geometric reasoning techniques.

Introduction

It is perhaps ironic that advances in geometric modelling, a subject that is generally agreed to be part of the field of Computer-Aided Design, have been more extensively taken up and used in Analysis and Manufacturing applications. Indeed, the concept of a product model as a collection of data describing a product, with a geometric model as the underlying core, seems to have been developed for this very purpose. It is, however, widely accepted that costs of a producing an artefact are largely determined in the design phase, even if they are actually only incurred at a later stage during manufacturing. Thus it is during design that the greatest influence can be exerted on the product

---

1 School of Industrial and Manufacturing Science, Cranfield University, UK

introduction process in order to reduce costs. The same argument also applies to reduction of lead times. It follows that it is highly desirable that designers be made fully aware of the implications of their decisions for downstream processes.

There is scope for argument as to how best to achieve the goal of better informed decisions at the design stage. The viewpoint taken on this must to a certain extent depend on the model of the design process that is adopted and the role foreseen for computer tools within it. Much of the recent literature on assembly modelling [GuMä94, ShRo93, Mä91, RoLi88] has concentrated on support for the early stages of design and the decomposition of a product into assemblies and sub-assemblies and so on. In other words it has assumed a "top-down design" process in the terminology used by Sodhi & Turner [SoTu94]. The focus of attention here will not be on discussion of "top-down" or "bottom-up" processes, but on defining the product models necessary to support those design evaluation tools which are, hopefully, applicable within any paradigm. This is a different type of activity from devising models to capture design intent and representing the function of components within a product. It is concerned with models needed to underpin the assessment of the implications for manufacture, with special reference to costs, of the present state of a design. Since small perturbations of a design can result in large changes, beneficial or otherwise, in manufacturing costs, such design evaluation must play an important role.

The type of information needed for Design for Manufacture (hereafter abbreviated to DFM) evaluation techniques is diverse. There is some common ground with the content of the models, mentioned above, proposed to support "top-down" assembly design, but there is also a significant geometric content. Thus there is clearly a tension between the desire to use DFM at as early a stage in the design process as possible and the need for the techniques to have some definite geometric data to work with.

However, designers tend to carry more than one candidate design through to a significant level of refinement before making a final choice, computerised tools can therefore enhance the critical evaluation of options. In the discussion that follows it is taken as axiomatic that there are benefits to be gained from using design evaluation tools at the stage of the process known as "concept development" [PaBe84]. It is also taken as read that these tools should be provided as an integral part of the CAD environment.

DFM and DFA

DFM is commonly understood as an umbrella term covering many techniques which address considerations relating to product quality and manufacturing systems as well as the production processes. Design for Assembly (hereafter abbreviated to DFA) is usually used to indicate those techniques which focus mainly on the more restricted domain of the assembly processes involved in the production of an artefact.

There are a number of DFA techniques in current industrial use or documented in the published literature. Although they have diverse origins they have some common aims and share similar characteristics. It is therefore perhaps reasonable to assume that the lessons drawn from an examination of how one of these methodologies can be integrated with CAD have the potential for wider application. In the text that follows the DFA methodology concerned is that described in [Mile89].

The cost of assembling a product is often dominated by the number of operations to be carried out which is, in turn, related to the number of components involved. Thus a major aim of DFA techniques is to drive down part count by eliminating "redundant" components or by forcing amalgamation.

Another major factor in determining assembly costs, especially for products that are to be assembled automatically by dedicated machines or by robots, is the cost of the machinery itself. The need for more sophisticated assembly systems often incurs an apparently disproportionate increase in the cost. Thus DFA techniques also include a rigorous and detailed examination of the feeding, gripping and insertion processes used in assembling a product.

The ultimate conclusion of driving down part count might be to design products as one single complex component. DFA techniques must therefore include some consideration of the cost of component manufacture to provide an effective counterbalance to this. Such estimation of component cost usually takes into account factors such as the manufacturing processes to be used and the tolerances that have to be achieved.

Each analysis area - function, feeding, gripping, fitting and manufacturing - provides feedback to the designer in terms of a scoring system for each candidate design. Those aspects of a design which have given rise to poor scores can then be the focus of re-design effort.

DFA methodologies can be implemented as "paper-based" systems through the use of workbooks and questionnaires or as software. They may be used by a single user or by teams working on a particular product design. Historically, DFA was used more in a posteriori design analysis role, but lately its use has become increasingly a more integrated part of the design process. Whatever the intended mode of use there has been a trend toward software implementations. This is driven by a desire for systematic application, a need to ensure that all issues are addressed and a wish for consistency in the process and its results.

Early DFA software tended to be procedural implementations of questionnaires, but the knowledge intensive nature of the methodology led to the production of knowledge-based expert systems. Whichever paradigm is used for implementation the user must potentially provide a significant amount of data about a candidate design. However, there are various factors which militate against the intensive user interaction demanded by this. Firstly, designers have many other tasks to attend to and, secondly, such re-inputting of data gathered from elsewhere is tedious and error-prone. Last, and by no means least, the designer may not understand questions relating to manufacturing considerations and may therefore give incorrect answers.

A brief examination of ways of avoiding intensive user interaction leads to the hypothesis that much relevant information may be contained, either explicitly or implicitly, in some product data models analogous to those developed for other applications. This is plausible since much of the data necessary for DFA analyses concerns component geometry and other information that might be inferred from it. In such a scenario much of the interaction with the designer would be replaced by automatic extraction or inference of the necessary data. A more in-depth analysis of the product data needs of DFA confirms the hypothesis, as will become clear later.

Linking DFA and CAD software

Both CAD systems with facilities for product modelling and knowledge-based implementations of DFA are inherently fairly large pieces of software. This, together with the conflict between procedural and declarative paradigms, were initially perceived as a major barriers to integration stretching from the conceptual down to the practical implementation level. However, as it turns out, useful links can be built.

Firstly, some consideration has to be given to the nature of the necessary linkage. Is passive data transfer from CAD to DFA sufficient? Is it a question of "filtering" existing entities used in the CAD representation to find the data relevant to DFA? It might be possible to use existing geometric functions provided in the CAD system to compute the information needed by DFA. Some kind of specification of the product data requirements, albeit formulated in terms meaningful in the DFA domain, can be produced by a detailed examination of the user interface of existing standalone software.

This latter approach, for example, has been used in the past [Swif87] to implement a CAD to DFA link in which the drawing file of a 2D CAD system is post-processed by a knowledge-based DFA implementation to build a simple model within the knowledge-based system environment. This is in turn used to perform some simple reasoning to provide information to some parts of the DFA analyses. Such an approach gives a demonstration of feasibility, but is not felt to be worth pursuing for several reasons. Firstly, its is not easily extensible - it is a considerable leap from handling the 2D geometric entities representing simple components to the full 3D implementation necessary to handle all components that the DFA analysis can be used on. Secondly, the PROLOG language used in the knowledge-based system is inappropriate for implementation of processes which are effectively duplicating, rather poorly, those of a geometric modeller.

However, a more suitable software architecture can be derived from the earlier attempts just described in the following manner. The functions necessary to provide the product data needed for DFA analyses are divided into three categories: firstly, those that belong in the geometric modelling arena - some may already be implemented in most existing geometric modellers; secondly, functions that can be provided in a "geometric reasoning" environment which has access to geometric modelling facilities through some programming interface; and, lastly, those functions that can be implemented in the DFA knowledge-based system environment - again assuming access to geometric reasoning functions and (possibly) geometric modelling functions. The complexity of such an arrangement reflects both the breadth of aspects of a product design that are relevant to DFA and also the high geometric content of the criteria used in DFA evaluation. The resulting software architecture is shown in Figure 1.

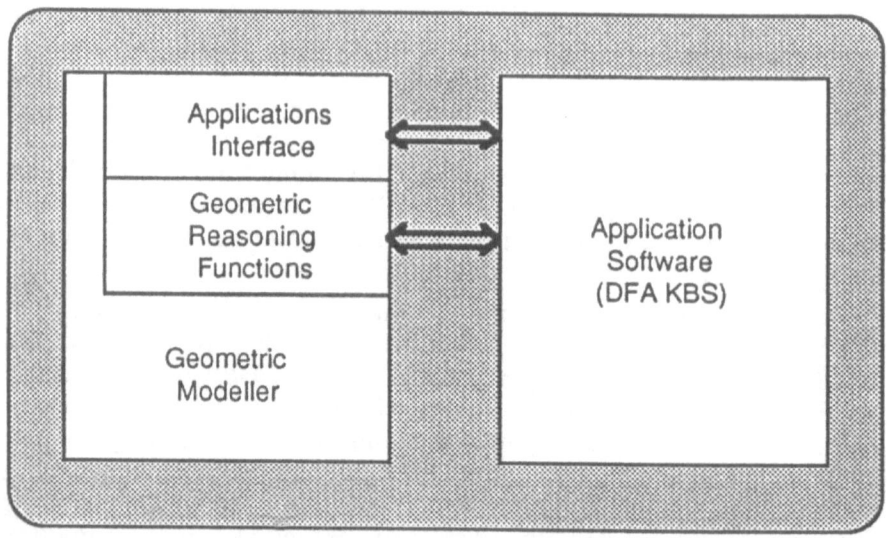

Fig. 1: Linking CAD and DFA systems

In order to actually map out in detail the functions needed in the three categories just described it is necessary to have both a thorough understanding of the underlying intent of the formulations used in the DFA analysis and the potential and actual functionality of geometric modellers. Such understanding is generally only available through collaborative projects involving researchers from both topic areas.

It is still too early to base any CAD to DFA link on such emerging interface standards as the ISO STEP SDAI for two reasons. Firstly, the current state of the art of geometric modelling and geometric reasoning (even assuming that this is captured in STEP) is not able to fully implement support for DFA methodologies as they currently stand. Secondly, DFA itself is a developing area and evolution of the methodologies will call for further development of geometric modelling and geometric reasoning. At least efforts to develop a standard geometric modelling application programming interface such as, for example, DJINN [BCJM95] for the research community are taking some of the present needs of DFA into account.

Methods to define the product modelling requirement

As already intimated the goal of defining the product modelling functions necessary to support DFA cannot be reached through a simplistic examination of user interactions with existing knowledge-based system implementations. What is needed is an examination of the intent of the formulations used in the DFA analyses in order to generate, wherever necessary, revised formulations for an integrated CAD and DFA environment. The outcome of such revision may fall into one of more of the following four categories: it may define a need for further additions to the knowledge-base, a demand for better engineering science formulae to predict the behaviour of components, a specification of a geometric reasoning function, or a value to be extracted directly from the geometric model. Only the latter two of these cases will be considered here.

Any DFA methodology must cover a large range of issues - the one discussed here [Mile89] has five general areas of analysis, each with several different formulations potentially needing evaluation; there are a total of forty seven to be examined in the manner just described. The task is in fact even larger than this figure might suggest because the products to be analysed by DFA may contain components of any geometric category, including shapes bounded by free-form surfaces. Furthermore, a range of manufacturing processes may be considered for each component - not only metal removal, but casting, forging and others. This in turn has implications for the geometric representations employed. The work reported here was only concerned with components represented by solid models. It may be that many components and processes might be more appropriately supported by lower dimensionality models, such as wireframes or surfaces. Thus any attempt to implement an integrated CAD / DFA environment with truly global coverage would have to address problems, such as those examples given in Figure 2 below, in a multi-dimensional modelling context - a fairly awesome task! It is therefore necessary to present the results of any study of the linkage of CAD and DFA in a structured manner with a careful definition of the boundaries of the domain considered. Even within the restricted domain of solid modelling, it is possible to differentiate between geometric reasoning tasks which could easily be accomplished using existing modellers and algorithms and those whose implementation depends on the result of further research. Figure 2 illustrates this by tabulating the perceived degree of difficulty of various geometric modelling tasks against the geometric domain -

rotational parts, prismatic parts and so on. The table entries reflect a
view at a particular point in time. However, it is still fair to say that
geometric reasoning with objects bounded by free-form surfaces is
perceived as a difficult area. It also remains a tenable view that the
analysis of symmetry of objects from their geometric models has only
been seriously addressed for a limited geometric domain.

	PURELY ROTATIONAL COMPONENTS	ROTATIONAL COMPONENTS + OTHER	PURELY 2.5D COMPONENTS	2.5D MULTI-AXIS COMPONENTS	3D FREE FORM COMPONENTS
SHAPE REP-RESENTATION	0	1	0	1	3
FEATURE RECOGNITION	0	1	2	3	4
VOLUME DET-ERMINATION	0	1	1	1	3/4
OTHER MASS PROPERTIES	0	1	1	1	3/4
STABILITY CRITERIA	1/2	3	2/3	3	4
SYMMETRY ANALYSIS	1/2	3	2/3	3	4
ATTRIBUTE ATTACHMENT	0	2	2	2	3/4

DEGREE OF DIFFICULTY SCALE 0-4
0. All the knowledge required to accomplish this aspect is currently available
1. Solutions to specific problem cases still remain for this area.
2. Still requires a dedicated research effort to achieve a viable solution.
3. Research is only at the conceptual stage
4. Only the problem has been identified.

Fig 2: Perceived degree of difficulty of geometric tasks
for different component types

Implementation issues

What follows is a discussion, based on the results of a recent research project., of the some of the implementation issues relating to providing product modelling support for DFA, A more general overview of this work and its application with a case study product are reported elsewhere [JLSS94]. A prototype software implementation of a DFA system was built in PROLOG (this will not be described in detail here) and integrated with a product modelling system based around the BUILD-4 geometric modeller [Stro89b]. The latter is a rather "long in the tooth" boundary representation modeller which has acted as research vehicle for geometric modelling for many years. Although BUILD-4 is a direct ancestor of several current commercial products, it does retain some unique characteristics which justified its continued existence and its use in the work reported here.

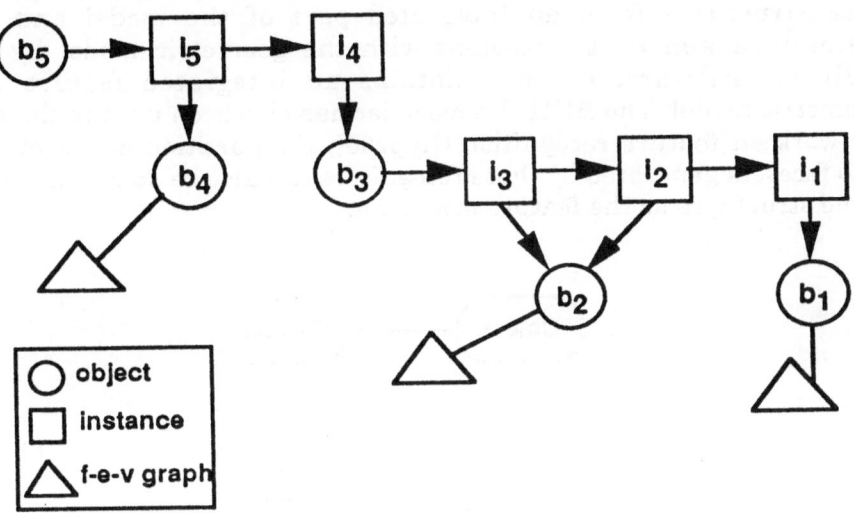

Fig 3: Final assembly model implemented as an "instance tree"

The major advantages of the use of BUILD-4 were that it already had, albeit often in a fairly rudimentary form, the facilities needed for the work. Thus, for example, it was capable of representing assembly and sub-assembly structures through an "instance tree" data structure [Brai80]. In this objects are represented as being made up of either a face-edge-vertex graph or a linked list of instances of other objects each with an associated co-ordinate transformation. Thus a product may be represented as a tree with all interior node being objects of the "linked list of instances" type and the leaf nodes being objects containing the face-edge-vertex graph and geometry (see Figure 3). It should be noted that this structure, known as the Final Assembly Model, can only model the positions in space of the components of a product in its finally assembled form. It does not contain any information about the sequence of assembly or the relationship between components, this function is performed by other structures which will be described later.

At the Component Model level (i.e. single objects) BUILD-4 has data structures that allow the modelling of features as collections of faces and the simultaneous holding of multiple feature decompositions of an object [Stro89a]. This is implemented by representing features as collections of faces in which faces may occur in more than one feature, and by using the concept of a decomposition of an object made up of a collection of features. Each object modelled by BUILD-4 has one face-edge-vertex graph, but can have many feature decompositions or "partitions" associated with it (see Figure 4). These feature modelling data structures form an integrated part of the model and are maintained and kept consistent with the geometric model by the BUILD-4 software, i.e. it maintains an integrated feature and geometric model. The BUILD-4 modeller has also been used in the past for work on feature recognition [Kypr80], the partitionings of objects into facesets generated by these recognisers can also be stored using the same structures as the feature modelling.

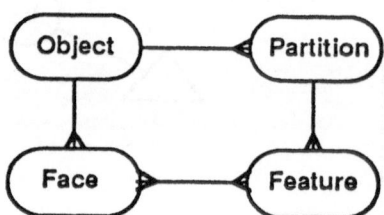

Fig. 4: Relationship between objects and their feature decomposition in BUILD-4

Finally, again mainly as the result of previous work in other application areas such as CAPP [Jare86], BUILD-4 has facilities to attach attribute data to basic modeller entities such as faces and also to features. This mechanism can be used to associate such information as material properties with objects, surface finishes with faces and / or features and so forth. It also allows a fairly crude approach to representation of tolerances within the geometric model although it is heavily reliant on the user's co-operation in assigning tolerances attributes to the appropriate structures.

All the BUILD-4 facilities described above are needed to provide product model support for DFA, but this is far from sufficient to achieve the objective of comprehensive coverage of all the data requirements. Out of those remaining, some have elements in common with those types of model developed to support assembly design, but a significant remainder are specific to DFA.

As previously mentioned, DFA techniques involve a thorough examination of the assembly process under the headings of feeding, fitting and gripping. Each of these analyses potentially needs information about the configuration of components at intermediate stages of the assembly process and also the operations to be used in proceeding to the next stage. This information is provided from data stored in two further layers of the product model, known as the "Component Interaction Model" and "Assembly Plan Model". Both of these models are also integrated into the BUILD-4 environment so that they may directly reference each other and also data held in the Final Assembly and Component Models (see Figure 5).

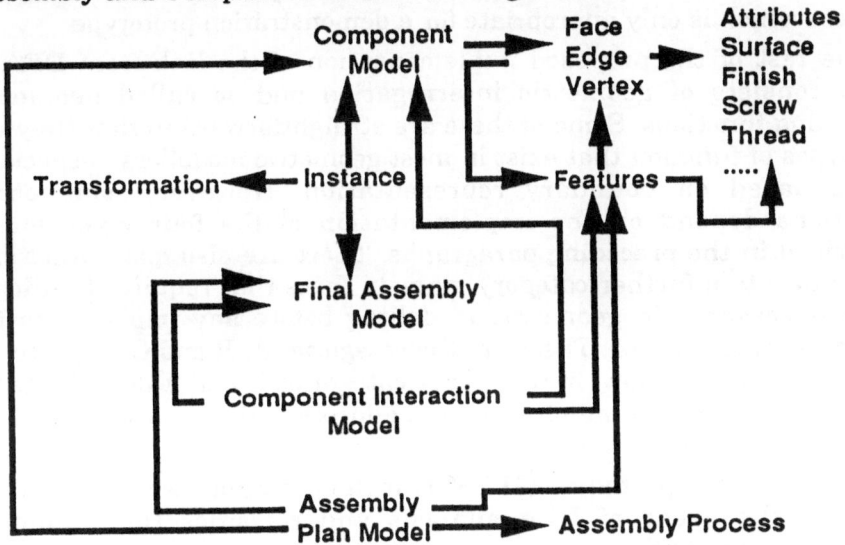

Fig 5: Relationships between four layers of product model

The Component Interaction Model stores information about which features of components are involved in a particular step of the assembly. Thus it is made up from structures that provide an association between an "assembly operation" in the Assembly Plan Model and the relevant the component(s) and their features that take part. The Component Interaction Model uses references to entities within the Final Assembly Model to indicate which components are being assembled and into the Component Model to show which features are involved. An "Assembly Operation Code" is used to indicate the type of operation being carried out.

The Assembly Plan Model is composed of structures representing the steps of the assembly process. It is made up of structures which indicate, by reference to the Final Assembly Model, the components used in each sub-assembly created in building up to the final product. Some concept of timing is kept within this model so that, for example, operations that involve the simultaneous mating of more that one feature can be accurately represented.

Both the Component Interaction and Assembly Sequence Models can be decomposed into list or list of lists type data structures and this is exploited in the mechanism used in passing them over to the PROLOG implementation of the DFA software. At present, the models are constructed within the BUILD-4 environment by a laborious interactive process which is only appropriate for a demonstration prototype.

The rest of the proposed implementation of the link from DFA to CAD consists of geometric interrogation and so called geometric reasoning functions. Some of these are straightforward in that they are the types of function that exist in most geometric modellers - especially those based on boundary representation. However, some other functions depend on the implementation of the four layer model described in the preceding paragraphs. There are also many functions that fall into a further category, namely those that require significant further research in geometric modelling before any implementation could be contemplated. These are the categories A, B and C respectively used in Figure 6 below; in this figure categories D and E describe those functions considered inappropriate to address and those considered too difficult to address.

The results reported in [JLSS94] include a study which examines each of the areas of DFA analysis and classifies the geometric interrogation and reasoning functions needed according to the categories just described.. Figure 6 reproduces in tabular form a summary of the numbers of functions in each category for the whole DFA methodology and a breakdown for each of the areas of DFA analysis described in a previous section. Examples of category A functions might be: the calculation of mass properties (volume, moments of inertia etc.) or interrogations of the type of geometry of faces (planar, cylindrical etc.). Category B corresponds closely to the second one described above, i.e. it mostly relates to extraction of information from the four layer model.

	Number of criteria in section	Number of criteria in A / B / C	Number of criteria in D / E	Percentage analysis covered by groups A&B	Percentage analysis covered by groups A, B & C
Functional analysis	7	0/2/0	4/1	29	29
Manufacturing analysis	9	2/4/0	3/0	67	67
Feeding analysis	14	1/5/5	1/2	43	79
Fitting analysis	9	0/5/3	0/1	56	89
Gripping analysis	4	0/2/2	0/0	50	100
All DFA analyses	43	3/18/10	8/4	49	72

Fig. 6: Table of geometric reasoning functions for each analysis area

The table of Figure 6 represents a generic result for products within the geometric domain considered - the implementation of a system covering all A and B criteria within the Manufacturing and Fitting Analyses is described in [JLSS94] together with a case study of a specific product.

There are several interesting challenges to geometric modelling research in the list of category C functions. The first of these is the detection of symmetric shapes through examination of their geometric model and also the isolation of those features which make an otherwise symmetric shape into an asymmetric one. A second topic which appears to need further study is the rapid detection of components that might be crushed or broken during assembly. It is clearly undesirable to engage in a fully-fledged stress analysis of a component when it is often the case that a simple rule of thumb based on geometric criteria could give an adequate answer for the purposes of DFA.

Other problem areas for geometric reasoning are concerned with the interactions of two or more instances of the same component during the feeding process. Examples of these are "tangling" and "nesting". The first of these describes a situation often encountered when trying to remove one paper clip from a pile of them - it is common to find one or more clips have become chained together. Nesting refers to a situation exemplified by a pile of paper cups, stacked one inside the other. Any attempt to remove the item on top of the stack leads to the removal of several items together.

No satisfactory solutions to any of these problems: symmetry, delicacy, tangling or nesting, appear to be available at the moment. Furthermore, it is far from clear how an approach to the solution of these problems might be developed based on boundary representation. However, methods which assume a set theoretic model, such as Woodwark's Algorithm [PBBo95], may well provide one in the near future.

Concluding Remarks

It has clearly been demonstrated that design evaluation techniques like DFM and, in particular, DFA present some significant challenges for product modelling. These fall into two categories: firstly, the provision of appropriate models of products and the process of assembling them; and, secondly, the extension of geometric reasoning to implement some fairly sophisticated geometric criteria used in DFA analyses. It is still the case that, due to the breadth of knowledge required, further progress in providing product model support for DFA will continue to depend on close collaboration between researchers in the two areas.

It is also clear that further work may be needed on appropriate methods for developing feasible assembly sequences.- the laborious, interactive model building is only sensible within the context of proving of a concept. It appears more than likely that recent research on the top-down approach to assembly design will provide some promising directions for solution.

Finally, it is worth noting that DFA methodologies continue to develop, in particular in the range of products and processes that can be addressed. This will in turn dictate a requirement for product models to be able to handle the appropriate shape representations. The necessary capabilities might be achieved, for example, through the use of mixed dimensionality or non-manifold modelling where wire, sheet, solid and cellular entities can be handled in one integrated environment. This, of course, would in its turn demand further new developments in geometric reasoning.

Acknowledgements

The author gratefully acknowledges the support of the ACME Directorate of the UK SERC under grant GR/F 70785 and the contribution of his co-researcher, Professor Ken Swift of Hull University and research assistants Mark Limage and Ian Sherrin. The author also acknowledges the generous help of many industrial collaborators including: Keith Shaw of PAFEC Ltd., Brian Miles and Graham Hird of Lucas Engineering and Systems Ltd; Mike Houldsworth and colleagues at Lucas Assembly and Test Ltd (Buckingham), Geoff Parmenter and Paul Kronan at Lucas Diesel Systems (Sudbury).

References

[BCJM95]   Bowyer, A., Cameron, S.A., Jared, G.E.M., Martin, R.R., Middleditch, A.E., Sabin, M.A. & Woodwark, J.R.,: Introducing DJINN, a geometric interface for solid modelling, ISBN 1-874728-08-9, Information Geometers Ltd., Winchester, UK (1995)

[Brai80]   Braid, I.C.,: Notes on a Geometric Modeller, University of Cambridge, Computer Laboratory CAD Group Document 101 (1980)

[GuMa94]   Gui, J-K & Mäntylä, M.,,: Functional understanding of assembly modelling, CAD J., Vol. 26, No. 6, pp435-451 (1994)

[Jare86]   Jared, G.E.M.,: Feature recognition and Expert Systems in Operation Planning for NC Machining, Proc. Int. Conf. AI EUROPA 86, Wiesbaden, September 86, TCM Expositions, Liphook, UK (1986)

[JLSS94]   Jared, G.E.M., Limage, M.G., Sherrin, I.J. & Swift, K.G.,: Geometric reasoning and design for manufacture, CAD J., Vol. 26, No. 7,pp528-536 (1994)

[Kypr80]   Kyprianou, L.K.,: Shape Classification in Computer Aided Design, Phd Thesis, University of Cambridge (1980)

[Ma91]   Mantyla, M.,: WAYT: towards a modeling environment for assembled products,: in Yoskikawa, Arbab & Tomiyama (eds), Intelligent CAD III, Elsevier Science Publishers 1991, pp187-202.

[Mile89]   Miles, B.L.,: Design for Assembly - A Key Element Within Design For Manufacture, Proc. I. .Mech. E., Vol 203 (1989)

[PaBe84]   Pahl, G. & Beitz, W.: Engineering Design a systematic approach, The Design Council, London, 1988.

[PBBo95]   Parry-Barwick, S.J. & Bowyer, A.,: Multidimensional set-theoreticfeature recognition, CAD J., Vol. 27, No. 10, pp731-740 (1995)

[RoLi88]   Roy, U. & Liu, C.R.,: Establishment of functional relationships between product components in assembly database, CAD J., Vol. 20, No. 10, pp 570-580 (1988)

[ShRo93]   Shah, J.J. & Rogers, M.T.,: Assembly Modelling as an Extension of Feature-Based Design, Research in Engineering Design, Vol. 5, Nos. 3 & 4, pp 218-237 (1993)

[SoTu94]   Sodhi, R & Turner, J.U.,: Towards modelling of assemblies for product design, CAD J., Vol. 26, No. 2, pp 85-97 (1994)

[Stro89a]   Stroud I.A.,: Modelling with Features and Manufacturing Data, Internal Report, Solid Modelling Group, Cranfield Institute of Technology (1989)

[Stro89b]   Stroud, I.A.,: The bumper BUILD-4 funbook ...., Cranfield University CAE Group, internal report (1989)

[Swif87]   Swift, K.G., "Knowledge-based design for Manufacture", Kogan Page, UK (1987)

Extracting Reusable Product Data

Martti Mäntylä[1]

The competitive environment of industrial companies has changed dramatically during the last decade due to requirements of decreasing product life cycles, increasing product complexity, and rapid lead time. From product modelling viewpoint, this poses several challenges not effectively met by past and present research. These include adequate life-cycle support, including early stages of design; process support for different types of engineering processes; integration of different perspectives to product information. These issues are illustrated within the context of production preparation on the basis of the practical experiences gained from the process planning system MCOES++ developed at the Helsinki University of Technology.

Introduction

The present industrial environment is characterised by increasing demands on product customisability, short and dependable order delivery, and reduced product life cycle. Faced with these pressures, companies throughout the world are investigating, assessing, and re-engineering their operations in order to eliminate unproductive work, to streamline the core processes, and to find opportunities for improving their performance by use of automation and information technology.

Effective administration of information is a key ingredient in these activities. In the future, companies cannot survive solely by excelling the logistical management of the physical material flow through the

---

[1]Helsinki University of Technology, Espoo, Finland

various activities; they must also excel the logistical management of the various types of information flow. A key objective for the logistical management of information is *reuse of existing information*: ideally, all information created or learned should be made available to later use in a correct, useful, and timely fashion.

For industrial companies, the bulk of information which is needed by the core processes is related to the products of the company. Consequently, *product modelling* has been recognised as a key technology for improving the information logistics of companies, and thereby their overall competitive position. In brief, product modelling can be characterised as a *unified methodology of capturing and representing product information of various types, and of making these data available to various activities of a company*. This includes both formalised, computerised methods, and informal organisational methods; these two should form a harmonised union.

The development of product modelling methods reflects the development of the underlying processes utilised in product realisation. In the conventional Taylorian functional paradigm that still forms the mainstream of how industrial companies perceive themselves, various functions such as design, production planning, and actual production are functionally separate. As a consequence, "islands of automation", i.e., functionally independent CAD, CAPP, production management, and CAM systems have emerged, each with its own separate product modelling capabilities (e.g., geometric models, group technology codes, and bill-of-materials). The objectives of product modelling are viewed *a posteriori* as an interfacing problem, where some means of data exchange between the independent design, planning, and production systems needs to be introduced. As a result, neutral static file interfaces such as IGES and STEP have been developed.

What forms the motivation our work is that presently a "Copernican revolution" in the basic thinking about the overall layout of company functions (and consequently, information technology based systems supporting these functions) seems to be in progress. Many researchers in the field expect that the result will be a new manufacturing paradigm which is based on a complete departure from the Taylorian functional division of the operations of a company [Yosh93, Tomi94].

The objective of this contribution is to give an analysis of the essential requirements and issues for the new generation of product modelling systems, aimed at forming the backbone of future knowledge-intensive CAD systems and the new manufacturing paradigm. These topics are illustrated within the context of extracting reusable production information on the basis of product and process models.

Change Pressures

To understand the requirements of the new manufacturing paradigm, it is useful to first look at the qualitative changes in the competitive environment of industrial companies a bit further.

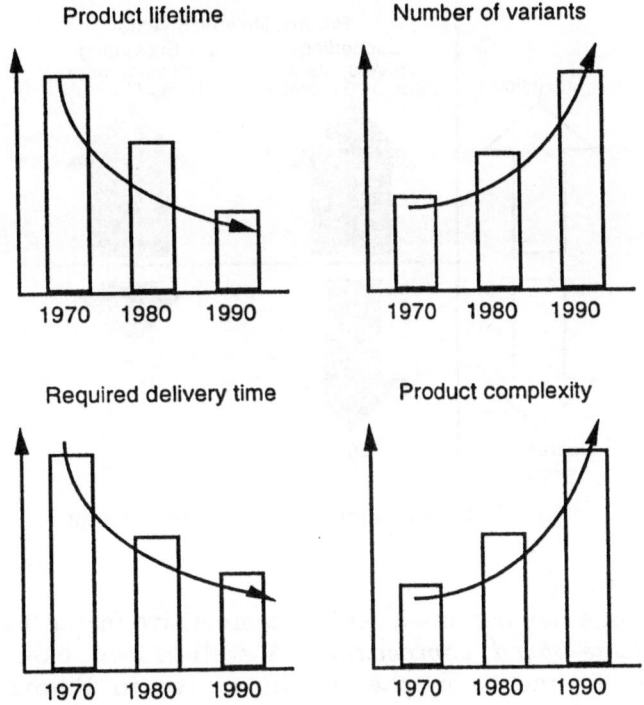

Fig. 1: Qualitative changes in the competitive environment

Some of the main qualitative changes in the competitive environment experienced by industrial companies are summarised in Figure 1. As indicated, *product life times* are getting shorter; a product which used to stay on the market for ten years must now be replaced after five years or even less. At the same time, the *number of product variants* is increasing; more and more customers demand products tailored for their particular needs (but are not willing to pay more). The case of a white goods company who reports that the number of product variants has increased from 200 in 1984 to 600 in 1992 is typical. The products are also more *complex* than before: increased demands on functionality, quality, durability, and environmental safety require more complex and integrated product designs where several types of engineering expertise are needed. A typical case is integration of mechanical and electrical engineering in mechatronics products. Last but not least, customers require the delivery of the products to take place more rapidly; the *required delivery time* which was measured in months or weeks in the early 1980's is now measured in days and even hours.

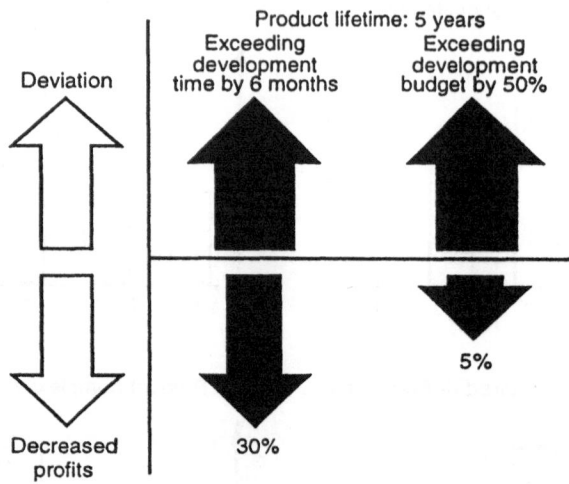

Fig. 2: Time to market as a competitive factor

In general, time has become a central competitive factor, leading to the concept of *time-based competition*. A well-known example of the importance of time to market is illustrated in Figure 2. Taking somewhat pessimistic stance, it depicts two scenarios of failure in product development, namely (i) exceeding the planned development time by six months (but staying within budget), and (ii) exceeding the development budget by 50% (but making it in time). On the basis of assumed product life time of five years, the overall decrease of profits computed over the whole lifetime of the product is in case (i) 30% and in case (ii) 5%. That is, given the choice, one should be prepared to spend more money to get the product to market in time. For further discussion on the importance of time to market, see [RoMB93].

Other significant change pressures are caused by the movements towards *Total Quality Management* (TQM) and the increasing concern over the environmental influences of a product and its manufacture [ToSU95]. Both of these require a holistic view of the product life-cycle from the early design stages to delivery, use, and dismantling.

Process-Based Paradigm

The roots of the new manufacturing paradigm may be found from the TQM approach. A core idea of TQM is that *the quality of a product is a result of the quality of the process which makes it*. The same observation holds for many of the other objectives discussed above such as reduction of lead time, improving total flexibility, and optimising the total environmental characteristics of the product.

Process improvement includes a sequence of activities according to the following outline:

Process modelling	A process must first be made visible by investigating the steps of the process, the actors performing these steps, the resources consumed by the various steps, and the sequencing and interfacing of the steps. Various models and notations for process modelling have been developed to help documenting the result.
Process simplification	Starting from a virgin state, a process often turns out to have unnecessary, non-value-adding steps which can be eliminated or merged with neighbouring steps. For any improvement effort to succeed, such process streamlining activities are typically needed.
Design of process improvement	A new, improved process is designed to replace the old process. New process design may include activities such as process benchmarking, aimed at identifying the "best practice" for the process. Investments needed to implement the new process are planned and analysed.
Process implementation	The new process is implemented. This may include a variety of activities from investments to information and automation technology to personnel training.
Process performance measurement	To assure that the new process works as intended, a measurement system for tracing process performance must be designed and implemented. The measures range from relatively abstract, high-level measures (such as total order lead time, total working capital requirements) to concrete, low-level measures (such as % of good parts made in a manufacturing step, % of orders handled within the specified time).

The whole sequence cyclically repeated. Major process renewals are augmented by continuous improvement activities such as Kaizen.

The result of applying the principles of process improvement to the activities of the whole company (or its core process) results in a *process-based view* [McCu93] of the company and its activities as shown in Figure 3. Instead on the functional division of the company, the emphasis is on the *business processes* of the company, in particular the *core process* (customer order satisfaction) and its *support processes* (such as new product development and production system development). The support processes are targeted at maintenance and improvement of the competence of the operative processes, and at holistic direction-setting for the whole company. Many of these processes will include other companies, such as customers, subcontractors, service providers, government bodies, and external experts.

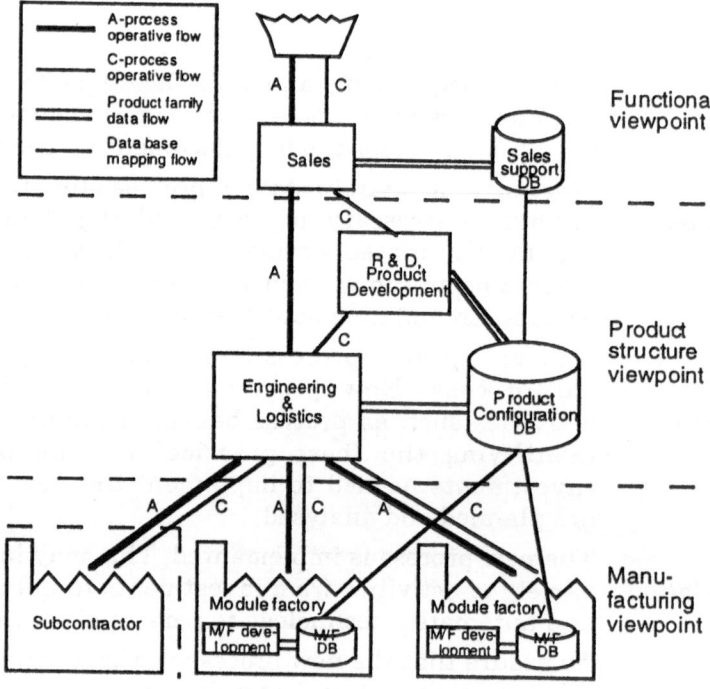

Fig. 3: Process-based view of a company

The customer order satisfaction process is typically the core process of any manufacturing company. This process starts from the customer (who is the "king", therefore denoted by the crown in Figure 3!) and ends in the shipment and successful installation of the product. The process often continues after these steps to include use, servicing, renovating and eventually dismantling the product.

Figure 3 is based on a simple ABC-classification of the customer order satisfaction process according to the degree of variability of the product being made. In particular, it makes a distinction between three types of the core process:

A-process   The customer order satisfaction process of a completely standard product ("No new drawings required").

B-process   The customer order satisfaction process of a non-standard configuration of the product made of standard modules ("New assembly drawings required").

C-process   The customer order satisfaction process of a non-standard configuration of the product which includes non-standard modules ("New detail drawings required").

The A-process should be simple and efficient. Information flow should be unidirectional to the extent possible, for instance on the basis of parametric designs and product configurators. The C-process should provide enough flexibility to support all intended customer needs. The B-process is intended to cover the middle ground.

Several support processes are also alluded to in the figure:

Product process   New products or modules are developed and released for sale and manufacture in a systematic schedule.

Production development process   The manufacturing capabilities of the company are systematically developed and improved by introducing new production machinery, tools, materials, and methods, and making automation or IT investments.

Marketing process   Products are systematically marketed to customers. Emerging customer requirements are systematically tracked and mediated to product developers.

After sales processes   Products are serviced, maintained, and renovated; related services are provided to customers. In some companies, these activities may constitute another core process, in addition to the customer order satisfaction process.

The various process steps are performed by *agents*. The following lists some of the most important agents and their tasks:

Customer   Customer requests a product or a service.

Salesperson   The salesperson translates a customer request (including the unstated customer requirements) to a specification of a product or service to be provided. In a support process, he or she transmits customer needs to product developers as a basis of development.

Product engineer	The product engineer configures a product satisfying the product specification and all applicable functional, technical, and economical criteria.
Manufacturing engineer	The manufacturing engineer specifies a production process which creates the product. The process should lead to a product with correct quality and cost while using the available resources effectively. In a support process, the manufacturing engineer develops the production facilities to improve cost effectiveness, quality, lead time, and throughput.
Product developer	The product developer designs a product platform and modules so that a wide variety of customer orders can be satisfied by combining and varying the modules, and the modules can be manufactured effectively.

Observe that the different agents assume different *viewpoints* to the product. Customer's viewpoint focuses on the function and behaviour of the product; salesperson's on the capture and translation of customer requirements as a specification; the product engineer's on the product structure; manufacturing engineer's on the manufacturing process; and product developer's on the optimal mapping of a set of functional needs to a product platform and related modules.

Figure 3 also includes several *data bases* containing product and related information. Ideally, these should be organised on the basis of the different agents' viewpoints to the product:

Sales database	The sales database should be based on customer-perceived functions of the product; its main objective is to support precise capture of customer needs.
Configuration database	The configuration database should be based on the product structure as modules and subassemblies; its main objective is to support concurrent engineering based on the recorded customer requirements.
Production database	The production database should reflect the production system; its main objective is effective production planning such that the resulting process plans use the available resources in an effective manner.

The databases must also support tactical and strategic processes. For instance, results of product development must be mappable to the configuration, sales, and production databases.

From the product modelling viewpoint, nearly every interface between the components of Figure 3 poses a challenge. For instance, the *specification mapping* from customer-perceived functional specification of a product to a structural specification has proved to be a tough nut to break. Another kind of mapping takes place between product development and configuration design: the objective of this mapping is to create a reusable product configuration model for use in the customer order satisfaction process on the basis of information created during the product development process.

A number of other significant issues and challenges raised by the architecture of Figure 3 include the following:

- The introduction of new products should be an orderly process, preferably based on a regular versioning cycle (e.g., new products are released twice a year). Observe that the "productisation" of a new product involves creating information for sales, configuration, and production databases as needed by intended process (A, B, or C).

- During the life cycle of a product, its customer order satisfaction process type may change. For instance, a product may first be introduced as a C-process product; later, it becomes a B-process product, and even later an A-process product. At the end of the product life it may again become B- or C-process product.

- Ideally, a complete trace of a customer order back to the original source of information should be created and saved. This includes the preservation of a "complete" design rationale. These data are needed, for instance, to fully implement ideas of Total Quality Management.

- Increasingly often, the design of a complex industrial product is no longer performed by a single, geographically centralised team of designers, but by several co-operating teams which divide the total design effort between themselves by some criteria, such as the engineering discipline involved (e.g., electronics design/mechanical design) or product structure (main modules). The teams may belong to different units of a single company, or increasingly often they come from several co-operating partner companies. Distributed operation opens a whole range of new issues such as concurrency control, change propagation, and negotiation protocols.

Process-Oriented Product Modelling

The process-based paradigm puts emphasis on the horizontal flow of information between the various agents of the core and the support processes. The "stone walls" between the various functions must be broken: Design will interact with later product life-cycle stages to exchange information and knowledge; manufacturing will utilise design information to aid its decision-making. The interaction crosses the boundaries of a single company to its suppliers and partners. It also bypasses ordinary hierarchical levels of company administration (many of which will disappear). To achieve these objectives, new methods of product modelling which support cross-functional work will be needed.

A central concept for the various levels of process-based product modelling is *reusability*. Reuse may involve engineering data at many levels, starting from the functional specifications and overall design rationale and ending with individual product modules, components, and their technical and geometrical details. A summary of possible reuse at stages of product development is given below:

Customer-perceived functions	What does the product do? What qualitative or quantitative requirements can be placed on its functions? What undesirable behaviours must be avoided?
Basic construction	What are the physical principles of the product? What functions are needed to realise customer-perceived functions? What functional subsystems are required?
Modules and subassemblies	What modules are required to implement the product? What are their functional and structural properties (parameters)? How are the modules interfaced?
Parts and components	Which parts are needed in the product? What requirements must they satisfy (geometric, materials, mechanical, electrical, etc.)? How are the parts joined?
Production processes	What production processes can be used to realise the product? Which production lines/cells can be used to implement the processes? Which resources (machines, tools, auxiliaries, etc.) are needed?

The extent of reusability may vary from one level to the other. For instance, physical realisation of two products may be quite different even when they are intended to satisfy a similar set of customer requirements. Even in this case, reuse of high-level product information should be possible. More commonly though, a set of reusable basic modules can be used to implement many combinations of customer-perceived functions. Effective implementation of this approach ("mass customisation") clearly requires product modelling facilities for reuse.

We conclude that new types of product modelling methods explicitly addressing the various issues of the new environment will be needed to support the process-based paradigm. Information flow and exchange between the stages of the core process must be viewed *a priori*: the processes and their supporting tools are designed to support and take advantage of knowledge flow. The realm of product modelling must also include the tactical and strategic processes of a company.

Therefore, the objectives of product modelling for the process-based paradigm are the union of the following three viewpoints:

Operative data: customer delivery process	Support flow and sharing of product data through the core process, that is, the customer order satisfaction process. In other words, deploy reusable information to facilitate effective execution of the various tasks of the operative process. [Short term]
Tactical data: product life-cycle modelling	Support the capture and sharing of product information covering the whole product life-cycle from design to manufacturing to eventual dismantling, reuse, and recycling. In other words, deploy information gathered from support processes in later operative process activities. [Medium term]
Strategic data: technology management	Support the capture and reuse of information from one product to another by capturing product data in a reusable form. That is, deploy (core) competence to product development. [Medium to long term]

As indicated, the focus of the operative viewpoint is on short-term management of information while the focus of tactical and strategic viewpoints is longer. The challenges of product modelling stem from the complex interaction of these three distinct viewpoints and time scales. The biggest gaps in present state of the art are between the stages of the various life cycles (customer order satisfaction, product life) and between the different levels of life cycles themselves. For instance, how can design process rationale information (tactical process) be used as a resource in creating product configuration models (operative process)?

Issues in Production Preparation

The challenges of product customisability, short and dependable order delivery, and reduced product life cycle discussed above culminate in production preparation. The puzzle to be solved includes seemingly contradictory elements: we should be able to produce a wide range of parts and modules with a rapid and dependable lead time from production order to delivery, and at the same time provide the capability of introducing new parts and modules to production.

The optimal balance between these desired characteristics depends on the business and products of a company and its core and support processes. Here we focus on one important scenario, namely *mass customisation*. In this approach, the product development creates a customisable product platform consisting of a range of variant modules and parts which can be combined in multiple ways to create a product instance satisfying the requirements of a customer. Production facilities are organised according to the main modules of the platform; as a result, "product-oriented" factories intended for the production of a predefined range of variants of a module are built.

The design and implementation of product oriented factories is not a one-shot effort; instead, mass customisation tasks are continuously performed to improve an existing factory and to adapt it to changing product platforms and manufacturing technologies. We may characterise these tasks and their requirements from different time scale perspectives using the three-level scheme discussed above:

Manage operative product data	Support rapid transformation of production orders to detailed instructions required for rapid execution of production processes. This includes process selection, routing, sequencing, and generation of NC programs. Very rapid lead time is desired, measured in minutes and hours instead of days. [Short term]
Product life-cycle modelling	Support rapid introduction of new products and product variants. This coincides with *product family modelling* and *process planning*. To satisfy the requirements of approaches such as DfM and Concurrent Engineering, a rapid lead time measured in hours is desired. [Medium term]
Technology management	Support reuse of production information from one product to another by capturing reusable production data. This requires facilities for characterising and representing recurrent processes and process sequences. Rapid introduction of new production methods for existing products must be supported; other important requirements are placed by quality management and tracability. [Medium to long term]

These viewpoints also match the different viewpoints of the personnel involved in production preparation. In particular, the operative flow of information matches the viewpoint of production cell operators and foremen; life-cycle modelling the viewpoint of process planners and NC programmers; and technology base management the viewpoint of engineers responsible of the development of production methods.

Production Data Reuse in MCOES++

MCOES++ is a new implementation of the MCOES feature-based process planning system originally developed in the Brite-Euram project no. BREU-3528 *Manufacturing Cell Operator's Expert System*. Like its predecessor, the prime objective of MCOES++ is to facilitate reuse of production data at various time scales on the basis of feature-oriented product and production process models. In particular, MCOES++ is intended to serve in the role of the module factory system of Figure 3.

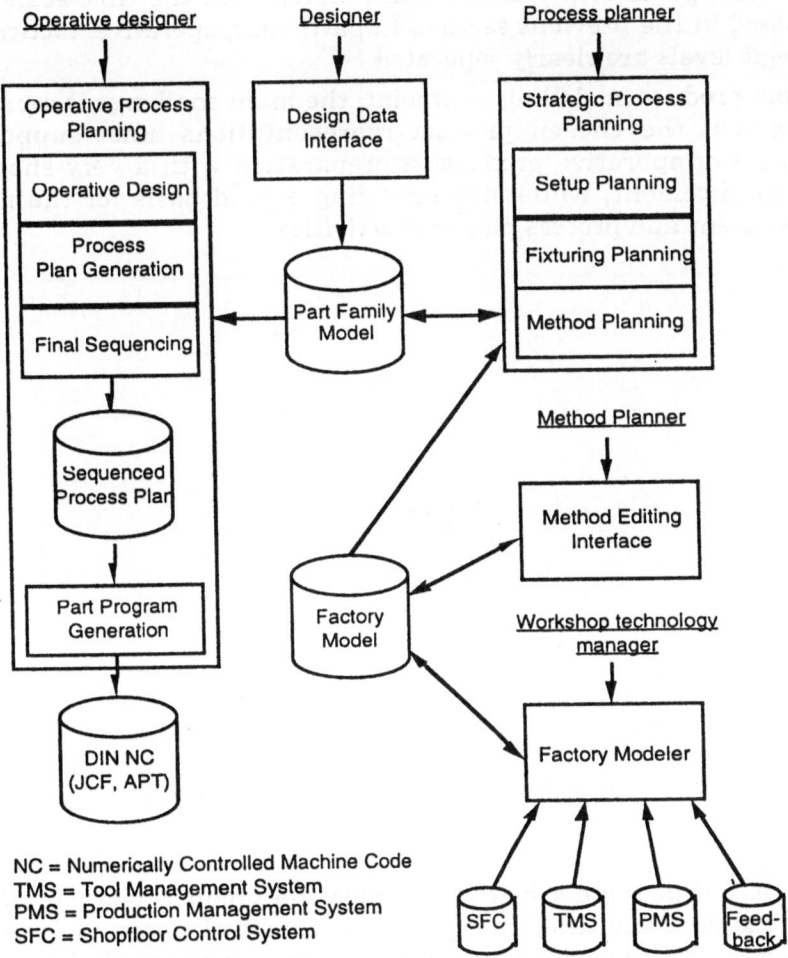

NC = Numerically Controlled Machine Code
TMS = Tool Management System
PMS = Production Management System
SFC = Shopfloor Control System

Fig. 4: The overall architecture of the MCOES system

The system architecture shown in Figure 4 is based on the various user roles in mass customisation:

- *product designer*, who originates the product descriptions
- *method planner*, who generates reusable information on the manufacturing processes available in the factory
- *process planner*, who generates process plans for the products
- *workshop technology manager*, who is responsible for the manufacturing resources in the workshop
- *operative designer*, who is responsible for creating actual process plans on the basis of a manufacturing order.

As seen, parts of the architecture match with the time scale levels discussed in the previous section. In particular, operative, tactical, and strategic levels are clearly separated.

From product modelling viewpoint, the main challenge is *separation of concern*: the chosen product representations must support the activities of operative production preparation with a very short lead time requirement, while also providing a good basis for the method development and process planning activities.

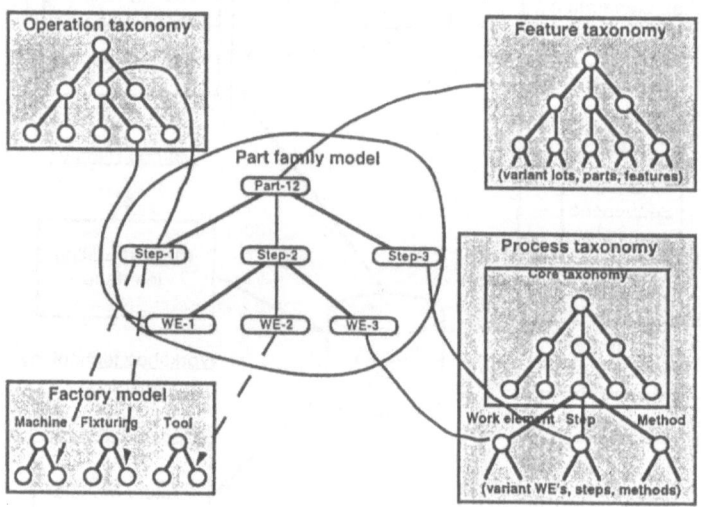

Fig. 5: Outline of the MCOES product model.

To satisfy this, we decided to organise the product model of MCOES along the lines indicated in Figure 5. The central element of the model is the *part family model*, consisting of a parametric description of a part in terms of its manufacturing features and a parametric process plan template [LaMä94]. The part family model is associated with various resource and knowledge models.

Process descriptions are the prime targets for reuse in a process planning system. In addition, the process model of MCOES was designed to support division of tasks. In particular, designers do not need to be bothered about manufacturing processes, and manufacturing engineers do not want (or need) to know about product details. As a result, we decided to use the concept of a *method* as the core entity of our process model [MäPu91].

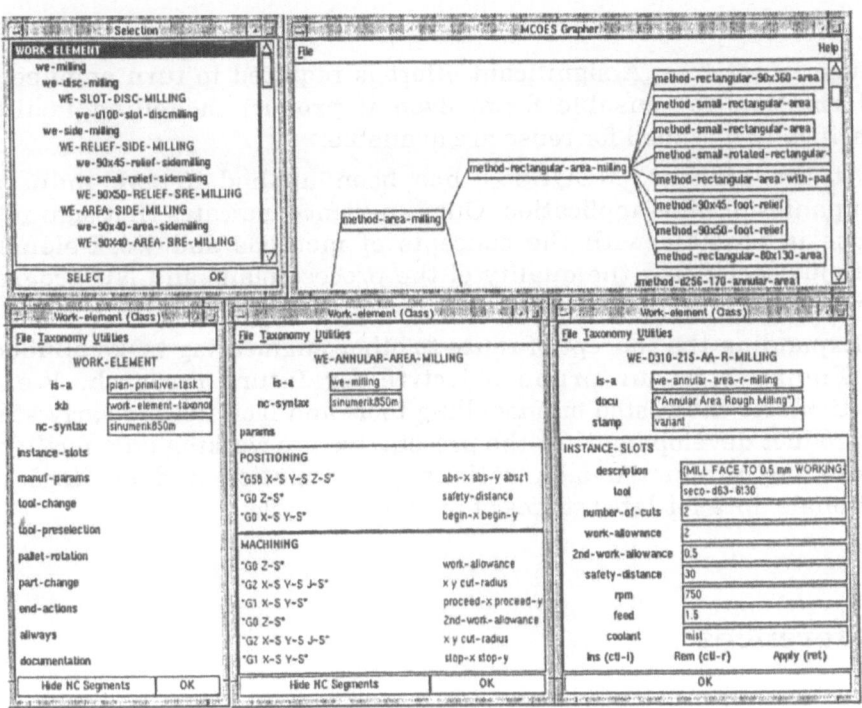

Fig. 6: Method editing interface

Methods are defined by a manufacturing specialist using the interface shown in Figure 6. As seen in Figure 6, a method consists of a (parametric) sequence of primitive processes, termed *work elements*. The bottom half of the figure gives a sample work element definition. Work elements store the detail information of a process such as tool information, machining parameters, and a NC macro for part program generation [OpMä95]. A (parametric) sequence of methods applied in a single setup on a machine is termed a *step*.

Methods are assumed to represent tested and trusted process sequences, for the execution of which the manufacturing system is optimised. Process planning decisions by a process planning specialist centralise on method selection; the planner will not try to reinvent them.

Conclusions

Reuse is not free. A significant effort is required to turn engineering information to reusable form, even if product modelling facilities specifically intended for reuse are available.

At the present, MCOES++ has been applied in two industrial companies in pilot application. Our experience indicates that significant reuse is possible with the concepts of methods and work-elements without sacrificing the quality of the process plans and NC programs generated. Nevertheless, each pilot required several months work.

Expanding the concept of reuse to other engineering tasks alluded to in Figure 3 is our prime objective for future research. We are particularly interested on modelling tools and facilities for early stages of product development. At the present, we are working on a facility for capturing product design rationale information and on deploying rationale data for later stages of product life cycle.

References

[LaMä94]   T. Laakko and M. Mäntylä, Feature-based modeling of product families, in K. Ishii et al., editor, *Proc. of The 1994 ASME International Computers in Engineering Conference, Volume 1*, pages 45–54, New York, September 1994. ASME.

[McCu93]   T. McCusker, Workflow takes on the enterhprise, Datamation 39(Dec. 1), pages 88-90, 1993.

[MäPu91]   M. Mäntylä and J. Puhakka, *Process Plan Model Representation*, BRITE-EURAM Project No. BREU-3528, MCOES, Deliverable WP6-D1(R), 1991.

[OpMä95]   J. Opas and M. Mäntylä, Techniques for automatic part program generation, *Advances in Engineering Software*, 20:141–155, 1995.

[RoMB93]   A. Rolstadås, B. Moseng and D. Blankenburg, Improved competitiveness through concurrent activities and handling of product changes, in *Towards World Class Manufacturing* (ed. M. Wozny and G. Olling), pages 119–133, Elsevier Science, 1994.

[Tomi94]   T. Tomiyama, From General Design Theory to Knowledge-Intensive Engineering, *Artificial Intelligence for Engineering Design, Analysis and Manufacturing* 8(4), pages 319-333, 1994.

[ToSU95]   T. Tomiyama, T. Sakao, and Y. Umeda, The post-mass production paradigm, knowledge intensive engineering, and soft machines, in *Life-Cycle Modelling for Innovative Products and Processes* (ed. H. Jansen and F.-L. Krause), pages 369–380, Chapman & Hall, 1995.

[Yosh93]   H. Yoshikawa, Systematization of design knowledge, in *Annals of CIRP*, Vol. 42/1/1993, pages 131-134.

Virtual Prototyping - An Open System Environment to Support the Integrated Product Development Process

Joachim Rix[1] and Holger Kress[1]

The ability to rapidly prototype a proposed design is becoming a key contributor towards fulfilling the business requirements embodied in a short time-to-market, in cost-effective and high quality manufacturing, and in easy support and maintenance. Reorganizing the design and development process along the lines implied by the concept, *Concurrent Engineering*, means that advanced information technologies must be taken advantage of. However, most of today's generic, commercial, off-the-shelf technologies have to be extended and adapted to the needs of the product development process. The integration of existing technologies in CAD modelling, design, analysis, simulation, networked cooperation, and virtual reality leads to a distributed desktop-environment which provides the basis to take the greatest advantage of the Virtual Prototyping technique.

Introduction

The use of physical prototypes is a widely adopted technique to verify the design and the functional behaviour of complex products. Especially in the automotive and aircraft industry physical prototypes, also called mock-ups, are built to check aesthetical details and overall appearance of a product, to confirm that products are easy to assemble and disassemble or to prove the ergonomical design of cars and aircraft. In the development cycle of these products a huge series of different

[1]Fraunhofer-Institut für Graphische Datenverarbeitung (IGD), Darmstadt, Germany

prototypes is produced. Normally these prototypes are made by hand in specialised departments, which makes this technique especially expensive and time-consuming. Consequently the industry tries to establish new processes which reduce both costs and production time.

In the past several years, the development of powerful computing hardware led to an increasing number of sophisticated engineering applications. Especially in the area of mechanical systems design an immense progress in the development of modelling, analysis, and simulation software has been achieved. 3D CAD systems provide high-level modelling operations in combination with kinematics, NC simulation or FEM analysis. Real-time analysis and simulation of multi-body systems has been realized in specialized applications. The need for a neutral representation of the different data sets related to one product has been identified. Therefore concepts for the covering of all these information arising during a product's life cycle have been defined in the STEP project of the International Organization for Standardization [ISO94]. The information is represented by a conceptual information model, called product model. By means of the STEP product model and rules for the handling of these models it will be possible to describe product data in a unified way and to share product data between different systems without any loss of information.

These developments led to a vision of a computer based prototype. While the occurrence of a physical prototype represents a realistic first model of a part, a computer based prototype realizes the functional behaviour of the underlying product model by means of computer based simulations. In this context the term *Virtual Prototype* has been formed. It is defined e.g. by Haug et al. [HKT93] as "a computer based simulation of a prototype system or subsystem with a degree of functional realism that is comparable to that of a physical prototype". This phrase emphasises as one of the most important characteristics of a Virtual Prototype the realistic, dynamic simulation of the functional behaviour. The simulation can either be an off-line simulation without human action involved or a real-time operator-in-the-loop simulation including human interaction.

The Virtual Prototyping Process can be regarded as an important method to shorten the product development time and to reduce or eliminate the use of real physical mock-ups. The greatest advantage of this process can only be taken if a full integration in the whole engineering process is achieved [Kre95]. The realization goes along the lines implied by the concept, *Concurrent Engineering*, which can be regarded as a systematic approach to an integrated product development which embodies parallel work, cooperation and information sharing among designers, mechanical engineers, manufacturing engineers and project managers.

Scenario

The improvement of the product development process is a major goal for companies and enterprises to remain competitive. Organizational changes and the use of innovative software tools are inevitable to reduce product development time and costs. A key concept used to achieve this goal is Concurrent Engineering. Focusing on the design phase of a product, the notion of Concurrent Engineering has to be mapped on the requirements in this phase. The project management requires a continuous coordination of the teams and the involved persons. Designers, mechanical engineers, and analysts have to be assigned to their work, as well as tasks and deadlines have to be communicated and checked. Hence a computer-based environment provides an optimized base for the execution of these tasks. Only if the team members and their leaders have the possibility to keep track of the work-in-progress of their colleagues and check their own work against the efforts of the others, the concept of parallelised work in a group can be realized.

The variety of the information handled in the design process and the complexity of the decision-making require graphical-interactive applications based on user-friendly concepts for the visualization of the information. Characteristical data handled and created in the design process are e.g. information about person and organization structures, the design progress, the approval status of specific parts, the product structure or the product's shape. According to the structure of the information units different modes of presentation are chosen. A product structure can be visualized as a tree structure, administrative information are schemed in panels, and 3D CAD data is presented by interactive 3D viewing applications. To realize the idea of a virtual prototype, additional visualization capabilities have to be provided. Virtual reality (VR) technology offers the possibilities to create such interactive environments. They are defined as real-time interactive graphics with three-dimensional models combined with a display technology that gives the user immersion in the model world and direct manipulation [BiFu92]. This technology is especially suited for design activities, because of the iterative analyse-refine cycle. Any method which aids the designer during this process will improve the entire activity. Because a strength of VR is the capability for direct manipulation of objects within the virtual space, design activities should benefit greatly from this technology [BiFu92]. A system incorporating real-time simulation of the functional behaviour, direct manipulations, and VR display technology realizes the interactive visualization of the virtual prototype.

Several implementations have been realized in the area of the aircraft and automotive industry. The Advanced Technology Center at Boeing Aircraft in Seattle investigates full immersive VR with the goal of integrating it into the design, test and mock-up process [PiTe93]. In October 1991 a first virtual prototype of the tilt-rotor aircraft V-22 has been shown [AuBl92]. Broad use of VR technology has been accomplished in the development of the commercial aircraft Boeing 777. The number of physical mock-ups for assembly verification has been reduced to one item for the extremely complex cockpit section. Automotive manufacturers like Chrysler [Bei94], Ford [Dei95], Mercedes-Benz [GrMa95], VW, or BMW are examining the VR technology for the virtual prototyping of cars. In Europe the research in this area is driven by the AIT Consortium, an alliance of the European automotive and aircraft industry [AIT94]. The goal is to establish research projects within the fourth research framework of the European Community. The research will focus on applications for styling, ergonomics, and assembly simulation.

The scenario illustrates the complexity of the virtual prototyping process and the numerous applications, data flows and organisation structures involved. Therefore an integrated computer-based environment is needed to support the synthesis of all these aspects.

Integrated Environment for Virtual Prototyping

The environment represents an open, extendable framework for the integration of engineering applications. It is based on the CoConut (**Computer** Support for **Con**current Design **u**sing STEP) environment, which has been developed by the Fraunhofer-IGD. A detailed description of the CoConut environment is given in [JKSU94]. Originally tailored as a system for the realization of Concurrent Engineering concepts in the design phase, it has been extended to cover the additional requirements of the virtual prototyping process. The system architecture is shown in Fig. 1.

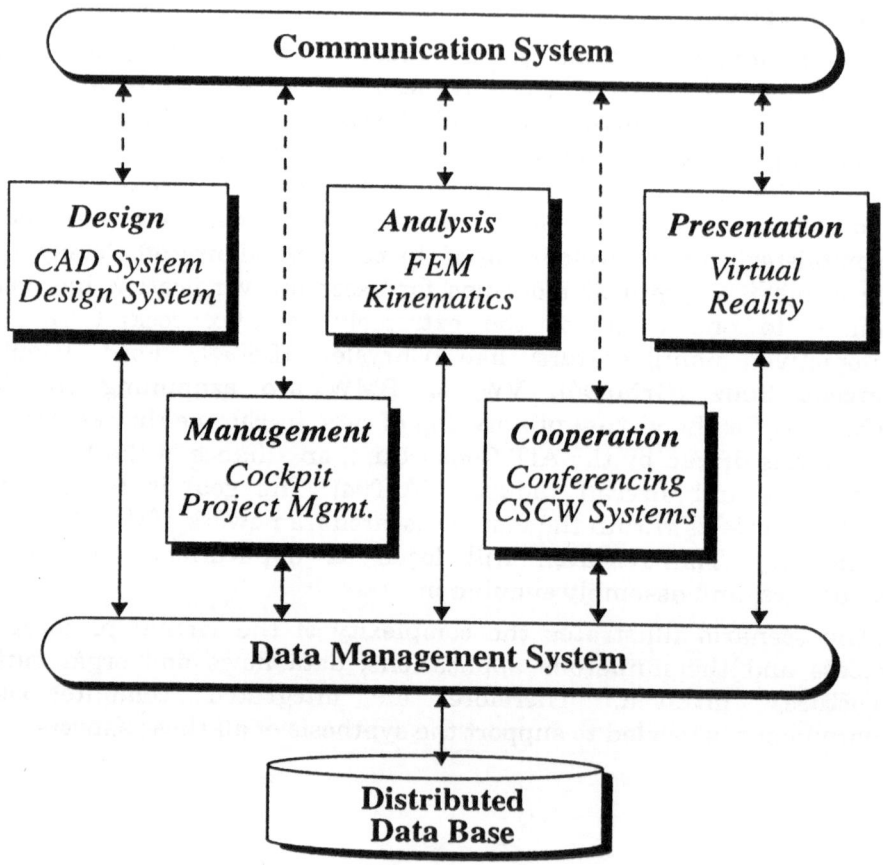

Fig. 1: System architecture

The environment provides services to couple different components which are essential for an integrated environment. The following components and services are incorporated in the environment:

- the management applications
- the design applications
- the analysis applications
- the presentation applications
- the cooperation applications
- the communication service
- the data management service

A prototypical implementation of the environment has been completed and the concepts have been approved using original data set of the automotive industry. A brief overview of the components and services is given in the following chapters.

System Components

The Management Applications

The category of the management applications embodies all administrative, managing and planning applications in the environment. These applications handle the data which is directly related to the user's environment, the application administration and the project planning and management.

The most important component of this category is the cockpit. It is responsible for setting up the user environment, starting of applications, and for message tracking within the environment. To be able to fulfil these tasks, the cockpit works closely together with the communication system. Furthermore the cockpit displays continuously the actual status of the user's environment. A typical configuration of the cockpit shows the projects the user is involved in, a still image of the colleagues which are currently working in the distributed environment, and the running applications the user is currently using.

Graphical interactive tools like the Person and Organization Tracking

System (POTS) and the Project and Product Tracking System (PPTS) are both information browsers and editors to create and view data. Using these tools a project leader is able to set up projects and assign designers and engineers to specific tasks within these projects. Part of the PPTS is a visualizer for product structures. A tree-like representation of the structure allows for interactive creation and refinement of complex assembly structures. The POTS and PPTS are directly interfaced to the underlying distributed object-oriented data base. The concurrent access of multiple users to the data is controlled by logging mechanisms of the data base.

The Design Applications

During the design process the design applications are those systems which are used by industrial and mechanical designers to create the shape and structure of the product. E.g. in the automotive industry these are CAD systems with high-level modelling capabilities for the design of complex 3D objects.

In our environment the commercial 3D CAD/CAM system *CATIA Solutions* has been integrated. CATIA is an advanced CAD/CAM system developed by Dassault Systemes, France [Das95] and is widely used in the automotive and aircraft industry. The system provides freeform surface and solid modelling capabilities, and preliminary digital-mock-up functionality. In the CoConut environment any other 3D CAD system with the appropriate interfaces could be used.

The Analysis Applications

According to the concept of virtual prototyping computer based prototypes realize the functional behaviour of the underlying product model by means of computer based simulations. The simulations focus on the following characteristics: optical appearance, spatial presence and dynamical behaviour. In [DaGö94] a description is given, how these characteristics can be integrated in a virtual prototyping environment. Qualitative analysis, which does not represent the physical behaviour of the product in all details, allows for real-time simulations. The virtual prototype can be manipulated directly and the functionality of kinematic structures can be experienced interactively. Quantitative analysis are usually time-consuming and have to be performed off-line. The results can be prepared for presentation in VR with tools for scientific visualization [DaGö94].

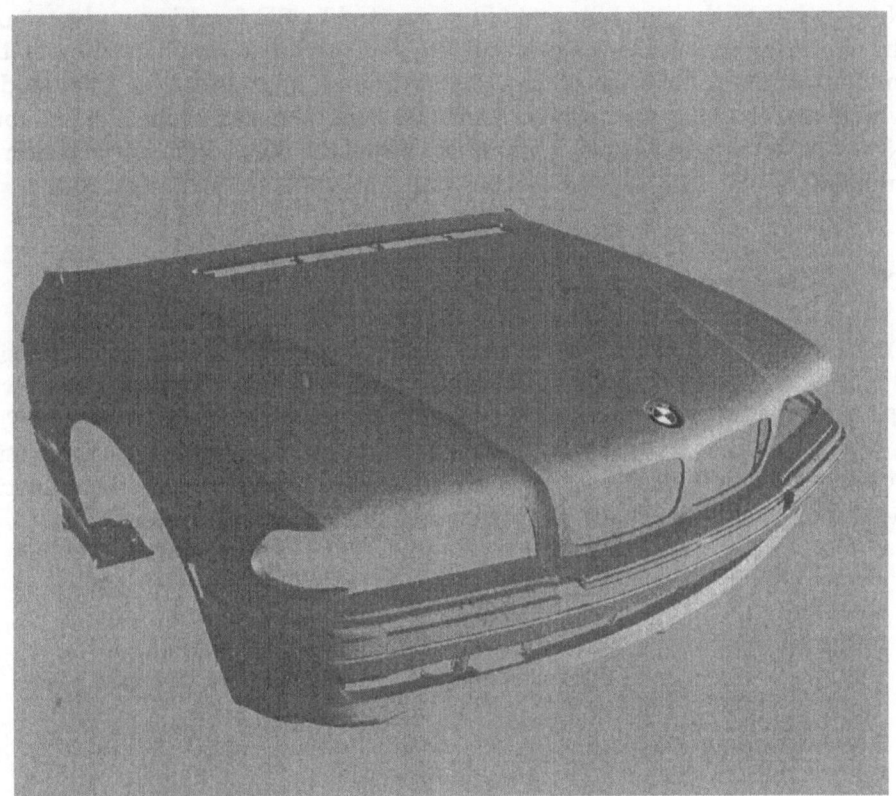

Fig. 2: Virtual prototype of a 7 series BMW (AIT project)

The Presentation Applications

For the final presentation of the results of the ESPRIT project No. 7704 *Advanced Information Technology in Design and Manufacturing* [AIT94] the Fraunhofer-IGD in close cooperation with BMW has realized a Virtual Prototyping demonstration. A virtual prototype of a 7 series BMW (Figure 2) has been prepared for interactive assembly and disassembly of different generators in the engine compartment. The demonstration included real-time collision detection, kinematic simulations, and the simulation of flexible parts. For the demonstration

IGD's Virtual Reality software Virtual Design [ADF95] has been used for visualization and interaction with the virtual prototype. Virtual Design is a general purpose VR system for industrial applications. It provides realistic audiovisual presentation and direct manipulation features. Navigation in the virtual world is supported by 3D tracking and gesture-driven interactions using a dataglove. A stereoscopic projection of the presentation generates a three-dimensional impression of the model, which permits a realistic examination of the functional behaviour. Navigation in the scene is possible while the kinematic simulation is running.

The Cooperation Applications

One of the main purposes of the environment is to share information during the design process. Information sharing should be possible, even if the members of the design teams are geographically divided. This implies the availability of CSCW (Computer Supported Cooperative Work) tools within the environment allowing synchronous cooperative work like that provided by a desktop video conferencing system.

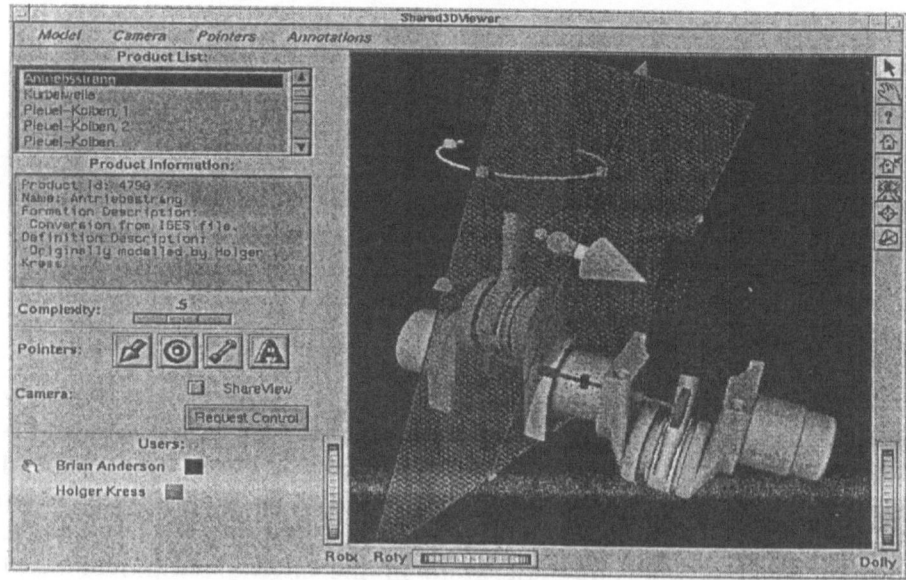

Fig. 3: Shared 3D Viewer

Based on the cockpit and the communication services of the environment a contact between the participants of the virtual team can be established. Audio and video communication in combination with CSCW tools give a proper support for the communication and cooperation within design teams [ScKr93]. A distributed viewing tool for 3D CAD data, the Shared 3D Viewer, has been integrated into the environment. The Shared 3D Viewer is a viewing system especially designed for discussions and conferences about 3D CAD Models between geographically divided CAD users. It interprets standard CAD exchange formats which permits CAD data input from different CAD systems. The graphics capabilities allow the visualization of complex 3D CAD models and the interactive modification of viewing parameters. Different 3D markers and multimedia annotations can be added to the model. The modifications and markers are transmitted to all partners simultaneously. Fig. 3 shows the Shared 3D Viewer with a sub-assembly of a driveshaft loaded and four markers styled as arrows, a circle and a dimensioning slider.

System Services

The Communication System

The Communication System embodies different levels of functionality. The cockpit communication level, the data base communication level, and the communication level of the cooperation applications. Every level fulfils the specific requirements made by the applications using this service.

The administrative communication of the environment, handled by the cockpit, is responsible for the message distribution and broadcasting services. For this communication level SunSoft's ToolTalk is used as the kernel communication system. It solves the requirements for messaging and is also able to operate in a heterogeneous environment. The data base communication level controls the massive data exchange in the environment, e.g. exchange of large CAD files. In this case the functionality of the underlying commercial data base is used. The communication of the cooperation applications is based on a specialized client-server architecture for distributed applications. This level is adapted to the needs of real-time communication with multiple users.

The Data Management System

Two concepts of data management are combined in the environment: a data sharing component based on an object-oriented data base and a data exchange component using physical files.

For the data sharing component we use as the underlying data base the VERSANT system developed by Versant Object Technology, Inc. Besides other criteria, this object-oriented data base offers a distributed data base management in a heterogeneous environment. It provides a generic and a specific interface to the persistent data in the distributed data base. Currently, the CAD system uses the physical file exchange for the data communication. The ST-Developer toolkit (STEP Tools, Inc.) is used to realize data exchange processors to convert the native CAD data in a STEP physical file and vice versa. STEP Tools Utilities handle the import of product model data contained in a STEP physical file into the data base and the export of the data to a STEP physical file.

The ST-Developer is a software toolkit to build STEP based applications. The main features of the toolkit are as follows. A STEP working form, called ROSE++, which offers main memory C++ structures to deal with STEP objects (Entity instances, etc.). Meta data and application data can be accessed by methods on C++ classes. There exist both, a generic and a generative, type specific access. STEP Utilities, a variety of utilities, are provided to work with ROSE++. A tool scans/parses the STEP information models, configures the working form according to the schema and generates schema dependent C++ classes to instantiate the information models. Further tools realize the reading of a STEP physical file into the working form and vice versa.

In the CoConut environment the data management has been developed to fulfil the requirements of the design process focusing on data sharing and exchange between CAD systems. With the integration in a virtual prototyping scenario the data management has to be extended with functionalities for data conversion and data enrichment to accomplish the needs of the analysis and presentation applications [KKR95].

Conclusion

An overview of the concepts and the user scenario of the Virtual Prototyping process was given. An environment for the integration of management, design, analysis, presentation and cooperation applications has been described and the results of the prototypical implementations have been presented. The proposed architecture for a Virtual Prototyping environment combined with the advantages of a common information model will lead to a full integration of the Virtual Prototyping process into the product development process.

Future developments should concentrate on a common data model for the Virtual Prototyping process and automatic conversion procedures for design and presentation applications, so that real-time data exchange will be achieved.

References

[ADF95]   Astheimer, P., Dai, F., Felger, W., Göbel, M., Haase, H., Müller, S., Ziegler, R.: Virtual Design II - An Advanced VR System for Industrial Applications, in proceedings of Virtual Reality World '95, Stuttgart, Germany, February 1995.

[AIT94]   AIT Consortium: Management Overview of the First Project Phase, ESPRIT Project 7704 Advanced Information Technology in Design and Manufacturing, 1994

[AuBl92] Aukstakalnis, S., Blatner, D.: Silicon Mirage. The Art and Science of Virtual Reality, Peachpit Press, Berkeley, CA, 1992

[Bei94]   Beier, K.-P.: Virtual Reality in Automotive Design and Manufacturing, University of Michigan, SAE-Congress 1994

[BiFu92] Bishop, G., Fuchs H. et al.: Research Directions in Virtual Environments, Computer Graphics, Vol. 26, No. 3, pp. 153-177 (1992)

[DaGö94] Dai, F., Göbel, M.: Virtual Prototyping - An Approach using VR-Techniques, in proceedings of the ASME International Computers in Engineering Conference, September 11-14, 1994, Minneapolis, Minnesota, USA

[Das95]   Dassault Systemes: CATIA Solutions Version 4 Release 1.5,
           Softcopy Collection Kit, SK2T-5219-06, 7th Ed., August 1995

[Dei95]   Deitz, D.: Real engineering in a virtual world, Mechanical
           engineering, Vol. 117, No. 7, pp. 78-85 (1995)

[GrMa95]   Grebner, K., May, F.: Applications of Virtual Reality
           Techniques in the Industry - Selected Examples, in
           proceedings of Virtual Reality World '95, Stuttgart, February
           1995, pp. 451-468

[HKT93]   Haug, E.J., Kuhl, J.G., Tsai, F.F.: Virtual Prototyping for
           Mechanical System Concurrent Engineering, in Concurrent
           Engineering: Tools and Technologies for Mechanical System
           Design (ed. E. J. Haug), Springer, 1993

[ISO94]   ISO/IS 10303-1: Industrial automation systems and
           integration - Product data representation and exchange -
           Part 1: Overview and fundamental principles, International
           Organization for Standardization, Geneve (Switzerland),
           1994

[JKSU94]   Jasnoch, U., Kress, H., Schroeder, K., Ungerer, M.: CoConut:
           Computer Support for Concurrent Design using STEP, in
           proceedings of the Third IEEE Workshop on Enabling
           Technologies: Infrastructure for Collaborative Enterprises,
           April 17-19, 1994, Morgantown, West Virginia, USA, IEEE
           Computer Society Press

[KKR95]   Kress, H., Kiolein, I., Rix, J.: CAD data preparation in a
           virtual prototyping environment, in proceedings of the IFIP
           Conference on Life-Cycle Modelling for Innovative Products
           and Processes, PROLAMAT '95, Berlin, Germany, November
           1995

[Kre95]   Kress, H.: Integration Aspects within a Virtual Prototyping
           Environment, in proceedings of the 5th International
           Conference on Flexible Automation and Intelligent
           Manufacturing, FAIM '95, Stuttgart, Germany, June 28-30,
           1995

[PiTe93]   Pimentel, K., Teixeira, K.: Virtual Reality: through the new
           looking glass, Windcrest Books, McGraw-Hill, 1993

[ScKr93]   Schroeder, K., Kress, H.: Distributed Conferencing Tools for
           Product Design, in proceedings of the IFIP-Workshop on
           Interfaces in Industrial Systems for Production and
           Engineering, March 15-17, 1993, J. Rix, E.G. Schlechtendahl
           (Editors), pp. 283-294, Elsevier Publishers, 1993

Chapter 3

Feature Technology

Overview

Feature validation and conversion

Klaas Jan de Kraker, Maurice Dohmen and Willem F. Bronsvoort[1]

A new approach to feature modeling that supports multiple feature views of a product is presented. Each view has its own feature model, which is validated by maintaining all constraints in the view. Consistency between the views is maintained by feature conversion.

A feature model is represented at two levels: specification and maintenance. At the specification level, a shape type and validation constraints are combined in a generic feature definition. The set of generic features of each view is extendible. At the maintenance level, a central cellular model, which stores all feature intersections, and a central constraint graph, which stores all constraint instances, are maintained. The cellular model links the feature models from the different views.

The product model, which contains each view's feature model, is initially specified from one view: generic features are instantiated by specification of parameter values. When another view is opened, feature conversion is performed using the central cellular model and view-specific information.

Introduction

Traditional solid modeling only deals with information about the geometry of a product. For application in a product engineering

---

[1] Faculty of Technical Mathematics and Informatics, Delft University of Technology, The Netherlands

environment this is a shortcoming, because here also non-shape information, e.g. functional information, is involved. This is, for example, the function of some part of the product for the user, or information about the way some part of the product is manufactured or assembled [BrJa93]. Besides shape information, feature modeling also deals with the relevant non-shape information, which are both represented in features.

Features can be used by several engineering applications. In particular in process planning for manufacturing, which has been the main motivation for the development of the feature concept, features play a prominent role. Here features can identify areas in a product that can be manufactured in one operation with one type of equipment. An example would be a slot that can be milled with a particular milling machine. Applications in other areas are also emerging now. For example, in analysis applications, features can identify areas of objects that require special attention in the analysis. In assembly process planning, features can identify connections between parts. In the design of products, features can also be used: design by features allows designers to model products with entities that are on a higher level, and closer to their way of thinking, than the geometric entities used in traditional solid modeling.

Each feature in any application has a well-defined meaning that can be expressed by constraints describing feature validity conditions. Maintaining this meaning, i.e. *feature validation,* is an important aspect of feature modeling.

Each application has its own *view* of a product—its own way of looking at it. Each view contains the features relevant for the specific application. An example of two views of one object is given in Figure 1. In the design view, it is the ribs on a plate that are regarded as features. If the object is manufactured by starting with a somewhat thicker plate and milling slots, then in the process planning view it is the slots that are regarded as features.

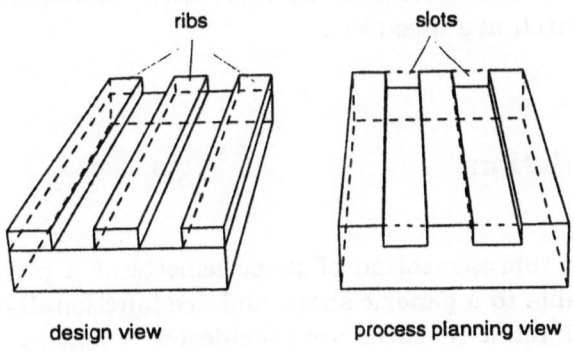

Fig. 1: Multiple views of a product

One way to obtain the features for a particular view is to use *feature conversion*, the process of converting features from one view of a product into features relevant in another view of the product.

In the ideal engineering environment, engineers from different disciplines can work simultaneously on the design of a product. This approach is called *concurrent* or *simultaneous engineering*. Concurrent engineering requires multiple views of one product to be supported simultaneously. Many of the activities in a concurrent engineering system will result in modifications of the design. For example, stress analysis may show that dimensions of some part need to be modified. Modifications should preferably be made in the view in which the need for them arises, and all modifications in any view should be reflected in all other views. This requires conversion between features in arbitrary views. Such feature conversion comprises management of the product's shape, which is represented by different features in each view, and management of the constraints, which specify validity conditions of the features.

Here, an approach to such feature conversion is described. First, the importance of feature validation is emphasized, and validation constraint types are presented. Then, current approaches to feature conversion and our new approach are described. The three following subsections present our feature validity specification and maintenance methods, and elaborate on the representation and maintenance of the product's shape. Then, our current method to obtain features in a newly opened view is described. Finally, conclusions and directions for future research are discussed.

Feature validation

A *feature* is the representation of shape aspects of a physical product that are mappable to a generic shape and are functionally significant. Here, only volumetric features are considered. A feature is characterized by a number of parameters. A parameterized description of a feature is called the *generic definition* of the feature. A generic feature can be instantiated multiple times by specifying values for its parameters. The topologic entities of a feature, such as vertices, edges, faces, and volume, are called *feature elements*.

The meaning of a generic feature is defined by its *feature validation constraints*. These include geometric relations within the feature, relations with other features, and validity conditions for feature elements. When a feature is instantiated, instances of its validation constraints are created automatically. After feature instantiation, it is possible to specify additional relations between feature elements, possibly of different features, i.e. *model validation constraints*. A collection of feature instances and their relations is called a *feature model*.

When a feature model is edited, i.e. when a feature parameter is changed or when a feature instance is added or deleted, validity of all features has to be maintained. If editing affects the way features intersect geometrically, feature validation is particularly difficult. Current feature modeling systems do not support such feature validation.

The remainder of this subsection presents the generic constraints that can be used to specify feature and model validity. Shape and attach constraints are used only for specifying feature validity; the other constraints can be used for specifying either type of validity [DKB95].

Shape constraints correspond to the type of feature shape, e.g. a block for a slot. They are used to control the relations between feature parameters and feature geometry.

Attach constraints specify the attachment of a feature to a feature model. A hierarchical relation is specified between two feature elements, e.g. faces, including the remaining degrees of freedom of the attached elements. These attachments are used instead of the parent-child relations between features, that are used in many other systems. This has the advantage that a feature instance does not necessarily have only one parent feature; it can be attached to feature elements of several features. An example is a thru hole attached to a block with a protrusion, intersecting both features, see Figure 2. The top face of the hole is attached to the top face of the protrusion, the bottom face of the hole is attached to the bottom face of the block.

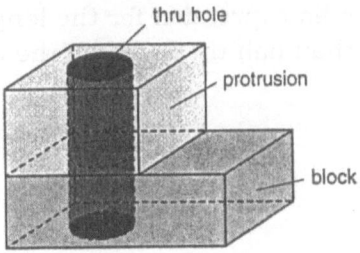

Fig. 2: Attach example

Semantic constraints specify topologic properties of feature elements. We use semantic constraints similar to those defined by Bidarra and Teixeira [BiTe94]. For a vertex, edge or face, a semantic constraint specifies the extent to which the element must lie on the product boundary. For example, the bottom face of a blind hole has to lie completely on the product boundary. For a volume, a semantic constraint specifies the extent to which the volume is allowed to intersect other feature volumes. Assume, for example, that a blind hole is represented by a cylinder that is subtracted. Its bottom face must be completely on the product boundary. The side face, on the other hand, must at least be partly on the boundary, and the top face must not be on the boundary. This may be the specification of a blind hole, in a design view. If a blind hole is part of a pen-hole connection feature in an assembly view [HBJ95], a semantic constraint on its volume may be imposed that declares that no additive feature instantiated later may intersect the hole.

Geometric constraints specify geometric relations, such as parallelism and distance, between feature elements. When used as a model validation constraint, geometric constraints can dimension a feature model. An example is a geometric constraint specifying a distance between two parallel slots.

Dimension constraints specify an interval for the value of a parameter of a feature. An example of a dimension constraint in a manufacturing view, is a constraint on the width of a slot, declaring it to be within some specified range, because slots with smaller or larger widths cannot be manufactured.

Algebraic constraints specify equations containing feature parameters. An example is an expression for the length of the protrusion in Figure 2 to be larger than half the length of the block.

Feature conversion

There are three methods to obtain a feature model: *feature recognition, design by features,* and *feature conversion.*

The first applications in which features were used, were based on *feature recognition*. Feature recognition is the process of deriving feature instances from a geometric model given a set of generic features. Most feature recognition algorithms are restricted in their domain. One reason for this is that the classes of generic features that can be recognized, and the order in which they are recognized, are integrated with the recognition algorithms. Another is that they are not capable of recognizing all types of feature intersections.

In the second method to obtain a feature model, *design by features,* a feature model is constructed by designers using features. In this case, assignment of a (functional) meaning to parts of a product is not done by feature recognition after creating a geometric model, but during the design phase: designers puts their intent for parts of the product into a feature model. Also, this method makes it possible to construct a model with high-level entities instead of the low-level geometric entities as in a geometric modeling system, which is considerably easier for designers.

The third method is *feature conversion*, also called *feature transformation* and *feature mapping*, which is the process of deriving a new feature model in one view from the feature models specified in the other views. The advantage of feature conversion over feature recognition is that it uses feature information from the other views to derive a feature model, whereas feature recognition only uses a geometric model. Because different applications require different feature models, feature conversion can be very useful in an engineering environment, in particular a concurrent engineering environment.

Before discussing current approaches to feature conversion, a typology of feature transformation types is given. For conversions from a view A to a view B, Shah distinguishes four types of transformations between (groups of) features [Sha88]:

- *identity transformation*: a feature from A is converted into a feature in B with equal geometry; an example is the conversion of a design hole into a manufacturing hole

- *projection transformation*: a feature from A is converted into a feature in B with less information; an example is the conversion of a blended corner into a sharp corner

- *adjoint transformation*: a feature from A is converted into a feature in B that is logically associated with it; an example is the conversion of a design rib into a load feature for finite-element analysis

- *conjugate transformation*: a (group of) feature(s) from A is converted into a (group of) feature(s) in B by rearranging the topologic entities of the features; an example is the conversion of the rib features into the slot features of Figure 1.

If only volumetric features are considered, the identity and conjugate transformation are relevant. Since views can be complementary, i.e. mainly constructive or destructive, such as a design view or a manufacturing view, respectively, the conjugate transformation is the most interesting one.

In current approaches, conversions are one-way: the features in an application view are derived from the features in a primary view, in most cases the design view. A designer has to input a primary view, and conversion modules are available to generate application-dependent feature models, for so-called secondary views.

This leads to the architecture of a feature modeling system depicted in Figure 3 [CuDi88]. If a modification in the model is required on the basis of the outcome of an application, this modification has to be entered in the primary view, after which new secondary views can be generated when needed.

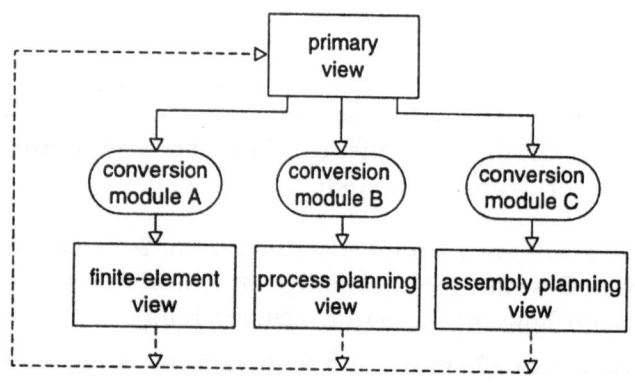

Fig. 3: Architecture of a feature modeling system
with primary view and secondary views

Recent research has focused on one-way conversion [AnCh90, VaRe94, SSS94]. It converts a feature-based design into process planning features.

If concurrent engineering with multiple views has to be supported, the solution with a primary view and a number of secondary application views is far from ideal. If an engineer running an application program discovers that, for example, a dimension of the designed product has to be adjusted, he has to switch from his application view to the primary view to make the adjustment. In this view, however, the feature model is different from the one in his own view, and it may be difficult to find the right adjustments of the feature parameters in that view. We have therefore developed an approach that supports all different feature views simultaneously, and performs multiple-way feature conversion between these views [KDB95].

When supporting different views simultaneously, two types of operations can be identified that correspond with two types of feature conversions. Firstly, it is possible to *open* a view. Feature conversion to the opened view is then performed, making all views consistent. Views are consistent if they represent the same product geometry. In the view that is opened, a new feature model is built by instantiating features, on the basis of the feature models as already specified in all other views. Secondly, in line with the design by features approach, it is possible to *edit* a view. Feature conversion is then performed by propagating the changes from the view edited to the other views. Either parameters can be changed, or feature and constraint instances can be created or deleted. These changes are reflected in the other views.

We are currently working on a prototype implementation of a system, called SPIFF[2], to test our approach. In SPIFF, a *product model* contains the different views and their feature models, see Figure 4. The feature models of the different views are linked by the product geometry.

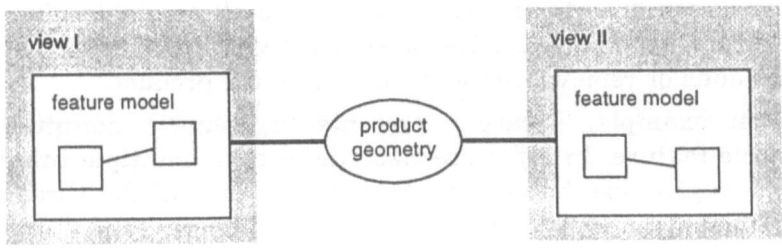

Fig. 4: The product model

The representation of features consists of two different levels: *specification* and *maintenance*. At the specification level, features and their properties are specified, such as application-specific

---

[2] Named after Spaceman Spiff, interplanetary explorer *extraordinaire*.

parameters and attributes and constraints, including relations with other features. At the maintenance level, feature validity is maintained. There are two advantages of such declarative feature specification, which separates feature validity specification and maintenance. Firstly, it provides a clean way of feature specification. Secondly, it gives the opportunity to test several techniques to maintain feature model validity.

Feature validity specification

At the specification level, shape information and constraints are combined in feature classes that are specified in the object-oriented language LOOKS [Pee93]. Features are specified using predefined types of feature constituents and using inheritance. Three types of feature constituents are provided in LOOKS: *shape type*, *validation constraints* and the *nature* of a feature.

The shape type of a feature denotes the type of generic shape of the feature. Since only volumetric features are considered, the generic shape of a feature is represented by a parameterized solid. The validation constraints presented earlier are all available. The nature of a feature is either additive or subtractive, specifying whether the feature adds or removes material to or from the product.

As an example, Figure 5 presents the generic definition of a ThruHole feature. In a feature class definition, multiple inheritance is used to give the feature the properties of two of the three feature constituents, shape type and nature, here Cylinder and Subtractive. With inheritance in LOOKS, renaming can take place: since for a hole a cylinder's height has the meaning of depth, it is renamed with: Cylinder(height>depth).

After the validation constraint declarations in the private part, an initialization method is declared in the public part. In a call to this method, formal parameters face1 and face2 are face instances from the feature model to which the ThruHole instance will be attached. The two coordinates posX and posY indicate the position of the top face in the coordinate system of face1.

```
class ThruHole inherit
  Volumetric,
  Cylinder(height>depth),
  Subtractive
private
  attachTop               :   CoPlanarEqual;
  attachBottom            :   CoPlanarEqual;
  semanticTop             :   NotOnBoundary;
  semanticBottom          :   NotOnBoundary;
  semanticSide            :   OnBoundary;
  dimensionDepth          :   Dimension;
  dimensionRadius         :   Dimension
public
  initialize(face1:Face; posX,posY:real;
      face2:Face; radiusValue:real):void
implementation
  initialize(face1:Face; posX,posY:real;
      face2:Face; radiusValue:real):void
  begin
    Cylinder:initialize();
    semanticTop.initialize(top,completely);
    semanticBottom.initialize(bottom,completely);
    semanticSide.initialize(side,partly);
    attachTop.initialize(top,face1);
    attachBottom.initialize(bottom,face2);
    dimensionDepth.initialize(depth,0);
    dimensionRadius.initialize(radius,1,10);
    radius.setValue(radiusValue);
    top.setPosition(face1,posX,posY,0);
  end
endclass
```

Fig. 5: Generic feature definition

The initialization method initializes validation constraints, and sets values for the radius of the feature and its relative position. For this, the feature's elements and parameters are used, which are inherited from its shape. Semantic validation constraints have a parameter with a value either equal to completely or partly. This parameter expresses the extent to which the feature face must or must not lie on the product boundary, depending on the constraint class. The position of the ThruHole instance is declared with attachments of its top and bottom faces. A CoPlanarEqual attach constraint positions a planar face with respect to another, by making it coplanar with equal normal direction. Values for available degrees of freedom are specified in a call to top.setPosition(face1,posX,posY,0). Since a cylinder's top and bottom faces are opposite faces, here values for the position of the bottom face and a value for the hole's depth are not required; these are implicitly specified by the attachments.

An instance of class ThruHole can now be created by defining a variable of class ThruHole, and calling its method initialize() with two feature faces, a relative position, and a desired value for the radius. After initialization, the feature is added to the product model, and is validated as explained in the next subsection.

Feature validity maintenance

At the maintenance level, feature validity is maintained. This is implemented using three managers, see Figure 6. The Feature Manager takes care of the communication with the LOOKS interpreter that processes the feature specifications. The Constraint Manager and Feature Geometry Manager store validation constraints and feature shapes, respectively, in their data structures, and they maintain those.

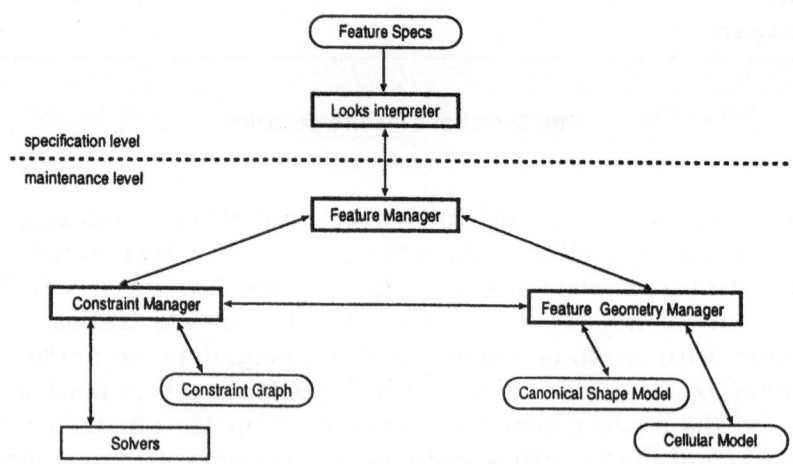

Fig. 6: Feature representation

The Constraint Manager stores all constraint instances in a bipartite constraint graph, in which two types of nodes represent constraints and variables, and edges connect constraints to associated variables [Doh95]. The constraints specify n-ary relations. The variables are feature elements and feature parameters. Hierarchical relations are represented by uni-directional constraints, non-hierarchical relations by multi-directional constraints.

Figure 7 depicts an example, showing part of the constraint graph for the model shown in Figure 2. The features each have a shape constraint associated that connects the various feature elements occurring as constraint variables. Furthermore, some dimension and semantic constraint instances are depicted. The constraints are grouped into clusters, one for each feature. Clusters are connected by attach constraints and by model validation constraints between features. In this example, a DistFaceFace model validation constraint is included, specifying a distance between two faces.

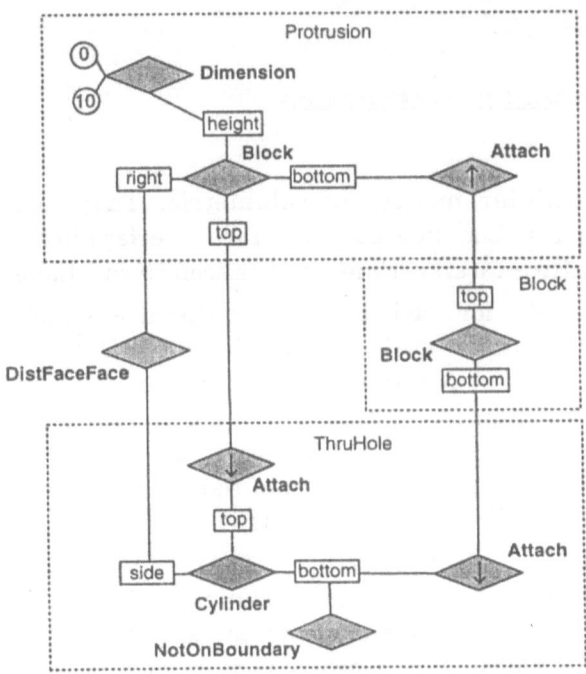

Fig. 7: Constraint graph

All constraints in the graph are maintained, both after changing the sets of instantiated features or model validation constraints, and after a feature parameter has been changed when those sets are fixed. The constraints are solved by the Constraint Manager, which handles the various constraint types by calling dedicated solvers. Constraints in the constraint graph are therefore mapped by the Constraint Manager onto dedicated constraint graphs, one for each solver [DKB95].

The Feature Geometry Manager maintains two geometric models for the feature geometry representation: a canonical shape model and a cellular model. The canonical shape model stores the feature shapes from a view in a CSG tree, which is an unevaluated representation. We use it for generating shaded images, and plan to use it for performing direct manipulation. The cellular model, on the other hand, is an evaluated representation and stores all feature intersections. We use it for checking semantic constraints and, when a view is opened, for performing feature conversion.

Cellular model maintenance

Cells in the cellular model are volumetric. They can have overlapping boundaries, but they can not have overlapping volumes. They reflect all feature intersections, and therefore can have any shape.

With each cell, for each view, it is stored to which features it belongs. This information is stored with the cell volume and all its faces in an *ownerlist* for each view. An ownerlist is an ordered list of feature element names. The nature of a cell with respect to a view, is defined as the nature of the last feature in the cell's volume ownerlist. A cell is consistent if it has the same nature for each view. All views are consistent if all cells are consistent.

For simplicity of explanation, 2D examples with only volume owners will be used. See for example Figure 8, depicting two consistent views and their cellular model. In view I, the product is represented by a base with a protrusion. In view II, it is represented by a stock with a step. In the cellular model, the grey cells are additive; the white cell is subtractive.

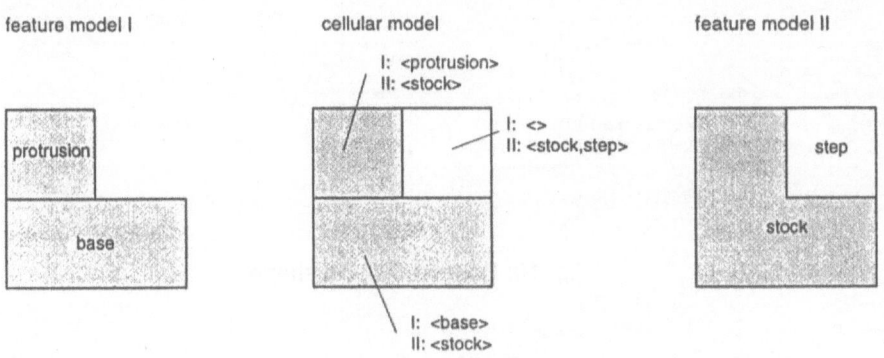

Fig. 8: Feature models and cellular model

The two basic operations on the cellular model are insertion and removal of a feature shape.

In Figure 9, a slot's shape is inserted, creating new cells that are used for feature conversion. The shape is labeled with an ownerlist containing one element. First, the shape is positioned, and then it is inserted into the cellular model by a Boolean operation. This is a nonregular union, which establishes a cellular structure. In this case, the stock's cell is split, and 'slot' is appended to the ownerlist of the new cell.

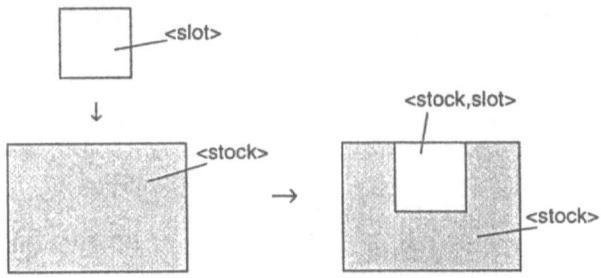

Fig. 9: Insert feature shape

When a feature shape is going to be removed from the cellular model, first it is removed from the ownerlists that contain it. Then cells with the same ownerlists are merged by removing and merging faces, see Figure 10.

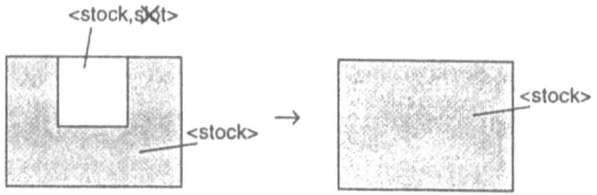

Fig. 10: Remove feature shape

Inserting shapes creates cells, but does not create all cells needed to perform feature conversion. Some cells still need to be added or split. For this, three cell creation procedures are used.

Firstly, to create a stock for a manufacturing view, a bounding shape, for example a bounding box, is computed and inserted. This creates negative cells that are not part of the product, and will have to be removed by manufacturing features.

Secondly, concave cells are split along their planar surfaces. For example, if we want to describe the product in Figure 11 as a smaller block with a protrusion on it in some view, we need a cell for the protrusion. If the grey cell is split along its surfaces, such a cell is obtained.

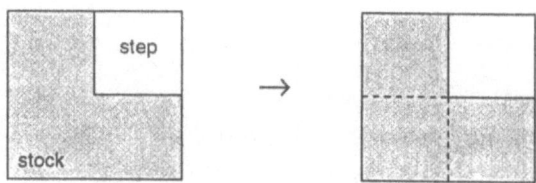

Fig. 11: Split concave cell

Thirdly, optional volumes [VaRe94] are created. These are used in a manufacturing view to choose a manufacturing order. Assume that the object in Figure 12 has been designed. In the manufacturing view, we could choose to drill the hole first. Therefore the step cell needs to be split. Optional volumes are created by splitting all negative cells by the surfaces of their adjacent negative features. In this case the step cell is split by the hole's cylindrical surface.

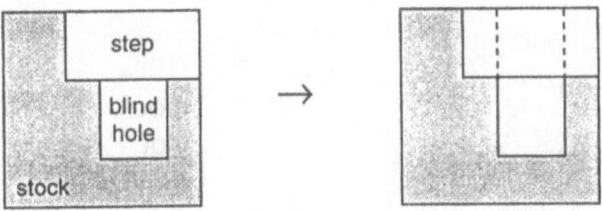

Fig. 12: Create optional volumes

For the implementation of the cellular model, we use Acis [Aci95]. Its Cellular Topology husk maintains the cellular model's nonmanifold topology, and its attribute mechanism provides functionality to maintain the ownerlists.

Open a view

After the product model initially has been specified from one view, another view can be opened. Therefore, feature conversion is performed using the central cellular model and view-specific information. It is assumed that all cells needed in the cellular model are available. A new feature model is now built by instantiating features one by one, until the opened view is consistent with the other views.

Given a set of generic features of a view and a cellular model, still many interpretations in terms of features exist. One approach is to generate all possible interpretations and choose one but, since there can be exponentially many interpretations this is not a satisfactory solution. Therefore, we try to find a good interpretation for each view directly.

For finding a good interpretation, we assign to each view a *strategy* for identifying feature instances in the cellular model. Such a strategy uses the view's generic features, and it reflects the view's function. Of the latter, the most important is the order in which the features are to be identified. For example, if we want the feature interpretation of the model in Figure 13 to be a stock with a slot and a protrusion in the slot, then these have to be identified in this order.

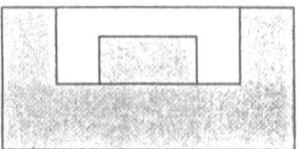
stock
slot
protrusion

Fig. 13: One feature interpretation

Thus, to open a view, its strategy provides a feature class, and it is tried to identify instances of this class. This is repeated until the view is consistent.

To identify an instance of a feature class, an instance of its shape must be identified. Currently, the identification of a feature's shape is done manually by the user by identifying feature elements in an image of the cellular model. After this, values for the feature's parameters are derived. If all its validation constraints are satisfied, a valid feature instance has been created.

We illustrate the opening of a view with an example. Assume that the product in Figure 14.a has been created in a design view, by starting with a base, and adding a protrusion and a hole. First, as explained in the previous subsection, all cells needed for the conversion are created, see Figures 14.b and 14.c. Now, a feature model in the manufacturing view is built. First, a stock is identified automatically by adding the bounding box of the designed object to the cellular model, see Figure 14.d. Assume that the strategy prescribes to identify a hole. The user identifies the hole's cylinder by selecting its top and bottom edges, see Figure 14.e; in Figure 14.f the hole has been added. Next, the strategy prescribes that a step must be identified. Its shape is identified by selecting four vertices, see Figure 14.g; in Figure 14.h the step has been added. Now, since each cell has the same nature for all views, and thus the manufacturing view is consistent with the design view, the opening of the manufacturing view has been completed.

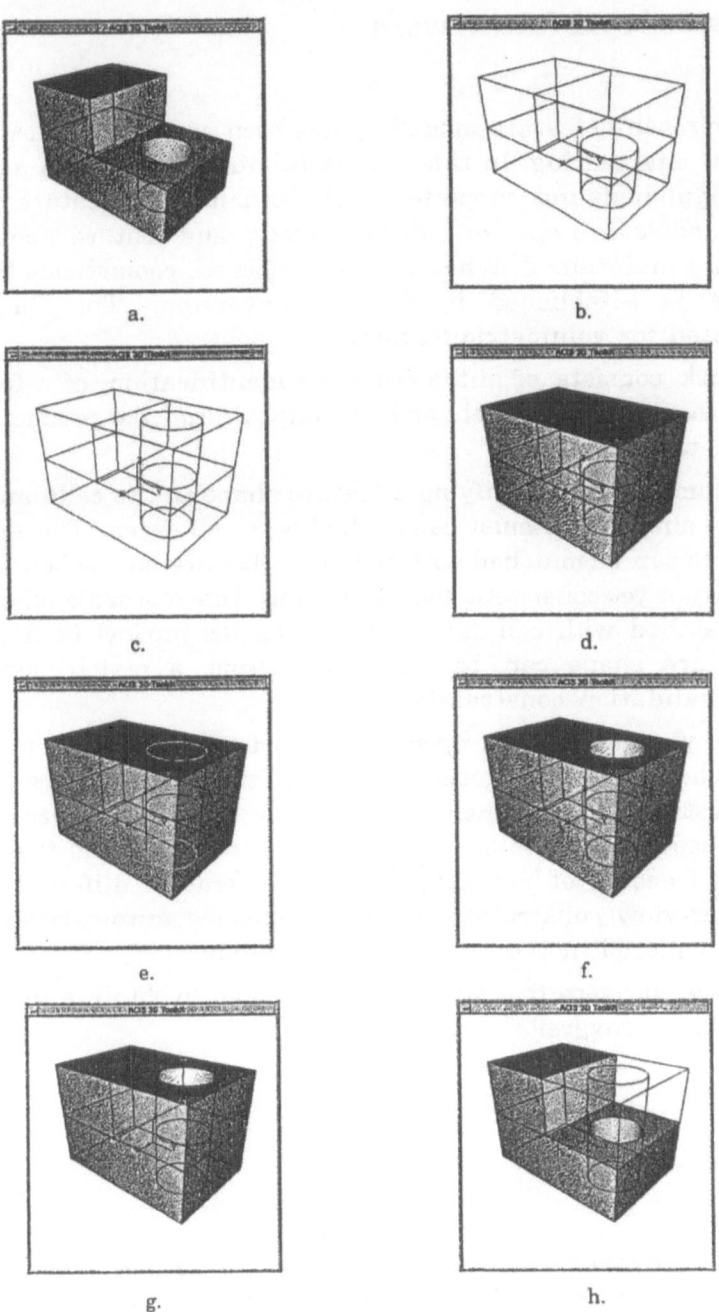

Fig. 14: Manual identification of feature shapes

Conclusions and future work

A new approach to feature modeling has been presented that supports concurrent engineering. In this approach, multiple views of a product are distinguished and supported, each with its own feature model. Feature models are specified declaratively, and feature and model validity are maintained. When a view is opened, consistency between the views is established by feature conversion. This has been implemented for volumetric features.

Future work consists of automating the identification of a feature's shape in the cellular model, and of maintaining the product model when a view is edited.

For automatically identifying a feature shape in the cellular model, the feature shape faces must be matched with cell faces. The feature's attach faces can be matched with cell faces that are on the boundary of the view's not yet consistent feature model. The feature's other faces can be matched with cell faces that are on the product boundary. A valid feature shape can be constructed from a match, using the feature's validation constraints

After a view has been opened and before a parameter can be changed, the link with the other views implicitly stored in the cellular model must be made explicit in geometric constraints between the views. These constraints are called *link constraints*, and they couple degrees of freedom of boundary feature elements of different views. These inter-view constraints will be established automatically, and will be considered in the constraint maintenance.

These are the steps that still have to be taken to obtain a fully automatic feature conversion system.

Acknowledgements

Klaas Jan de Kraker's work is supported by the Netherlands Computer Science Research Foundation (SION), with financial support from the Netherlands Organization for Scientific Research (NWO). Thanks to the Department of Mathematics and Computing Science of Eindhoven University of Technology for providing the LOOKS interpreter software.

References

[Aci95]   Geometric Modeler Programmers Reference, Version 1.7, Spatial Technology, Inc., Boulder, Colorado, USA, 1995

[AnCh90] Anderson, D.C., Chang, T.C.: Geometric reasoning in feature-based design and process planning, Computers & Graphics, Vol. 14, No. 2, pp. 225-235, 1990

[BiTe94]   Bidarra, R, Teixeira, J.C.: A semantic framework for flexible feature validity specification and assessment, Proceedings of the 1994 ASME International Computers in Engineering Conference, Volume 1, pp. 151-158, 1994

[BrJa93]   Bronsvoort, W.F., Jansen, F.W.: Feature modelling and conversion - Key concepts to concurrent engineering, Computers in Industry, Vol. 21, No. 1, pp. 61-86, 1993

[CuDi88] Cunningham, J.J., Dixon, J.R.: Designing with features: the origin of features, in: V.A. Tipnis, E.M. Patton (eds), Proceedings of the 1988 ASME International Computers in Engineering Conference and Exhibition, Volume 1, pp. 237-243, 1988

[Doh95]   Dohmen, M.: A survey of constraint satisfaction techniques for geometric modeling, Computers & Graphics, Vol. 19, No. 6, pp. 831-845, 1995

[DKB95]   Dohmen, M., de Kraker, K.J., Bronsvoort, W.F.: Constraint techniques for feature validation, in: T. Tomiyama, M. Mäntylä, S. Finger (eds), Knowledge Intensive CAD-1, Preprints of the First IFIP WG 5.2 Workshop, pp. 179-192, 1995

[HBJ95]   van Holland, W., Bronsvoort, W.F., Jansen, F.W.: Feature modelling for assembly, in: W. Straszer, F. Wahl (eds), Graphics and Robotics, Springer-Verlag, Berlin, pp. 131-148, 1995

[KDB95]   de Kraker, K.J., Dohmen, M., Bronsvoort, W.F.: Multiple-way feature conversion to support concurrent engineering, in: C. Hoffmann and J. Rossignac (eds), Proceedings of the Third Symposium on Solid Modeling and Applications, pp. 105-114, 1995

[Pee93]   Peeters, E.A.J.: Design and implementation of an object-oriented, interactive animation system, in: C. Mingins, W. Haebich, J. Potter, B. Meyer (eds), Technology of Object-Oriented Languages and Systems, TOOLS 12 & 9, Prentice Hall, pp. 255-267, 1993

[Sha88]   Shah, J.J.: Feature transformations between application-specific feature spaces, Computer-Aided Engineering Journal, Vol. 5, No. 6, pp. 247-255, 1988

[SSS94]   Shah, J.J., Shen, Y., Shirur, A.: Determination of machining volumes from extensible sets of design features, in: J.J. Shah, M. Mäntylä, D.S. Nau (eds), Advances in Feature Based Manufacturing, Elsevier Science, pp. 129-157, 1994

[VaRe94] Vandenbrande, J.H., Requicha, A.A.G.: Geometric computation for the recognition of spatially interacting machining features, in: J.J. Shah, M. Mäntylä, D.S. Nau (eds), Advances in Feature Based Manufacturing, Elsevier Science, pp. 83-106, 1994

Classification of generic shape features for the recognition of specific feature instances

T. De Martino[1,2], B. Falcidieno[1], F. Petta[1,2]

More recent releases of CAD systems adopt feature-based modeling to include functional and behavioural information in the product model and to support the designer's activity with high level semantic modeling entities. However, these systems are still far from satisfying the industrial need to support an automatic flow from design to production in a concurrent engineering environment. To improve CAD systems in this direction, current research proposes the integration of feature recognition techniques with the design-by-features approach.

The realization of an integrated feature-based modeling system is the aim of a joint research project between the Istituto per la Matematica Applicata, Genova, Italy, and the Fraunhofer Institut für Graphische Datenverarbeitung, Darmstadt, Germany.

Here the feature recognition system, which is based on a feature classification strategy, is presented. This system supports the recognition of classes as well as specific instances of features and allows the whole system to derive different context dependent views of the product.

Introduction

Computer-aided design tools have an increasing importance in efficient industrial product development processes. Innovative and competitive product design depends on the suitability of the used CAD system to support an intuitive design process and to allow

---

[1] Istituto per la Matematica Applicata del CNR, Genova, Italy
[2] Fraunhofer Institut für Graphische Datenverarbeitung, Darmstadt, Germany

communication with the other downstream phases of the product development in the new perspective of *concurrent engineering*. As a matter of fact, the main goal of concurrent engineering (CE) is the reduction of costs and time for product development obtained by considering design, installation, organisation and control of the production activities as a whole, and in such a way that all the decisions to be taken can be evaluated in consistency with each other during the design phase. This new paradigm assumes an ideal environment, where engineers from different disciplines simultaneously work on the product design. After an initial conceptual model has been defined, several engineers should be able to work at the same time on the product definition, modifying or adding details to the design and also running application programs (e.g. stress analysis, cost analysis, process planning) [BrJa 93] [DFG 95]. For the realization of such CE approach it is important that the CAD system is able to represent a product in a complete way, including application dependent information besides the geometric and topological description. Such information, which is necessary to *understand* and to *reason* on the product parts, usually is referred to portions of the object shape, the so called *form features* of the object features are considered in the engineering community as semantic entities which associate functional meaning to the shape and allow high level product descriptions. Since features are context-dependent, through feature-based modeling it is possible to represent an object from different viewpoints. As an example, two different feature-based descriptions of the same object are depicted in fig. 1.

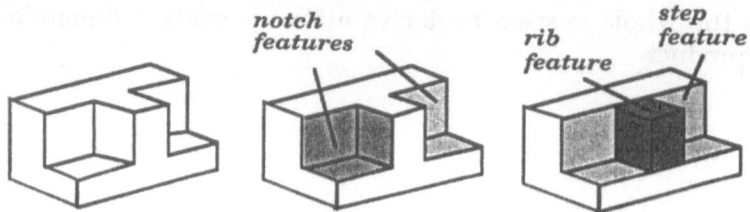

Fig. 1: Different feature-based descriptions of the same object

To create a feature-based model, two main approaches have been defined, called *design-by-features* and *feature recognition*. Systems based on the design-by-features approach allow the designer to create the product model by using directly features as high level modelling entities, thus supporting intuitive design processes which reflect the designer's way of thinking [DiLi 90] [OvHa 91] [ChLe 94]. The main disadvantage of this approach derives from the fact that features are domain specific and once a feature-based model has been defined, the model could not be appropriate in other application contexts. For example, a part can be modelled with design features that could be totally different from machining features, like in fig.1 where the description in terms of two notch features is meaningful for machining while the description in terms of a rib and a step features is meaningful for the design context. In feature recognition approach, features are extracted from the geometric model and by changing the recognition rules it is possible to derive different views of the same product [ReVa 89] [SaGo 90] [DFG 91] [CoCl 93]. The main weakness of this strategy is that the domain of recognizable features is limited and depends on the adopted recognition criterion.

New work is now investigating how to integrate the design-by-features approach with feature recognition [LaMä 92] [DFGHO 93] [KPKSK 93]. An integrated feature-based modeling system seems to be promising to support CE: in such a system the user can both design by features and use the solid modeler according to the complexity of the object, while feature recognition techniques are integrated in the core of the system and used to derive a feature-based model from the object solid model, in order to update the feature model after solid modeling operations, to define and to keep consistent different feature-based descriptions for specific application contexts.

In the following a new feature recognition mechanism based on an original classification of generic protrusion and depression features is presented. The proposed approach has been defined according to the requirements of an integrated feature-based modeling system, which is currently under development at the Istituto per la Matematica Applicata del CNR (IMA-CNR), Genova, Italy, in co-operation with the Fraunhofer Institut für Graphische Datenverarbeitung (FhG-IGD), Darmstadt, Germany.

An Integrated Feature-based Modeling Approach

The integration of a design by features system developed at FhG-IGD and a feature recognizer developed at IMA-CNR is the goal of a joint research project between the two institutes supported by the

European Communities within the HCM programme. The integrated system allows the user to generate a feature-based description by using both features and geometric primitives and provides a mechanism based on feature recognition techniques to derive and to keep consistent different context-dependent feature-based descriptions of the product [DFGHO 94]. The key points on which the integration is based are the use of a common feature library for the definition of design and application dependent features useful for both modeling and recognizing specific feature instances, and a single shape feature-based model, called Intermediate Model, which is a multiple view representation shared by all the considered application contexts.

The Intermediate Model results from merging two representation schemes: the Feature Entity Relation Graph (FERG) which specifies the shape feature semantics by geometric constraints between feature entities [BDFH 95], and the Shape Feature Object Graph (SFOG++) which keeps the adjacency relations between feature entities necessary to perform geometric reasoning and analysis [DFGG 94]. In the integrated system, the feature recognition can be activated not only after solid modeling operations for the creation of a feature-based model, as an alternative to the design by features approach, but it can be used also to derive different application dependent feature-based models of the product. These requirements have brought to the definition of a flexible recognition process which can be performed at different levels of detail in order to identify general classes of features as well as specific feature instances.

The Feature Recognizer

A feature recognition process has to take into account the association between shape and function which is intrinsic in the concept of feature. Geometric and topological reasoning is the basis for the identification of form features, but this process has to be driven by the application when specific instances of features are required. The basic idea of the approach here described is to use a classification of form features as an intermediate step in the process of mapping geometric models into context dependent feature based models. The classification is the result of geometric and topological reasoning, thus it can be considered context independent. The definition of equivalence classes is based on the type of topological interaction between the feature entities and the rest of the object, moreover it is independent on those shape variations which may affect the recognized feature without changing its main properties. Whether these variations have to be considered as significant elements for the feature identification or just "noise" on some invariant properties of the feature this strongly depends on the context of the application. Only fixing the context and providing the related information, the classified form features can be interpreted in a way meaningful for further analysis in that particular context.

The recognition system consists of three main components: the Form Feature Recognizer, the Form Feature Classifier and the Feature Interpreter. The Form Feature Recognizer is based on a revised version of Kyprianou's approach and analyzes the B-rep of an object in order to identify face sets corresponding to generic protrusions and depressions. The recognised face sets are stored in a hierarchical structure, called Shape Feature Object Graph (SFOG++). Then the Form Feature Classifier analyses each face set represented in the SFOG++ model and identifies the Class and the Sub-Class the feature belongs to. Finally the Feature Interpreter identifies specific feature instances performing a recognition at different levels of detail on the basis of the classification results and according to the requirements of the specific application. The system architecture is depicted in figure 2.

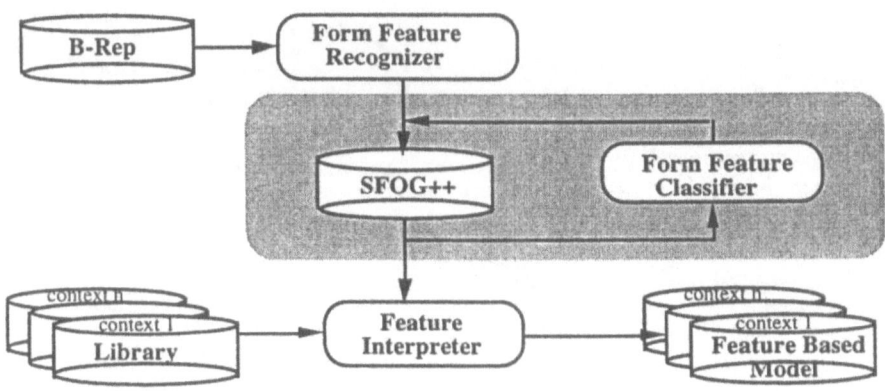

Fig. 2: The recognizer architecture

The Shape Feature Object Graph

The Shape Feature Object Graph (SFOG++) is a hierarchical graph structure where the nodes correspond to the object form features and the arcs, named *macro-links*, represent adjacency relationships between the feature face sets. Each macro-link is then expressed by a set of *micro-links*. A micro-link between two face sets *fs1* and *fs2* is described as a triple <*a, b, ab*>, where *a* and *b* are adjacent entities belonging respectively to fs1 and fs2 and *ab* is the intersection between them. Both macro-links and micro-links are oriented. The direction of the macro-links defines the hierarchy of the structure. They are unidirectional when they express a parent-child relation or bi-directional when the connected nodes are at the same level in the hierarchy.

The hierarchy of the model is defined during the form feature recognition step and depends on the type of adjacency between the feature face sets. Further details on the model are in [DFGG 94]. In figure 3, the SFOG++ representation of an object with two protrusions and one depression is shown. In the graph, the arcs between the main shape and the features correspond to a parent-child relation while the bidirectional arcs between the depression and the protrusions indicate that these components are at the same level in the model hierarchy.

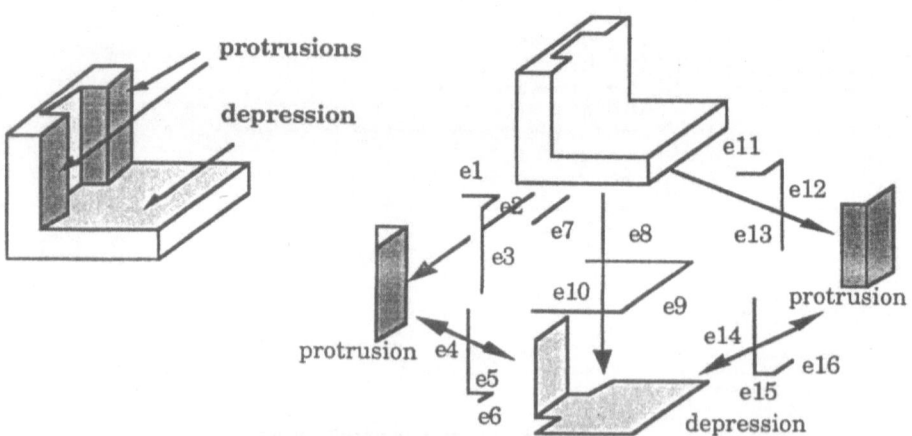

Figure 3: SFOG++ of an object with a depression and two protrusions

Feature Classification

The main requirement that the feature classification has to satisfy within the Recognition System is the capability of grouping features according to shape similarities without referring to the application context. At the same time a certain selective power on the shape has to be kept. The data stored in the SFOG++ representation are used by the Form Feature Classifier as neutral information for reasoning on the shape characteristics and for analysing the type of interaction between adjacent features. Classes and subclasses of features are defined by considering the hierarchical and adjacency relationships between the graph nodes and the so called *connection faces*. A connection face of a feature A is each face of the object which is adjacent to A through at least one edge without belonging to A. See fig. 4.

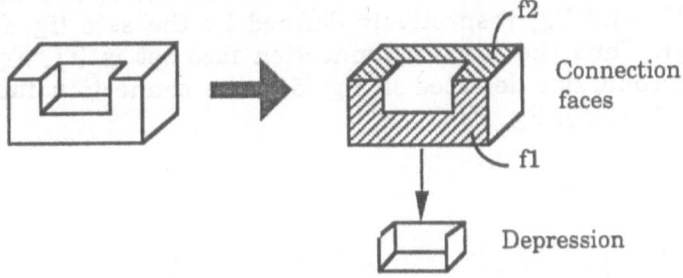

Fig. 4: Connection faces of a notch feature

By reasoning on a particular set of connection faces it is possible to evaluate the type of interaction between adjacent face sets and to derive hints to characterize the shape of a feature. The hierarchy in the SFOG++ model drives the identification of the *connection face set* of a feature, defined by all the connection faces of the feature that belong to parent or sister features. The connection faces which belong to child features are ignored. Since more than one occurrence of a same connection face can result in the connection face set, formally it is a multi-set.

The connection faces which belong to this set are further analyzed and distinguished in primary and secondary connection faces. *Primary connection faces* are those faces which are adjacent to more than one face of the feature face set while those connection faces which are adjacent to only one face are considered *secondary connection faces*. Since primary connection faces interact with a bigger number of feature entities, they are assumed to be more influent on the shape of the feature than secondary ones.

The information coming from secondary connection faces can be optimised by grouping them into *connection macro-faces*. A connection macro-face is the result of a collapsing operation on a connected set of secondary connection faces adjacent to a same face of the feature. The sets of secondary connection faces defining the macro-faces are not physically collapsed. The macro-faces are abstract entities which substitute the occurrences of the collapsed faces in the connection face set of the feature. The example in figure 5 shows the effect of the collapsing operation on the connection face set of a slot feature. In the slot depicted in fig. 5(a), f_1 and f_5 are primary connection faces since they are adjacent to three faces of the features, while f_2, f_3, f_4, f_6, f_7, f_8 are secondary ones. The secondary connection faces can be collapsed in two macro-faces F_2 and F_4, respectively defined by the sets $\{f_2, f_3, f_4\}$ and $\{f_6, f_7, f_8\}$. Thus the feature connection face set is $\{f_1, F_2, F_4, f_5\}$. For the second slot depicted in fig. 5(c) the connection face set will be simply $\{F_1, F_2, F_3, F_4\}$.

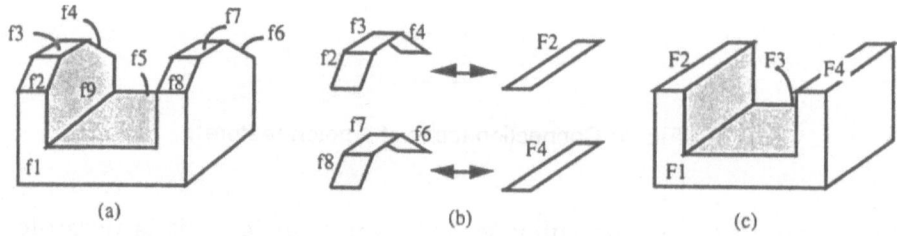

Figure 5: Equivalent slot features (a, c) by collapsing secondary connection faces

Feature Classes

Feature classes are identified by the following relationship of equivalence: *two features are equivalent if and only if their connection face sets have the same cardinality.*

The definition of feature classes follows easily as the result of this grouping operation on the set of all possible form features. More precisely with *Class n* , $n \in N$, we will indicate the set of equivalent form features having the number of connection faces equal to n. Formally the classes are the elements of the quotient set $\Phi/\sim$, where $\sim$ is the previous equivalence relationship and Φ is the set of all possible form features. Features with only one connection face belong to Class 1, features with two connection faces belong to Class 2, in general features with n connection faces belong to Class n.

To classify a feature on the basis of the cardinality of the set of its connection faces gives the advantage that the resulting classification is independent of the number of faces that belong to the feature. In figure 6 different instances of a slot feature are depicted: they have a different number of faces but each one has four connection faces, then they belong to Class 4.

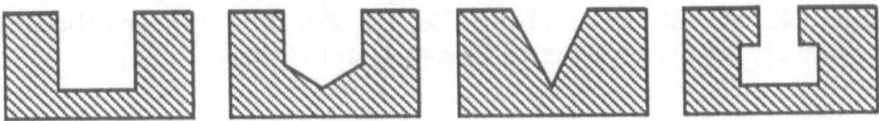

Fig. 6: Different instances of slot feature

In this sense, the connection faces allow to analyse the interaction between the form feature and the rest of the object. Furthermore, the collapsing step and the identification of connection macro faces allow the method to classify feature instances in a way as much as possible independent on the particular shape of the object on which the feature is positioned thus reaching a higher level of abstraction. In the example of fig. 5 the two slot features belong both to Class 4. The class of the slot in fig. 5(a) is obtained by adding the two primary faces and the two macro-faces F2 and F4. For the slot in fig. 5(c) the evaluation of the class is easier: there are four connection faces, two are primary and two are secondary but since they are isolated there is no need for a collapsing operation.

Sub-Classes

The proposed feature classification satisfies the requirement to be enough independent on the number of faces of the feature and on the shape of the object part which is interested by the feature. However, this classification groups together features which may affect the topology of the object in completely different ways, like the two features of class 2 depicted in figure 7.

In order to consider in the classification also the topological properties of the features, a further level of specification is performed. Within each class, sub-classes are defined analysing the set of the edges belonging to the boundary of the feature face set and considering the number of connected components of this set. More formally *features belonging to a same Class n are equivalent if and only if the set of boundary edges have the same number of connected components*. If m is the number of connected components, the features belong to the *Sub-class m*. Features belonging to Class n and Sub-class m are indicated in short with *Class n-m*. The example in fig. 7 shows two depressions belonging to Class 2. In (a) the boundary loop of the feature is a single chain of edges [e1, e2, e3, e4, e5, e6], while in (b) the boundary loop is composed by the two chains [E1, E2, E3, E4] and [E5, E6, E7, E8] thus they are classified respectively as depressions of Class2-1 and Class2-2.

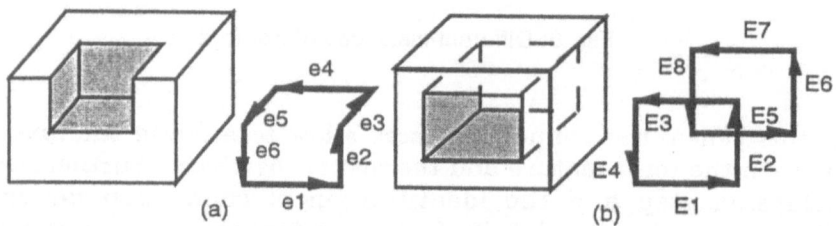

Fig.7: Two features belonging to (a) Class 2-1 (b) Class 2-2

Interpretation of Context Dependent Features

The result of the classification is stored in the SFOG++ representation and it is used by the Form Feature Interpreter for the recognition of specific instances of features. The information on the feature class, provides a necessary but not sufficient condition for the recognition of specific feature instances. For example, a squared slot is necessarily a Class4-1 depression but not all the Class 4-1 depressions are the right candidates to be a square slot (see fig.6). However the classification allows the feature interpreter to reject as candidates all the features which are not depressions of

Class4-1. Finally the interpreter performs on a reduced set of candidates, i.e. only the depressions of Class 4-1, the geometric checks necessary to identify all the occurrences of a specific feature instance in the given context.

The Interpreter is based on a teaching by examples technique [DFG 91]. User-defined features, described by the boundary representation and by context dependent technological information, are shown through simple examples to the system which automatically identifies the feature classes and browses the SFOG++ structure of the object looking for the face sets belonging to the same class of the example feature. If the system does not find any face set this means that no instances of the example feature are present in the object. If one or more face sets are found, the system considers also the information associated to the example feature, which includes parameters, geometric constraints, attributes. According to the level of specification required by the user, this information is processed and directly mapped or checked on the recognised face sets. This system component is currently under development.

Conclusions and future work

A flexible feature recognition process which can be performed at different levels of detail has been presented.

The recognition process is based on a context-independent feature classification which groups generic protrusion and depression features according to invariant shape characteristics. Then, context dependent information is used to process the results of the classification for the identification of specific feature instances. The main advantage of this approach is the selective power of the classification, used in the system to reduce the set of entities on which context dependent reasoning has to be performed. The validity of the use of the classification results independent on the recognition techniques adopted for the identification of specific feature instances. As a limit of this approach, it is important to point out that polyhedral representations take better advantage from this method while non polyhedral or sculptured surface representations do not completely exploit the selective power of the classification. An example of the system which has been realised on top of ACIS solid modeler in C++ language is shown in fig. 8. The recognition process has been applied to the object depicted in the window on the left, finding some depressions and protrusions represented in the SFOG++ graph (on the right side of the picture) respectively with dark and light grey nodes. The result of the classification is shown on the right side of the picture, in the bottom part.

The process here described has been defined within a feature-based modeling system which integrates feature recognition and design-by-features approaches. In the integrated system the recognizer is used to derive different context dependent views of the same object, while the relations between the views are maintained in a representation structure, called Intermediate Model, by means of attributes definition. Future developments of the system will show how this structure and the recognition mechanism can be used to support product design with concurrent engineering. In particular we are currently investigating the problem of modification propagation from one view to the others. At this regard the Intermediate Model will serve as the communication link between the different contexts while the recognizer will keep consistent the different feature-based models when a modification is performed.

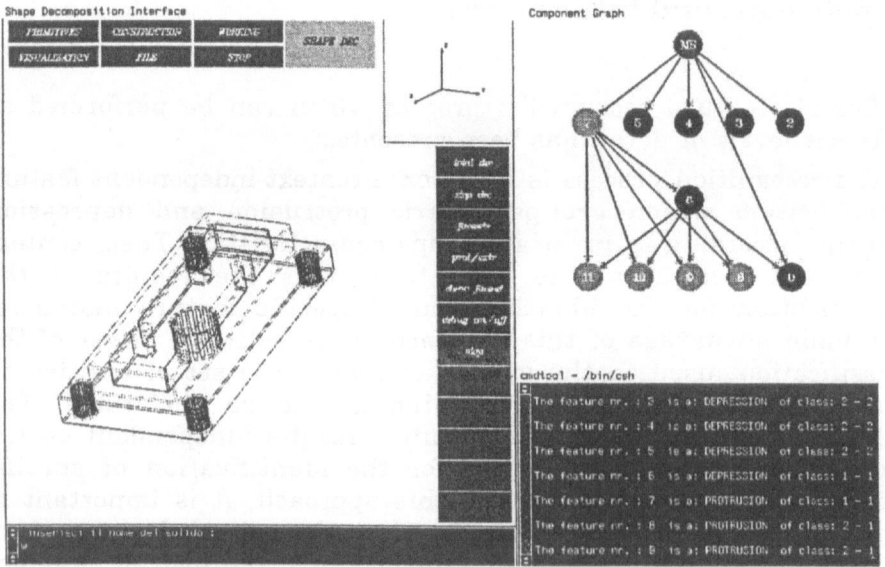

Fig.8: An example of feature classification

Acknowledgements

This work has been partially supported by the European Communities within the Human Capital and Mobility program, HCM Institutional project n. ERB CHBG CT930380. The authors thank Franca Giannini for the helpful discussions on the topic.

References

[BDFH 95]   Brunetti G., De Martino T., Falcidieno B., Haßinger S.: A relational model for interactive manipulation of form features based on algebraic geometry, Third ACM Solid Modeling'95, Salt Lake City, Utah USA, May 17-19 (1995), pp. 95-103

[BrJa 93]   Bronswoort W., Jansen F.: Feature modelling and conversion - Key concepts to concurrent engineering, Computers in industry, Elsevier, n. 21, 1993, pp. 61-86

[ChLe 94]   Chen C.L.P., Le Clair S.R.: Integration of design and manufacturing: solving setup generation and feature sequencing using an unsupervised-learning approach, Computer-Aided Design Vol. 26 N. 1, Jan 1994, pp. 59-75

[CoCl 93]   Corney J., Clark D.E.R.: Efficient Face-Based Feature Recognition:, 2nd ACM Solid Modeling '93, May 1993, Montreal, Canada, pp. 313-322

[DFG 91]   De Martino T., Falcidieno B., Giannini F.: Feature-based Model transformations between different Application Contexts, Proceedings of Computer Applications in Production and Engineering, Bordeaux, France, 10-12 September 1991, pp. 361-368

[DFG 95]   De Martino T., Falcidieno B., Giannini F.: Sharing Product Information in Concurrent Engineering environment through a Reference Model, Proceedings of ILCE'95, Integrated Logistic and Concurrent Engineering, Paris, France, Febr. 1995, pp.181-188

[DFGG 94]   De Martino T., Falcidieno B., Gamba F., Giannini F.: Feature Kernel Model: a reference model for integrated feature-based modeling systems,

Proceedings of AICA '94 annual conference, Palermo, Italy, Sept. 1994, Vol. 2

[DFGHO 94] De Martino T., Falcidieno B., Giannini F., Hassinger S., Ovtcharova J.: Feature based modeling by integrating Design and Recognition approaches, CAD journal vol. 26 nr. 8, August 94 pp. 646 - 653

[DiLi 90] Dixon JR., Libardi EC.: Unresolved Research Issues in Development of Design with Features Systems, Geometric Modeling for Product Engineering, North Holland, IFIP1990, pp. 183-196

[JoCh 88] Joshi S., Chang T.: Graph-based heuristics for recognition of mechanical features from a 3D solid model, Computer Aided Design 20, No 2, 1988

[KPKSK 93] Ko H., Park M, Kang H., Sony Y., Kim H.S.: Integration Methodology for Feature based Modeling and Recognition, Proceedings of Computer in Engineering, ASME 1993, pp 23-34

[LaMä 92] Lakko T., Mäntylä M.: Feature-based Modelling of Families of Machined Parts, Proceedings of the IFIP TC5/WG5.3 Eighth International PROLAMAT Conference, Tokyo, 24-26 June 1992, pp. 351-360

[OvHa 91] Ovtcharova J., Haßinger S.: Feature-Based Reasoning in Product Modeling, Proceedings of the Fourth International IFIP TC5 Conference on Computer Applications in Production and Engineering, Integration Aspects, CAPE'91, Bordeaux, France, Sept. 1991, pp.379-387

[ReVa 89] Requicha A.A.G., Vandenbrande J.H.: Features for Mechanical design and Manufacturing, Computer and Engineering, Book n.G0502A, 1989, pp.376-381

[SaGo 90] Sakuray H., Gossard D.C.: Recognizing Shape Features in Solid Models, IEEE Computer Graphics & Applications, Sept. 1990, pp. 22-32

Stability Features for Free Form Surfaces

Hans Hagen[1] and Stefanie Hahmann[2]

Feature based techniques are a key factor for successful producting modelling. There is strong demand in many application areas for free form features. This paper describes stability features for free form surfaces. The concept of stability is derived from the kinematic meaning of a special vector field with respect to infinitesimal bending.

Introduction

A very competitive international market forces companies to increase the quality of their products by simultaneously reducing their costs and the development time. Today's CAD systems are not able to fully support these goals. Therefore, a further development of tools supporting the product development process is marked by an enormous varity of variants for products and supplementary parts. There are no efficient mechanics for storage and retrevieval of these variants because the underlying semantics can't be stored today. Feature-based design is a novel approach to overcome these problems: features are used to store not only the form of an object but also its semantics. However, currently this approach is limited to relatively simple objects, no theory for features of complex shape parts exists.

There is a strong demand for fundamental research in the field of Free Form Features.

In many applications special information about the semantics of parts of the geometry and topology is needed to "automate" the link to subsequent design applications. Such information subsets abouts a mechanical part like slots, blind holes, bolts etc. are commonly called features. A very well suited formal definition for such features is Dieter Roller's [Rol89] approach:

---

[1] Fachbereich Informatik, Universität Kaiserslautern, Germany
[2] Laboratoire LMC-IMAG, Université INPG Grenoble, France

feature = form feature + feature semantics

In the last twenty years most of the research efforts concentrated on form features, but there are very important feature semantics issues in geometric modelling. The purpose of this paper is to present stability features for free form surfaces.

Stability Features

The design of free form objects is in most cases a feature based process. Points as output of a scanning process for example have to be interpolated or approximated under certain constraints like special energy functionals [BHS93, BH94]. After the construction of free form surfaces the quality control is an important step. Surface interrogation methods [HH92] test certain form features, like flat points, continuity, technical smoothness or simply aesthetic aspects, which are not always guaranteed by the design process.

Another aspect of shape control is the stability of surfaces with respect to their bending behaviour. Therefore the notion of stability in this paper is related to the geometry of free form surfaces.

The stability features presented in this paper are based on infinitesimal bendings. We will present an analysis tool for the detection of unstable regions on a surface. The notion of stability which will be developed in the following is related to infinitesimal bendings of free form surfaces. An infinitesimal bending of a surface is a small continuous deformation of the surface without stretching or compressing it. In other words, infinitesimal bendings are surface deformations which "keep" the length of any arbitrary surface curve unchanged in first order during the deformation.

Once the definition of infinitesimal bendings is known we will show that there is a special vector field associated to each infinitesimal bending. This special vector field, the so-called rotation vector field has a kinematic meaning which allows to understand intuitively what happens in the beginning of a deformation. It is therefore very well suited for stability investigations. It turns out, that while visualizing such a vector field, one is able to say which region on the surface is more likely to bend than other.

Infinitesimal bendings

First a short introduction to the theory of infinitesimal bendings is given. A general survey can be found in [Vek63, Efi57].

We represent surfaces in $\mathbf{R}^3$ as vector valued functions of class $\mathbf{C}^2$

$$X : G \to \mathbf{R}^3 \ , \quad (u, w) \mapsto X(u, w) \tag{1}$$

where G is a connected domain in $\mathbf{R}^2$.

Definition 1:   *A continuous one-parameter family $\{X_t\}$ of mappings $X_t : G \to \mathbf{R}^3$ with $t \in I := [0, a)$, $a > 0$ and $X_0 = X$, is called* **deformation** *of X.*

A parametric representation is given by

$$X_\varepsilon(u, w) := X(u, w) + \varepsilon Z(u, w) , \quad \varepsilon \in \mathbf{R} . \tag{2}$$

$Z(u, w)$ is called **deformation vector field** of an infinitesimal bending.

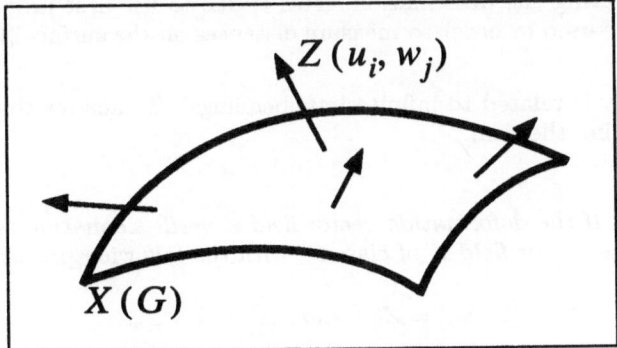

Figure 1:   Deformation vector field

The basic concept of an infinitesimal theory is to neglect all infinitesimal small quantities of the surface X_e of higher order in ε. This leads to the following definition.

Definition 2:   *The deformation X_ε (2) is called an* **infinitesimal bending** *of first order of the surface X if the length L of any arbitrary curve on the surface X keeps unchanged to first order in ε, for $\varepsilon \to 0$, i.e., $L(c_\varepsilon) = L(c) + o(\varepsilon)$, where $c(t) = X(u(t), w(t))$ is an arbitrary smooth surface curve and c_ε the deformed curve.*

The vector field Z can be interpreted as **velocity field** of the deformation. This means that infinitesimal bendings also describe the bending behaviour of a surface in the beginning of a deformation.

The following theorem characterizes the infinitesimal bendings by the coefficients of the first fundamental form.

Theorem 3: *Let Z be a deformation vector field of the surface X. Let $\tilde{g}_{ij}$ be the coefficients of the first fundamental form of the deformation $\tilde{X} = X + \varepsilon Z$ and denote the first partial derivatives of X and Z by $X_u := \partial X/\partial u$ and $Z_u := \partial Z/\partial u$. The following statements are equivalent:*

i)   *Z defines an infinitesimal bending of first order of X*

ii) $\frac{\partial \tilde{g}_{ij}}{\partial \varepsilon}|_{\varepsilon=0} = 0 \quad i, j = 1, 2$ (3)

iii) $< dX, dZ > = 0$ (4)

where $<\ ,\ >$ denotes the dot product.

Proof: see [Efi57].

Remarks:

- Equation (4) is also called the differential equation of the infinitesimal bendings.
- Equation (3) means that the length of any surface curve doesn't change in first order in ε during the deformation. This is due to the first fundamental form which can be used in order to measure distances on the surface [CoC76].

How stability is related to infinitesimal bendings? To answer this question we need the following theorem.

Theorem 4: *If the deformation vector field Z verifies equation (4), then there exists an unique vector field Y of class C^1 with the following properties:*

$$[Y, X_u] = Z_u \quad \text{and} \quad [Y, X_w] = Z_w\,,$$ (5)

where $[\ ,\ ]$ denotes the vector product.

The vector field $Y(u, w)$ is called **rotation vector field**.

Surfaces which don't allow bendings are called infinitesimal rigid surfaces. We now characterize infinitesimal rigid surfaces by means of the rotation vector field.

The differential equation $< dX, dZ > = 0$ (4) has always the trivial solution $Z = [C, X] + D$, where C, D are arbitrary constant vectors. These deformations don't cause inner deformations of the surface, because they define a rigid (infinitesimal) motion of the surface.

Definition 5: *If $X_\varepsilon = X + \varepsilon Z$ is an infinitesimal bending with $Z = [C, X] + D$, where C, D are constant vectors, i.e. $Y = C = const$, then X_ε is called **trivial infinitesimal bending** (or infinitesimal motion) of the surface X.*

All the bundles of line elements have the same momentary rotation if the rotation vector field is constant. This context leads to the following definition.

Definition 6: *A surface which allows only trivial infinitesimal bendings is called* **infinitesimal rigid** *under infinitesimal bendings.*

A classical theorem of infinitesimal bendings says that all closed convex analytic surfaces which are connected are rigid [Lie00]. Open surfaces are generally not rigid. They are nevertheless more or less stable depending on their shape. Definition 5 and 6 show that the notion of rigid surfaces is defined by the rotation vectors, more precisely by constant rotation vector fields. The next step is now to use this vector field in order to visualize the bending behaviour of free form surfaces with respect to infinitesimal bendings. We call it *stability*.

To record quantitatively, how a surface is likely to bend (i.e. how it is stable), is possible by using the rotation vector field. The next theorem gives the kinetic meaning of this vector field and shows what happens geometrically during the deformation.

Theorem 7: $\varepsilon Y(u, w)$ *is the rotation vector field of the infinitesimal bending of the surface* $X(u, w)$ *into the surface* $X_\varepsilon(u, w)$.

The direction of the rotation vector is the axis of the rotation of the surface element in the point (u, w) during the bending.

The norm and the orientation of the rotation vector determine the angle of rotation, except for quantities of higher order.

Proof: see [HH96]

One can therefore think of Y as a rotation vector of a rigid body attached to the surface $X(G)$ at the point $X(u_i, w_j)$ during the deformation.

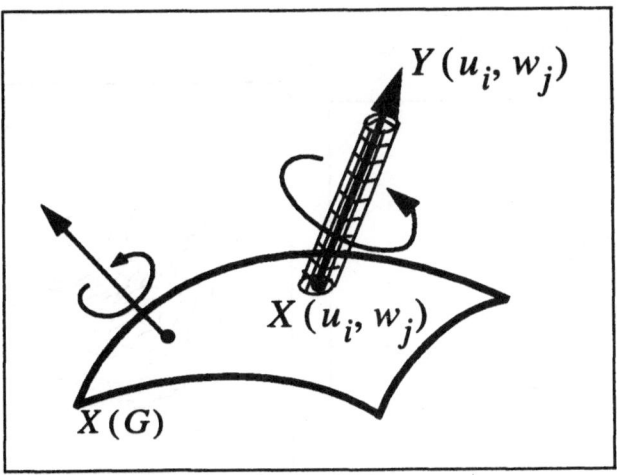

Figure 2:   Rotation vectors

Stability as an analysis tool

To define "stability" as a geometric property of free form surfaces, we will refer to theorem 7. The kinematic meaning of the rotation vectors leads to the statement, that the more the rotation vectors of a surface region vary in their directions and lengths, the more the surface is likely to bend in this region, i.e. the less the surface there is *stable*. On the other hand, if the rotation vectors are nearly constant, the surface behaves as a rigid one in this region, i.e. it produces stability there.

Stability is therefore defined (locally) in a region of a given surface whereas it is also possible to take the behaviour of the whole rotation field as a global feature (see [HH96]). Nevertheless, in the present paper, non-stable regions are detected by large local variations of the rotation vectors. This statement is basic for the stability concept and underlines the importance of the rotation vectors in this concept. In order to detect non-stable surface regions one can think of different vector field visualization techniques, like arrows plots, color maps, etc. The simplest technique is employed in the following examples. The vectors are attached on the surface and pin point directly to the non-stable regions.

Examples

We now study the stability of two test surfaces. The first surface is a bi-cubic Bézier patch (Figure 3 and 4). And the arrow plot on the right shows the rotation vector field, *i.e.*, some rotation vectors attached on their corresponding surface points.

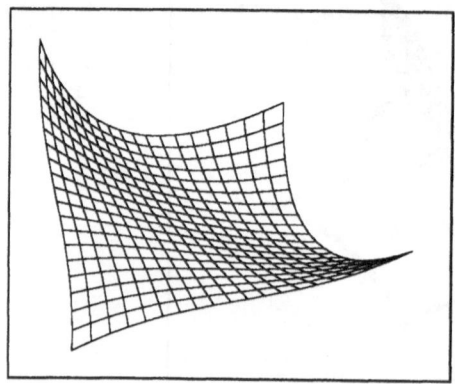
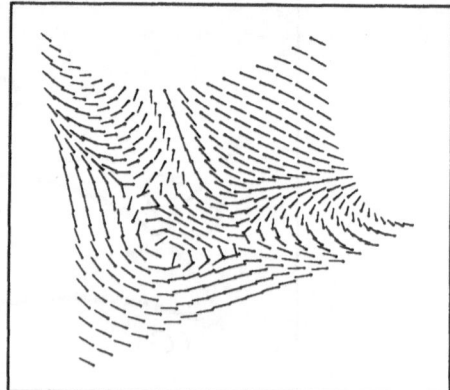

Figure 3. Surface   Figure 4. rotation vector field

In the second example we also have a bi-cubic Bézier patch (Figure 5). And we show the rotation vectors attached on on their corresponding parameter values in the parameter domain (Figure 6).

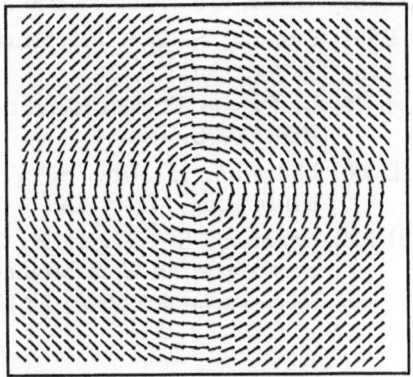

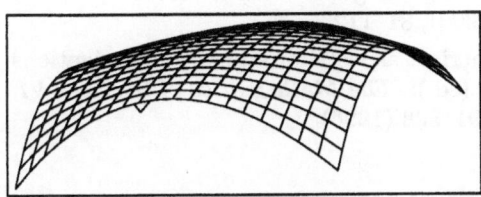

Figure 5. Surface   Figure 6. rotation vector field

It is easy to see where the regions of biggest inner deformations are. As stated out before, this are the regions where the variation of the rotation vectors are big with respect to other regions on the same surface. This means, that the test surface of Figure 5 tends to deform first in the middle.

Stability features presented below are therefore an analysis tool for free form surfaces, *i.e.*, for complex shapes. They can detect unstable surface regions by visualizing the momentary bending behaviour.

Remark:

The calculation of the vector fields of a surface is not an easy task, if we don't want to calculate the corresponding infinitesimal bendings, too. A solution can be found by a least-square fitting with a B-Spline representation for Y [HH96]. We don't want to go in this detail here.

References

[Rol89] Roller, Dieter: Design by features: an approach to high level shape manipulations Computers in Industry 12, 185–191, (1989)

[BHS93] Brunnett, G., Hagen, H., Santarelli, P.: Variational design of curves and surfaces, Surv. Math. Ind. 3, 1–27, (1993)

[BH94] Bonneau, G.-P.; Hagen, H.: Variational design of rational Bézier curves and surfaces, in Laurent, Le Méhauté, Schumaker (eds): Curves and Surfaces II, 51–58, (1994)

[HHS92] Hagen, H; Hahmann, S; Schreiber, T; Nakajima, Y; Wördenweber, B; Hollemann, P.: Surface interrogation algorithms, IEEE CG & Appl. 12(5), 53–60, (1992)

[Vek63] Vekua, I. N.: *Generalized analytic functions, (1963)*

[Efi57] Efimow, N. W.: *Flächenverbiegungen im Großen*, §21-24, Akademie-Verlag, Berlin, (1957)

[DoC76] Do Carmo, M.P.: *Differential Geometry of Curves and Surfaces* Prentice Hall, (1976)

[Lie00] Liebmann, H.: Über die Verbiegung der geschlossenen Flächen positiver Krümmung, Math. Ann. 53 (1900), 81–112

[HH96] Hahmann, St.; Hagen, H.: Numerical aspects for stability investigations on surfaces, in Glen Mullineux (ed.): *The Mathematics of Surfaces VI*, IMA conference Series Nr.58, 291–308 (1996)

Representation Scheme for Feature-based Parametric Design

Ana Sofia Vieira[1] and Gino Brunetti[1]

Feature-based parametric design (FbPD) is an approach to CAD that integrates the advantages of design-by-features and parametric design. The realization of FbPD systems requires an appropriate representation scheme. Here, a parametric feature representation (PFRep) is introduced that incorporates the application data of a feature-based model with the generic data of a parametric model. The PFRep represents explicitly features, feature relationships, form entities, as well as geometric and non-geometric parameters and constraints.

12 Introduction

Design-by-features and parametric design are two design methodologies being adopted by most of the current commercial and research CAD systems [CAT95, DKB95, DFGH94, SBRU94, ChSc90]. The objective is to provide systems with facilities to capture, maintain, and exchange the engineer's design intent and to support an efficient generation of valid model variations. From the designer's point of view, design features are seen as information units, which enrich the traditional geometric representation of a product with semantic knowledge. The use of these information units helps to optimize both, the design quality and the product design costs, thus reducing the product time-to-market. It also allows to link different phases of the product life cycle, such as detailed design, process planning and manufacturing. On the other side, the CAD system has to model this semantic knowledge and has to provide

---

1. Fraunhofer-Institut für Graphische Datenverarbeitung (IGD), Darmstadt, Germany

efficient methods for the generation of correct model variations. An approach to realise these objectives is the integration of design-by-features and parametric design leading to a design paradigm that we call Feature-based Parametric Design (FbPD) [Vie95].

In order to support feature-based parametric design, the development of an appropriate representation scheme is essential. In this contribution we introduce a parametric feature representation that describes explicitly features, features relationships, form feature entities, as well as geometric and non-geometric parameters and constraints. It retains all the information needed to evaluate a traditional BRep model.

This work is organized as it follows: After giving an overview of related works, the fundamental ideas of the feature-based parametric design approach are outlined. Based on this foundation an appropriate representation scheme is introduced and discussed by an example.

Related Work

Several authors have presented different approaches for defining and representing features and feature-based models.

Sheu and Lin [ShLi93] proposed a representation scheme for defining and operating form features. Five basic constituents are used to represent a single form feature: a solid component (represented by a volume associated with a BRep solid), measure entities (are the interfaces used to attach dimension to the solid component; they refer to real faces, edges, etc. stored in the solid component or to artificially created geometric entities), size dimensions (control an intrinsic size of a form feature referring two measure entities), location dimensions (represent relative position relationships between two features), and constraints (are directed chains of measure entities linked by bounded and implicit dimensions). Dimensions are associated with geometric preconditions, e.g. parallel. The feature-based model is maintained in a graph. Nodes are form features and position operators, which represent the relative position between two features using location dimensions.

Shah *et al.* [SBRU94] have moved from a procedural approach of feature-based modelling to a declarative one. Features are defined by explicitly stating the spatial relationships between its geometric entities. A minimal set of geometric constraints is used to orient and position geometric feature entities. Feature-based models are represented as graphs where nodes are geometric entities and arcs geometric constraints.

Following the declarative approach, Brunetti *et al.* [BDFH95] described a parametric model, which maps feature shape semantics into a geometric model and provides facilities for interactive feature manipulation. The model is expressed as a graph called Feature Entity Relation Graph (FERG). It specifies the shape semantics of features by geometric constraints between feature entities. The model maintains real and virtual feature entities as well as intrinsic and extrinsic feature relations. Similar results have been presented by Dohmen *et al.* [DKB95].

Presently, we can observe that many authors recognize the importance of the alliance between parametric and feature-based modelling. However, we verify that the potential of this alliance is being rarely used to define and represent more powerful feature-based models. Specially, in what respects to the representation and maintenance of more high level semantic (non-geometric) data and constraints. This aspect is, therefore, an important focus of this work.

Feature-based Parametric Design

In *Feature-based Parametric Design (FbPD)*, design features are defined on the basis of a combination of feature-based and parametric design methodologies. Following the proposal in [Ovt92], our FbPD approach structures design feature data into three levels: an application level, a generic level, and a geometric level (Figure 1).

In the *application level*, feature-based models describing a product part are specified. *Design features* are defined by design specific data over combinations of sets of application independent generic components. *Feature relationships* reflect relations that exist between various generic components of different features. These relations concern requirements for feature positioning and orientation, as well as for parameter dependencies. Feature relationships define sometimes new parameters, which do not belong to any particular feature but to the model itself. Such parameters are called *model parameters*.

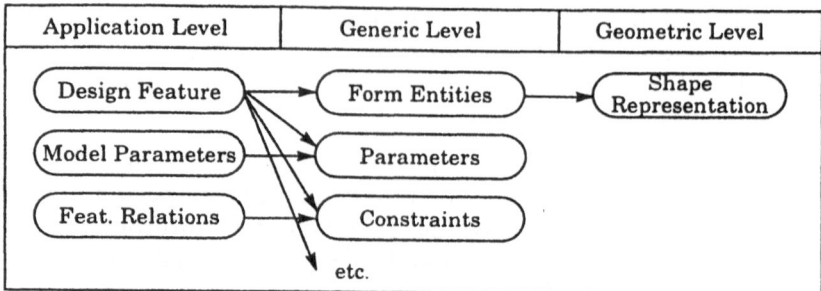

Figure 1: Feature data structured in three levels.

Generic components describe properties of products in a general way. They are represented in the *generic level* and regard *parameters, constraints, form, material, tolerances*, etc. Form features are represented and maintained in a parametric model [BDFM95]. Shapes, which concern the dimensional and proportional appearance of forms, are derived from this representation. Constraints work on the basis of the parametric definition of the features. They comprise both geometric and non-geometric feature requirements and are used to describe the form, the shape, the location, and the engineering semantics of features. Constraints are defined and represented generally and independently from features. Instances of these constraints are linked to features describing their meaning and behaviour in the part model.

Finally, in the *geometric level*, the *shape representation* of the feature-based model is stored in a BRep scheme.

The Parametric Feature Representation

Bringing together the advantages of design-by-features and parametric design allows to define a powerful model where both the geometry and the engineering meaning of features can be consistently managed. This model is called *Parametric Feature Representation* (PFRep). To illustrate the following discussion of its components, Figure 2 summarizes its object-oriented specification and class relationships.

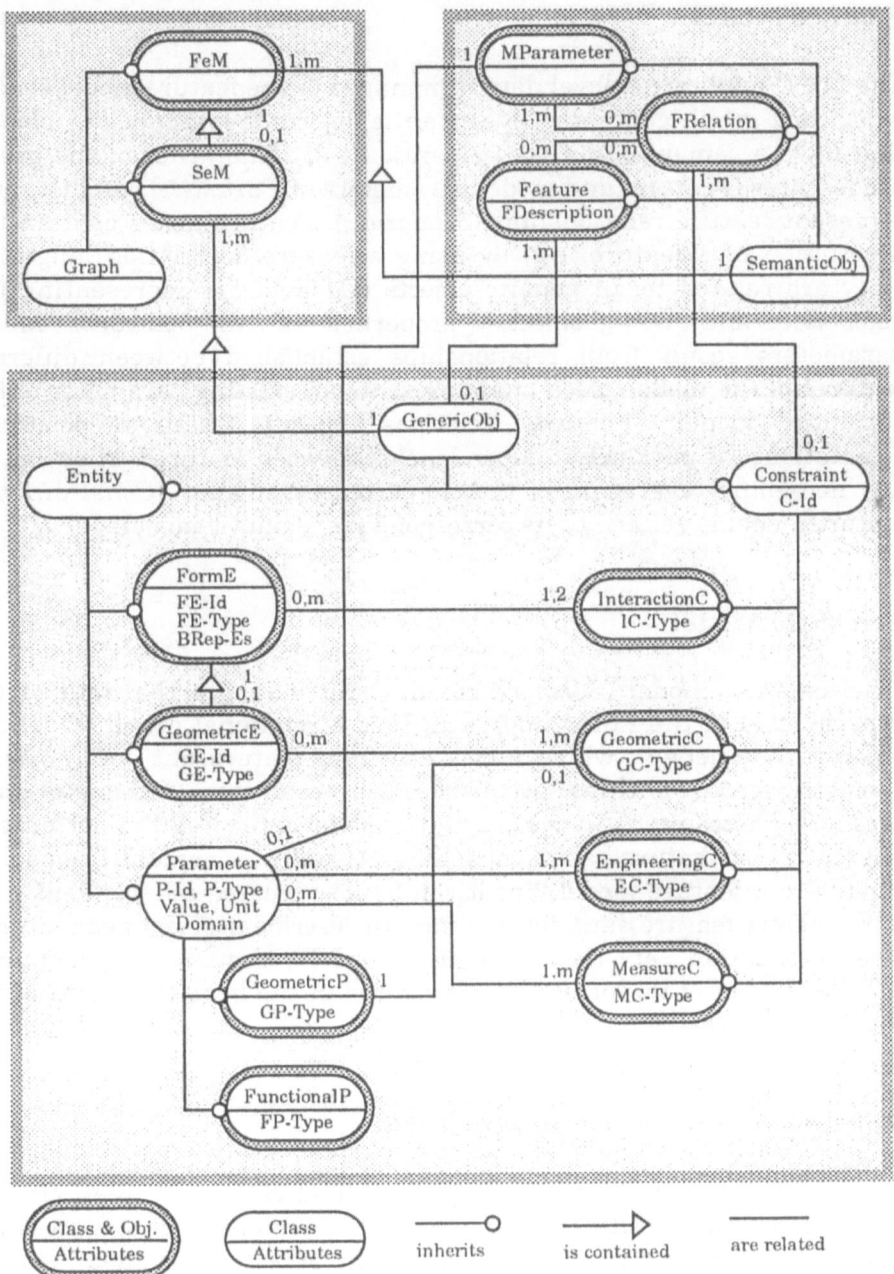

Figure 2: The class hierarchy and class relationships of the Parametric Feature
Representation (PFRep). Syntax by Coad & Yourdon [CoYo91].

Feature Model

The FbPD application level data is managed in the feature model (*FeM*), which is a graph generated by semantic objects (*SemanticObj* - objects that have a semantic, not the semantic itself). The nodes of the graph are features (*Feature*) and model parameters (*MParameter*) and the arcs represent feature relationships (*FRelation*). Feature nodes contain the description of a feature, e.g. by using a feature description language. They are related to all generic objects (*GenericObj*), representing the geometric and non-geometric properties of the feature. Model parameters result from relationships established between different features of the model. Each one represents an existing parameter of the semantic model. Feature relations specify relative positions, orientations, or parametric dependencies between features. They can be any non-empty aggregate of the supported constraints (*Constraint*). A feature model is related to its corresponding semantic model.

Semantic Model

The semantic model (*SeM*) represents and manages the data of the generic level of the FbPD approach. It is a relational graph of generic objects (*GenericObj*), which nodes are form feature entities (*FormE*), geometric feature entities (*GeometricE*) , or parameters (*Parameter*), and arcs are constraints. It is a parametric model extending the declarative approach for feature-based modelling. Usually, a semantic model is related to a feature model, but it can be also created independent from any concrete feature data, for instance, to describe user-defined features. The evaluation of the semantic model creates the boundary representation of the part, which is stored in the geometric level of the FbPD structure.

Entities

Form entities (*FormE*) are classified in three categories: real, closure, and construction entities. They express the semantics of a form entity with respect to its role in the definition of a feature. Real entities correspond to an entity of the evaluated BRep. Closure entities are entities completing the volume of a feature, for instance, the top face of a rectangular slot. They may be boundary evaluated, e.g. for editing, but they never belong to the authentic boundary of the model. Construction entities are used as auxiliary entities for the creation of the feature form, *e.g.* the principal axis of a cylinder or the centre of a sphere.

Each form entity is always associated to its correspondent geometric description (*GeometricE*). Geometric entities are currently restricted to implicit algebraic equations generated by irreducible polynomials of first and second order. In 3D they build up the halfspace decomposition of the form feature. The interior of the halfspace is defined by the opposite direction of the surface normals. Geometric entities are linked to each other by several types of spatial relations expressed as geometric constraints. These relations are important for describing the entities relative positions. Finally, the form of the feature is obtained from a union of volumetric and convex cells, which are derived from the intersection of the halfspaces of the geometric entities.

Another type of entities are the geometric and functional parameters, which are both derived from the parameter class (*Parameter*). Parameters are mainly defined by a value, a unit, and a domain. The value and the domain of a parameter can be constrained by engineering and measure constraints. Parameters can represent metric, angular, quadric, or cubic measures according to the specified unit. If no unit is specified, they represent simply coefficient values. Geometric parameters (*GeometricP*) are always related to a geometric constraint, which control their geometric role (distance, angle, radius) in the part. Functional parameters (*FunctionalP*) are defined by engineering constraints, e.g. the volume of a depression or the weight of the part.

Parameters are also grouped in three different categories: *bound* , *derived*, and *fixed*. Bound parameters are parameters whose values can be manipulated by the user. If these parameters are engaged in a design modification, it is sure that their value will not be altered. If a parameter is derived, its value can be dynamically updated during the design process when the parameter is affected by some design operation. The value of the parameter is derived from the associated constraint. Fixed parameters are used to describe standardized feature shapes, material properties, etc. Their value can be modified neither by the user nor by the evaluation of some constraints.

Geometric Constraints

The spatial dependencies between features and their geometric entities are described by geometric constraints (*GeometricC*). A geometric constraint can be associated with a geometric parameter, which then helps to control the validity of the value of its measure. Currently, the supported geometric constraints are Coincident, Complement, Parallel, Intersecting, Perpendicular, Concentric, and Coaxial [BDFH95].

Geometric constraints controlling the form of a feature are called intrinsic constraints, those controlling the relative position and orientation between features are called extrinsic constraints. If extrinsic constraints define a parent/child relation, they are directed from the child (target) to the parent (reference) entity.

Measure Constraints

Parameters are controlled by domain and value constraints, which are derived from the measure constraint class (*MeasureC*).

A *domain constraint* is defined by a domain $D \subseteq [min, max]$ and specifies how the value of the constrained parameter varies within *min* and *max*. Variations can be performed linearly, in equidistant steps, or by selecting values out of a concrete set (Figure 3).

A *value constraint* determines internally the value of a parameter, which is then automatically replaced. The value calculation is based either on generic algorithms dedicated to solve concrete feature problems or it is obtained directly from the designer as a need.

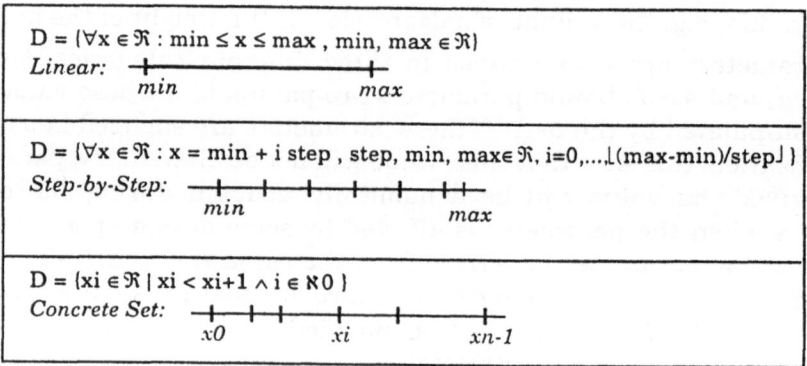

Figure 3: Parameter variation types.

Interaction Constraints

Interaction constraints (*InteractionC*) specify the way form entities of features behave in relation to their intersection, attachment, and covering.

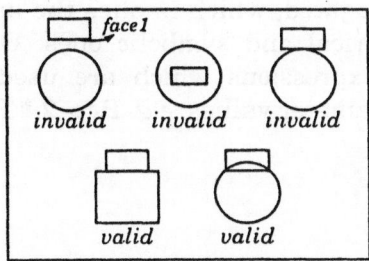

Figure 4.1: Valid and invalid
positioning of positive features.

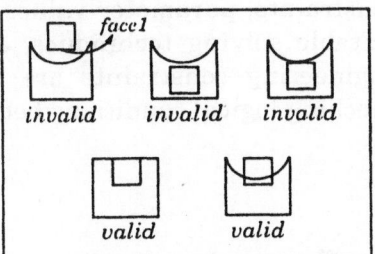

Figure 4.2: Valid and invalid
positioning of negative features.

The objective of an *intersecting constraint* is to force an entity to keep touchable or untouchable by other entities of the part model. Certain features by definition do not allow intersections in some of their faces. Others, in order to be correctly positioned, have to intersect the part model with specific form entities. A parameter specifies which type of intersection (vertex, edge, face, volume) is or is not allowed. In the examples of Figure 4, face f_1 is forced to intersect the model. The result of the intersection with the model has to be either a face or a volume different from the one of the feature.

An *attachment constraint* establishes a relation between two form entities. It is satisfied, if the two entities are geometrically coincident or complement and if the intersection between them is not empty. It is one of he most used constraints for controlling feature positioning.

When a *covering constraint* is applied, it avoids that the constrained form entity becomes invisible. A flag determines if the constraint has to check total or partial covering (see Figure 5).

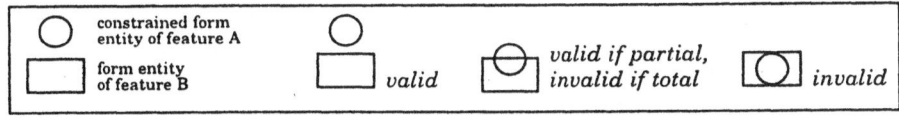

Figure 5: Evaluation of a covering constraint (top view).

Engineering Constraints

Engineering constraints (*EngineeringC*) control the value and behaviour of parameters. They are expressed by analytic equations and build a system of non-linear equation. An example is the constraint specifying that a pocket should always keep a volume of 1/4 litre. Using such constraints, parameter values are propagated, which implies the use of suitable solving techniques, *e.g.* numerical and symbolic ones. Other engineering constraints are boolean expressions which are used for checking logical conditions between parameter values, *e.g.* $P_1 > 2 * P_2$.

An Example

In this paragraph the introduced PFRep will be discussed by an example. Its goal is to round off the explanations given before.

The underlying part is a doorknob as shown in Figure 6. Its dimensions are illustrated in Figure 7.a,b. The doorknob is modelled by three features, a cylindrical main shape, a cylindrical blind hole and a doorknob slot. The corresponding feature model as well as the semantic model are illustrated in Figure 8.a,b, where features are drawn with a gray background embedding their corresponding semantic model as it is derived from the feature description.

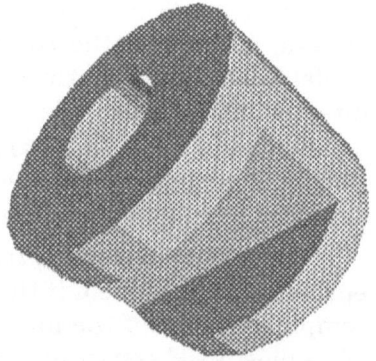

Figure 6: Doorknob

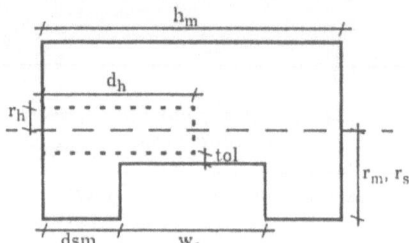

Figure 7.a: Side view

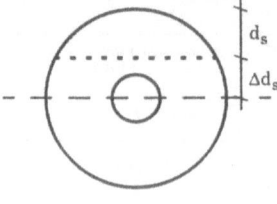

Figure 7.b: Back view

The form of the main shape is composed by three form entities, i.e. the cylindrical face cyl_m, the top face top_m, and the bottom face bot_m. The position of the cylinder is determined by the position of its two

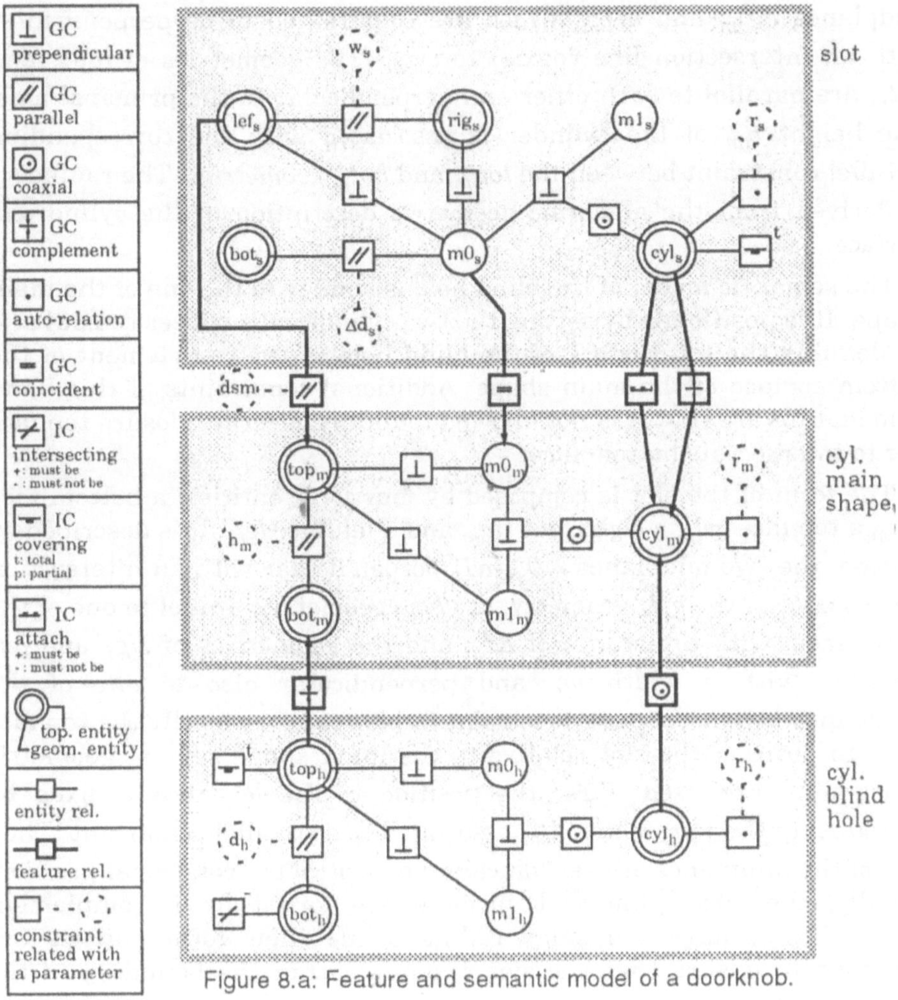

⊥ GC
prependicular

// GC
parallel

⊙ GC
coaxial

⊞ GC
complement

• GC
auto-relation

▬ GC
coincident

✗ IC
intersecting
+: must be
-: must not be

▭ IC
covering
t: total
p: partial

⊷ IC
attach
+: must be
-: must not be

top. entity
geom. entity

entity rel.

feature rel.

constraint
related with
a parameter

slot

cyl.
main
shape

cyl.
blind
hole

Figure 8.a: Feature and semantic model of a doorknob.

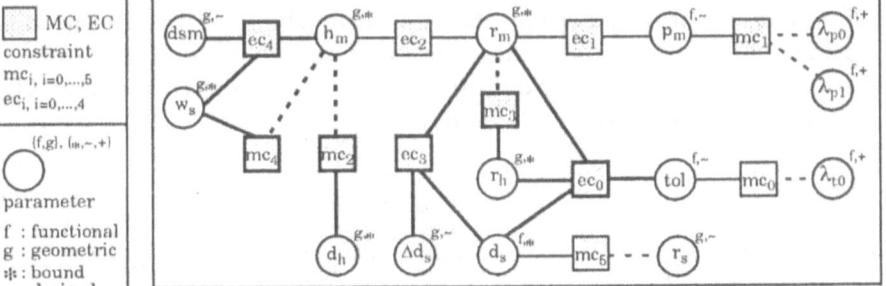

MC, EC
constraint
$mc_{i, i=0,...,5}$
$ec_{i, i=0,...,4}$

{f,g}, {*,~,+}

parameter

f : functional
g : geometric
* : bound
~ : derived
+ : fixed

Figure 8.b: Parametric relationships of a doorknob.

midplanes $m0_m$ and $m1_m$, which are constrained to be perpendicular with an intersection line coaxial to cyl_m. The geometries of top_m and bot_m are parallel to each other and perpendicular to the principal axis. The height h_m of the cylinder is associated with the corresponding parallel constraint between the top_m and bot_m geometries. The radius r_m is derived from the algebraic geometric description of the cylindrical surface.

The semantic model of the blind hole is similar to the one of the main shape. It is positioned by setting the two cylindrical surfaces coaxial and by defining the top surface of the blind hole as the complement of the bottom surface of the main shape. Additional constraints of this blind hole feature are that it is not allowed to totally cover its closure top face nor to intersect its bottom face.

The form of the slot is composed by four form entities: a bottom face bot_s, a top face cyl_s, a right face rig_s, and a left face lef_s. It is described by setting: the two midplanes $m0_s$, $m1_s$ perpendicular with an intersection line coaxial to the cyl_s geometry; the bot_s geometry parallel to one of the midplanes, with a distance of Δd_s; and the geometries of rig_s and lef_s parallel, with a width w_s, and perpendicular also to one of the midplanes. An interaction constraint forbids to cover totally the top face cyl_s. To position the slot relative to the main shape several geometric constraints are used. First the position of the lef_s face is fixed by introducing the parameter d_{sm} associated to a parallel constraint. Then two of the midplanes are set coincident to control the rotational position. Finally, the two cylindrical surfaces are forced by a complement constraint to have the same radius, while their form entities are attached to ensure that the slot remains within the boundary of the main shape.

Having defined the form and the interaction semantics of the doorknob it is now necessary to constrain the generation of model variations by introducing some functional parameters (see Figure 8.b and the list below) and their defining engineering constraints, as well as constraints on the parameter domains.

ec_0: $tol = r_m - r_h - d_s$	mc_0: $[\lambda t_0, \infty [$	mc_3: $] 0, r_m [$
ec_1: $p_m = 2 \, \Pi \, r_m$	mc_1: $[\lambda p_0, \lambda p_1]$	mc_4: $] 0, h_m [$
ec_2: $r_m = 1/3 \, h_m$	mc_2: $] 0, h_m [$	mc_5: $] 0, r_s [$
$ec3$: $\Delta d_s = r_m - d_s$		
$ec4$: $d_{sm} = (h_m - w_s) / 2$		

The functional parameter *tol*, for instance, is defined by the engineering constraint ec_o and must be greater then a given λt_0 that depends on the used material. Another functional parameter is p_m, which is a measure for the perimeter of the doorknob. Its lower and upper bound are given by λp_0 and λp_1, which have a reasonable relation to the size of human hands.

Conclusions

In this work a representation scheme for a feature-based parametric design (FbPD) system is presented. It is called parametric feature representation (PFRep) and benefits from the integration of feature-based and parametric design. PFRep allows the explicit representation of semantics in a feature-based system by incorporating constraints on the geometry, the form, and the parameters.

The PFRep is the base for the realization of our FbPD system, which is formed by the integration of three IGD developments: SINFONIA, a feature-based design kernel providing a consistency management for FbPD [OHVJ94, Vie95], the declarative form feature modelling tool FERG (Feature Entity Relation Graph) [BDFH95], and ARCADE (Advanced Realism Computer Aided Design Environment), which provides constrained 3D interaction techniques [SBV96]. Furthermore, the PFRep is influenced by an EU-project for the integration of design-by-features and feature recognition [DFGH94], being realized within a cooperation between IGD and the Istituto per la Matematica Applicata, C.N.R., in Genova.

Currently, we are working on the development of a declarative and object-oriented feature description language [BVO96] and developing and testing different methods and algorithms based on the PFRep. Constraints are expressed in different ways and hence solved by different constraint solvers. Engineering constraints are expressed by algebraic sets of equations and inequalities. They are solved using numerical or symbolic techniques. If they describe boolean expressions an operational solving approach is applied [DKB95]. Measure constraints are expressed by real intervals and boolean operations on those intervals. Measure and interaction constraints can also be represented by algorithms, which may take advantage of the functionality of the modeller. In this case, the operation approach is applied for solving them. Finally, geometric constraints represent spatial relations between geometric entities and are solved using an incremental propagation technique. Current research at IGD concerns also the development of a consistency mechanism, which combines the above mentioned solving techniques in order to solve the existing design constraints and preserve consistent the semantic of the model.

Future work regards the extension of the PFRep for supporting assembly modelling and for the integration of material properties, and tolerances.

Acknowledgments

The authors want to thank Prof. J. L. Encarnação and Dr. J. Rix for their guidance and for making this work possible. We want also to thank the colleagues and students of the department for Industrial Applications at the Fraunhofer Institute for Computer Graphics, as well as the colleagues from the Istituto per la Matematica Applicata, C.N.R., in Genova, that are involved in the realization of this work.

References

[CAT95]   Dassault Systemes: CD-ROM: "CATIA Solutions Version 4 Release 1.5", Softcopy Collection Kit, SK2T-5219-06, 7th Ed., August (1995)

[DKB95]   Dohmen, M.; Kraker, K. J.; Bronsvoort W. F.: "Constraint Techniques for Feature Validation", IFIP WG5.2 Workshop in Knowledge-Intensive CAD-1, Helsinki University of Technology, Espoo, Finland, Sep. 26-29 (1995)

[DFGH94] De Martino, T.; Falcidieno, B.; Giannini, F.; Haßinger S.; Ovtcharova, J.: "Feature-based Modelling by Integrating Design and Recognition Approaches", Computer-Aided Design, Vol. 26, No. 8, August (1994)

[SBRU94] Shah, J.; Balakrishnan, G.; Rogers, M.; Urban, S.: "Comparative Study of Procedural and Declarative Feature-based Geometric Modeling", IFIP International Conference: Feature Modeling and Recognition in Advanced CAD/CAM Systems, San Diego, Valenciennes, pp. 647-671, May (1994)

[ChSc90] Chung, J. C. H.; Schussel, M. D.: "Technical Evaluation of Variational and Parametric Design", Computers in Engineering, Vol. 1, pp. 289-298, (1990)

[Vie95] Vieira, A. S.: "Consistency Management in Feature-based Parametric Design", ASME'95, Computer Aided Concurrent Design Symposium of the Design Technical Conferences of ASME, Boston, MA, pp. 977-987, Sep. 17-21 (1995)

[ShLi93] Sheu, L.-C.; Lin, J. T.: "Representation scheme for defining and operating form features", Computer-Aided Design, Vol. 25, No. 6, June (1993)

[BDFH95] Brunetti, G.; De Martino, T.; Falcidieno, B.; Haßinger S.: "A Relational Model for Interactive Manipulation of Form Features based on Algebraic Geometry", Solid Modeling'95, Third ACM/IEEE Symposium on Solid Modeling and Applications, Salt Lake City, Utah, pp. 95-103, May 17-19 (1995)

[Ovt92] Ovtcharova, J.: "An Approach to the Form Feature-Based Modelling in Computer-Aided Design", PhD thesis, Technical University of Sofia, Bulgaria, March (1992)

[CoYo91] Coad, P.; Yourdon, E.: "Object Oriented Analysis", 2nd Edition, Prentice Hall, Englewood Cliffs, NY (1991)

[OHVJ94] Ovtcharova, J., Haßinger S., Vieira, A. S., Jasnoch, U., Rix, J.: "Sinfonia, An Open Feature-based Design Module", 14th ASME International Computers in Engineering (CIE'94) Conference, Minnesota, Sept. 11-14 (1994)

[SBV96] Stork, A.; Brunetti, G.; Vieira, A. S.: "Intuitive Semantically Constrained Interaction in Feature-based Parametric Design", Submitted to CAD 96 - Distributed and Intelligent CAD Systems, Kaiserslautern, Germany, March 7-8 (1996)

[BVO96] Brunetti, G.; Vieira, A. S.; Ovtcharova, J.: "Towards a Feature Description Language", 29th International Symposium on Automotive Technology & Automation (ISATA'96), Florence, Italy, Juni 3-6 (1996) (to be published)

Chapter 4

Complex Surface Design

Overview

Transfinite B-spline Interpolation with Derivatives

E. Gschwind [1] and H. Hagen [2]

Cross-sections are a simple but powerful method to define complex shapes. We present a method which analyzes a given grid of B-spline curves to determine cross-boundary derivatives, such that G^1 or G^2-continuous tensor-product B-spline surfaces interpolating the given curve grid can be determined. The transfinite (curve interpolation) problem is converted to an equivalent point interpolation problem with well known solution techniques.

Introduction

Tensor-product B-spline surfaces have become one of the most often used representations in computer-aided geometric design. The B-spline tensor-product surface is defined as:

$$\mathbf{S}(u,v) = \sum_{i=1}^{n} \sum_{j=1}^{m} N_{i,k,t}(u) \cdot \mathbf{P}_{i,j} \cdot N_{j,l,s}(v) \tag{1}$$

where n is the number of control vertices, k the order, and t the knot vector in u-direction, and m the number of control vertices, l the order, and s the knot vector in v-direction. A number of techniques for direct B-spline interpolation surfaces are known. B-spline surface interpolation of a recti-linear grid of points is described in algorithmic detail in de Boor [Boor 78] and Barsky et al. [Bars 88]. Additional derivative information may be given at the grid points. This method interpolates the grid

[1]Hewlett-Packard GmbH, Mechanical Design Division, Böblingen, Germany

[2]Computer Science Department,University of Kaiserslautern, Kaiserslautern, Germany

only at specific points, the interpolation of a bounding curve grid with or without derivatives is not achieved.

We would like to present a direct transfinite (i.e curve interpolation) method to determine tensor product B-spline surfaces, considering additional tangential or curvature information along the surface bounds. This technique can be used to smoothly cover a grid of B-spline curves given for example by a set of of cross-sections defining a complex shape. In the further considerations of this section we assume that a given grid of cross-sections can be split into rectilinear sub-grids, and all given curves can be expressed as B-splines with a common basis.

Determining Cross Boundary Derivatives

Continuity at a Vertex

G^1 **Continuity at a Vertex** Given a number of curves meeting at a common vertex, G^1 continuous surfaces are possible at this point, only if all curve tangents at this point lie in a common plane.

G^2 **Continuity at a Vertex** All surfaces S_i adjacent to a vertex, are G^2 continuous at this vertex, if they share a common osculating paraboloid. An equivalent characterization of this property is the existence of a common Dupin's indicatrix at this point (see DeRose/Hagen [Dero 91]). This means that G^2 continuous surface must have common principle curvatures at this vertex.

The definition for the principle curvatures using the first and second fundamental forms (see Lipschutz [Lips 69]) is:

$$(E \cdot G - F^2)\kappa^2 - (E \cdot N + G \cdot L - 2F \cdot M)\kappa + (L \cdot N - M^2) = 0 \qquad (2)$$

Equation 2 actually contains a free parameter to achieve G^2 continuity; E, F, G, L and N are defined by the curve grid at the vertex, but M, the normal component of the twist vector, is independent of the bounding curves of adjacent surfaces and therefore can be determined to achieve G^2 Continuity. For n surfaces with a common vertex, coefficient comparison of Eqn. 2 leads to a system of equations to determine the normal twist vector component of each individual patch around the surface.

If no solution is possible for this system of equations, then the curve situation does not allow all surfaces to be joined G^2 continuous at this vertex. A trivial solution, i.e. zero normal twist components, may be a correct and useful solution to achieve G^2 continuity.

A final twist vector can be set by addition of the normal twist component and the horizontal component of the Adini twist as Hagen presented in [Hage 90].

Continuity along Curves

Many authors have been concerned with the continuity of surface patches. (See Verron et al. [Verr 76], Watkins [Watk 88], Jones [Jone 88], Hahn [Hahn 89], and DeRose / Hagen [Dero 91].) Verron's considerations are followed in a form suitable for determining the cross boundary derivatives for the B-spline interpolation of surfaces.

G^1 **Continuity**   The most general form of tangent (G^1) continuity (i.e common normals or common tangent plane) along the common boundary of two surfaces is:

$$\gamma(u) \cdot \mathbf{T}_2(u) = \alpha(u) \cdot \mathbf{C}_u(u) + \beta(u) \cdot \mathbf{T}_1(u) \tag{3}$$

assuming the common boundary C is parametrized in u and α, β and γ are polynomials. The $\mathbf{T}_i$ for $i = 1, 2$'s are the cross boundary derivatives of the left and right surfaces along the common boundary.

G^2 **Continuity**   In a similar fashion the most general definition of curvature or G^2 continuity is:

$$\begin{aligned}
\epsilon(u) \cdot \kappa_2(u) &= \alpha^2(u) \cdot \mathbf{C}_{uu}(u) + 2\alpha(u)\beta(u) \cdot \mathbf{S}_{1uv}(u) + \beta^2(u) \cdot \kappa_1(u) \\
&\quad + \gamma(u) \cdot \mathbf{C}_{1u}(u) + \delta(u) \cdot \mathbf{T}_1(u)
\end{aligned} \tag{4}$$

with $\alpha, \beta, \gamma, \delta$ and ϵ being polynomials and κ denoting a 2nd order cross boundary derivative.

Compatibility at patch corners   The curves and cross boundary derivatives meeting at patch corners must fulfill specific compatibility conditions. The following discussion assumes a given corner point of the surface at u_0, v_0, with $\mathbf{C}_1(u)$ and $\mathbf{C}_2(u)$ being patch boundary curves.

- Positional compatibility at a patch corner u_0, v_0 of a surface S(u, v) needs:
$$\mathbf{C}_1(u_0) = \mathbf{C}_2(v_0) = \mathbf{S}(u_0, v_0) \tag{5}$$

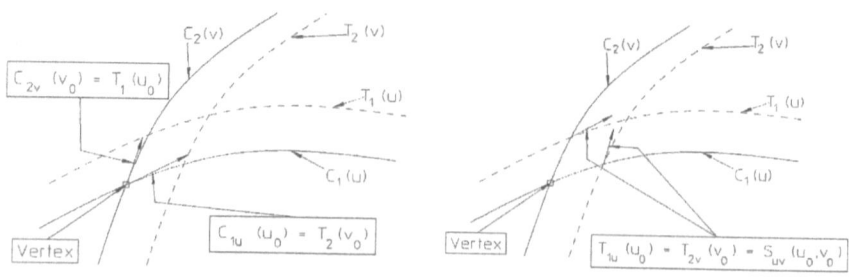

Figure 1: Tangent compatibility   Figure 2: Twist compatibility

which is automatically given, as a curve mesh naturally is defined by intersecting curves.

- As can be seen in Fig. 1 tangential or G^1 compatibility requires in addition:

$$\begin{aligned} \mathbf{T}_1(u_0) &= \mathbf{C}_{2v}(v_0) = \mathbf{S}_v(u_0, v_0) \\ \mathbf{T}_2(v_0) &= \mathbf{C}_{1u}(u_0) = \mathbf{S}_u(u_0, v_0) \end{aligned} \tag{6}$$

and

$$\mathbf{T}_{1u}(u_0) = \mathbf{T}_{2v}(v_0) = \mathbf{S}_{uv}(u_0, v_0) \tag{7}$$

- A curvature (i.e. G^2-continuous) compatible surface definition at this point demands in addition to positional and tangential compatibility:

$$\begin{aligned} \kappa_1(u_0) &= \mathbf{C}_{2vv}(v_0) = \mathbf{S}_{vv}(u_0, v_0) \\ \kappa_2(v_0) &= \mathbf{C}_{1uu}(u_0) = \mathbf{S}_{uu}(u_0, v_0) \end{aligned} \tag{8}$$

Further investigation leads to:

$$\kappa_{1u}(u_0) = \mathbf{T}_{2vv}(v_0) \tag{9}$$

assuming that the mixed derivatives $\mathbf{S}_{uvv}(u_0, v_0), \mathbf{S}_{vuv}(u_0, v_0)$, and $\mathbf{S}_{vvu}(u_0, v_0)$ are equal at any given point, which is the case for tensor-product B-spline surfaces. In the same manner,

$$\kappa_{2v}(v_0) = \mathbf{T}_{1uu}(u_0) \tag{10}$$

assuming that the mixed derivatives $\mathbf{S}_{uuv}(u_0, v_0) = \mathbf{S}_{uvu}(u_0, v_0) = \mathbf{S}_{vuu}(u_0, v_0)$, which again is valid for tensor-product B-spline surfaces.

Finally:

$$\kappa_{1uu}(u_0) = \kappa_{2vv}(v_0) \tag{11}$$

as the fourth order derivatives $\mathbf{S}_{uuvv}(u_0, v_0) = \mathbf{S}_{vvuu}(u_0, v_0)$

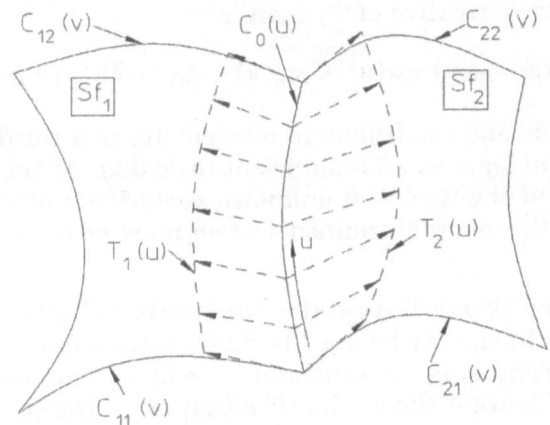

$C_{12}(v)$ $C_0(u)$ $C_{22}(v)$

Sf_1 Sf_2

$T_1(u)$ u $T_2(u)$

$C_{21}(v)$

$C_{11}(v)$

Figure 3: Situation for G^1 continuity

Determining Cross Boundary Derivative Curves

G^1 **Continuous Cross Boundary Derivative Curves**   Figure 3 shows the situation at the common boundary of two surfaces. $C_0(u)$ is their common boundary; $C_{11}(v)$ and $C_{12}(v)$ are boundaries of surface S_1 and $C_{21}(v)$ and $C_{22}(v)$ are boundaries of surface S_2.

This approach does not require that the surface boundary curves $C_{11}(v)$ and $C_{21}(v)$ or $C_{12}(v)$ and $C_{22}(v)$ be tangent continuous. Any configuration is valid, except $C_{11}(v)$ or $C_{21}(v)$ being tangent continuous to $C_0(u)$ at $u = u_0$. The same restriction also applies at the other end of $C_0(u)$; $C_{12}(v)$ or $C_{22}(v)$ must not join continuously to the common boundary $C_0(u)$.

Assuming surface S_1 has already been calculated (for example by using the method described in the next section), can a cross boundary derivative for surface S_2 be determined, such that the surface is tangentially continuous to surface S_1? Taking into consideration the compatibility conditions of Eqn. 6 and Eqn. 7 the end conditions that a first derivative T_2 for surface S_2 must fulfill are:

$$
\begin{aligned}
\mathbf{T}_2(u_0) &= C_{21v}(v_0) \\
\mathbf{T}_{2u}(u_0) &= S_{2uv}(u_0, v_0) \\
\mathbf{T}_2(u_m) &= C_{22v}(v_0) \\
\mathbf{T}_{2u}(u_m) &= S_{2uv}(u_m, v_0)
\end{aligned}
\tag{12}
$$

Without loss of sufficient freedom the polynomial $\gamma(u)$ of Eqn. 3 is set to one and the first derivative of T_2 then is:

$$T_{2u}(u) = \alpha_u(u) \cdot C_{1u}(u) + \alpha(u) \cdot C_{1uu}(u) + \beta_u(u) \cdot T_1(u) + \beta(u) \cdot T_{1u}(u) \quad (13)$$

There are four end conditions to interpolate, so a third degree, fourth order polynomial for α and β is sufficient to do this. As there are $4 \cdot 3 = 12$ equations to find the $2 \cdot 4 = 8$ unknown coefficients of the polynomials, the solution of this overdetermined system must be checked for validity.

G^2 Continuous Cross Boundary Derivative Curves   An approach along the same lines may be used to find a second order cross boundary derivative guaranteeing G^2 continuity along the common boundary of two surfaces. Figure 4 shows the G^2 situation at the common boundary

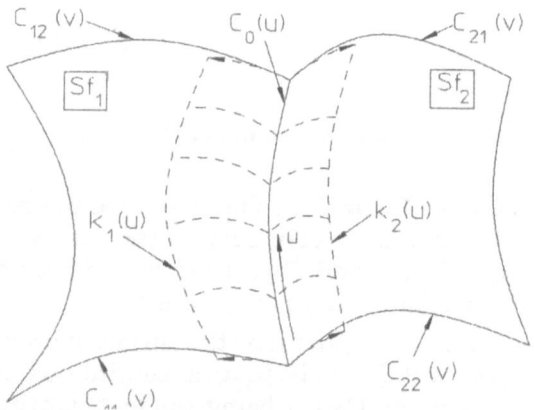

Figure 4: Situation for G^2 continuity

of two surfaces. $C_0(u)$ is the common boundary; $C_{11}(v)$ and $C_{12}(v)$ are boundaries of surface S_1 and $C_{21}(v)$ and $C_{22}(v)$ are boundaries of surface S_2. It is also assumed that surface S_1 has already been calculated (for example with the method described later in this section), and that its first and second cross boundary derivatives $T_1(u)$ and $\kappa_1(u)$ along the common boundary may be extracted. The tangential derivative $T_2(u)$ has been calculated as described in the previous section. Now the goal is to determine the second cross boundary derivatives $\kappa_2(u)$, such that surfaces S_1 and S_2 join curvature continuously. With regard to second order compatibility (see Eqn. 8 , 9, 10 and 11) the end conditions of $\kappa_1(u)$ are set up to be:

$$\kappa_2(u_0) = C_{21vv}(v_0)$$
$$\kappa_{2u}(u_0) = T_{21vv}(v_0)$$

$$\kappa_{2uu}(u_0) \;=\; 0 \tag{14}$$
$$\kappa_{2}(u_m) \;=\; C_{22vv}(v_0)$$
$$\kappa_{2u}(u_m) \;=\; T_{22vv}(v_0)$$
$$\kappa_{2uu}(u_m) \;=\; 0$$

The second derivative of $\kappa_2(u)$ at the corner points vanishes; this equivalent to a fourth order derivative of the surface and it is common practice set them to zero. Without loss of sufficient freedom the polynomial $\epsilon(u)$ of Eqn. 4 is set to one and the polynomials $\gamma(u)$ and $\delta(u)$ are set to zero (as Verron et al. does it in [Verr 76]). The derivative of the G^2-continuity condition for surfaces along common curves then is:

$$\begin{aligned}
\kappa_{2u}(u) \;=\; & 2\alpha(u)\cdot\alpha_u(u)\cdot C_{1uu}(u) + \alpha^2(u)\cdot C_{1uuu}(u) \\
& + 2\alpha_u(u)\cdot\beta_u(u)\cdot S_{1uv}(u,v_c) + 2\alpha(u)\cdot\beta_u(u)\cdot S_{1uv}(u,v_c) \\
& + 2\alpha(u)\cdot\beta(u)\cdot S_{uvu}(u,v_c) + 2\beta(u)\cdot\beta_u(u)\cdot\kappa_1(u) \\
& + \beta^2(u)\cdot\kappa_{1u}(u)
\end{aligned} \tag{15}$$

A polynomial of fifth degree, sixth order is sufficient to interpolate the six end conditions for $\kappa_2(u)$: There are $6 \cdot 3 = 18$ equations to find the $2 \cdot 6 = 12$ coefficients of the unknown polynomials.

Transfinite B-spline Interpolation with Derivatives

We have now a given set of boundary curves and have determined additional cross boundary derivatives in order to guarantee G^1 or G^2 continuity.

Now we solve the curve interpolation problem by converting it to an equivalent point interpolation problem, which can easily by solved by using the techniques described in De Boor [Boor 78], Chapter XIII on Spline Interpolation.

Simultaneous Representation and Interpolation

The transfinite interpolation input contains two sets of curves, one determining the surface shape in the u parameter direction and the other controlling the shape in v parameter direction. The investigation of the boundary situation shows, that for each boundary of one curve set a curve

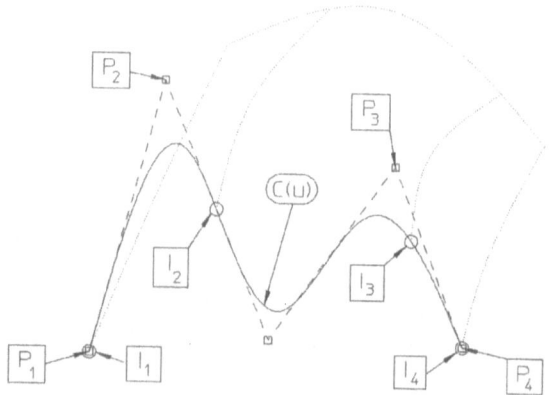

Figure 5: Simultaneous representation and interpolation

representation

$$C(u) = \sum_{i=1}^{n} N_{i,k,t}(u) \cdot P_i \qquad (16)$$

is given, as well as a number of interpolation points, which are the intersections of this boundary curve with all curves in the other set.

$$C(u_j) = I_j, \quad j = 1, m \qquad (17)$$

Can an curve interpolation of points I_j be set up such that the result of the interpolation is exactly the curve $C(u)$? This is what is meant by a simultaneous representation of curve $C(u)$ and an interpolation of points I_j. The interpolation points as well as the control points of the curve are already known. The question can be reformulated: What parameter values u_i must be chosen so that the solving of the interpolation results in the given curve $C(u)$?

First of all there have to be the same number of interpolation points as control points. The next section shows how this may be achieved in the transfinite interpolation of curves. Secondly, if the values of these parameters u_i correspond to the parameter values of the interpolation points I_i on the curve $C(u)$, then and only then will the resulting curve be $C(u)$. That is, a simultaneous interpolation and representation is achieved by a correct choice of the parameter values for the interpolation points.

Transfinite Interpolation of a Recti-linear Curve Mesh

The results of the simultaneous curve interpolation and representation observations are applied in a surface interpolation context.

Given are two sets of B-spline curves (it is assumed that all curves in one set have already been expressed in the same basis, which is done by well-known knot insertion and degree raising techniques):

$$\mathbf{C}_a = \sum_{i=1}^{n_1} N_{i,k_1,t_1}(u) \cdot \mathbf{P}_{i,a} \quad for \quad a = 1, m_1 \tag{18}$$

and

$$\mathbf{C}_b = \sum_{j=1}^{n_2} N_{j,k_2,t_2}(v) \cdot \mathbf{P}_{j,b} \quad for \quad b = 1, m_2 \tag{19}$$

where m_1 and m_2 are the number of curves in the respective curve set. Find the tensor-product B-spline surface

$$\mathbf{S}(u,v) = \sum_{i=1}^{n_1} \sum_{j=1}^{n_2} N_{i,k_1,t_1}(u) \cdot \mathbf{P}_{i,j} \cdot N_{j,k_2,t_2}(v) \tag{20}$$

which interpolates both curve sets $\mathbf{C}_a$ and $\mathbf{C}_b$.

The transfinite surface interpolation problem can be set up as:

$$\mathbf{S}(u, v_b) = \mathbf{C}_a(u) \tag{21}$$
$$\mathbf{S}(u_a, v) = \mathbf{C}_b(v)$$

If this can be converted to an equivalent point interpolation of the form:

$$\mathbf{N}_i \cdot \mathbf{P} \cdot \mathbf{N}_j^t = \mathbf{I} \tag{22}$$

a well-known technique exists to solve this system of equations efficiently (see de Boor [Boor 78] and Barsky et al. [Bars 88]).

A number of conditions have to be fulfilled, so that the point interpolation problem is truly equivalent to the transfinite curve interpolation.

- As can be seen from the matrix notation, curve set $\mathbf{C}_a$ and $\mathbf{C}_b$ must form an isoparametric, topologically recti-linear net. In the setting of this discussion, this is always the case as only boundary curves and derivatives along boundaries are considered, which are always guaranteed to be isoparametric.

- The B-spline basis functions $N_{i,k_1,t_1}(u)$ are the basis functions of the curves in curve set $\mathbf{C}_a$, which have all been expressed in the same basis (same parameter interval, same order and same knot vector).

The B-spline basis functions $N_{j,k_2,t_2}(v)$ are the basis functions of the curves in curve set C_b, which have also all been expressed in the same basis. The matrices N_i and N_j are called Gramian matrices and must be totally positive or invertible in order to find a solution to the linear system of equations. This may be achieved, if a certain dependency between order, knot vector and parameter values u_i and v_j is maintained.

- The simultaneous representation and interpolation shows, that the parameter values u_i must correspond to the parameter values of curve set C_a at their intersections with curve set C_b; in the same manner the parameter values v_j correspond to the parameter values of curve set C_b at their intersections with curve set C_a.

- Simultaneous representation and interpolation assumes, that the number of control points in a given direction is equal to the number of interpolation points. In this case the number of control points in one set must be equal to the number of curves in the other set. If the number of interpolation points I_i is greater than the number of control points (i.e. the number of curves in one curve set is larger than the number of control points in the other set), then knot insertion is used to generate more control points. This is of course applied to all curves in the curve set, so that they always have the same basis. The knot insertion is done at appropriate values, taking care to fulfill the Schoenberg-Whitney condition respectively the Karlin-Ziegler condition so that the Gramian matrices are always invertible. Schoenberg-Whitney states that for a given strictly increasing sequence of interpolation parameters u_i for $i = 1, n$ a knot sequence must be chosen, such that $t_i < u_i < t_{i+k}$ for $i = 1, n$, so that $N_{i,k,t}(u_i) \neq 0$ and therefore the Gramian matrix is invertible. The Schoenberg-Whitney condition requires strictly increasing parameters, which is only true for interpolation without derivatives. The Karlin-Ziegler condition takes care of interpolation with additional derivative information. Given a set of non-decreasing interpolation parameters $u_i < u_{i+k}$, for all $i = 1, n$. For any given parameter u_i, the number r of interpolation conditions plus the number s of knots t_j must be $r + s \leq k$, with k the specified order. For the Gramian matrix to be invertible, (the Gramian matrix contains not only B-spline basis functions $N_{i,k,t}(u_i)$, but also their derivatives $N^d_{i,k,t}(u_i)$) the following condition must prove true: $t_i < u_i < t_{i+k}$ for all $i = 1, n$. Essentially both Schoenberg-Whitney respectively Karlin-Ziegler ensure that the Gramian matrices do not have vanishing components in the main diagonal.

De Boor [Boor 78] in Chapter XIII describes an optimal knot sequence for interpolation at given parameters u_i guaranteeing total positivity (i.e. fulfilling the Schoenberg-Whitney respectively the Karlin-Ziegler conditions), and therefore the invertibility of the Gramian matrix:

$$t_{k+i} = \left(\frac{u_{i+1} + \ldots + u_{i+k-1}}{k-1} \right) \qquad (23)$$

where k is the order.

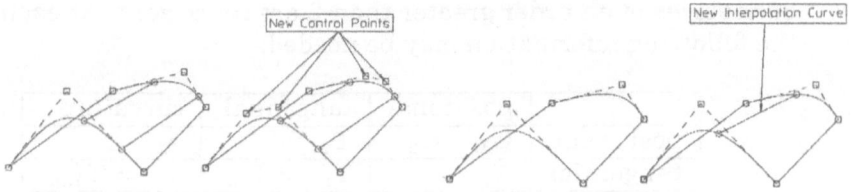

Figure 6: Adding control points   Figure 7: Adding interpolation curves

- If on the other hand the are not enough interpolation conditions (i.e there are more control points in one curve set than there are curve in the other), additional interpolation conditions must be found at appropriate parameter values. Again it is important that the Schoenberg-Whitney respectively the Karlin-Ziegler conditions are fulfilled. De Boor [Boor 78] in Chapter XIII describes a recommended parameter sequence:

$$u_i = \left(\frac{t_{i+1} + \ldots + t_{i+k-1}}{k-1} \right) \qquad (24)$$

if a knot vector t is given. For each additional parameter value, curves of the opposite set are evaluated and new curves are interpolated and added to the curve set. Care is taken that the new curves are at least quadratic and not linear as this would result in less smooth surfaces.

- The interpolation conditions need not be restricted to positional information; derivatives may be interpolated. The Gramian matrices now contain not only B-spline basic functions, but also their derivatives. Appropriate parameter values are determined by the corresponding positional curve.

- It is common knowledge for B-splines that even order B-splines generate smoother curves and surfaces than odd order ones; therefore at least fourth order splines are used for tangent continuous surfaces and at least sixth order B-splines are used for curvature continuous surfaces. Well-known degree-raising algorithms exist to achieve this (see e.g. Cohen et al. [Cohe 85]).

- If derivatives have been specified, high order mixed derivatives are involved in the point interpolation. The are directly determined by calculating the derivative of the derivative curves at this point, or if no derivatives are given, Adini twists are calculated from the curve mesh (see Barnhill et al [Barn 78]). In this case all mixed derivatives of an order greater than 2 are set to zero. At each point the following information may be needed:

	positional	tangential	curvature
positional	$C_1 = C_2$	T_2	κ_2
tangential	T_1	$T_{2v} = T_{1u}$	$\kappa_{2v} = T_{1uu}$
curvature	κ_1	$T_{2vv} = \kappa_{1u}$	$\kappa_{2vv} = \kappa_{1uu}$

The control points of the resulting surface are now determined by inverting equation Eqn. 22.

$$P = N_i^{-1} \cdot I \cdot \left(N_j^t\right)^{-1} \qquad (25)$$

which can be solved efficiently in a two staged process. First solve an intermediate problem for:

$$\bar{P} = N_i^{-1} \cdot I \qquad (26)$$

and then solve the actual problem using the intermediate result:

$$P = \bar{P} \cdot \left(N_j^t\right)^{-1} \qquad (27)$$

Each separate system Eqn. 26 and Eqn. 27 can be solved efficiently by the method described in detail by De Boor's book [Boor 78] in Chapter XIII.

Results and Summary

In this section some examples, which verify the findings of the tangentially smooth surface generation techniques are shown.

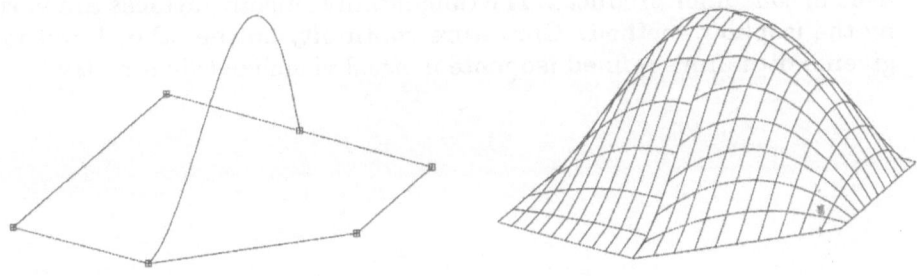

Figure 8: Example 1: Wire frame   Figure 9: Example 1: Surfaces

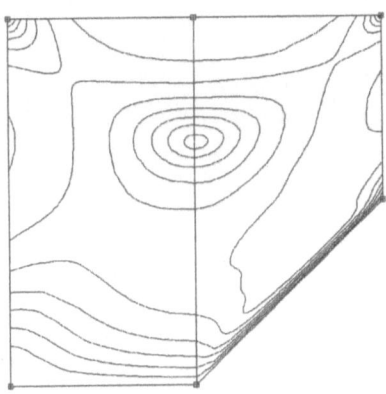

Figure 10: Example 1: Isophotes

For each example there is a picture of the wire frame and the result-ing surface geometries drawn in a mesh form. The surfaces in mesh form sometimes give the impression of being highly discontinuous, this is due to an optical illusion. G^1 continuity of surfaces does not demand that isoparameter lines (i.e the mesh boundary lines) of adjacent surfaces also join continuously. Furthermore a surface quality analysis depicting isophotes show that the surfaces are truly tangentially continuous. The isophotes may have tangent discontinuities at the surface boundaries, which is a sign of curvature discontinuity, but they may not have gaps, which would mark tangent discontinuous surfaces.

Example 1 shows two adjacent faces with a varying surface bound curve continuity at common vertices.

Example 2 shows a practical example from industry, a plastic bottle used in consumer products. The tangentially smooth surfaces are verified by the isophote method. Curvature continuity on the other hand is not given; Pottmann's refined isophote method visualize this directly.

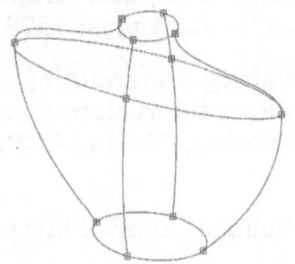 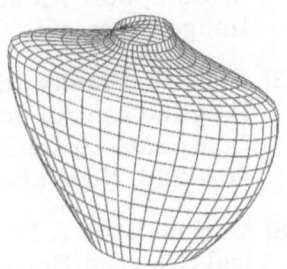

Figure 11: Example 2: Wire frame   **Figure 12: Example 2: Surfaces**

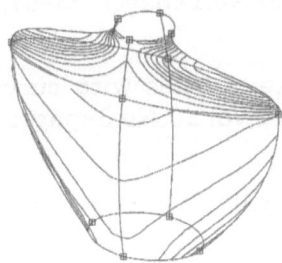 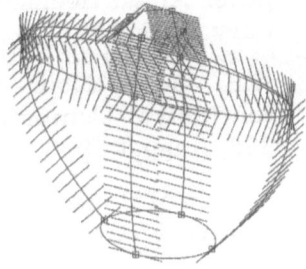

Figure 13: Isophotes in orthotomic view   **Figure 14: Refined isophotes**

References

[Barn 78] R. E. Barnhill, J. H. Brown, and I. M. Klucewicz. A new twist in Computer Aided Geometric Design. Computer Graphics & Image Processing, Vol.8(No.1):pages 78–91, August 1978.

[Bars 88] Brian A. Barsky and Donald P. Greenberg. Determining a set of B-spline control vertices to generate an interpolating surface. Computer Graphics & Image Processing, Vol.14(No.3):pages 203–226, November 1980.

[Boor 78] Carl de Boor. A Practical Guide to Splines. Applied Mathematical Sciences. Springer Verlag, 1978.

[Cohe 85] Elaine Cohen, Tom Lyche, and Larry L. Schumaker. Algorithms for degree-raising of splines. Association for Computing Machinery Transactions on Graphics, Vol.4(No.3):pages 171–181, July 1985.

[Dero 91] Anthony D. DeRose and Hans Hagen. Curvature continuity of parametric surfaces. Computer Aided Design, to be published.

[Hage 90] Hans Hagen. Twist estimation for smooth surface design. In Proceedings of the Conference: The Mathematics of Surfaces, Bath 1990, 1990.

[Hahn 89] Jörg M. Hahn. Geometric continuous patch complexes. Computer Aided Geometric Design, Vol.6(No.1):pages 55–67, January 1989.

[Jone 88] A.K. Jones. Nonrectangular surface patches with curvature continuity. Computer Aided Design, Vol.20(No.6):pages 325–335, August 1988.

[Lips 69] Martin M. Lipschutz. Theory and Problems of Differential Geometry. McGraw-Hill Co., 1969.

[Verr 76] M. Verron, G. Ris, and J.-P. Musse. Continuity of biparametric surface patches. Computer Aided Design, Vol.8(No.4):pages 267–273, October 1976.

[Watk 88] Michael A. Watkins. Problems in geometric continuity. Computer Aided Design, Vol.20(No.8):pages 499–502, October 1988.

Surface reconstruction and variable offset

Siegfried Heinz[1]

Surface reconstruction is currently a main research topic in several application areas. In this section we discuss a method for surface reconstruction based upon a variational design principle. The construction algorithm combines a weighted least-square fitting with an automatic smoothing process. This algorithm for calculating technical smooth surfaces directly from scattered point data can be used for many other applications. We illustrate the method by applying it to generate a variable offset surface. For the definition of the variable offset we use a law surface.

Introduction

In many applications only point data are available without additional information such as tangents or curvatures. Also inaccuracies have to be considered, for example material roughness, when digitising an original model with worn out parts. Furthermore, by a surface reconstruction of many engineering objects it is impractical to get a regularly grid of points. Regular data is often incomplete or insufficiently accurate when curvature varies over its extent. We present an algorithm appropriate for these situations and use this general algorithm for a *cloud of points* to get a new possibility to generate a surface for a special case of engineering. Sometimes in the phase of design an engineer has to build a surface with a variable normal displacement to an existing surface. An example for such a variable offset surface is the design of inner components of a car near the car body. The designer needs surfaces with variable distances to the car body. To define the distances over a given base surface (e.g. a car body surface) we use a law surface. The distance from a point of the law surface to a plane defines the offset value in the corresponding point of the base surface.

---

[1] TransCAT GmbH, Karlsruhe, Germany

Surface reconstruction

Algorithm for surface reconstruction

The algorithm for surface reconstruction is designed to approximate and smooth given point data which do not necessarily represent surface isoparametrics or arbitrary curves lying on the surface. To achieve this we use a multipatch tangent continuous surface representation with a polynomial degree 5. For the mathematical description of the polynomials a B-Spline representation was chosen. This allows to consider the surface as one entity and to have the point continuity and tangent continuity implicit given by an appropriate choice of the knot vectors. The degree 5 is a balance between oscillation and complexity of higher degrees and less degrees of freedom of lower degree polynomials.

Thus the surface can be represented as follows:

$$X(u,v) = \sum_{i=1}^{4n+2} \sum_{j=1}^{4m+2} d_{ij} N_i^5(u) N_j^5(v)$$

with the knot vectors

$$(\underbrace{u_1,\ldots,u_1}_{6\times}, \underbrace{u_2,\ldots,u_2}_{4\times}, \ldots, \underbrace{u_n,\ldots,u_n}_{4\times}, \underbrace{u_{n+1},\ldots,u_{n+1}}_{6\times})$$

$$(\underbrace{v_1,\ldots,v_1}_{6\times}, \underbrace{v_2,\ldots,v_2}_{4\times}, \ldots, \underbrace{v_m,\ldots,v_m}_{4\times}, \underbrace{v_{m+1},\ldots,v_{m+1}}_{6\times})$$

where $N_i^5(u)$ and $N_j^5(v)$ are the quintic B-Spline base functions, d_{ij} the control points, n the number of segments in u–direction and m the number of segments in v–direction The set of the knot vectors guarantees the C^1-continuity of the surface. This algorithm has to determine the (4n+2)*(4m+2) parameters d_{ij}.

As a first criterion we use a least-square fitting to get the best possible match of the point data. This is done by

$$LS \; := \sum_{k=1}^{n_p} (\sum_{i=1}^{4n+2} \sum_{j=1}^{4m+2} d_{ij} N_i^5(u_k) N_j^5(v_k) - P_k)^2 \;\to \min$$

where n_p is the number of points, P_k the given point data and (u_k,v_k) are the point parameters on the surface.

By this least-square fitting we obtain good results when the point data is already smooth by itself. Otherwise terms have to be added to smooth the surface; eg. compensation of inaccurate measuring or material roughness.

Therefore the second criterion is an approximate minimisation of the variation of curvature of the surface isoparametrics in both directions. This can be expressed by

$$
SM \ := \ \sum_{p=1}^{n} \sum_{q=1}^{m} \left(\int_{v_q}^{v_{q+1}} \int_{u_p}^{u_{p+1}} \left\| \frac{\partial^3 X(u,v)}{\partial u^3} \right\|^2 du\, dv + \int_{v_q}^{v_{q+1}} \int_{u_p}^{u_{p+1}} \left\| \frac{\partial^3 X(u,v)}{\partial v^3} \right\|^2 du\, dv \right) \to \min.
$$

A convex combination of the least-square fitting criterion and the smoothing criterion results to the final surface computation

$$
(1 - ws) \, LS + ws \, SM \to \min
$$

with a smoothing weight $ws \in [0,1]$.

The input for the received linear system of equations for the control points are the point data, the point parametrization and the smoothing weight. The number of segments in u and v direction are determined through the definition of the knot vectors. For more details of this algorithm see [San94].

Example - Shower head

This method has been used to reconstruct the shower head shown in figure1-3. Figure 1 shows point data digitised from an existing designer model. Figure 2 shows the necessary parametrization and figure 3 the reconstructed surface. For more examples see [SW91].

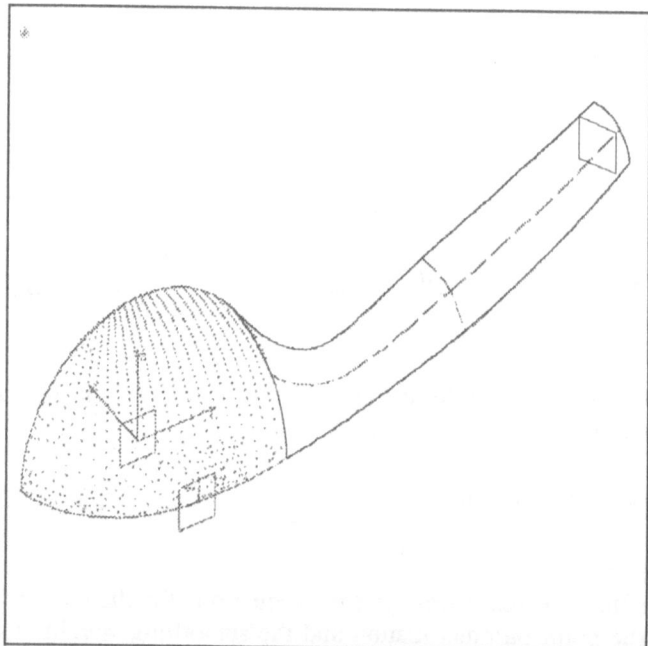

Fig. 1: Digitising

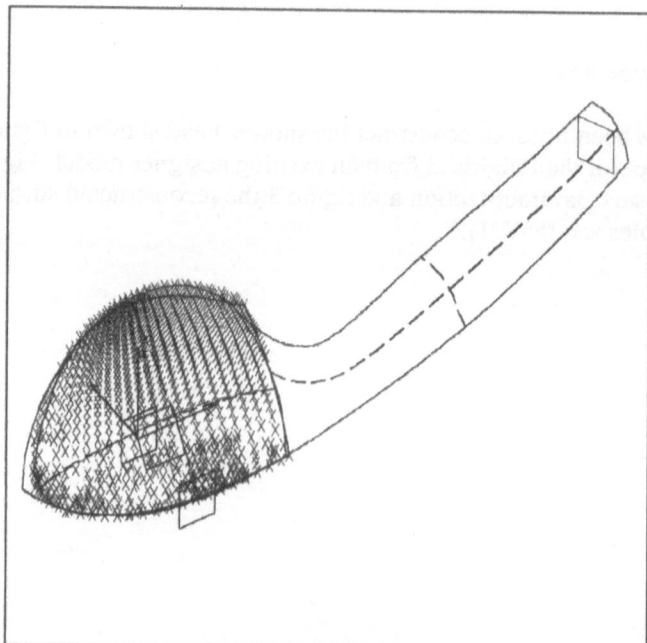

Fig. 2: Parametrization

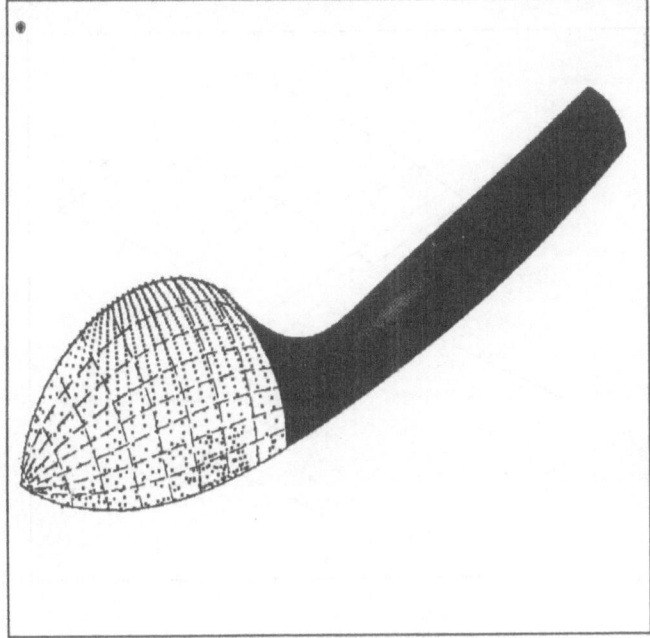

Fig. 3: Generated Surface

Variable offset

Definition of a law surface for variable offset

To define different offset values in each point over a given base surface we use a law surface. This means that the distance of a point on the law surface normal to a planar surface defines the offset value in a corresponding point on the base surface. The correspondence between the base surface and the planar underlying surface of the law surface is given by an appropriate choice of the planar surface. This planar surface is a visualisation of the uv-parametrization of the base surface (see Figure 4).

A definition of the law surface is done by defining the distances for several points to the base surface, or using arbitrary curves on the base surface by defining an offset value for each curve. In this way we get a point cloud over the planar surface with a given parametrization for the points from the base surface (when the curve data is transformed in point data). Then the law surface can be generated with the above algorithm for surface reconstruction through the given point data which defines the law surface (see Figure 5).

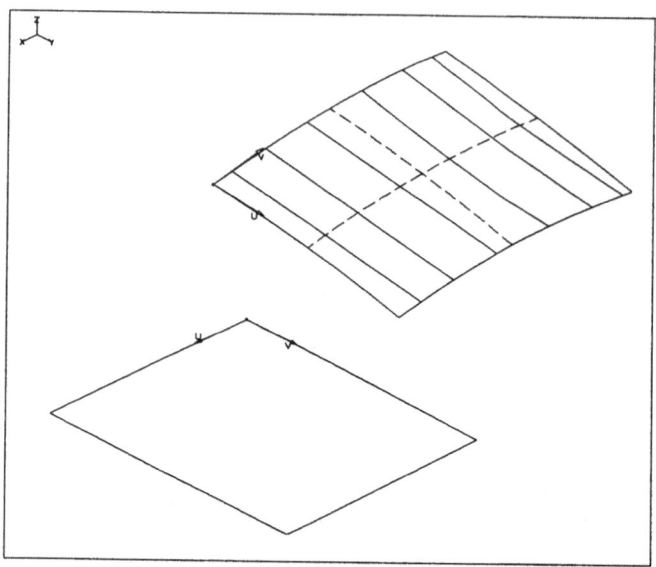

Fig. 4: Visualisation of the parametrization

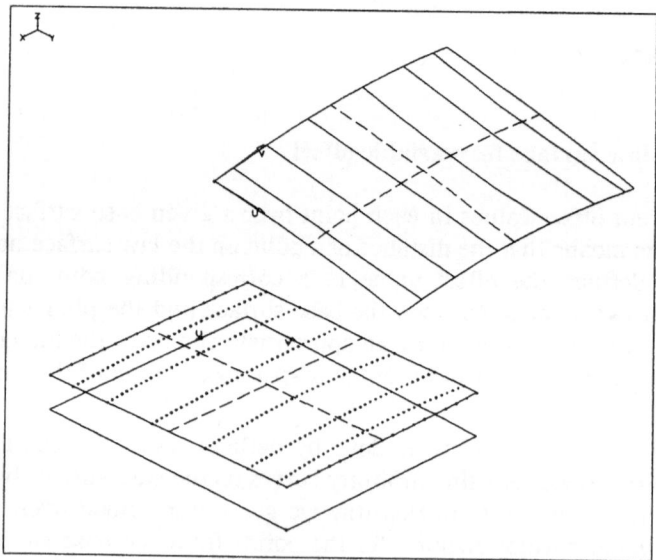

Fig. 5: Law Surface defined through points

Generating a variable offset surface

The offset surface is determined point by point through a given base surface and a given law surface defining the variable offset values. Point data can now be generated independent from the original point data defining the law surface. Through this point data a technical smooth surface can be calculated with the algorithm for surface reconstruction. The parametrization of the point data is given through the base surface and the offset surface can be smoothed by an iterative process. In every step of the iteration the smoothing weight and the patch distribution (knot vectors) can be changed.

Example - Generating a variable offset surface

One possibility to get the point data for the law surface is to determine points on the base surface with offset values in each point. This can be replaced by arbitrary curves on the starting surface and defining offset values for each curve. For the curves with the given offset values a number of points can be generated to define the law surface. Once the law surface exists the point data for the variable offset surface can be generated and the offset surface through this point cloud can be calculated.

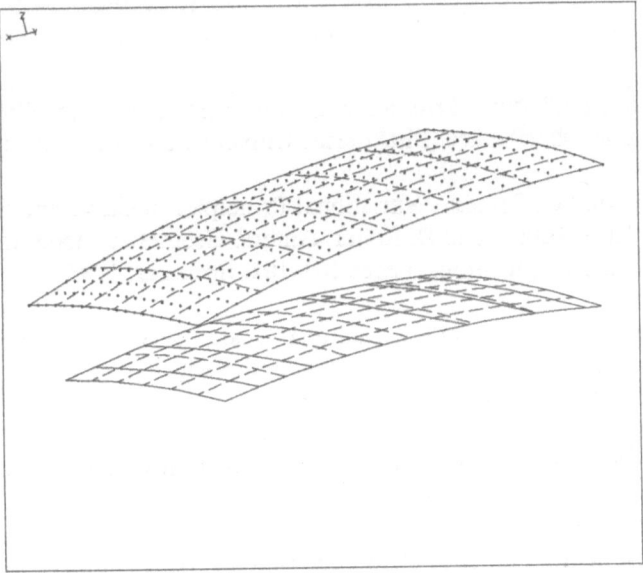

Fig. 6: Generated variable offset surface

Conclusions

The necessary point parametrization for the surface reconstruction can be done with an *underlying* surface. This could be an already existing surface in the CAD/CAM-System which has been machined or a surface generated with standard functions of the CAD/CAM-System. So the parametrization can be calculated by an approximate curve length of the isoparametrics passing through the projected points of the underlying surface.

Acknowledgements

With the presented algorithms for surface reconstruction and for variable offset two programs were implemented in the CAD/CAM-System CATIA® in a joined co-operation development with HELLA KG Hueck & Co. in Lippstadt/Germany.

References

[San94] P. Santarelli. Glättungskriterien und Algorithmen zum Modellieren von Kurven und Oberflächen. PhD thesis, Universität Kaiserslautern 1994.

[HS91] H. Hagen and G. Schulze. Variational Principles in Curve and Surface Design. In H. Hagen and D. Roller, editors, Geometric Modelling: Methods and Applications, pages 161-184. Springer, 1991.

[HS92] H. Hagen and P. Santarelli. Variational Design of Smooth B-Spline. In H.Hagen, editor, Topics in Surface Modelling, pages 85-92. SIAM, Philadelphia, 1992.

[SW91] P. Santarelli and B. Wördenweber. Digitising sculptured surfaces. Paper held at the Centre for Applied mathematics, Pfalz-Akademie Lambrecht 1991 Summerschool on practice of computer-aided geometric design.

[BH93] G. Brunnett, H. Hagen and P. Santarelli. Variational design of curves and surfaces. Surv. Math. Ind. 1993, pages 1-27.

Variable-Order Surface Reconstruction Through Region Growing

Nickolas S. Sapidis[1]

Today's highly accurate range image sensors are able to expeditiously measure a dense *cloud of points* on a surface and produce an "electronic replica" of any physical object. Making productive use of this technology in CAD/CAE/CAM requires robust software for transforming a dense point-cloud into a CAD surface-model, appropriate for *styling, detailed design,* or *reverse engineering.* The solution proposed here borrows from *Computer Vision* the ideas of "variable-order fitting" and "region growing", which are adapted to the problem of CAD-surface generation. The resulting methodology succeeds in using the rich "surface information" encompassed in an accurate image in contrast to existing techniques that employ only positional information and rely on the efficiency of a least-squares fitting procedure to construct a high-quality surface.

Introduction

An algorithm is proposed for segmenting a dense, highly-accurate set of 3-D points (e.g., measured with a scanner on a physical surface) into *a small number* of *regions* (subsets), each approximated by a single-polynomial surface $z = z(x, y)$. The algorithm is based on the techniques of *variable-order fitting* and *region growing* [Besl88][BeJa88] and puts effort at (i) forcing each surface to represent as a large region as possible, (ii) making each region as "square" as possible, and (iii) keeping the polynomial degree of each surface low. More specifically, the algorithm is based on the *local region-growing* procedure in [SaBe95], which, for a given *seed-region* $\mathcal{R}$ and a fixed polynomial degree τ (in our implementa-

---

[1] Department of Naval Architecture and Marine Engineering, Ship-Design Lab, National Technical University of Athens, Greece.

tion: $\tau \leq 4$), fits a polynomial $z = z(x, y)$ of degree $\tau \times \tau$ to the points in $\mathcal{R}$ and subsequently grows both $\mathcal{R}$ and $z = z(x, y)$ in the following iterative manner. First, $\mathcal{R}$ is redefined to include all points of the image that in a certain sense are compatible with $z = z(x, y)$, and then $z = z(x, y)$ is re-evaluated as a least-squares fit to the new region $\mathcal{R}$.

The above procedure was used in [SaBe95] as the backbone of an interactive surface-reconstruction method, where seed-regions are specified by the user and surfaces are restricted to be of degree 4×4. In addition to these two disadvantages, the method [SaBe95] also lacks any provision for correcting position- and/or tangent-plane-discontinuities between surfaces produced by local region-growing. The main part of the present work describes a fully automatic surface-reconstruction method, which combines the *local region-growing* procedure [SaBe95] with *variable-order fitting* [Besl88][BeJa88], an automatic *seed-region selector*, and a post-processor for alleviating tangent-plane discontinuities between polynomial surfaces. The final part ("Discussion") highlights the primary bottlenecks in surface-reconstruction and compares the solutions proposed here to those discussed in the current literature.

From Dense Range Images to Surfaces

One of the standard range-image forms used in Industry is the *gridded Dense Range Image (DRI)*, i.e., an image constructed by measuring a matrix of heights of object points above a plane [Besl88] [Besl89a] [Besl89b]. More specifically, a DRI I is defined to be a set of points (see Fig. 1) $I = \{p_{ij} \equiv (x(i), y(j), z(i,j))\}$, where

$$x(i) \approx a_x + s_x * i \quad \text{and} \quad y(j) \approx a_y + s_y * j. \tag{1}$$

Here, the *column number* i takes values $0, 1, ..., K$, the *row number* j takes values $0, 1, ..., L$, $a = (a_x, a_y)$ is an offset vector, and $s = (s_x, s_y)$ the increment vector. The measured value $z(i, j) > 0$ is the distance from p_{ij} to the plane $z = 0$. An image location (i, j) not corresponding to a point on the object produces $z(i, j) = 0$. Finally, the use of "$\approx$" instead of "$=$" in (1) is due to the fact that often the current image I is produced from some other denser (and thus larger) image by applying certain "thinning" procedures (see detailed discussion in p. 474 of [MBVW95]).

(1) makes obvious that we can also represent I as a collection of quadrilaterals (in short, quads) $\{Q_{ij}; \ 0 \leq i \leq K - 1, \ 0 \leq j \leq L - 1\}$, where Q_{ij} has as vertices the points $p_{ij}, p_{i+1,j}, p_{i+1,j+1}, p_{i,j+1} \in I$. When

all vertices of Q_{ij} are object points, Q_{ij} is characterized as an object (or visible) quad, otherwise Q_{ij} is considered a background (or invisible) quad. The above classification is recorded in the integers $\{V_{ij}\}$ (called *visibility labels*), where $V_{ij} \geq 0$ if Q_{ij} is a visible quad, and $V_{ij} = -1$ otherwise. During the surface reconstruction process, visibility labels are also used for describing subsets of I, which here are called *regions*: The quad Q_{ij} belongs to the region R_q ($q = 1, 2, 3, \ldots$) if and only if $V_{ij} = q$. Finally, each region R_q is associated to a quadruple of integers $d(R_q) = \{dd_q, du_q, dl_q, dr_q\}$, called the *domain* of R_q with the min/max row- and column-numbers of the points p_{ij} in R_q.

Below, we use the same symbol I to represent both the point-set and quad-set representation of the DRI, and we assume that I is always accompanied by a set of visibility labels $I_v \equiv \{V_{ij}\}$. Also, we assume that I is accompanied by the *positive normal vector* "image" $I_{pnv} \equiv \{n_{ij}\}$, where n_{ij} is an estimate (produced using *convolution operators* [Besl88][BeJa88]) of the normal vector of the "physical" surface underlying I at the point $p_{ij} \in I$.

The Surface Reconstruction Problem

Existing methods aim at producing, from an image, a complete surface model of patches meeting at edges and vertices with prescribed continuity [Dietz95][GuYa95][MBVW95]. We take a different approach that puts less emphasis on the continuity between surface patches and aims at producing high-quality *fair surfaces* (: characterized by a gradually varying curvature, free of unwanted "wiggles" [Sapi94]), appropriate for demanding applications like automobile styling. More accurately, we consider the following [SaBe95]:

PROBLEM S. **Given input:** the DRI I, a distance-error tolerance T, a normal-compatibility tolerance V ($0 < V < 1$), and a maximum permissible degree t for bivariate polynomial approximations. **Decompose** I into N quasidisjoint regions (i.e., nonoverlapping regions that may intersect only at their boundaries) R_q, $q = 1, 2, \ldots, N$, and define N polynomial functions $z_q = z_q(x, y)$, $q = 1, 2, \ldots, N$, such that:
(i) For every point p in a particular region R_q

$$\text{the distance of } p \text{ to the surface } z_q \text{ is smaller than } T, \text{ and} \qquad (2)$$

$$n_{ij} * N_{z_q}[p_{ij}] > V, \qquad (3)$$

where $N_{z_q}[p_{ij}]$ denotes the positive normal vector of z_q evaluated at the orthogonal projection of p_{ij} onto $z_q = z_q(x, y)$, and the symbol "$*$" denotes here the vector inner-product operation.

(ii) The total number of regions (and surfaces) N is as small as possible.
(iii) Each region R_q should include as few interior boundaries (holes) as possible. (Ideally, each interior boundary of R_q should correspond to a cavity or hole or sharp edge in the physical object.)
(iv) Each region R_q should correspond to a domain $d(R_q)$ that is as close as possible to a square. Also, for any two regions R_q, R_l that intersect (at their boundaries) the projection of $R_q \cap R_l$ onto the plane $z = 0$ should be as close as possible to a straight line.

Regarding the parameters involved in the description of Problem S, we note that typically the maximum permissible degree for polynomials is 4×4, and, for high-quality DRIs, one uses $T \approx 0.1 - 0.5$ mm and $V \approx 0.96 - 0.995$.

Variable-Order Surface Fitting & Region Growing based on Surface Coherence

Table 1 gives a pseudocode description of the algorithm *Variable-Order-FittingbyRegionGrowing (VOFRG)*. It produces regions and associated polynomial surfaces that exactly satisfy requirement (i) of Problem S and approximately fulfil requirements (ii), (iii), and (iv). While regions are defined using the visibility labels (cf. definition of DRI), the polynomials $\{z_q\}_{q=1}^N$ are represented in terms of the *discrete orthogonal polynomials* (see, e.g., Appendix C of [Besl88]), since this representation suppresses numerical problems during least-squares fitting (ibid. §C.2) and can be easily transformed into the B-spline representation.

Following the specification of a seed-region (a related procedure is given below) for growing the region $R_{n,d}$ --- wherever a second subscript appears in R_n or z_n, this denotes the degree of the fitted polynomial --- *variable-order fitting (VOF)* is performed. As the original VOF procedure [Besl88][BeJa88] has such a high complexity that renders it inapplicable to large images, we propose the following simplified version (see loop marked with {♮} in Table 1): First, a polynomial of degree 1×1 is fitted to the seed-region, followed by iterative application of *LocalRegionGrowing* (see below for a description), for polynomial degree $d = 1$, producing the region $R_{n,1}$ and the associated surface $z_{n,1}$. These are used as the seed-region (and starting surface) for reapplying *LocalRegionGrowing* with a polynomial degree $d = 2$, and so on. The result $\{R_{n,d}, z_{n,d}\}$ of the dth iteration, for $d = 2, 3, 4$, is compared with that of the previous

Algorithm *Variable-OrderFittingbyRegionGrowing (VOFRG)*

Input: $I, I_{pnv}, t, T, V;$ Output: $\{R_q, z_q\}_{q=1}^{N};$

{ Symbols are defined in the description of Problem S }

Working Variables/Symbols/Procedures: n: number of regions, d: degree of surface $z_{q,d}$, H: threshold, *RegionGrows*: flag, *RemainingQuads*: integer, D_q: domain of R_q, $NQ(R_q)$: Number of Quads in R_q, $\not\gg$: "not significantly larger", $r(R_{q,d}, z_{q,d})$: regions-test procedure;

$n = 0;$ *RemainingQuads* = number of object quads in $I;$
while *RemainingQuads* > 0 **begin** {$}
  Increment $n;$ $d = 1;$ *SelectSeedRegion*$(I, I_{pnv}, R_n, D_n);$
  while $d \leq t$ **begin** {♮}
  LeastSq.PolynomialFitting$(R_n, d, z_n);$
  ThresholdSelection$(R_n, z_n, H);$ *RegionGrows* = *true;*
  while ([*RegionGrows* == *true*] **or** [$H < T$]) **begin** {§}
   LocalRegionGrowing$(R_n, D_n, z_n, d, H, V, T, RegionGrows);$
  end {§}
  if ([$NQ(R_{n,d}) \not\gg NQ(R_{n,d-1})$] **or** [$r(R_{n,d-1}, z_{n,d-1}) \not\gg r(R_{n,d}, z_{n,d})$])
   then recreate $R_{n,d-1}, z_{n,d-1}$ and set $d = t + 1;$ **else** $d = d + 1;$
  end {♮}
  RemainingQuads = *RemainingQuads* - $NQ(R_n);$
end {$}
CorrectContinuity$(\{z_q, R_q\}_{q=1}^{N});$ *CreateFilesIGES144*$(\{z_q, R_q\}_{q=1}^{N});$
End.

Table 1: Surface-Reconstruction Algorithm

iteration on the basis of two criteria: the size of the regions and the *regions-test*. If the result of the dth iteration fails to be superior to that of the previous iteration, with respect to *either one* of these criteria, the process is terminated and the final result is that of the iteration $d - 1$, i.e., $\{R_{n,d-1}, z_{n,d-1}\}$. While Table 1 clarifies the first criterion, the second criterion, *regions-test*, needs explanation. This test is a direct result of the fundamental assumption of *surface coherence* underlying both the present and the original version of *VOFRG* [Besl88][BeJa88]. Surface coherence implies that

> *the image data may be interpreted as random noisy-samples*
> *of a free-form, piecewise-smooth "physical" surface $z_f(x, y)$.*

Thus, an ideal fit should correspond not only to a small error but also to a continuously alternating *sign-of-residual* (the residual for the point $p_{ij} = (x_i, y_j, z_{ij})$ is: $z_{n,d}(x_i, y_i) - z_{ij}$). Based on this and certain results from statistics, Besl materializes the *regions-test* in the form of a quantity $r(R_{n,d}, z_{n,d})$ (calculated by formula (4.13) of [Besl88]) that approaches zero as the fit improves.

A second consequence of the assumption of *surface coherence* is the following. In order for the growing surface z_n to closely approximate the underlying "physical" surface z_f, examination of compatibility of an image point to z_n (according to requirement (i) of Problem S) should be based on an estimate of the *noise* in the DRI I instead of the arbitrary limit T [Besl88]. Indeed, whenever the procedure **LocalRegionGrowing** examines the validity of the distance-error criterion (2), T is replaced by a *threshold H* measuring how well z_n should fit I near the specified seed-region. H is calculated by multiplying the RMS fit error, between the seed-region and the corresponding surface, by a factor W depending on the quality of I. The tests reported in [Besl88] suggest $W = 2.5$ for good-quality images, which is the value used here.

Completion of region/surface growing is followed by application of the procedure **CorrectContinuity** aiming at reducing position- and tangent-plane-discontinuities between adjacent polynomial surfaces. The surface-reconstruction process is concluded by the routine **CreateFilesIGES144** that converts each polynomial z_q to the IGES 144 [SaBe95] format, i.e., to a parametric B-spline trimmed in accordance to R_q.

Automatic Seed-Region Selection Using Recursive Domain-Decomposition

A prerequisite for employing the iterative procedure **LocalRegionGrowing**, to grow the nth region/surface, is determination of the seed-region $R_n^{k=0}$ --- k denotes the iteration number for the loop {♮} in Table 1 --- out of which R_n will grow. The original publication [BeJa88], where region-growing was first proposed, offers a seed-region selection algorithm that is impractical for large images as it involves *discrete-curvature* estimation at every point of I and various image-processing operations applied to the whole image. A much more economical method, which gives comparable results, is used here:

A quadtree subdivision of the *image domain* (i, j) is constructed, where at every step and *for each cell ("sub-domain") of the quadtree:* all points p_{ij} corresponding to quads with a visibility label equal to 0 are found and, if they are more than 10, they are fitted with a polynomial of degree 2×2 and the corresponding RMS error is calculated. As soon as this error becomes smaller than $10*T$, the recursive subdivision is terminated and the terminal cell with the least RMS fit-error specifies the seed-region.

The Procedure *LocalRegionGrowing*

This procedure takes as primary input a seed-region $R_n^{k=0}$, for creating the nth region, a fitted surface $z_n^{k=0}$, and a threshold H (see discussion above). Growth is attempted first within $d(R_n^{k=0})$ and then outside this domain considering only quads with a visibility label equal to zero (i.e., quads that already belong to a region are not examined). In both cases, growing is an iterative process, where first quads that are compatible with the current surface z_n^k are found and collected in the new region R_n^{k+1}, to which a new surface z_n^{k+1} is fitted, in the least-squares sense. The procedure, which is a simplified version of that in [Besl88], is detailed in the paper [SaBe95]; below only a short overview is given.

GrowRegionIN (growing a region within its domain): Here, only points p_{ij} with (i,j) in $d(R_n^k)$ are considered. Those satisfying (2) --- with T replaced by the current threshold H as explained above --- and (3) are collected in R_n^{k+1} and a new surface is calculated by least-squares fitting. This process is iterated until a sufficiently large percentage of the points corresponding to $d(R_n^k)$ are in R_n, or R_n has stopped growing.

GrowRegionOUT (growing a region outside of its domain): This routine grows R_n outside $d(R_n^k)$, towards "left" (: smaller column numbers), "right" (: larger column numbers), "down" (: smaller row numbers), and "up" (: larger row numbers); see Fig. 1. Rules are employed that specify appropriate growth directions so that the region grows uniformly towards the four possible directions and does not create "gaps" (by skipping quads) as implied by requirements (iii) and (iv) of Problem S.

Completion of *GrowRegionIN* and *GrowRegionOUT* is followed by a comparison of the number of quads in R_n to that before applying these two procedures to evaluate progress. When this is found unsatisfactory, the threshold H is increased and local region-growing is reapplied to R_n. Local growing is terminated when the region has stopped growing or H has reached the user-specified limit T.

The Procedure *ContinuityCorrection*

Adjacent surfaces, produced by VOF and the procedure *LocalRegionGrowing*, meet in general with a position- (and, of course, tangent-plane-) discontinuity, although the amount of discontinuity is often small and sometimes even within the limits set by industrial applications (this is true for the examples in [SaBe95]). The **ContinuityCorrection** procedure uses the **GrowRegionOUT** routine (highlighted previously) to further reduce such discontinuities as follows:

(1) For each surface z_q and region R_q: the normal vector of z_q is evaluated at a finite number of locations on the boundary of R_q and compared to that of neighboring surfaces. Of all surfaces that do not satisfy the user's requirements the one corresponding to the largest total-discontinuity is specified.

(2) The surface z_w and region R_w identified above are grown by a variant of **GrowRegionOUT** which allows growing to consider all visible quads, i.e., even quads that belong to neighboring regions. These quads are not added to R_w but they are included in the point-set supplied to the least-squares fitting routine. The new surface z_w is a "weighted" least-squares fit where points belonging to R_w are assigned a weight equal to 1 and the rest of the points a weight < 1, where the further a point is from the domain-limits of R_w the smaller its weight is.

As expected, the above heuristic does reduce discontinuities between adjacent surfaces as these are better fitted to their common boundary area.

Discussion

Variable-Order Fitting (VOF) and *Region Growing (RG)* were proven efficient for fitting surfaces to images and solving problems related to Range Image Understanding [Besl88] [BeJa88]. Recently, the author and Besl [SaBe95] [Besl89a] [Besl89b] have been experimenting with these techniques for producing "CAD quality" surfaces from xyz-range images. Although the original codes by Besl [Besl88] give acceptable results, excessive revision of both methodologies (VOF, RG) was required for them to produce, from highly dense images, fair surfaces in a reasonable amount of time. (The original algorithms in [Besl88] targeted images with 128×128 or 256×256 pixels while the new ones operate on xyz-data with hundreds-of-thousands or even millions of points.) The new (local) region-growing method has been detailed in [SaBe95], while here a new, combined *Variable-Order Fitting by Region-Growing (VOFRG)* methodology is described, appropriate for CAD and reverse-engineering applications. One of the major improvements introduced --- limitations of space do not allow a complete comparison of the new vs. the old VOFRG method --- is that while the original method, after completing the iteration with degree d, performs a detailed analysis/evaluation of the fit $\{R_{q,d}, z_{q,d}\}$ to determine whether a degree $(d+1)$ fit should be attempted, here we take advantage of a very efficient RG algorithm to always try the degree $(d+1)$, and directly compare the two results to decide about continuing with the iterations.

The new VOFRG algorithm has been applied, among others, to the images presented in [SaBe95]. The obtained results are indistinguishable, regarding the regions identified, from those in [SaBe95], produced by an interactive surface-reconstruction procedure also highlighted in the Introduction. The new procedure requires for the images in [SaBe95], 5-15% more CPU time but up to 60% less elapsed real-time as no user interaction is required for seed-region selection.

We conclude with a short account of principal issues in surface reconstruction, some of which seem to be ignored by recently proposed algorithms. These issues are also used as criteria to evaluate VOFRG and competing methods.

Principal Issues in Free-Form Surface Reconstruction

• *Automatic Segmentation of Range Images:* Industrial applications produce DRIs that most often cannot be represented by a single CAD surface (= assembly of tangent-plane- or curvature-continuous polynomial segments). Thus, the image must be *segmented* into regions (sub-images), where each region can be approximated by a single surface with the required accuracy. Existing techniques either (i) ignore this issue [GuYa95], or (ii) try to fit the whole image with a single surface having many polynomial patches [Dietz95], or (iii) rely on the user's expertise to segment the image [MBVW95], or (iv) use *edge detection* to identify regions [SaMe91]. Only this last approach deserves further commenting. We feel that this is not a reasonable approach as (a) it attempts to derive "surface information" from rapid changes in point-data, (b) the fact that certain part of an image is surrounded by an edge does not guarantee that it can be correctly approximated by one surface, and (c) often the transition area between regions has been "rounded" making edge-detection impossible. Region growing provides a robust approach to Image Segmentation as it uses *smooth* reliable data (away from edges) to derive surface information, and it *de facto* guarantees that identified regions can be represented by a single bivariate polynomial.

- *Shape Quality of Surfaces:* Existing techniques rely either fully [Dietz95][GuYa95][SaMe91] or to a significant degree [MBVW95] on the user for specifying the number of polynomial segments in the surface-model used for approximating the given point-set (or its regions). This is an extremely important decision as redundant degrees-of-freedom (d.o.f.s) lead to local undulations that can be fatal regarding the shape quality of the constructed surface. Region growing, on the other hand, guarantees that the final surface has no redundant d.o.f.s as the model is a single polynomial "stretched" to represent as many data-points as possible.

- *Direct Control of Point-Surface Error:* Region Growing guarantees *a priori* that every point of the region R fitted by the surface z is at a distance smaller than any given bound. All other methods first identify regions and construct the corresponding surfaces and then *a posteriori* measure point-surface distances. Regarding a remedy to the problem of excessive point-surface error only [SaMe91] suggests one which is the obvious "brute force" idea of increasing the number of polynomial segments in the surface and repeating the fitting process.

- *Exploiting High Accuracy of Images:* Current laser sensors produce, in a few minutes, *electronic replicas* of physical prototypes, where the density of the measurements can be extremely high and the maximum error < 0.1 mm, as confirmed, e.g., by numerous tests at GM Research. This allows us to apply standard image-processing algorithms on a DRI to derive accurate orientation-information (normal vectors) as well as curvature-estimates. Region Growing employs this information while all other methods use only position measurements (points).

- *Wide Geometric Coverage:* Although most often surface reconstruction involves "functional" xyz-images, where each pair (x, y) is associated to a single z measurement, the fact that [Dietz95], [GuYa95], [MBVW95] and [SaMe91] produce parametric surfaces is an advantage over the present version of VOFRG. However, one must note that even parametric B-splines do not cover all industry's requirements. Sometimes other representations are preferable, e.g., the implicit form of quadrics for images extracted from quadric physical surfaces. Extending the methods [Dietz95], [GuYa95], [MBVW95], [SaMe91] to implicit quadrics is not straightforward as these rely solely on least-squares fitting (LSF) for creating a surface, a procedure that is quite problematic when applied to implicit quadrics [GGS94] [MoWa90] [SaBe95].

Region Growing combines LSF with an iterative refinement of the fitted point-set, that may be used for increasing the robustness of a quadric-LSF procedure. The present version of our Quadric Region-Growing (QRG) algorithm differs from the one for polynomials (Table 1) in that a much "less-aggressive" strategy is used in increasing the threshold H which controls local region-growing. This causes a much slower growth of a region but has succeeded in eliminating failures of the technique occurring for quadrics with "extra branches" (these failures were reported in [SaBe95] and are also discussed by many others [MoWa90]). Still, there are cases where QRG fails to converge, e.g., for a point-set lying closely to an almost flat ellipsoid or to a cylinder with a very large radius. *Our current work* focuses exactly on these problematic cases. One of the approaches investigated is the development of an improved quadric-fitting routine according to the ideas described in [GGS94]. Also, work is under way towards an RG algorithm for parametric B-spline surfaces.

Acknowledgements: This text builds on the work [SaBe95] and has greatly benefited from discussions with P.J. Besl. Personal communications with G. Golub on quadrics-fitting are gratefully acknowledged. I thank Prof. P. Kaklis and the director of NTUA's Ship-Design Lab, Prof. A. Papanikolaou, for their support and assistance. This research was also supported by the hellenic *Ministry of Industry, Energy and Technology* through a PENED'91 research-grant awarded to P. Kaklis.

References

[Besl88]   Besl, P.J.: Surfaces in Range Image Understanding. Springer-Verlag, New York, 1988.

[Besl89a]   Besl, P.J.: Geometric Signal Processing. In: Jain, R., Jain, A. (eds), Range Image Understanding, Springer-Verlag, 1989.

[Besl89b]   Besl, P.J.: Active Optical Range Imaging Sensors. In: Sanz, J. (ed), Advances in Machine Vision: Architectures and Applications, Springer-Verlag, New York, 1989.

[BeJa88]   Besl, P.J., Jain, R.C.: Segmentation through variable-order surface fitting. IEEE Transactions on Pattern Analysis and Machine Intelligence, 10, pp. 167-192, 1988.

[Dietz95]   Dietz, U.: Erzeugung Glatter Flachen aus Mepunkten. Preprint-Nr. 1717, FB Mathematik, TH Darmstadt, Febr. 1995.

[GGS94]   Gander, W., Golub, G.H., Strebel, R.: Fitting of Circles and Ellipses--Least Squares Solution. To appear in BIT.

[GuYa95]   Gu, P., Yan, X.: Neural Network Approach to the Reconstruction of Freeform Surfaces for Reverse Engineering. Computer-Aided Design, 27, pp. 59-64, 1995.

[MBVW95]   Milroy, M.J, Bradley, C., Vickers, G.W., Weir, D.J.: G^1 Continuity of B-spline Surface Patches in Reverse Engineering. Computer-Aided Design, **27**, pp. 471-478, 1995.

[MoWa90]   Moore, D., Warren, J.: Approximation of Dense Scattered Data Using Algebraic Surfaces. Technical Report TR90-135, Department of Computer Science, Rice University, 1990.

[Sapi94]   Sapidis, N. (ed): Designing Fair Curves and Surfaces: Shape Quality in Geometric Modeling and CAD. Society for Industrial and Applied Mathematics (SIAM), Philadelphia, 1994.

[SaBe95]   Sapidis, N., Besl, P.J.: Direct Construction of Polynomial Surfaces from Dense Range Images through Region Growing. ACM: Transactions on Graphics, **14**, pp. 171-200, 1995.

[SaMe91]   Sarkar, B., Menq, C.-H.: Smooth Surface Approximation and Reverse Engineering. Computer-Aided Design, **23**, pp. 623-628, 1991.

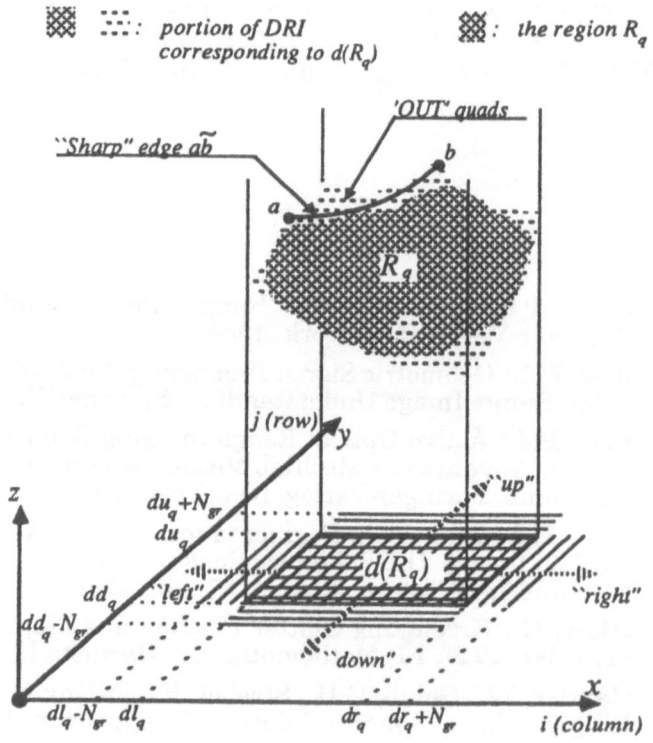

Figure 1: A Region R_q and its domain $d(R_q)$.

On the Conversion of Dupin Cyclide into Principal Patches

Xiaolin Zhou[1] and Dieter Roller[2]

The rational parametric representation of Dupin cyclide given by Forsyth [For12] and that of the principal patches introduced by de Pont [DeP84] are the two most practical representation forms for cyclide modeling in CAGD. They represent the same kind of patches, but have different parametrizations. We discuss these two representations from the application point of view and present a method to convert the Dupin cyclide patch into a principal patch.

Introduction

Cyclides have attracted the interest of researchers in Computer Aided Geometric Design (CAGD) due to some useful analytical and geometrical properties. Such properties include low algebraic degree, circular lines of curvatures, the constant angle between the surface normal and the normal of the line of curvature which enable the use of cyclide as blending surface between natural quadrics, tori and cyclides. It has been shown [Boe90] [ChDH88] [Pra90] [Pra95a] that as blending surface cyclides can provide a simple and precise solution for some situations where other methods fail. The suitable mathematical formulations for the use of cyclides as blending surface are the construction method given by Maxwell [Max68] in 1868, the rational parametric representation by Forsyth [For12]. We will discuss this issue later in detail. The NURBS-formulation presented in [ZhSt91] and [Zho92] enables an easy integration of the cyclides into an available modeler. On the other hand, it is well-known that all natural quadrics (plane, sphere, cylinder, cone) and torus are subclass of cyclides. Therefore through the introduction of cyclides in CAGD it is possible to treat these primitives uniformly. For theses purpose the construction method of prin-

---

[1] Nemetschek Programmsystem GmbH, Munich, FRG
[2] Institut für Informatik, Universität Stuttgart, FRG

cipal patches from the differential geometry point of view given by Martin [Mar82] and the rational parametric representation by de Pont [DeP84] are proper tools. In order to distinguish these two representations here we call the rational representation given by Forsyth the Dupin Cyclide Representation (DCR) and the representation by de Pont the Principal Patch Representation (PPR). The theory about patches of a single cyclide is well established, yet these two representations are treated rather separately. Their relationship is rarely considered. As the focus of the research work on cyclides shifts gradually from theory to the implementation and practical application issues, it is naturally desirable that these two representations are convertible. The conversion of a principal patch into a Dupin cyclide patch has been considered by Martin. Here we discuss the inverse problem, namely, how to get the equivalent PPC if a DCR is given.

Here is a short overview of the contents of the following paragraphs: First we give a brief description of Dupin cyclide and show the fact that the construction method by Maxwell and the DCR given by Forsyth are especially suitable for blending. Then we consider the PPR from the aspect that it enables an uniform treatment of natural quadrics and torus. Further we present a formulation to convert a DCR into its equivalent PPR In the last paragraph we summarize the results and indicate further research direction. In general we stress on the applications rather than the mathematical foundations.

The Dupin cyclide

The Dupin cyclide was first discovered by the French mathematician C. Dupin in 1822 [Dup22]. He defined a cyclide as "the envelop of a variable sphere that touches three fixed spheres in a continuous manner". Later there were also several other definitions. The details can be found in [ChDH89]. Yet the most intuitive and straightforward way to construct a Dupin cyclide was given by Maxwell [Max68]:

"Let a sufficiently long string be fastened at one end to one focus f of an ellipse E, let the string be kept always tight while sliding smoothly over the ellipse, then the other end z will sweep out the whole surface of a cyclide".

From this construction the function of the ellipse E become conspicuous. It is a "spine curve" of the Dupin cyclide. In the definition of a blending surface such a spine curve plays an important role. Recall the popular "rolling ball" method, the spine curve is actually the locus of the center of the ball.

Forsyth [For12] has given the following formulations for a cyclide in a standard location (see fig.1):

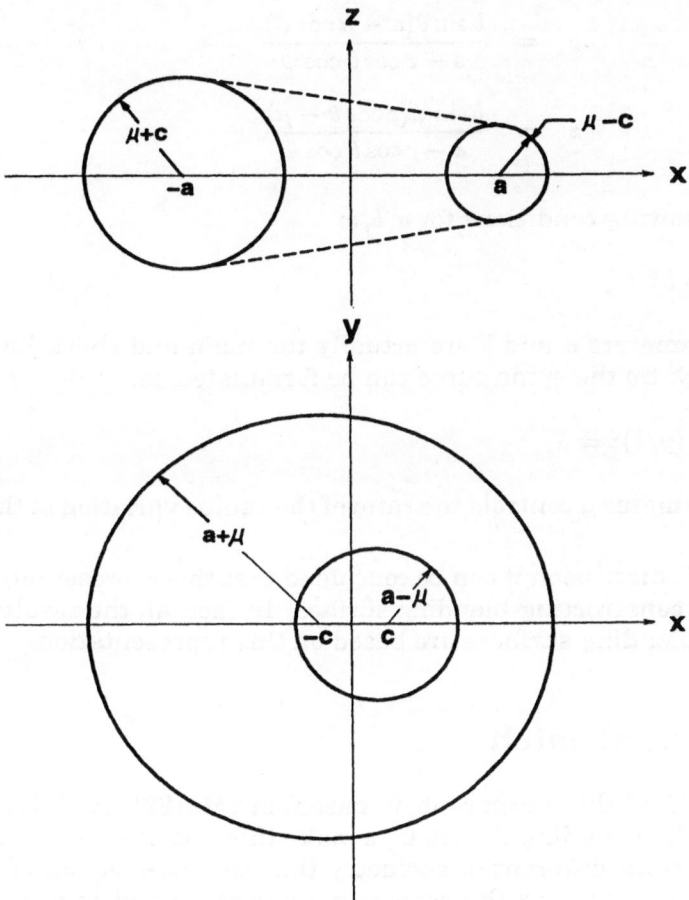

Fig. 1: The cross-section of a Dupin cyclide

Two implicit forms:

$$(x^2 + y^2 + z^2 - \mu^2 + b^2)^2 = 4(ax - c\mu)^2 + 4b^2y^2$$

$$(x^2 + y^2 + z^2 - \mu^2 - b^2)^2 = 4(cx - a\mu)^2 + 4b^2z^2 \tag{1}$$

and a parametric form:

$$x = \frac{\mu(c - a\cos\theta\cos\psi) + b^2\cos\theta}{a - c\cos\theta\cos\psi}$$

$$y = \frac{b \sin \theta (a - \mu \cos \psi)}{a - c \cos \theta \cos \psi}$$

$$z = \frac{b \sin \psi (c \cos \theta - \mu)}{a - c \cos \theta \cos \psi} \qquad (2)$$

with the following conditions for a, b, c:

$$c^2 = a^2 - b^2$$

The parameters a and b are actually the main and short diameters of the ellipse E. So the spine curve can be formulated as:

$$(x/a)^2 + (y/b)^2 = 1$$

The parameter μ controls the ratio of the radius variation of the "rolling ball".

From this discussion it can be concluded that this representation is very suitable for constructing blending surface. In fact, all the results of using cyclides as blending surfaces are based on this representation.

The principal patch

The material of this paragraph is based on [Mar82], [DeP84], [Sha85]. The reason for including it here is to make this article self–contained. Remembering from differential geometry that the intersection of a surface with a plane containing the surface normal at a point is a plane curve, the curvature of this curve at this point is the normal curvature of the surface in the direction of the plane. At any point on a surface there are infinitely many of these planes, each of which will give a different value for the normal curvature. The normal curvature takes on minimum and maximum values for a pair of directions which are orthogonal. These are called the principal directions at this point. The normal curvatures in these directions are called the principal curvatures. On any surface we can draw curves whose tangents are always in one of the principal directions. Such curves are called lines of curvature. There are two families of these curves and they intersect orthogonally (except for umbilical points, where they need to be treated specially). A four–sided patch whose boundary curves are lines of curvature is called a principal patch. If all the lines of curvature on a principal patch are circular arcs, this patch is a cyclide patch. In order to distinguish from the Dupin cyclide, we use the name principal patch in this section.

One important property of a cyclide patch is that its four corners lie on a single circle. This means that if we take two adjacent sides of the patch as being given, the fourth corner of the patch is constrained to move around on the circle defined by the three given corners, and there is only one degree of freedom (see fig. 2). Martin has shown that 7 parameters are needed to define a cyclide patch. They are the geodesic curvature g, normal curvature n and the chord length l of sides 1 and 2 as well as a shape parameter P, where P ranges from 0 to 1 and determines the position of the fourth corner on the circle (see fig. 3).

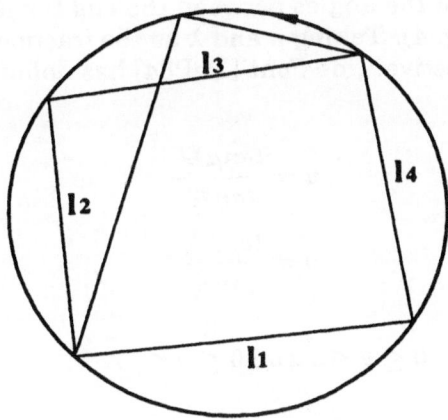

Fig. 2: The four corners of a cyclide patch lie on a circle

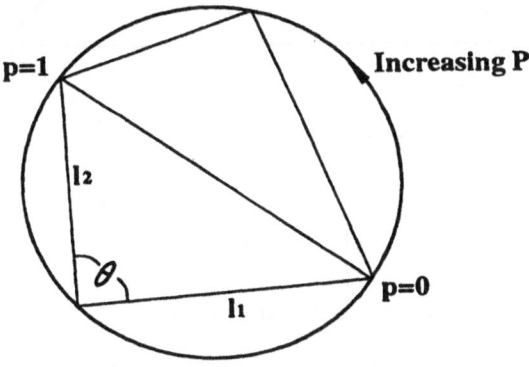

Fig. 3: The parameters P and θ

Considering side 1, we have:

$$g_1 = \kappa_1 cos\phi_1$$
$$n_1 = \kappa_1 sin\phi_1$$
$$l_1 = \frac{2sin\frac{\psi_1}{2}}{\kappa_1}$$

where κ_1 is the curvature of side 1, ϕ_1 is the angle between the space curve binormal and the surface normal. The same is also valid for side 2.

Let ψ_1 and ψ_2 be the angles between the end tangents of sides 1 and 2 respectively (see fig. 4). Taking μ and λ as the fractional arc lengths along sides 1 and 2 respectively, de Pont [DeP84] has defined two parameters u and v:

$$u = \frac{tan\mu\frac{\psi_1}{2}}{tan\frac{\psi_1}{2}}$$

$$v = \frac{tan\lambda\frac{\psi_2}{2}}{tan\frac{\psi_2}{2}}$$

It is obvious that $0 \le u \le 1$ and $0 \le v \le 1$.

Side 1

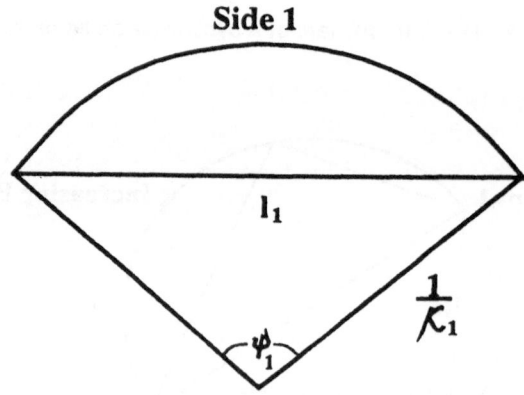

Fig. 4: Some parameters of side 1

Using u and v as variables, a principal patch in the location shown in fig. 5 can be described by the following parametric form:

$$x(u, v) = \frac{a_1 u(A_2 l_1 - B_2 l_2) - b_2 v^2 (A_1 l_2 + B_1 l_1)}{A_1 A_2 + B_1 B_2}$$

$$y(u, v) \quad = \quad \frac{b_1 u^2 (A_2 l_1 - B_2 l_2) + a_2 v (A_1 l_2 + B_1 l_1)}{A_1 A_2 + B_1 B_2} \tag{3}$$

$$z(u, v) \quad = \quad \frac{c_1 u^2 (A_2 l_1 - B_2 l_2) + c_2 v^2 (A_1 l_2 + B_1 l_1)}{A_1 A_2 + B_1 B_2}$$

where

$$
\begin{aligned}
b_i &= \cos\phi_i \sin\frac{\psi_i}{2} = \frac{g_i l_i}{2} \\
c_i &= \sin\phi_i \sin\frac{\psi_i}{2} = \frac{n_i l_i}{2} \\
a_i &= (1 - b_i^2 - c_i^2)^{1/2} \quad i = 1, 2
\end{aligned}
\tag{4}
$$

are the parameters of sides 1 and 2 respectively. A_i, B_i $i = 1, 2$ can be calculated as follows:

$$
\begin{aligned}
A_1 &= a_1^2 + (b_1^2 + c_1^2)u^2 \\
B_1 &= pu^2 + 2b_2 a_1 u(1 - u) \\
A_2 &= a_2^2 + (b_2^2 + c_2^2)v^2 \\
B_2 &= qv^2 + 2b_1 a_2 v(1 - v)
\end{aligned}
\tag{5}
$$

In order to calculate p and q, we define a parameter θ. The geometric meaning of θ can be found in fig. 3 and can be calculated by:

$$\cos\theta = -a_1 b_2 + b_1 a_2 + c_1 c_2 \tag{6}$$

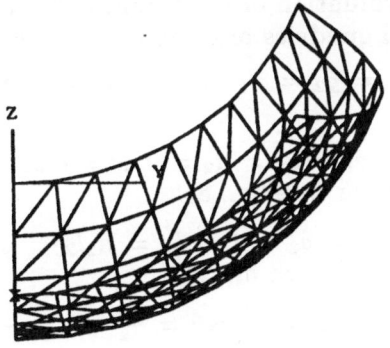

Fig. 5: A cyclide patch with $g1 = 0$

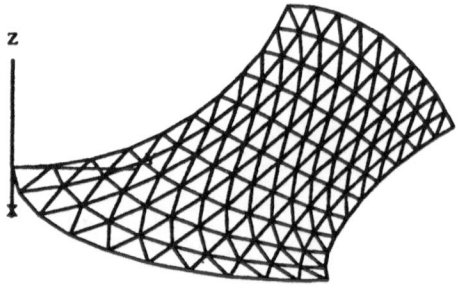

Fig. 6: A cyclide patch with $n1 = 0$

p and q can be obtained:

$$p = \frac{-l_1 l_2 + 2P(l_1 l2 - l_2^2 \cos\theta)}{(1 - P)l_1^2 + Pl_2^2}$$

$$q = \frac{-l_1 l_2 + 2(1 - P)(l_1 l_2 - l_1^2 \cos\theta)}{(1 - P)l_1^2 + Pl_2^2} \tag{7}$$

We call the formula 3 the Principal Patch Representation (PPR). It enables us to construct a cyclide patch by controlling the curvatures of side 1 and side 2. The parameters g_i and n_i $(i = 1, 2)$ have clear geometric meanings. Fig. 5 and fig. 6 show two cyclide patches defined be formula 3. They have different $g1$ and $n1$. Other parameters of both patches are equal.

Through the evaluation of the formula 3, we can easily get the representation of natural quadrics and the torus. For example:

- Plane: let $g_1 = g_2 = n_1 = n_2 = 0$, Formula (3) yields a plane (see fig. 7).

- Cylinder: Let $g_1 = g_2 = n_2 = 0, P = 0.5$. In this case (3) represents part of a cylinder (see fig.. 8).

- Sphere: Let $g_1 = g_2 = 0, n_1 l_1 = n_2 l_2 = \sqrt{2}$. Here (3) represents a octant of a sphere (see fig. 9).

- Cone: Let $g2 = n2 = 0, \cos\theta = \frac{g_1 l_1}{2}, P = \frac{l_1}{2(l_1 - l_2 \cos\theta)}$. In this case (3) represents a cone (see fig. 10).

- Torus: Let $g2 = 0, n2 \neq 0, \cos\theta = \frac{g_1 l_1}{2}, P = \frac{l_1}{2(l_1 - l_2 \cos\theta)}$. In this case (3) represents part of a torus (see fig. 11).

From the discussion in this section it can been seen that the PPR enables an uniform treatment of natural quadrics and torus.

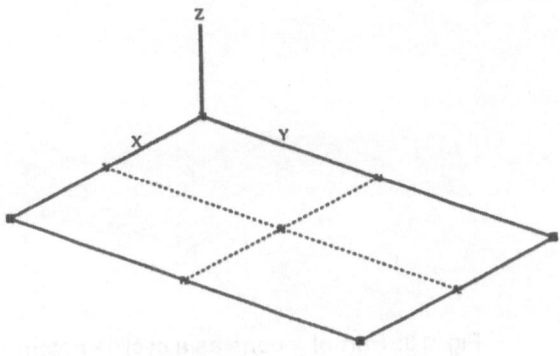

Fig. 7: A rectangular plane as a cyclide patch

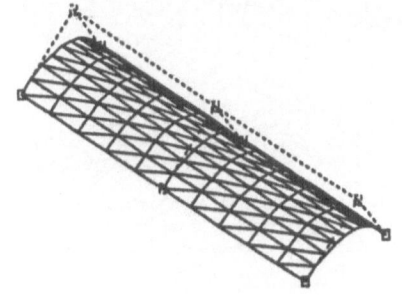

Fig. 8: Part of a circular cylinder as a cyclide patch

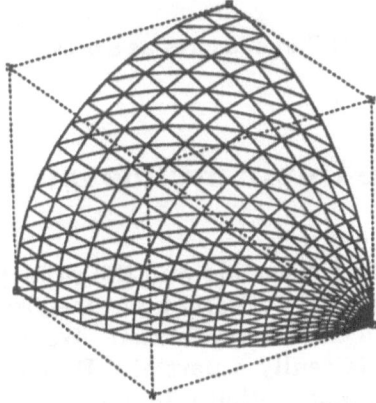

Fig. 9: Part of a sphere as a cyclide patch

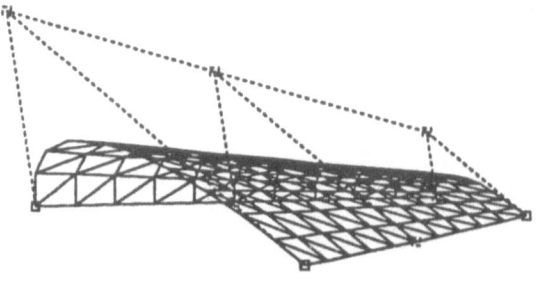

Fig. 10: Part of a cone as a cyclide patch

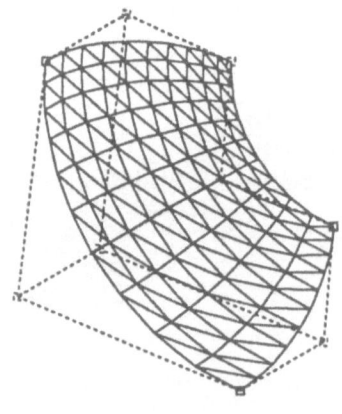

Fig. 11: Part of a torus as a cyclide patch

Conversion of the Dupin cyclide into principal patches

As shown above, the Dupin cyclide and the principal patch meets different requirements and possess different parametrization. The choice of the representation depends on the application. We have also shown the fact that a principal patch is really a part of a Dupin cyclide. It is desirable to convert from one representation into another. We discuss here how to get the equivalent PPR if a DCR is given. The inverse problem has been treated by Martin [Mar82].

The problem can be described as follows:

Given is a DCR in the form of 2 with the known parameters $a, b, c, \mu, \theta_1, \theta_2, \psi_1, \psi_2$ where $\theta_1 \leq \theta_2$ and $\psi_1 \leq \psi_2$. Wanted is a PPR in the form of 3 with the parameters $g_1, g_2, n_1, n_2, l_1, l_2, P$.

For Dupin cyclide there exist the following equations [For12]

$$\kappa = \frac{\sqrt{a^2 \sin^2 \theta + b^2 \cos^2 \theta}}{b(\mu - c \cos \theta)} \tag{8}$$

for ψ = constant and

$$\kappa = \frac{\sqrt{a^2 \sin^2 \psi + b^2 \cos^2 \psi}}{b(\mu \cos \psi - a)} \tag{9}$$

for θ = constant and

$$\cos \phi = \frac{c \sin \theta}{\sqrt{a^2 \sin^2 \theta + b^2 \cos^2 \theta}} \tag{10}$$

for ψ = constant and

$$\cos \phi = \frac{a \sin \psi}{\sqrt{a^2 \sin^2 \psi + b^2 \cos^2 \psi}} \tag{11}$$

for θ = constant, where κ is the curvature of the curve. ϕ is the angle between the surface normal and the binormal of the curve.

The conversion process includes the following steps:

Step 1: calculate the κ_i and $\phi_i (i = 1, 4)$ of the 4 boundary curves of the given Dupin cyclide patch.

Step 2: based on the κ_i and ϕ_i calculate the geodesic and normal curvatures of the $g_i, n_i (i = 1, 4)$ of the 4 boundary curves of the wanted principal patch.

Step 3: calculate the l_1, l_2 and P using g_i and n_i, we will then obtain the PPR.

From (3), (8) and (9) we have

$$\begin{aligned} g_i &= \kappa_i \cos \phi_i \\ &= \frac{c \sin \theta_i}{b(\mu - c \cos \theta_i)} \end{aligned}$$

$$
\begin{aligned}
n_i &= \kappa_i \sin \phi_i \\
&= \frac{1}{\mu - c \cos \theta_i}
\end{aligned}
\tag{12}
$$

where $i = 1, 3$ and

$$
\begin{aligned}
g_i &= \kappa_i \cos \phi_i \\
&= \frac{a \sin \psi_i}{b(\mu \cos \psi_i - a)} \\
n_i &= \kappa_i \sin \phi_i \\
&= \frac{\cos \psi_i}{\mu \cos \psi_i - a}
\end{aligned}
\tag{13}
$$

where $i = 2, 4$.

We have now the geodesic and normal curvatures of the 4 boundary curves. For convenience we use 4 help–parameters to investigate l_1, l_2 and P Γ, Δ, f_1 und f_2 where

$$
f_1 = \frac{2a_1}{l_1}, \qquad f_2 = \frac{2a_2}{l_2}
\tag{14}
$$

are called auxiliary curvatures and Γ as well as Δ are called blending parameters and they are defined as [NuMa88]:

$$
\begin{aligned}
\Gamma &= \frac{l_1}{(l_1 + q l_2)} \\
\Delta &= \frac{l_2}{(l_2 + p l_1)}
\end{aligned}
\tag{15}
$$

Comparing of (7) and (15) it can be seen that Γ und Δ are actually another definition of the shape parameter P.

[NuMa88] shows the following equations:

$$
\left\{
\begin{aligned}
g_3 &= -\Gamma g_1 - (1 - \Gamma) f_2 \\
n_3 &= \Gamma n_1 + (1 - \Gamma) n_2 \\
g_4 &= -\Delta g_2 - (1 - \Delta) f_1 \\
n_4 &= \Delta n_2 + (1 - \Delta) n_1 \\
\Gamma &= \frac{P}{1 - P} \Delta
\end{aligned}
\right.
\tag{16}
$$

For a detailed description of (16) please refer to [NuMa88].

From (16) follows:

$$
\left\{
\begin{aligned}
\Gamma &= \frac{n_3 - n_2}{n_1 - n_2} \\
f_2 &= \frac{g_3 + \Gamma g_1}{\Gamma - 1} = \frac{(n_1 - n_2)g_3 + (n_3 - n_2)g_1}{n_3 - n_1} \\
\Delta &= \frac{n_4 - n_1}{n_2 - n_1} \\
f_1 &= \frac{g_4 + \Delta g_2}{1 - \Delta} = \frac{(n_2 - n_1)g_4 + (n_4 - n_1)g_2}{n_2 - n_4} \\
\Gamma &= \frac{P}{1 - P} \Delta
\end{aligned}
\right.
$$

Together with (14) we hve the following results:

$$
\begin{cases}
P &= \dfrac{\Gamma}{\Gamma+\Delta} = \dfrac{n_3-n_2}{n_3-n_2+n_1-n_4} \\[2mm]
l_1 &= \dfrac{2}{\sqrt{f_1^2+g_1^2+n_1^2}} \\[2mm]
&= \dfrac{2(n_2-n_4)}{(g_4 n_2+g_2 n_4-(g_4+g_2)n_1)^2+(g_1^2+n_1^2)(n_2-n_4)^2} \\[2mm]
l_2 &= \dfrac{2}{\sqrt{f_2^2+g_2^2+n_2^2}} \\[2mm]
&= \dfrac{2(n_3-n_1)}{(g_3 n_1+g_1 n_3-(g_1+g_3)n_2)^2+(g_2^2+n_2^2)(n_3-n_1)^2}
\end{cases}
\tag{17}
$$

with g_i, n_i, $i = (1,2)$ from (9) and (13) we have the complete PPR.

Conclusion

The two rational parametric representations of cyclides describe the same class of surface and have different uses. The relationship between them has been rarely considered. In this section we take this issue into account. We have shown why the DCR is suitable for blending whilest the PPR can lead to an uniform treatment of the natural quadrics and torus. Also a method for converting the DCR into the PPR has been represented. This work enables us, for instance, to choose adequate representations for different applications and at the same time to keep just an unique internal representation in a modeler. Ongoing work currently includes building a user–friendly interactive environment to deal with cyclides; the use of cyclide for variational design [Rol88]; the investigation of combining more generalized cyclide form to gain more degree of freedom [Deg91] [Pra95b].

References

[Boe90]   Wolfgang Boehm. On cyclides in geometric modeling, Computer Aided Geometric Design, 7:pp. 243–256, 1990.

[ChDH88] V. Chandru, D. Dutta, and C. M. Hoffmann. Variable radius blending using Dupin cyclides. In K. Preiss M. J. Wozny, J. U. Turner, editor, NSF–IFIP Working Conference on Geometric Modeling, pp. 39–60. North-Holland, 1988.

[ChDH89] V. Chandru, D. Dutta, and C. M. Hoffmann. On the geometry of dupin cyclides. The Visual Computer, (5):pp. 277–290, 1989.

[DeP84]   de Pont. Essays on the Cyclide Patch. PhD thesis, Cambrige University, Cambrige, UK, 1984.

[Deg91]   W. L. F. Degen. Generalized cyclides for use in CAGD. In the IMA Conference Proceedings Series. Oxford Press, 1991.

[Dup22]   C. P. Dupin. Applications de Géometrie et de Méchanique. Bachelier Paris, 1822.

[For12]   A. R. Forsyth. Lectures on DIfferential GEometry of Curves and Surfaces Cambridge University Press, 1912

[Max68]   J. C. Maxwell. On the Cyclide. Quaterly Journal of Pure and Applied Mathematics, pp. 111–126, 1868

[Mar82]   R. R. Martin. Principle Patches for Computational Geometry. PhD thesis, Cambrige University, Cambrige, UK, 1982.

[NuMa88] W. Nutbourne and R. Martin. Differential Geometry Applied to Curve and Surface Design. Ellis Horwood, 1988.

[Pra90]   M. J. Pratt. Cyclides in CAGD. CAGD, 7:221–242, 1990.

[Pra95a]   M. J. Pratt. Cyclides in CAGD II. CAGD, 1995.

[Pra95b]   M. J. Pratt. Quartic Supercyclides I: Basic Theory CAGD, to be published.

[Rol88]   D. Roller. An Approach to Computer Aided Parametric Design CAD, (5): pp.81-86, 1988

[Sha85]   T. J. Sharrock. Surface Design with Cyclide Patches. PhD thesis, Cambrige University, 1985.

[ZhSt91] Xiaolin Zhou and Wolfgang Straßer. A NURBS Representation for Cyclides. In T. L. Kunii, editor, Modeling in Computer Graphics, Proc. of the IFIP 5.10 Working Conference, pages pp. 77–92. Springer-Verlage, 1991.

[Zho92] Xiaolin Zhou. Representing and modeling of cyclide patches using NURBS In B. Falcidieno I. Hermann and Pienovi, editors Computer Graphics and Mathematics, pp. 45-60, Springer–Verlag, 1992

Chapter 5

Parametric Modelling

Overview

Extension of STEP for the Representation of Parametric and Variational Models

M. J. Pratt[1]

The International Standard STEP (ISO 10303) is intended to facilitate the exchange of data between CAD systems. The first release of the standard, which occurred in 1994, allows the transfer of geometric product models in terms of geometry and topology alone. Since most CAD systems now allow the creation of parametric, constraint-based and feature based models, it is necessary to extend STEP to take into account these newer capabilities. What follows is a discussion of some of the considerations which have arisen in the early stages of this work.

Introduction

The topic addressed here is the problem of developing enhancements to the international standard ISO 10303[Int94], informally known as STEP. At present STEP is not capable of transferring parametrized geometry, constrained geometry or feature-based representations[Eas94]. Since most major CAD systems currently generate product models having these characteristics, an effort has recently started to extend the standard to accommodate them. For readers unfamiliar with the details some information on the organization of the STEP development work is given in Appendix 1. For the moment, it is sufficient to say that the information actually exchanged by STEP in a particular application context is specified by an Application Protocol (AP), and that at a lower level Integrated Resources (IRs) are provided which are are in general referred to by multiple APs. The IRs fall into the 40-series parts of the overall standard, and the APs into the 200-series. Refer to the Appendix for further details.

Since the early days of CAD there have been two approaches to product

[1]National Institute of Standards and Technology, Gaithersburg, MD, U.S.A.

modeling. One is the procedural approach, epitomized in former years by constructive solid geometry (CSG). The product description generated by a procedural modeler is a sequence of instructions for creating a model of the product; it therefore embodies a history of the process of model construction.

The other approach does not capture the constructional history of the model, but rather records explicit details of it at any one time during its construction. The boundary representation approach to solid modeling is an example of this approach. At any time during the modeling process what is stored by such a modeler may be regarded as a 'snapshot' of the model at whatever particular stage of its construction has been reached. No constructional history is recorded by, or can be inferred from, such a model.

In what follows the two types of models will be referred to as *implicit* and *explicit*. The justification for this is that in the first case it is not possible to obtain detailed information about the model until the constructional procedure has been followed through, while in the second case the full details are known although the constructional history is lost.

In its present form, STEP is almost exclusively concerned with the transfer of explicit product models of the boundary representation type. Furthermore, in the released parts AP201, AP203 and in other APs still in preparation, no provision is made for the transfer of parametrised entities or of models based on the use of constraints or features. Some future APs, notably AP214 and AP224, will allow the representation of feature-based models, but in the latter case these are machining features and in the former their intended application area in the overall product realization process is left indeterminate. No generic mechanism currently exists in STEP for the representation of features.

Although its current emphasis is on explicit models, STEP does make some concessions to the implicit or procedural approach. Part 42, for example, provides for the representation of CSG models built from primitive volumes by the use of Boolean operations. However, this is at present only possible using numerically rather than parametrically dimensioned primitives, because of the lack of parametric capabilities in the standard. Furthermore, none of the currently released parts of the standard actually make use of this latent capability. It is also worth noting that certain specialized geometry definitions may also be regarded as procedural, notably offset curves and surfaces, which are customarily defined in terms of a base entity and an offset distance. It may therefore be seen that STEP as it currently exists is something of a compromise, with implicit and explicit representations mixed up in a not very logical manner, the emphasis being strongly on the explicit forms. An alternative implicit or procedural means for the exchange of product models has been proposed by Hoffmann and Juan[HJ92].

Despite the apparently fundamental differences in approach between implicit and explicit modeling, most of the practical CAD systems of the last twenty years or so have in some sense provided both types of capability. Any procedurally-based system has needed the capability for generating explicit versions of its models, if only for the fundamental purpose of creating graphical renderings of them. Conversely, any explicit modeling system has provided the means for storing the set of modeling commands actually invoked by the system user in creating the explicit model. These commands are an implicit description of the model, and thus, in a very real sense, any CAD system may be regarded as a hybrid. There may be greater or lesser degrees of coupling between the two forms of the model. In the worst case there is no coupling at all. Thus, in early CSG systems, the explicit model was not generated until the implicit modeling process was complete, whereas later a higher degree of coupling was achieved through incremental evaluation of the explicit model during the construction of the implicit model. Similarly, in early boundary representation systems there was no coupling between the explicit model and the file of commands compiled; to change the model it was necessary to edit the command file and then re-run it from the beginning. Nowadays it is on many cases possible to 'roll back', i.e. undo the effects of the most recent commands, make a modification to some previous command and then roll forward again to generate the modified model.

Ideally, once a product model has been transferred from System A into System B, it should be possible to continue modeling with it in the receiving system just as though it had originally been created there. To enable this to be so regardless of the underlying nature of the sending and receiving systems is a major challenge to the developers of STEP, and whether it is even possible is an open question. However, we can take some comfort from the fact established earlier that all CAD modelers are in some sense hybrid, and thus they all share some common ground.

Current Directions for the Representation of Parametric and Variational Models in STEP

There are several teams working within ISO TC184/SC4 (see Appendix 1) who have an interest in parametric and constraint-based modeling. The ISO Parametrics Group hopes to coordinate the efforts of these teams to achieve a uniform approach across all the various parts of the STEP standard. The Parametrics Group is composed of two subgroups. One is concerned with a specific short-term issue, namely the urgent requirement to extend STEP so that it can handle the parametric, variational and feature-based information generated by modern CAD systems. The emphasis at present is primarily on explicit models, since it is felt that these are characteristic of the native models generated by such systems. Only the short-term issues will be covered here; the interests of the other ('long-term') Parametrics subgroup lie in such topics as knowledge representation and non-geometric constraints.

One other Working Group (WG) within ISO TC184/SC4 has aleady done some significant work on parametric modeling, and that is WG2, the developers of the future ISO 13584 Parts Library standard. This group has a requirement for parametric models that can be instantiated with appropriately chosen parameter values to represent any member of an entire family of parts. The approach taken has been an implicit one, part representations being specified in the form of a sequence of parametrized operations on geometric elements[Pie94]. For purposes of data transfer it is proposed that the implicit model description is transmitted together with a 'current instance', i.e. an example member of the family.

Numerous further SC4 teams have expressed an interest in the work of the Parametrics Group, with a view to using the capabilities it develops in new or revised parts of the standard. There is strong interest in the AEC area, for example, and potential application areas in mechanical engineering include all those where form features are likely to be used, including tolerancing, various manufacturing processes, assembly and inspection.

The Parametrics short-term subgroup is currently working closely with WG3/T1, the Shape Representation team, to develop the initial basic variable parameter and constraint capability in an extended STEP context. The declared aims of this work are to cover the capabilities of current CAD systems and to meet the needs of the WG2 Parts Library team. However, since this requires an explicit approach on the one hand and an implicit approach on the other it may be necessary to follow two different paths initially before achieving convergence in the future.

There are numerous liaisons with other groups in the STEP community, since extensions are now being made to various parts of the standard that have already been released. Ongoing discussions concern what changes need to be made in several parts of the STEP to facilitate provision of the new Parametrics capabilities, and the best ways of achieving upwards compatibility with the current version.

External liaisons will also be very important. Several projects are currently running, mainly in the USA, Germany and Japan, which will generate results useful to the ISO Parametrics work. It will also be necessary to circulate Parametrics proposals around the CAD vendor companies to obtain informed technical feedback on compatibility with the capabilities of their various systems.

The work of the Parametrics Group has only recently started, and efforts are currently under way to develop representations for parametrized entities and for constraints. Some of the relevant issues are discussed in what follows.

Parametrized models

The Generic Resource Part 42 of STEP provides definitions of a variety of geometrical and topological entities for use in building product model representations. At present these require all defining dimensions to be of type LENGTH_MEASURE, where LENGTH_MEASURE is an entity of type REAL defined in Part 41. In order to provide a parametric capability compliant with the current version of STEP it has been found necessary to define *parametric* geometric entities paralleling each of the types defined in Part 42, and to construct a schema defining variables and algebraic expressions for use in assigning variable dimensions to them. However, it has been determined that a comparatively small change in Part 41, to allow LENGTH_MEASURE to be either of type REAL or type VARIABLE, will allow the Part 42 geometric entities as currently defined to be used in a parametric manner. This provides a simple solution, without the need to double the number of geometric entities, but at the cost of changing an existing part of the standard. This is one example of the type of tradeoff which has to be made in revising STEP.

Another example relates to the need for a variables/functions schema. Such a schema has been developed in compliance with the standard as it currently exists[Int95], but it is fairly complex. The possibility is now being investigated that comparatively small changes in the EXPRESS information modeling language, the foundation of the whole edifice of STEP, may provide what is needed in a much less complex way. Since EXPRESS is already part of the current standard, any changes will need to be upwards compatible with the previous version.

Changes of the kind envisaged will also affect Part 21, which specifies the manner in which STEP information is actually stored in a physical file. Once again, upwards compatibility must be the aim.

It will be seen that the decisions to be taken are of a delicate nature. What is desired is a compromise between representational power, conciseness, and degree of compliance with the existing released version of the STEP standard.

Constraints

It appears that the provision of constraint representations in STEP will give rise to fewer interactions with the existing parts of the standard, since these are essentially new entity types rather than variants of existing ones. The following discussion is based upon the simple 2D profile shown below. The geometry of the profile is composed of the entities listed below (they are not given in STEP format):

l_1: line from (1,0) to (4,0)
l_2: line from (1,4) to (8,4)
l_3: line from (0,1) to (0,3)
l_4: line from (4,0) to (8,4)
c_1: circular arc with center (1,1), start (1,0), end (0,1)
c_2: circular arc with center (1,3), start (0,3), end (1,4)

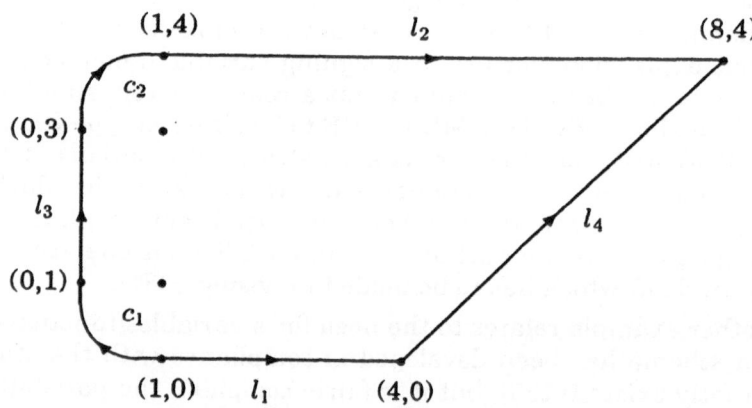

Some constraints which might be applied to the profile include

1. l_1 and l_2 are parallel

2. $l_1.start$ and $l_2.start$ are 4 units apart

3. the (oriented) angle between l_1 and l_4 is 45°

4. the (oriented) angle between l_2 and l_4 is 45°

5. $c_1.center$ is equidistant from l_1 and l_3

6. $c_2.center$ is equidistant from l_2 and l_3

7. c_1 and l_1 are tangent at $c_1.start$ and $l_1.start$

8. c_1 and l_3 are tangent at $c_1.end$ and $l_3.start$

9. c_2 and l_2 are tangent at $c_2.end$ and $l_2.start$

10. c_2 and l_3 are tangent at $c_2.start$ and $l_3.end$

11. $l_1.end$ and $l_4.start$ coincide

12. $l_2.end$ and $l_4.end$ coincide

13. $l_1.start$ is fixed at (1,0)

14. l_3 is perpendicular to l_1

There is of course redundancy in this set, and in a practical situation only a subset of these constraints would be imposed. Since the emphasis here is primarily on the provision of mechanisms, the list is intended to be illustrative rather than to provide exhaustive coverage of all types of 2D constraints that will be needed in practice.

As STEP currently exists, only cases 1, 11 and 12 can be represented. Since a line is represented in terms of a point and a direction, the parallelism of l_1 and l_2 can be captured implicitly by making them share the same direction entity in the STEP file. An argument is given below as to why this probably not a good idea. The coincidence of end-points as expressed in Constraints 11 and 12 will be captured by making the specified bounding vertices of the edges in question lie at the same point, which is a standard connectivity mechanism in boundary representation modeling.

It may be noted that Constraints 2, 3, and 4 in effect specify *dimensions*, and any provision in this area should therefore be compatible with other STEP capabilities for the representation of dimensions. At present these occur mainly in the context of 2D drawings. The 'oriented angles' mentioned in Constraints 3 and 4 give the counterclockwise change in direction required to rotate from the direction of the first line specified to that of the second. If we regard perpendicularity as a special case of an angular dimension, as seems reasonable, then the same remark also applies to Constraint 14. In this case it will be logical to deal with parallelism as an angular dimension constraint in the same way.

As has been shown, some specific types of constraints in the above list bear some relation to existing Part 42 capabilities. Others do not, and some of the new capabilities required seem to be

1. The capture of tangency between specified end-points of two geometric entities (Constraints 7, 8, 9 and 10). This could be dealt with by a combination of a coincidence and a parallelism constraint, though for reasons mentioned below this would be undesirable.

2. The statement that a point is equidistant between two lines (Constraints 5 and 6).

3. The ability to state that a vertex of the profile is anchored at a fixed point (Constraint 13); this effectively allows other vertices to be moved during design modifications, but not the one at (0,1).

4. A concept of construction geometry.

5. The ability to reference subfields of geometric entities. The EXPRESS language does not currently permit this, and the examples above show a clear requirement for this facility in the next version of the language.

It must not be forgotten that STEP should also be able to deal with constraints involving *functional* relationships between entities. It was mentioned earlier, in the section on parametric modeling, that discussions are already under way on the best way of achieving this.

Since only a few of the desired constraint types can be handled by STEP as it currently exists, it seems best to provide a new and consistent treatment for all constraints, even at the expense of some slight redundancy in the information exchanged. In any case, employing the existing Part 42 capabilities mentioned above would really be misusing them, since their intention is essentially to capture the a *static* product model, not to impose restrictions on how it can be modified in the future.

Several considerations on the design of a constraint modeling capability in STEP are discussed in the following paragraphs:

What kinds of entities should constraints apply to? It is necessary to decide whether the constraints should apply to topological entities (e.g. edges) or to the underlying geometric entities (e.g. lines, or at a lower level, directions). The second alternative is probably most appropriate, since it seems to reflect what most CAD systems do in practice. Nevertheless, it may under some circumstances be useful to apply constraints to topological entities, and possible requirements for this should be examined.

Parallelism and other constraints on angular dimension: It was mentioned above that one way of handling constraints on the parallelism of lines is simply to define the lines concerned in terms of the same direction entity. The use of this implicit mechanism is consistent with existing Part 42 capabilities, but neverthless it does not seem to be a good idea. A parallelism constraint is a special case of an angular dimension constraint, and there is no comparable mechanism for handling the more general case, which includes the frequently occurring case of perpendicularity. In any case, CAD systems may replicate direction vectors rather than check for the pre-existence of the appropriate direction vector when each new line entity is created. Thus parallel lines may refer to different (albeit equivalent) direction vectors, and unless translators are designed to check for this kind of thing the implicit parallelism relationships may be lost. For these reasons, and also in the interests of consistency in modeling constraints, the initial conclusion is that explicit constraint representations are best.

Next consider the representation of a tangency constraint; this could in principle be done in terms of a coincidence and a (parallel) directional constraint. The problem with this approach is that it does not generalize to cases where (for example) second or higher order derivatives are required to be continuous across a join. In fact there is a tie-up here with one of the enhancements requested by AP developers in Part 42 ('Continuity Constraints'). It therefore seems desirable to treat tangency as one particular case of a more general 'geometric continuity' constraint.

Another question regarding tangency is whether STEP should capture only *apparent* continuity (i.e. the visual smoothness of the join in the diagram), or should take into account also the sense of the defined lines and arcs? In the latter case, Constraint 7 in list above would not count as a tangency, since the *directed* tangents are in opposite directions.

Mode of constraint representation:

Several different possibilities for the capture of constraint information have been suggested. These include

Declarative, e.g. **parallel**(l_1, l_2) — or, perhaps better, **angle**$(l_1, l_2, 0)$, which provides a unified way of handling parallelism, perpendicularity and general angular relationships. Here 'parallel' and 'angle' have been written in the form of PROLOG predicates[CM94].

Relational, e.g. **directionfn**(l_1) = **directionfn**(l_2). In this case **directionfn** is a vector-valued function to be evaluated. Alternatively, it would be simpler in this case to use $l_1.direction = l_2.direction$ in terms of attributes, but sometimes function evaluation is going to be needed.

Algebraic, e.g.

$$(l_1.end.y - l_1.start.y)/(l_1.end.x - l_1.start.x) =$$

$$(l_2.end.y - l_2.start.y)/(l_2.end.x - l_2.start.x),$$

which is equivalent to the two previous examples. It is probably a less desirable alternative, for two reasons. Firstly, its geometric significance is not intuitively apparent, and secondly it requires exceptions for special cases, for example when one or other denominator is zero. The second problem could be overcome by expressing the constraint in terms of projective coordinates, but the additional complexity makes the simplicity of the declarative and relational approaches seem increasingly alluring.

On the other hand, 'special-case' explicit algebraic constraints of the type

$$box.length = sqrt(box.height^2 + box.width^2)$$

are probably indispensable; it is true that they can also be expressed in a declarative form, but much is thereby lost in terms of comprehensibility.

Geometric. This category has been suggested for examples of the type 'The centre of circle c_1 is the perpendicular projection of the intersection of lines l_1 and l_2 onto line l_3.' This could be formalized in declarative terms, given a supply of predefined PROLOG predicates, as follows:

> **intersection**(l_1, l_2, p_1);
> **normproj**$(p_1, l3, p2)$;
> **center**(p_2, c_1)

Clearly an algebraic expression of this constraint is also possible, though it will be rather complicated. In relational terms we could use

$$c_1.center = \mathbf{projfn}(\mathbf{intfn}(l_1, l_2), l_3)$$

This is concise, but its meaning is not intuitively obvious.

Both the declarative and relational approaches have the virtues of conciseness, and both provide more comprehensible semantics than the algebraic formulation. There seems to be no virtue in identifying a separate category of 'geometric' constraints, since the other three representations are sufficiently flexible to cover situations that will arise in practice.

Different CAD systems doubtless represent constraints in different ways, and for purposes of data exchange it is important that the formulation used for them should capture their meaning or semantic content. The algebraic approach only does this at a very low level, in terms of relations (in STEP terminology) between individual attributes of entities; the 'engineering' intent of the constraints is lost. The declarative and relational approaches, on the other hand, are much more successful in expressing the meaning of constraints as they apply to entire modeling entities.

The issue of semantics is important, since however a constraint is represented in a STEP model it must be possible to translate it into whatever is the appropriate format for a receiving system. This requires that the translator must in some sense be able to 'understand' the nature of the constraint in order to reformulate it if necessary. In general that will be impossible for a constraint expressed algebraically in a STEP file, which can therefore only be passed on into the receiving system in algebraic form. This is not a problem in cases such as the box dimensions example given in 3) above, but for constraints involving relatively high-level geometric concepts such as 'parallelism' or 'tangency' it is highly desirable to capture those concepts in the information transferred. One possibility might be to require that any algebraically formulated constraint having one of a 'standard' set of geometric meanings should be transmitted together with a declarative or relational statement of that meaning.

These, then, are some of the considerations to be borne in mind when the modeling approach for STEP constraints is decided. Two further significant points are briefly discussed below:

1. All the examples given are two-dimensional. We will of course have to watch developments in the area of 3D constraints, and to try to accommodate new CAD capabilities as they arise.

2. One suggestion made during a recent ISO meeting is that constraints should be weighted or prioritized, so that in the event of conflicting constraints a 'best' compromise solution (in some sense) can be determined. At present there is probably little use for this capability, but it may become important in the work of the Long-term Parametrics Subcommittee when they come to discuss the handling non-geometric design constraints.

Features

The provision of feature capabilities in STEP will not be discussed in detail. It has been mentioned that feature representations are being developed in the context of two future APs, but these will be limited in extent. What is really needed is a generic capability in the standard for the flexible definition of feature classes, and this will become possible once mechanisms for parametrically defined entities and geometric constraints are in place. Features will therefore be addressed by the ISO Parametrics Group in the medium-term future.

Conclusions

Some preliminary considerations relating to the representation parametric and constraint information in the STEP standard have been presented. The whole discussion has been at a low level, but clearly any of the representations eventually chosen must be fitted into a hierarchical data structure and ultimately into one or more STEP schemas. Top-down analysis will therefore be needed to supplement the bottom-up approach whose initial stages are given here.

Acknowledgements

The author would like to thank members of the Parametrics Group and the Shape Representation Task Group of ISO TC184/SC4 for helpful discussions. In particular, Edward Clapp of Autodesk Inc. suggested an initial version of the constraints example analyzed earlier, and provided insightful comments upon it.

References

[CM94] W. F. Clocksin and C. S. Mellish. *Programming in Prolog (4th Edition)*. Springer-Verlag, 1994.

[Eas94] C. M. Eastman. Out of STEP? *Computer Aided Design*, **26**, 5, 338 – 340, 1994.

[HJ92] C. M. Hoffmann and R. Juan. EREP: An editable high-level representation for geometric design and analysis. In P. R. Wilson, M. J. Wozny, and M. J. Pratt, editors, *Geometric Modeling for Product Realization*. North-Holland Publishing Co., 1992. (Proc. IFIP WG5.2 Workshop on Geometric Modeling in CAD, Rensselaerville, NY, 27 Sep - 1 Oct 1992).

[Int94] International Organisation for Standardisation. *Industrial Automation Systems and Integration – Product Data Representation and Exchange*, 1994. (International Standard ISO 10303, informally known as STEP).

[Int95] International Organisation for Standardisation. *Industrial Automation Systems and Integration – Parts Library, Part 20: General Resources*, 1995. (Committee Draft ISO CD 13584-20).

[Pie94] G. Pierra. Parametric product modelling for STEP and Parts Library (V0.3). Working Document ISO TC184/SC4/WG2 N183, International Organisation for Standardisation, July 1994.

Appendix 1: ISO TC184/SC4 and STEP

The International Organisation for Standardisation (ISO) administers a range of committees, which in general are divided into subcommittees. ISO Technical Committee 184, Subcommittee 4 (TC184/SC4) is concerned with the development of International Standards for the digital representation of product data and manufacturing management data. This is the forum in which ISO 10303 (informally known as STEP: STandard for the Exchange of Product data) has been under development since 1984. The first release of the STEP standard[Int94] occurred in 1994. Earlier standards (for example IGES) were intended primarily for the exchange of pure geometric data between design systems, but STEP is intended to handle a much wider range of product-related data covering the entire life-cycle of a product.

ISO TC184/SC4 is also responsible for the development of ISO 13584 (Parts Library), a future standard for accessing libraries of standard part information for use by designers. Additionally, early work is in progress on a standard representation for manufacturing management data (MANDATE).

The development of STEP has been one of the largest efforts ever undertaken by ISO. Several hundred people from many different countries have been involved. The standard is being released in parts. Currently there are twelve of these, but many more are in preparation, dealing with specific product ranges (e.g. automotive, AEC, shipbuilding, electrical, ...) and different aspects of the product life-cycle (design, finite element analysis, process planning, ...).

The initial parts of STEP dealing with geometry transfer are two Application Protocols, AP201 (Explicit Draughting) and AP203 (Configuration Controlled Design). The first is concerned purely with 2D drawing information, while the second covers wireframe, surface and boundary representation solid models. The content of AP203 models is restricted to geometric and topological data, together with 'configuration' information relating to such matters as version control and release status.

STEP is designed to operate in the first instance as a 'neutral file' transfer mechanism. Each CAD system must be provided with a *preprocessor* and a *postprocessor*. Their functions are, respectively, to translate native data from the sending CAD system into the neutral STEP format, and to translate from the neutral format into the native format of the receiving system. This philosophy only requires the provision of $2n$ translators for exchange between any pair chosen from n systems, rather than $n(n-1)$ if 'direct' translators have to be written. As an alternative to file transmission, STEP information may be stored in a database, and a STEP Data Access Interface is being developed as part of the standard to allow the use of shared data access.

Many CAD vendors have developed or are developing STEP AP203 translators; some are already commercially available, while others are under test. Some third-party software vendors are also marketing STEP AP203 translators.

The currently released parts of the standard are

Part 1	Overview
Part 11	EXPRESS language (used in writing the standard)
Part 21	Physical file format
Part 31	Methodology and framework for conformance tools
Part 41	Fundamentals of product description and support
Part 42	Geometric and toplogical representations
Part 43	Representation specialisation
Part 44	Product structure configuration
Part 46	Visual presentation
Part 101	Application resources: draughting
AP (Application protocol) 201	Explicit draughting
AP (Application protocol) 203	Configuration-controlled design

The structure of the standard is fairly complex, but the lower numbers (100-series and below) define the infrastructure and a set of integrated resources. The actual data exchange standards are specified by the Application Protocols, and these are defined in terms of the lower-level resources. The EXPRESS language is an information modeling language, rather like a programming language, which is used for the formal definition of constructs in the exchange files.

Parts of the STEP standard still currently under development are freely available by anonymous ftp from the Solis information server at NIST (ftp.cme.nist.gov). Files which can be downloaded are in directory pub/step, listed under STEP Part numbers (e.g. part224).

A Generalised Segment Concept

Manfred Rosendahl[1], Roland Berling[2], Chun Du[3]

Introduction

The main issue of constraint-based geometric modeling is to use constraints to guarantee the consistenc of the geometric model. In purely algebraic modeling there are equations between the elements of the geometric model defined, which are solved to find the characteristic points of the model[LiGo82,LGL81,SeGo87]. Commercial CAD-systems using this approach are for instance I-DEAS Master Series from SDRC[ChSch90], I/EMS from Intergraph, Sigraph-Design developed by Siemens or Design-View from ComputerVision. To avoid iterations to solve the nonlinear equation systems in some cases algebraic methods can be used[BuPe93].

Another way is to use geometric reasoning mechanism in which the dimensions and geometric relationships are defined as either facts or rules [VSR92]. This can also be done in the form of Prolog clauses [Ald88, Arb88, ArWa91].

In some commercial system e.g. Pro/ENGINEER from Parametric Technology Corporation the method feature design is used.

In the RelCAD system a constructive approach to variational geometry is used,. to reduce the number of equations, which have to be solved. Another feature, which was introduced to the constraint based

[1] Institut für Informatik, Universität Koblenz, F.R.G.
[2] Institut für Informatik, Universität Koblenz, F.R.G.
[3] Navtel,North York Ontario, Canada

geometric modeling is the Segment-concept. In normal CAD-Systems collections of elements, called group, block or segment are either programmed or the parameters can only be insertion point, angle, size. In the RelCAD-System a segment is a collection of objects that not only logically belong together, but also have geometric/numerical relationships among each other. They can even have relationships to objects outside the segment and are thereby be dependent on them. Any object of a segment definition can be treated as a parameter, not only dimensions or points but also other items and even segments.

When creating a segment instance, actual parameters for the corresponding formal parameters of the segment definition are assigned and by inserting the actual parameters the segment instance can be computed. A segment instance is treated in RelCAD as a normal geometric object and can therefore also be an element of an other segment definition, since nested segments can easily be defined. In a CAD-model also access from outside to the local elements of a segment instance is needed. To realize this despite the fact, that in RelCAD the definition of a segment is only stored once, a replacement element is introduced, which holds the information to access a local element of a segment instance.

RelCAD Geometric modeling system

The RelCAD system was developed at the University of Koblenz as an application extension to the general 2D CAD-system VarioCAD, also developed there.

Each element of the geometric model is either an absolute one or defined by its relations to other geometric objects. So any changes in an object cause changes in all objects, which directly or indirectly depend on them. This is achieved because the dependencies built a directed acyclic graph (DAG). the method how to change an object, which is not a leaf in the graph, will be explained later.

The following objects are defined as absolute geometric and nongeometric objects:

Value (dimension)
   e.g. coordinate, length, distance, radius, angle but also nongeometric e.g. engineering values,
Point,

Line,
Circle,
Arc.

The relationships between the objects are typed according to these absolute object types. Only Arc is a subclass of Circle and can be used if a circle is required.

From these absolute classes, which have no relations the Constructive classes with relations are derived. The relations are defined in all directions e.g. a point can be derived from geometric elements and also geometric elements can be derived from points.

Some of the classes which are defined, with their corresponding absolute class:

- Value:
  Coordinate, Distance, Angle, Expression
- Point:
  Intersectionpoint, Tangentpoint, Centerpoint, Endpoint, Relativpoint
- Line:
  Tangential line, Perpendicular Line, Parallel Line, Axis parallel line
- Circle:
  Given by center and Radius, Tangential to 2 lines or circles and radius, Tangential to 3 lines or circles,
- Arcs:
  same arc circles

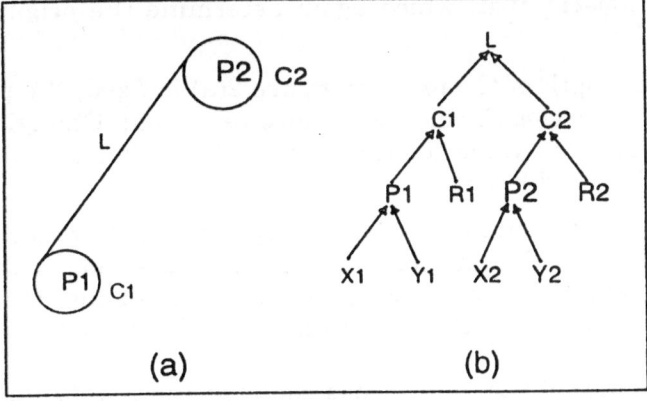

(a)   (b)

Figure 1

Figure 1 shows the definition of a derived element LINE_2O. This element has 2 support elements C1 and C2.

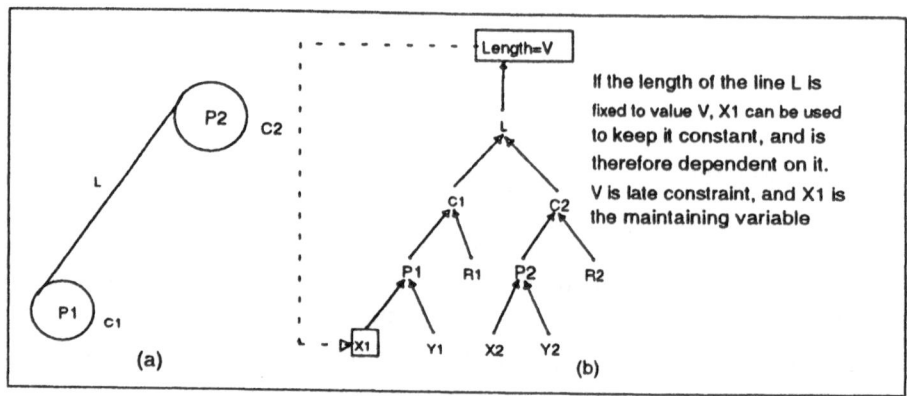

Figure 2

Up until now we have only discussed definitions with acyclic dependencies. There is also a class, which deals with cyclic dependencies. It is used to set extra dimensional restrictions on derived objects. For example, it could be used to fix the length of the line L in figure 2 This kind of constraint is called **late constraint,** because it is mostly assigned to the objects after they have been created. We call the derived object to which the late-constraint is assigned a **late-constrained-object**. A late constraint causes cyclic dependency among the geometric objects, because as an extra independent dimensional constraint it influences the original dimension of a late-constrained-object and thereby the support objects of it, which again determine the original dimension.

For example, if the length of the line L in figure 2(a) is fixed, the positions and radii of both circles $C1$ and $C2$ are also restricted. Changing of them leads to a irregular value for the length of the line L which does not agree with the fixed length.

Figure 2.(b) illustrates the situation of cyclic dependency. In order to maintain the consistency of the late constraint a free dimension which directly or indirectly supports the late-constrained-object should be selected as a maintaining variable. A maintaining variable of a late constraint has the following tasks:
1) When the value of the late constraint has changed the maintaining variable should also be changed so that one of the support objects of the late-constrained-object gets the new data which leads to a consistent late constraint.

2) When the support objects of the late-constrained-object have changed the maintaining variable should be changed so that the late constraint remains satisfied.

A dimension is no longer free if it is selected as the maintaining variable of a late constraint. Figure 2(b) shows an example where the coordinate X1 is selected to be the maintaining variable if the length of the line L is fixed to be the value V.

The evaluation of a late-constrained-object is more complicated then the evaluation of other geometric objects because of the cyclic dependency among the late-constrained object, its late-constraint, and the maintaining variable of the late-constraint. An iterative procedure is used to find an appropriate value for the maintaining variable to satisfy the late-constraint. More then one late constraint can exist in a model at the same time and some of them may be related to each other when the maintaining variable of one late constraint is the support object of another late-constrained-object. The related late constraints should be satisfied simultaneously, which means we have to solve a set of (non-linear) constraint equations, where the unknowns are the maintaining variables. For each geometric model there is one process to satisfy all late constraints (independent and related) by using Newton-Raphson iterative method. When evaluating a geometric model this process will not be run until all other objects of the model have been evaluated.

Because the late constraints are necessary only when the geometric model can not be constructed in sequential order any more and because they are assigned to the model after the main part of the model has been sequentially constructed, the number of the constraint equations which have to be solved simultaneously can be reduced by the user.

Late constraints are also used to change the data of conditioned objects, that means objects, which are not a leaf in the relation graph. If the user wants to change such an object, he has to choose, which independent objects(leaves) should be given free. Then a temporarily late constraint is solved to find a solution with the new values of the dependent objects.

Parametric design using segments

A family of design parts with various dimensions are often needed during the design. The concept segment serves this purpose.

About segments

The concept of the segment is similar to the concept of the *procedure* in high-level programming languages, *e.g.* Pascal. Therefore we introduce our segment by comparing it with the procedure concept concept.

The segment has two related aspects: segment scheme and segment instance. Segment scheme describes the inner structure of the segment. It determines what components the segment has, *e.g.* the number of the components, the type of each component and the relationships among the components. A segment instance is a graphical realisation of a segment schema. It is derived from the segment scheme and the actual parameters and is an appearance of the segment. Segment schemes correspond to *procedure declarations* and segment instances correspond to *procedure calls*.

In the following discussion we still use the word 'segment' when it is not necessary to differentiate the segment scheme from the segment instance. We say 'the components of the segment' when it is not necessary to know exactly how the components are defined within the segment scheme and the segment instance.

Another significant feature of the segment is that segment can also have parameters. Similar to the parameters of the *procedure* there are two different forms of parameters for the segment: formal parameters and actual parameters. The formal parameters exist in the segment scheme and determine the types and the sequences of the actual parameters. The actual parameters do not belong to the segment instance, but are used by the segment instances to determine the size, the variational shape and the position of the segment instance. The actual parameters define the relations of the segment to the rest of the model.

Each *procedure* can be called many times in a program. Similarly, a segment scheme can also be associated with many segment instances, which means that some segments may have different graphical representations. This can happen, when the data of the actual parameters are different for each segment instance with the same inner structure.

The class segment

The graphical representations of the segments are called 'segment instances' because they could be treated as the instances of the class 'segment scheme' from the point of view of the object-oriented methodology. In our approach we define these two concepts as separate classes and set up a connection between them.

Two new classes are defined. They are also called segment scheme and segment instance. A segment scheme contains
(a) a list of formal parameters, and
(b) a list of components.
The component objects are mostly related to each other and some of them have relationship with formal parameters.

A segment instance contains
(a) a list of actual parameters,
(b) a corresponding segment scheme
Segment scheme and segment instance are also treated as classes (or types) like the other classes. An instance of the segment scheme class is a concrete segment scheme with a definite number of geometric objects as components and a number of formal parameters of certain types. A concrete segment scheme does not appear in the geometric model. An instance of the segment instance class is the representation of a certain concrete segment scheme in the geometric model. Figure 3 shows the segment scheme class, segment instance class and their instances.

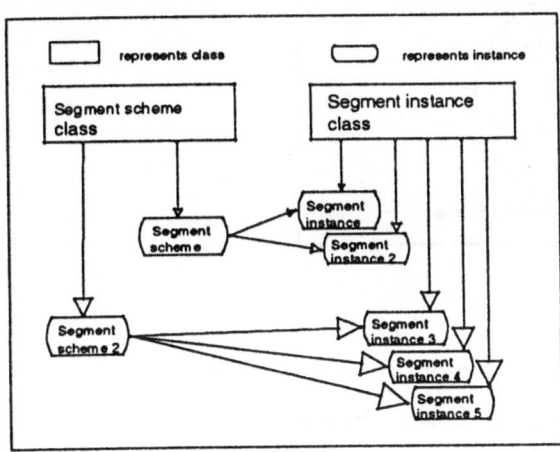

Figure 3

In the following discussion we call the instance of the segment scheme class **segment scheme** and the instance of the segment instance class **segment instance** when there is no misunderstanding.

The parameters of the segment

The formal parameters can be either
  (1) of any basic type, *e.g.* value, point, line, circle or arc.
  (2) of a segment instance.
Formal parameters are support objects of some component objects in a segment scheme. Therefore they determine the graphical data of these component objects.

An actual parameter must be of the same type with the corresponding formal parameter or a type derived from it, *i.e.* a object in the same absolute object-class. Therefore an actual parameter can be a derived object. Actual parameters do not belong to the segment instance. They are local geometric objects in the geometric model. If the formal parameter is a segment instance the actual parameter must be an instance of the same segment schema.

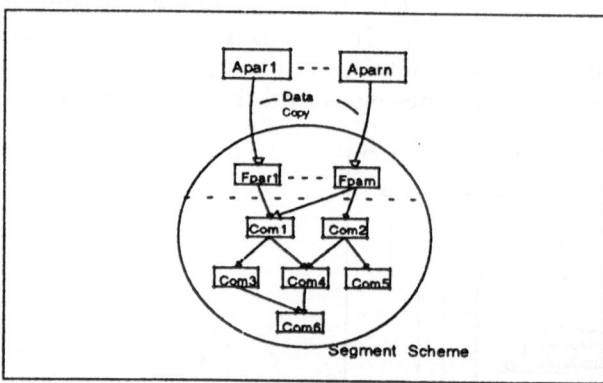

Figure 4

This is also the way compatible elements are defined.

Definition: 2 elements are compatible if they are either
  • Derived from the same absolute object class
  • Instances of the same object schema
The data of the actual parameters determine the size, the variational shape and the position of a segment instance through formal parameters. The computing process of a segment instance does the following operations:
(a) It copies the graphical data of the actual parameters into the formal parameters of the associated segment scheme;

(b) It runs all the computing processes of the component objects in the associated segment scheme to generate the graphical data for each component;

(c) It returns all the graphical data obtained in (b) to the segment instance.

Figure 4 shows the actual and formal parameters and the segment scheme. The arrows within the segment scheme illustrate the supporting relation of component objects.With different actual parameters variations on the segment scheme can be generated. When a segment instance uses local objects of a model as actual parameters it is fully embedded in the geometric model.

The external object of the segment

Although the component objects of the segment are geometrically related to each other it is still possible for them to access the objects outside the segment, which means that a component object of a segment has objects outside the segment as its support objects. Such 'outside' object is called **external object**.

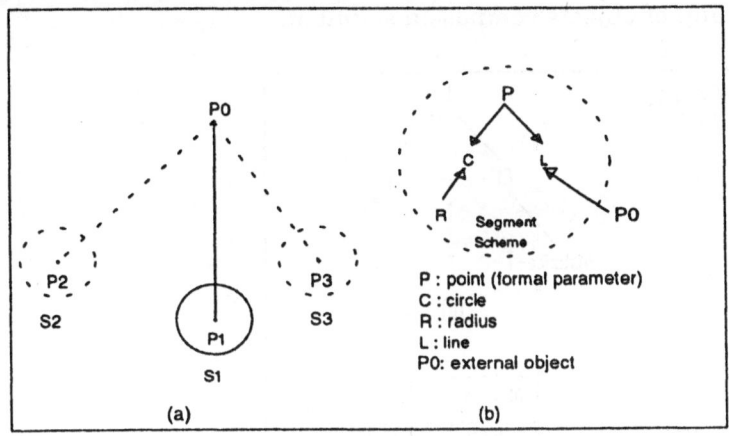

P : point (formal parameter)
C : circle
R : radius
L : line
PO: external object

(a)   (b)

Figure 5

Figure 5(a) shows an example, where *P0* is an external object of the segment instances *S1*, *S2* and *S3*. From the segment scheme shown in figure 5(b) we can see that *P0* is not the component object but is used to support a component object. *S1*, *S2* and *S3* are segment instances with the same segment scheme but different actual parameters *P1*, *P2* and *P3*.

The concept of the external object is similar to the concept of the global variables in a high-level programming language. The difference between external objects and actual parameters of the segment instance is that the external objects remain the same for each segment instance based on the same segment scheme, while actual parameters can be different objects of the same type.

Accessing component objects of a segment from outside

A segment instance exists as a single geometric object in the geometric model. This means that a component object of a segment can not appear as a real geometric object in the geometric model. Nevertheless it should be possible to access a component object of a segment from outside. For example, the user should be able to pick an object in the geometric model and use it as support object to create another object although the object he is picking might be a component object of a segment. This function is important because the user of the CAD system can see the graphical form of the single objects but has difficulty to recognize which group of objects compose a segment.

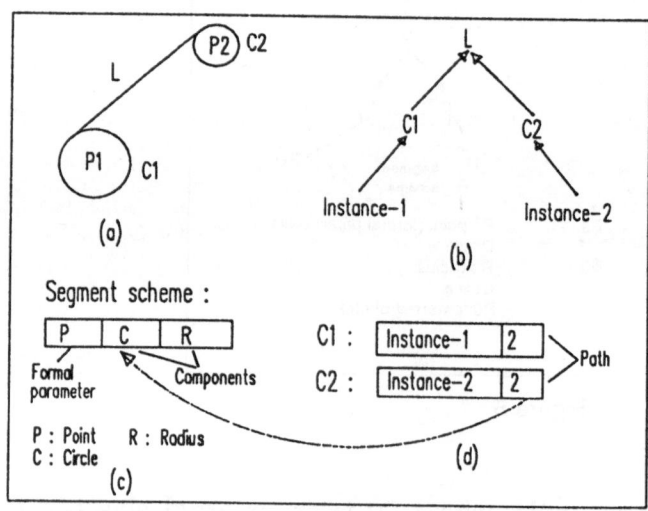

Figure 6

To make the accessing possible, five new classes are defined, which are called **substitute classes**. They belong to the five absolute-classes respectively. Each instance of these substitute classes contains a path to get the geometric values of the inside object of the segment instance. The first element in the path is the reference to segment instance in which the wanted component object appears. Then the position of this component object in segment scheme is stored. If the substituted object is a local element of a local segment the path goes further until the last element of the path. The process of getting geometric character finds the wanted component object by going along this path, gets its data and delivers the data to the substitute object.

An access to a component object of a segment is realized as an access to a substitute object of this component object. Figure 6 shows an example of substitute object where *C1* and *C2* are substitute objects of the circles in the segment instances *Instance-1* and *Instance-2* respectively.

Segments with Alternatives

Besides the parameters another concept used in programming languages is the concept of conditional statements. A conditional element can be introduced in the segment concept with the following class:

```
type condelement=object(tany)
    cond:valueptr;
    truepart:anyptr;
    falsepart:anyptr;
end;
```

Depending on cond the condelement results either in truepart^ or falsepart^. So far true- and falsepart could only contain one element. If they should contain more than one element a segment-instance had to be used. To simplify this, it is practical to define a grouping of elements too. This can be achieved by the following class:

```
type elementlist=object(tany)
    elements:reflistptr;
    function numberofelements:integer;
    function element(i:integer):anyptr;
end;
```

When defining a condelement it has to be insured, that there is no relation between the elements of the true part and the elements of the false part. Also it has to be defined, how a relation to the condelement from outside are invoked. It has to be insured that the invoked relation to the truepart and to the falsepart are compatible. If true- and falsepart have only one element these elements must be compatible. But in any other case, if one part has more than one element, the access has to be defined like the access to local elements of a segment was defined. This substitute element includes a path to truepart and a path to the falsepart. If there is no true- or no falsepart no relations from outside to the elements of a condelement may be defined. Otherwise under one condition this relation could not be evaluated.

Segments with Repetitions

The last concept of programming languages which was included in the RelCAD system was the concept of repetition. The definition of the class is

```
type loopelement=object(tany)
  kind:tloopkind;
  n:integer;
  first,second:anyptr;
  function element(i:integer):anyptr;
end;
```

The elements of then loop are numbered 0..n-1. Then a difference diff between first and second is computed. Depending on the value of kind the following elements of the loop are defined:

Type of loop(kind)	I th element
isforloop	first+i*diff
isuntilloop	first+i/((n-1)*diff)
iswhileloop	first+i/(n*diff)

A forloop is given by the first and second element. The difference is taken further to the other elements. A untilloop is defined by the first and the last elements. The elements between are defined though, such that the difference between the elements are equal. The whileloop is nearly the same, only second does not give the last element, but of that which would be the next one.

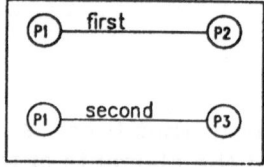

Figure 7

```
P2=polar(P1,r,0);
P3=polar(P1,r,360);
n-star:loopelement(iswhileloop,n,first,second);
```

E.g. in a 4-star the angles of the 4 lines would be: 0,90,180,270.

The last problem is to define the difference between 2 elements. From an element characteristic scalar values are derived and the difference between these scalar values define the difference of the 2 elements. The characteristic values according to the absolute type on an element are:

Type	Characteristic values
Value	Value
Point	Px, Py
Line	Length, Angle, P1x, P1y, P2x, P2y
Circle	Radius, Centerx, Centery
Arc	Radius, Centerx, Centery, Startangle, Endangle

For some derived types of elements additional characteristic values are needed. E.g. the angle of a polar point in the example above. So the difference between P1 and P2 in the example would be the angle-difference of 360. Because the n-star is defined as a whileloop the difference is divided by n

Conclusions

A system for constraint geometric design was explained. The characteristics different to other approaches are mainly the contained segments and the introduction of segments with alternatives and with repetitions.

References

[Ald88]   Aldefeld B, 'Variation of geometry's based on a geometric-reasoning method', CAD vol 20 no 3, pp 117-126, 1988.

[Arb88]   Arbab F, 'Examples of Geometric Reasoning in OAR', in Akman V, Hagen P.J.W.ten and Veerkamp P.J(Eds.) Intelligent CAD System II, Springer-Verlag, 1988, pp 32-57.

[ArWa91] Arbab F and Wang B 'A Geometric Constraint Management System in OAR' in Hagen P.J.W.ten and Veerkamp P.J(Eds.) Intelligent CAD System III,Springer-Verlag,1991,pp 205-231.

[BuPe93] Buchanan A. and Pennington A. 'Constraint Definition System: a Computer Algebra Based Approach to Solving Geometric-constraint Problems', CAD vol 25 no 12,pp 741-750, 1993.

[ChSch90] Chung J and Schussel M, 'Technical evaluation of variational and parametric design. Proceedings of ASME Conference in Engineering Conference, Boston, MA, 1990,pp 289-298.

[DRB93] Du C, Rosendahl M and Berling R, 'Variation of Geometry and Parametric Design', Proc. 3rd. international conference on CAD and computer graphics, Beijing, Aug. 23-26, 1993, pp 400-405,international academic publishers, 1993

[LGL81] Lin V C, Gossard D C and Light R A, 'Variational Geometry in CAD', Computer Graphics vol15, no3,1981,pp 171-177

[LiGo82] Light R and Gossard D, 'Modification of geometric models through variational geometry', CAD vol 14, no 4, 1982, pp 209-214.

[RBD92] Rosendahl M, Berling R, and Du C, 'Objektorientierte Implementierung eines relationalen CAD-Systems', Research report 4/92, University of Koblenz-Landau, 1992.

[RSV89] Roller D, Schonek F and Verroust A, 'Dimension-driven geometry in CAD: a survey' in Strasser W and Seidel H-P (Eds.) Theory and Practice of Geometric Modeling, Springer Verlag, 1989, pp 509-523.

[SeGo87] Serrano D and Gossard D, 'constraint Management in Conceptual Design' in Sriram D and Adey R A (Eds.) Knowledge Based Expert Systems in Engineering: Planning and Design. Computational Mechanics Publications, 1987.

[VSR92] Veroust,A Schonek,F, Roller,D, 'Rule oriented method for parametrized computer-aided designs, CAD, Vol.24, No.10, pp531-540.

A Hybrid Constraint Solver Using Exact and Iterative Geometric Constructions

Ching-yao Hsu and Beat D. Brüderlin[1]

We describe a geometric approach to constraint solving for Computer Aided Design. A graph representation based on the notion of degrees of freedom and valencies is introduced for geometric objects and geometric relationships. A hybrid constraint solver has been developed to find a solution from such a graph, in form of direct geometric constructions and iterative geometric constructions. The iterative construction method is an adaption of the multivariate secant method to the geometric nature of the problem. The approach combines the advantages of exact symbolic solutions with the universality of iterative numerical methods.

Introduction

Most modern Computer Aided Design systems provide some kind of design automation tool, often in form of a geometric design programming language which facilitates parametric modeling. Design automation tools improve the productivity of designers in creating new product designs, reuse previous designs, and exploring variations. Variational modeling goes one step beyond parametric modeling, by allowing the definition of two-way relationships (constraints) between the features of a geometric model. In this approach, usually a sketch is used as a first approximation of the shape of an object. While sketching, the designer only needs to concentrate on the approximate shape and the functionality of the design, and need not worry about the exact dimensions and details. Metric dimensions and relationships between the geometric features can be determined afterwards. A constraint solver is responsible for automatically

---

[1] Computer Science Department, University of Utah, USA

generating a solution satisfying all specifications, as well as for offering alternative solutions, when required.

An early implementation of constraint-based design, was the 'Sketchpad' system [Sut63]. Despite its promise and the many research efforts made in the past thirty years, since, constraint solving has remained a very difficult problem. There have been several different approaches developed, but there still isn't one that is general, efficient, and robust enough for commercial use.

Two major approaches, constructive methods and numerical methods have been used in constraint solving. Constructive methods [BFH+95, SB94, Bru93, Owe91, Rol91] solve the constraint problem in two phases, a planning phase, and an execution phase. In the planning phase a sequence of geometric constructions is determined, which is then carried out in the execution phase. Constructive methods are capable of handling simple cyclic dependencies and they can generate multiple solutions. However, they also sometimes fail in the case of more complex cyclic dependencies, even if a solution exists. On the other hand, numerical techniques such as Newton-Raphson iteration [LG82, SG86] are able to handle all cyclic dependencies, in principle. However, their convergence behavior is heavily dependent on a good initial guess, and there is no known theory to control this behavior. Consequently, the best approach may be to integrate the constructive approach and the iterative approach, in a way that combines the advantages of both methods.

A hybrid graph-based approach is developed in this section. The algorithm tries to satisfy the constraints by applying geometric constructions whenever possible. Iterative methods are used only when a cyclic dependence cannot be resolved by geometric construction operations. Instead of translating the geometric problem into algebraic equations (as it is necessary for the Newton-Raphson method and other numerical techniques) this approach remains in the geometric domain. The iterative part is a geometric version of the secant method [DS83].

Graph Representation

A *geometric model* in our approach is defined by a set of geometric objects $O = \{o_1, o_2, \ldots, o_n\}$ and the set of geometric relations (constraints) $C = \{c_1, c_2, \ldots, c_m\}$ between the elements of O.

Geometric objects such as points, lines, and circles listed in table 1 *own* degrees of freedom, which allow them to vary in shape, position, size, and

object type	degree of freedom
point	2
line	2
circle w. fixed radius	2
circle w. var. radius	3

Table 1: Object types and their degrees of freedom.

orientation. The set of degrees of freedom $DOF = \{dof_1, dof_2, \ldots, dof_l\}$ owned by the objects in O, represent different types of domains. Each domain, represents a set of allowable values. The cross product of these domains contains the possible states of the geometric model. The number of degrees of freedoms l is the dimension of the model (also called its total degree of freedom).

constraint type	arguments	valency
distance	pt, pt	1
incidence	pt, ln	1
incidence	pt, cl	1
angle	ln, ln	1
tangency	ln, cl	1
tangency	cl, cl	1
midpoint	pt, pt, pt	2

Table 2: Constraint types and their attributes.

Geometric constraints, such as those in table 2, define an n-ary geometric relation among a set of n objects, $c_i = c_i(o_{i_1}, o_{i_2}, \ldots, o_{i_n}, \lambda)$ where λ is the parameter of the constraint. Depending on the constraint type, the parameter may be a scalar, a vector, or empty. A constraint reduces the degree of freedom of the model by a certain number (called the *valency* of the constraint, as defined in [Ald88]).

We also introduce a special class of constraints, so-called *local (unary)* constraints, which *consume* all or part of the degrees of freedom owned by an object. For example, a constant x-coordinate constraint on a 2-D point fixes its x-coordinate in space (it consumes one degree of freedom owned by the point).

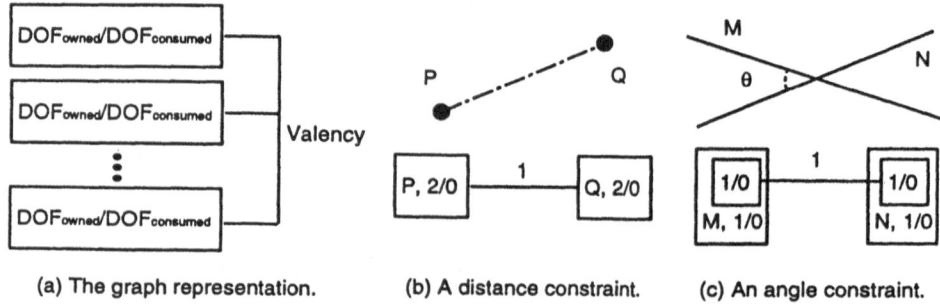

(a) The graph representation.   (b) A distance constraint.   (c) An angle constraint.

Figure 1: The nodes and arcs of a constraint network.

In the following, we will introduce constraint networks as the graph representation of geometric models. A *constraint network* is an undirected graph which consists of a finite set of nodes and arcs. A *node* in the network represents a geometric object, and is depicted as a rectangular box annotated with $DOF_{owned}/DOF_{consumed}$. An *arc* represents an n-ary relation and is therefore a general undirected arc with fan-out equal to n. We label the arc with the valency of the constraint, as shown in Figure 1. In the following, we will use the terms 'object' and 'node', as well we 'constraint' and 'arc' interchangeably.

Note that (depending on the representation) there are cases of constraints which only affect specific degrees of freedom of an object. For example, if a line is represented by one translational degree of freedom and one rotational degree of freedom, an angle constraint between two lines would only affect the rotational degree of freedom. We will therefore sometimes represent the different types of degrees of freedom in an object node by *sub-nodes* (depicted by small boxes inside the *master node*). The arcs representing the constraints may connect these small boxes directly as shown in Figure 1 (c). This type classification of degrees of freedom often helps in detecting degenerate cases of constraints (examples are described in [Hsu96]). In other cases, the degrees of freedom are affected indistinguishably (e.g the x-/y- coordinates of a point are both equally affected by a distance constraint in figure 1 (b)).

Hybrid Constraint Solver

First, we will introduce the concept of a *direct object constructor* to solve simple subgraphs which have closed form solutions. However, not in all cases can cyclic dependencies be broken by direct geometric constructions. In these cases, so-called *iterative constructors* are used. A *hybrid graph constructive algorithm* which combines these two types of constructors is developed for evaluating the constraint graphs and for finding a valid geometric model.

Direct Object Constructors

A *direct object constructor* is applied when there is a definitive way to construct a geometric object from other, already constructed objects. In other words, the geometric object becomes fully constrained with respect to its related objects. We explain the concept in terms of the nodes and arcs in the constraint graph.

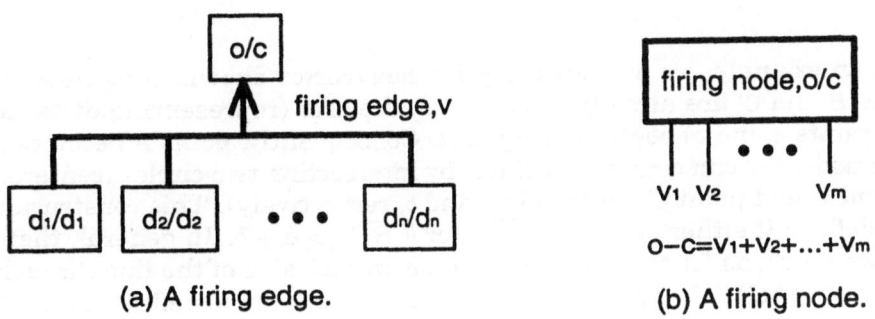

(a) A firing edge.   (b) A firing node.

Figure 2: Firing conditions for arcs and nodes.

When all but one node connected to an arc become fully constrained, the arc is ready to *fire*. A *firing arc* is depicted as a bold arc with an arrow pointing to the not yet fully constrained node, as show in figure 2 (a). Similarly, a *node* becomes ready to fire, when the sum of the valencies of the connected arcs that are ready to fire, is equal to the available degrees of freedom of the node ($DOF_{owned} - DOF_{consumed}$). We call this node a *firing node* (depicted as a bold-line box as show in figure 2 (b)).

Depending on the types of the the the firing arcs, different object constructors may be used to construct the firing node. Here, we use a geometric
method based on a combination of simple compass and ruler geometry,
vector analysis, geometric transformations, etc., to construct the object.
The notion of a geometric constructor may include the following functionality: Construction of general positions, construction of degenerate positions, and conditions indicating if the construction is defined for given parameters, and if so, the conditions specifying which of the several possible
solutions is chosen.

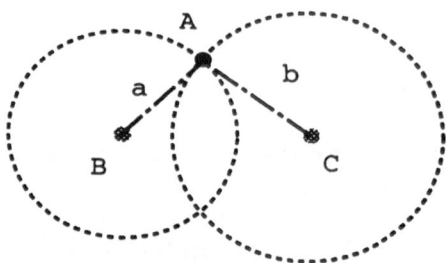

Figure 3: An object constructor for a point from distance constraints.

As an example, we discuss the point constructor shown in figure 3. If
points B and C are already constructed, the arcs (representing distance
constraints a and b) become firing arcs. Consequently, point A becomes a
firing node. We can construct point A by intersecting two circles (centered
at point B and point C, with radii a and b, respectively). This constructor
is undefined if either $|a - b| > \| \overline{BC} \|$ or $\| \overline{BC} \| > a + b$. In general, there
are two solutions for this constructor (one on each side of the line through
points B and C). The condition to select a solution can be defined by specifying the sign of $((A - B) \otimes (C - B)) \odot$ z-axis ($\otimes$ is the cross product, and
$\odot$ is the dot product for vectors)

If several constructors are involved in the construction of a geometric object, the number of valid solutions for a well-constrained problem
may grow exponentially with the number of geometric objects. To automatically generate a solution, the constraint solver can make the decision
based on the additional information extracted from the topological or geometric description of the sketch. This *root selection* process is similar to
the one discussed in [Fud95].

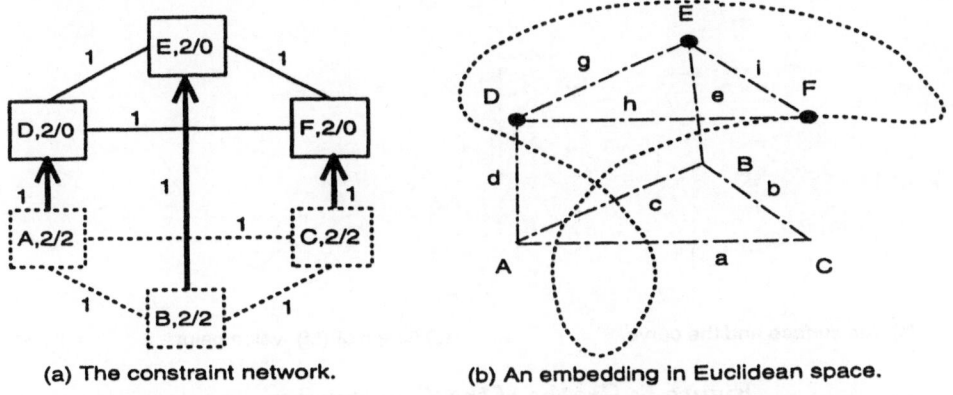

(a) The constraint network.   (b) An embedding in Euclidean space.

Figure 4: Constraint network with cyclic dependence.

Iterative Constructors

There are subgraphs with cyclic dependencies for which no sequence of firing arcs and nodes can be found to construct all nodes (an example is shown in figure 4). We assume, that points A, B and C are fixed. The arcs pointing to points D, E, and F are therefore firing arcs. Although the network is fully constrained, there is no firing node, and hence it cannot be satisfied further using direct object constructors alone. We will therefore introduce so-called iterative constructors.

An *iterative constructor* is a hybrid constructor which combines exact geometric constructors with a version of the secant method. (Please refer to [DS83] for information on the secant method used in numerical analysis.)

To visualize the method, we discuss figure 4 (b) (it is the same constraint network as shown in figure 4 (a) except that the distance constraint between points C and F has been removed temporarily). Therefore, the upper triangle DEF has one additional degree of freedom. We associate this degree of freedom with a parameter t. If we change the upper triangle continuously within its degree of freedom (observing consistent root selection for all direct object constructors) point $F = (x_F, y_F)$ will move along curve γ.

To reintroduce the distance constraint $d(C, F) = f$ we define the function $f(x_F, y_F) = (x_F - x_C)^2 + (y_F - y_C)^2 - f^2$ which represents the discrepancy between the constraint and the actual distance (shown as a 3-D surface, in figure 5 (a); the curve γ was mapped onto the surface). For each parameter value t, there is a corresponding f value. Figure 5 (b) graphs the (t, f)-value pairs. The parameter values t for which $f(t) = 0$ correspond

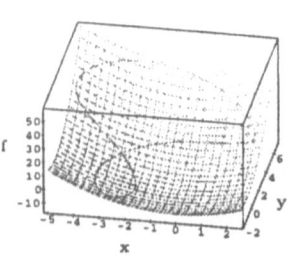

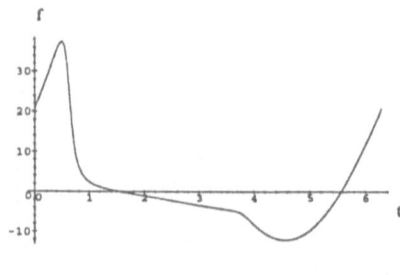

(a) The surface and the curve.   (b) Graph of (t,f)–value pairs.

Figure 5: Graphs of the f-constructor.

the points on curve γ that satisfy the constraint. It is therefore necessary, to find the roots of $f(t)$. In theory, the Newton-Raphson method could be used for that purpose. However, since the derivative of the function $f(t)$ is not explicitly available, we apply the secant method to find the roots of the function f, by iterating the geometric constructions of point F.

The *iterative constructor* (or i-constructor for short) is made up of three different kinds of constructors:

- t-constructor; it is used to construct a geometric object with one free degree of freedom. We will use the symbolic parameter t to represent the free degree of freedom (this is the same parameter used to parameterize the curve γ).

- o-constructor (or object constructor); it is an exact geometric constructor, as described above.

- f-constructor; used to measure the discrepancy between a defined constraint and the actual value.

These constructors are used in an i-constructor in a certain order, starting with a t-constructor, followed by a series of o-constructors, and ending with an f-constructor. To evaluate an i-constructor, we first choose two t values as initial guesses for the t-constructor. For each t value, all the o-constructors are evaluated in order. At last, the f-constructor is evaluated, yielding an f value for the t value. With two (t, f)-value pairs, we can linearly approximate the solution $f(t) = 0$ (*secant method*). In the iterative approach, the f-constructor is evaluated for the new value of t, and the secant method is repeated (each time with the last two (t, f)-value pairs) until a value for t is found, for which $f(t)$ is close enough to zero within a given tolerance. The choice of initial values for t is critical for achieving convergence at the desired solution. Often, the choice is an arbitrary value within the range of the parameter t. In an interactive situation, a value of t that is equal to the current value may be chosen (e.g. derived from a sketch) and usually leads to predictable solutions.

To illustrate the method, we discuss the example in figure 4 in more detail. The i-constructor to satisfy the constraint network consists of the following simpler constructors:

1. $t\_pt\_d(D, d)$: A t-constructor for point D with distance constraint d.

   Here, the locus of point D is the circle centered at point A with radius d. We express the circle in parametric form as follows:

   $$\begin{aligned} x_D &= x_A + d\cos(t) \\ y_D &= y_A + d\sin(t) \end{aligned}$$

   where the domain of t is from 0 to 2Π.

2. $o\_pt\_dd(E, g, e)$: An o-constructor for point E with distance constraints g and e.

   Point E can be constructed by intersecting two circles, with centers B and D, as described above.

3. $o\_pt\_dd(F, h, i)$: Construct Point F by intersecting two circles, with centers E and D. (Note that the result of the preceding o-constructor is used in this o-constructor.)

4. $f\_nl\_d(f)$: An f-constructor with distance constraint f.

   The constructor measures the discrepancy of the distance constraint f. That is,

   $$f(t) = \| \overline{CF(t)} \| - f$$

If we pick, for instance, $t_0 = 0.5$ and $t_1 = 0.6$ as arbitrary initial values for t, after 10 iterations, the error becomes less than 10^{-7} for $t = 1.570796327$ (see also figure 5(b)).

A critical issue in the evaluation of the i-constructor is the consistency of root selection. As we have mentioned before, there may be several solutions for each object constructor. If we do not make the choice of the roots in a consistent manner, the secant method may fail because the sample points are taken from different (t, f)-curves.

Another problem is that the evaluation of an o-constructor in an iterative constructor may not be defined for certain values of t. To handle this problem, we introduce a so called *error function* for each o-constructor which indicates if the constructor fails, and if so, provides a measure for the distance to a valid solution. For example, the error function δ for the circle-circle intersection $o\_pt\_dd(E, g, e)$ (above) can be defined as:

$$\delta(t) = \begin{cases} \| \overline{BD} \| - (e + g) & \text{if this value} > 0 \\ \| \overline{BD} \| - |e - g| & \text{if this value} < 0 \\ 0 & \text{otherwise} \end{cases}$$

Since this error function is defined everywhere in the domain, we can use the secant method to determine the values of t, for which the δ function becomes 0 (meaning the object can be constructed).

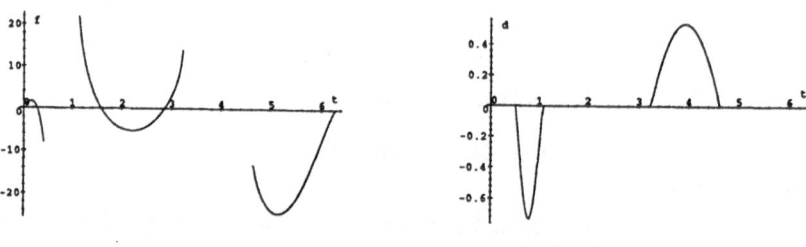

(a) Graph of (t,f)–value pairs.   (b) Graph of (t,d)–value pairs.

Figure 6: f-constructor and error function.

Figure 6 (a) shows a different plot of the (t, f)-value pairs for the same constraint graph as in figure 4 (b), however, with different values for the distances. The discontinuities indicate that the object constructor for point E is undefined for some values of t. Figure 6 (b) graphs the error function (the (t, δ)-value pairs) for that constructor. We observe that the non-zero regions of the (t, δ)-graph fill out the gaps in the (t, f)-graph.

To handle the undefined regions of the constructors, the evaluation of the i-constructor will be modified as follows: If one of the object constructors fails in an iteration step, we first find a zero for the error function of that constructor (using the secant method on that error function) until the evaluation of the object constructor succeeds again.

Table 3 shows an example for the convergence of such an i-constructor. In this example, we deliberately pick initial points for which the constructor $o\_pt\_dd(E, g, e)$ fails, e.g. $t_0 = 3.51$ and $t_1 = 3.50$. It takes only one iteration to find the zero of the function $\delta(t)$; t_2 and t_3 are the initial sample points for the function $f(t)$. It then takes seven more iterations to find a good approximation of a zero of function $f(t)$.

k	t	$f(t)$	$\delta(t)$
0	3.510000000	-	0.339264996
1	3.500000000	-	0.329652889
2	3.157044091	8.45449485	0.000000000
3	3.147044091	7.95166937	0.0
4	2.988904345	2.66215563	0.0
5	2.909314304	0.91466583	0.0
6	2.867655525	0.13327050	0.0
7	2.860550432	0.00767099	0.0
8	2.860116488	0.00006844	0.0
9	2.860112582	0.00000004	0.0
10	2.860112580	0.00000000	0.0

Table 3: The iteration steps (with error function).

Like the direct object constructors, the iterative constructors generally possess multiple solutions. However, root selection for iterative constructors is much more difficult to control. This could be a serious limitation for the iterative construction if we have iterative constructions nested inside one another. The reason is similar to the one given for direct object constructors used inside an iterative constructor. If we don't select the solutions of the constructions consistently, the sample points may be from different (t, f)-curves, and therefore represent a bogus secant. In the multivariate secant method the order of constructors will therefore be rearranged. Instead of letting the inside iterative construction converge for each sample point of the dependent, outer one, we only compute the first approximation of the inside construction to find two samples of the outside one, and let the two iterations converge simultaneously. Not only is this more robust, but it is also much more efficient. The total number of iterations necessary to approximate the solution to a bivariate secant problem within a given precision is often not much larger than it would be for the univariate secant method (using a sequential convergence the total number of steps would be roughly the product of the number of steps of the individual iterations). A detailed treatment of this subject can be found in [Hsu96].

Implementation

A prototype 2-D profile editor based on the hybrid geometric constraint solver has been implemented in C++. It is an interactive system with the graphical front-end realized with DI (version 1.5). The DI library [SSB92] is a portable graphical user interface toolkit. It provides 2-D gadgets and 3-D interactors and display functions, which are implemented as C++ classes in a portable way.

A model in the system is defined by a set of points, lines, and circles with fixed radii (listed in table 1), together with a repertoire of geometric constraints including distance, angle, incidence, and tangency between pairs of the geometric objects (listed in table 2). The points, lines and circles, can then be used as references for a profile consisting of line segments, and arcs.

The number of f-constructors in the system needs to be equal to the number of different types of constraints supported by the system. The number of t-constructors is equal to the total number of different types of constraints involving each object type. Both f-constructors, and t-constructors are relatively straight forward to implement. The number of o-constructors may vary with the particular implementation. The more o-constructors are available, the better the chance that the cyclical dependencies can be solved by a sequence of o-constructors. According to Galois theory, however, for any finite number of direct constructors we can always find situations that cannot be solved with a sequence of constructions of this set, and we need to resort to iterative constructors. The current implementation provides a total of 32 constructors. In addition to the basic circle and line intersection constructors, the system also provides higher level constructors to construct a line tangent to two circles, or to construct a circle with fixed radius, tangent to two lines, etc. The example in figure 7 shows three circles with fixed radius, and three lines. On the right side, each circle is tangent to three lines, and each line is tangent to three circles. This situation cannot be constructed by any sequence of constructions provided by the system. However, by relaxing one tangency condition (as shown on the left-hand side) the system may easily solve the problem with the available o-constructors, for instance, by first constructing the upper two circles in arbitrary position; then the three lines are constructed (each tangent to both circles), and at last, the third circle is constructed, tangent to two of the lines. There is one extra degree of freedom in this configuration (it may be represented by the distance between the upper two circles, as a parameter). By iterating the above construction over different values of the parameter, we may achieve tangency of the lower circle with the third line, as required.

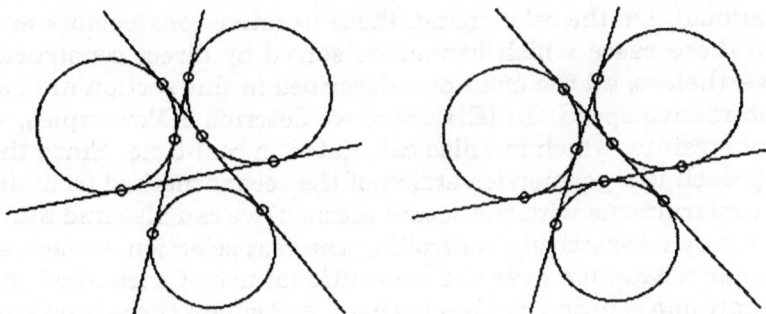

Figure 7: Two models consisting of points lines and circles.

The user interface of the system supports sketching and interactive constraint definitions. The system generates a unique solution based on the additional information extracted from the topological or geometric description of the sketch (e.g. which of four lines tangent to two circles is intended). An interactive mechanism similar to the one in [Fud95] is provided for the user to intervene, in case the system fails to deliver the desired solutions.

Conclusion

A new graph representation which is based on the notion of degrees of freedom and valencies, is introduced. A set of firing rules is applied to determine a corresponding geometric construction operation. The principles used here, are fundamental to a larger class of constraint problems. In [Hsu96, EHEB96] we have generalized the approach to solve problems involving two- and three-dimensional geometric constraints, in combination with algebraic equations between geometric dimensions (so called engineering equations).

Geometric constructions play the central role in the hybrid constraint solver, presented here. The direct geometric constructions are fast and can be applied to most common cases. We showed that the analysis phase can be done in time $O(n^2)$, where n is the number of objects in the constraint graph, and the evaluation time is linear in the number of objects, as long as only direct object constructions are involved [Hsu96].

The iterative geometric constructions make the evaluation roughly one order of magnitude slower than the exact constructions (due to the number of iterations). On the other hand, these iterative constructors enable us to solve those cases which cannot be solved by direct constructions alone. Nevertheless, all the examples described in this section are calculated at interactive speed. In [EHEB96] we describe 3D examples, with over 100 constraints, which are also calculated in real-time. Since the iterative approach is a geometric version of the secant method (combining geometric constructions with the secant method) we can also find alternative solutions by interactively controlling the root selection at each step. This is a clear advantage over the conventional use of numerical methods where only one solution can be obtained, and where there is no simple mechanism for the user to guide the constraint solver to another solution.

References

[Ald88]   B. Aldefeld. Variation of geometries based on a geometric-reasoning method. Computer Aided Design, 20(3):117–126, April 1988.

[BFH+95] W. Bouma, I. Fudos, C.M. Hoffmann, Jiazhen Cai, and Robert Paige. A geometric constraint solver. Computer Aided Design, 27(6):487–501, June 1995.

[Bru93]   B.D. Bruderlin. Using geometric rewrite rules for solving geometric problems symbolically. Theoretical Computer Science, 2(116):291–303, August 1993.

[DS83]   J.E. Dennis and Robert B. Schnabel. Numerical Methods for Unconstrained Optimization and Nonlinear Equations. Prentice Hall, 1983.

[EHEB96] L. Eggli, C. Hsu, G. Elber, and B. Bruderlin. Inferring 3d models from freehand sketches and constraints. Computer Aided Design, 1996.

[Fud95]   Ioannis Fudos. Constraint Solving For Computer Aided Design. PhD thesis, Computer Science Department, Purdue University, August 1995.

[Hsu96]   C. Hsu. Graph-Based Approach for Solving Constraint Problems. PhD thesis, Computer Science Department, University of Utah, May 1996.

[LG82]   Robert Light and David Gossard. Modification of geometric models through variational geometry. Computer Aided Design, 14(4):209–214, July 1982.

[Owe91]   J.C Owen. Algebraic solution for geometry from dimensional constraints. In Proceedings of the 1991 ACM/SIGGRAPH Symposium on Solid Modeling Foundations and CAD/CAM Applications, May 1991.

[Rol91]   D. Roller. An approach to computer-aided parametric design. Computer Aided Design, 23(5):385–391, June 1991.

[SB94]   L. Solano and P. Brunet. Constructive constraint-based model for parametric cad systems. Computer Aided Design, 26(8), 1994.

[SG86]   D. Serrano and D.C. Gossard. Combining mathematical models and geometric models in CAE systems. In Proc. ASME Computers in Eng. Conf., pages 277–284, Chicago, July 1986.

[SSB92]   M. Salem, S. Skowronski, and B. Brüderlin. DI Reference Manual. Technical Report UUCS-92-031, Computer Science Department, University of Utah, 1992.

[Sut63]   I. Sutherland. Sketchpad, a man-machine graphical communication system. PhD thesis, MIT, January 1963.

Chapter 6

Algorithmic Aspects

Overview

An Adaptive Algorithm to Compute the Medial Axis Transform of 2-D Polygonal Domains

R. Joan-Arinyo, L. Pérez-Vidal and E. Gargallo-Monllau[1]

An adaptive algorithm to compute the medial axis transform of 2D polygonal domains with arbitrary genus is presented. The algorithm is based on the refinement of a coarse medial axis transform by an adaptive subdivision of the domain. The algorithm yields the medial axis represented by a set of triangles of a predefined size and the closest boundary element. Examples of results are also presented to illustrate the method.

Introduction

The Medial Axis Transform (MAT) was introduced by Blum in [Blu67] as a means to describe shapes in biology and medicine. Currently the MAT is being used in a wide variety of fields like modelling growth, path planning, feature recognition, and finite element mesh generation. Since it provides a complete representation of a solid, attempts of using it as a representation scheme in solid modelling have been reported. For a recent and thorough review of work on MAT and related sets see [SPB95].

Lavender *et al.* [LBD+92], report an algorithm that exhibits some conceptual similarities with the method presented here. Their algorithm approximates Voronoi Diagrams of arbitrary set-theoretic solid models based on recursive subdivision of the object space using octrees. Goldak *et al.*, [GYKD91], and Sheehy *et al.*, [SAR95], have also proposed algorithms to compute the MAT based on domain Delaunay triangulations. The strategy applied in both papers is based on the classification of the cells resulting from partitioning the domain against the domain boundary.

---

[1] Departament de Llenguatges i Sistemes Informàtics. Universitat Politècnica de Catalunya. Barcelona.

A recursive algorithm to approximate the medial axis transform of 2D polygonal domains with arbitrary genus is presented. The algorithm has three main steps. First, a domain-compatible Delaunay triangulation of a set of points is computed. This set of points includes the set of vertices and a relatively sparse set of extra points generated on the boundary of the domain. In the second step, the edges of the triangulation that are interior to the polygonal domain are partitioned and labeled according to their closest boundary element. The computed set of labeled segments, which is a coarse MAT of the domain, is then adaptively refined. The algorithm is both conceptually simple and easy to implement.

Mathematical Fundamentals

This section gives some definitions and describes the properties of the medial axis that are important for the algorithm presented in the next section.

Medial Axis and Medial Axis Transform

Let us start by giving three basic definitions that are standard in the field, [Blu67, Wol92].

Definition The *medial axis* of a planar object is the locus of the centers of all maximal discs in the object, together with the limit points of this locus.

Definition The *radius function* of the medial axis of a domain is a continuous, real-valued function defined on the medial axis which value at each point is equal to the radius of the maximal disc centered in the point.

Definition The *Medial Axis Transform* (MAT) of a planar object is its medial axis along with its associated radius function.

From now on, we shall consider polygonal domains in a 2-D Euclidean space, with arbitrary genus, straight edges with no two adjacent, colliner edges in the boundary. In this context, the maximal discs that define the medial axis can be tangent only to edges and concave vertices in the boundary. Convex vertices represent limit points of the medial axis where the radius function is zero. The edges and concave vertices in the boundary will be called *active boundary elements*.

We classify the points in the medial axis according to the number of

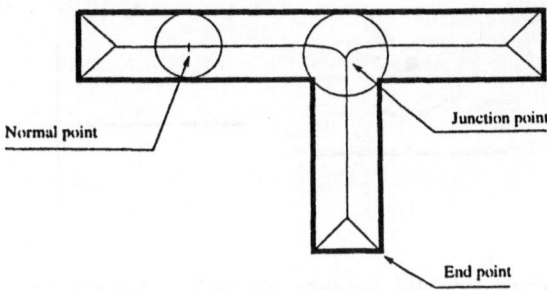

Fig. 1: Taxonomy of medial axis points.

active boundary elements which the maximal disc centered in the point is tangent to. The classification is as follows (see Fig. 1):

1. *Junction points* : The maximal disc is tangent to three or more active boundary elements. Several medial axis branches meet at a junction point.

2. *End points* : An end type point results when a medial axis branch runs into the domain boundary. These points are actually limit points of the medial axis where the radius function has zero value. In our context, these points are the convex vertices of the polygon.

3. *Normal points* : The maximal disc touches two different active boundary elements. Those points in the medial axis that are neither junction points nor end points are normal points.

Every connected subset of points of the medial axis limited by two points that are each of them either a joint point or an end point, defines a medial axis *branch*.

Voronoi Diagrams

Since all maximal discs centered in medial axis points, except for the end points, are tangent to two or more different boundary points, the junction and normal points on the medial axis are equidistant from two or more active elements on the domain boundary. This fact results in the existence of strong relations between the medial axis and point sets with some equidistance function defined on them. Among all these point sets, we are interested here in the Voronoi diagram, [Aur91, PS85]

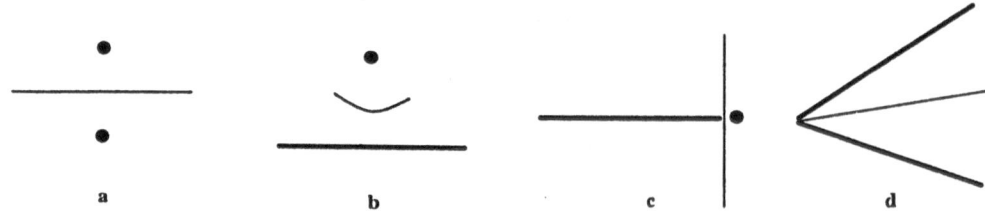

Fig. 2: Generalized Voronoi diagrams of points and open, straight edges.

Definition Consider a collection of sets $\{s_i\}$ in 2-D Euclidean space. The *Voronoi polygon* associated with s_i, denoted by $V(s_i)$, is the locus of points closer to s_i than to any other set. The *Voronoi diagram* of the collection, denoted as $Vor(\{s_i\})$, is the locus of points in the space belonging to two or more Voronoi polygons. The vertices of the Voronoi diagram are called *Voronoi vertices* and its line segments are *Voronoi edges*.

This definition is a generalization of the usual definition where each set s_i is an isolated point, [Kir79, PS85]. See Aurenhammer, [Aur91], for a survey of the Voronoi diagrams.

Since we focus on polygonal objects, it is convenient for our pourposes to consider that sets $\{s_i\}$ are made from points and open, straight segments, [Kir79]. They will represent respectively concave vertices and open, straight edges in the polygonal boundary. In this context, the generalized Voronoi diagrams associated with every possible pair of active boundary elements are (see Fig. 2),

1. *Point-point* pair: straight bisector of the segment defined by the pair of points. Fig. 2a.

2. *Segment-point exterior to the segment* pair: arc of the parabola defined by the point and the segment. Fig. 2b.

3. *Segment-endpoint of the segment* pair: perpendicular to the segment through the segment endpoint. Fig. 2c.

4. *Segment-segment* pair meeting at a convex angle: straight bisector of the convex angle. Fig. 2d.

We close this section with two definitions that will be used in our algorithm. Fig. 3 illustrates the definitions.

Definition Let e be an edge of a polygonal domain boundary. Let $V(e)$ be its Voronoi polygon and let (ve_i, ve_j) be the pair of edges in $V(e)$ through the endpoints of e. The *influence region* of e is the set of points bounded by edge e and the two halflines supporting the Voronoi edges (ve_i, ve_j).

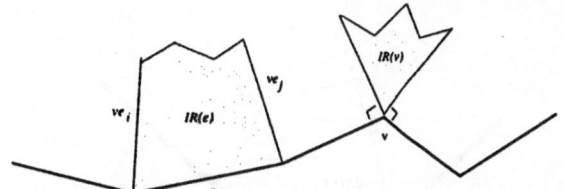

Fig. 3: Influence regions of active boundary elements.

Definition Let v be a concave vertex on a polygonal domain boundary. Let $V(v)$ be its Voronoi polygon and let (ve_i, ve_j) be the pair of edges in $V(v)$ incident to the vertex v. The *influence region* of v is the set of points bounded by the two halflines supporting the Voronoi edges (ve_i, ve_j).

We shall denote by $IR(b)$ the influence region of the active boundary element b.

The Algorithm

The algorithm we propose here is capable of determining the MAT of arbitrary 2-D polygonal domains. The algorithm has three major parts: 1) Triangulation of the domain, 2) Labeling of the triangulation edges that are inside the domain, and 3) Adaptive refinement of the labeling resulting from step 2.

Domain Triangulation

The algorithm starts with the computation of a domain-compatible Delaunay triangulation, that is, a Delaunay triangulation that covers exactly the polygonal domain and such that the domain boundary is a subgraph of the Delaunay triangulation.

The set of points to be triangulated is formed by all the vertices in the domain boundary and a relatively sparse set of extra points generated on the boundary. The question of how many points have to be placed on the domain boundary in order to force it to be a subgraph of the Delaunay triangulation is still open, [Aur91]. In our experiments we have placed on each domain boundary edge two addicionals points each point colser to each edge endpoint. The resulting set of points is then triangulated using

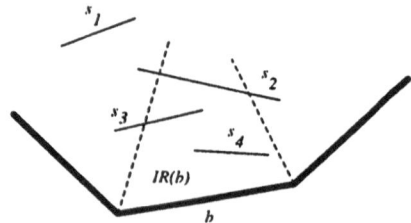

Fig. 4: Splitting by Voronoi edges. Only that part of the segment inside $IR(b)$ need to be considered.

a convenient method; we used the implementation reported in [Vig95] of the De Floriani and Puppo method, [FP92] In the sequel we will call *interior edges* those edges in the domain compatible triangulation that do not belong to the domain boundary.

Labeling interior edges

Those edges of the compatible domain triangulation that are interior, are partitioned and labeled according to their closest active element in the domain boundary. This is achieved by classifying every interior edge with respect to the influence region of every active domain boundary element.

Assume that a given segment s, belonging to one interior edge, has already been labeled with a closest active boundary element and that we want to update its labeling with respect to the active boundary element b. We start by classifying segment s with respect to $IR(b)$. See Fig. 4.

If $s \cap IR(b) = \emptyset$ then we are done. Otherwise two different situations can arise. First case: Assume that $s \subset IR(b)$. If the whole segment s is closer to b than to the previous label, b is the new label of s. If only a part of s is closest to b, segment s is split and labeled according to the Voronoi diagram (bisector) of the pair of active elements formed from b and the current label of s. See Fig. 5. Second case: If s is not a subset of $IR(b)$ but their intersection is not empty, segment s is split by the Voronoi edges of $IR(b)$ into a list with a maximum of three segments with only one of them being inside $IR(b)$. Then the process above applies to the segment interior to $IR(b)$. Now edges in the triangulation can be labeled by traversing the triangulation and running the process above for each interior edge.

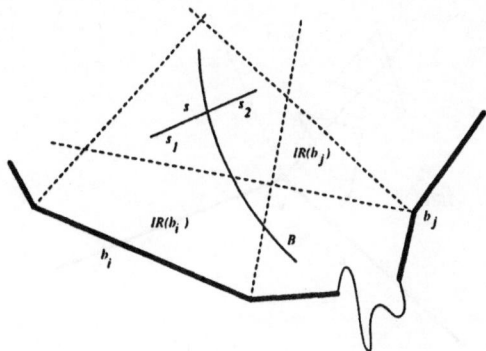

Fig. 5: Splitting by B, the bisector of b_i and b_j. Segment s is inside $IR(b_j)$ but only subsegment s_2 is closer to b_j than to the current label, b_i.

Adaptive Refinement

Note that the interior edges in the triangulation along with their labeling define a coarse Voronoi diagram of the polygonal domain. This coarse Voronoi diagram can be refined by subdividing adaptively the triangulation. Since the procedure is recursive we begin with the recursion. Then starting the recursion from the coarse Voronoi diagram will be clear.

Let the triangle t, defined by points (p_1, p_2, p_3) in Fig. 6, be a triangle of the Delaunay triangulation. Split triangle t into triangles t_1, t_2, t_3 and t_4 such that their vertices lie on the edges of triangle t and label each vertex according to the closest boundary element of the edge segment of triangle t where it lies.

It is easy to see that triangle t_i is crossed by a Voronoi edge if and

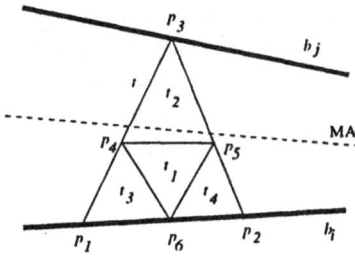

Fig. 6: Triangles crossed by Voronoi edges.

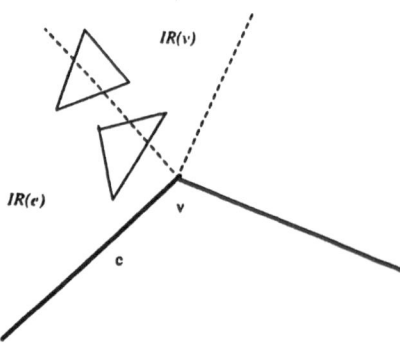

Fig. 7: Triangles crossed only by one Voronoi edge associated with a reflex vertex in the domain boundary.

only if at least two of its vertices have a different labeling. Then the algorithm has to traverse the triangulation and recursively subdivide all those triangles for which the Voronoi edge crossing condition holds, and label their vertices. The recursion stops when no branch of the Voronoi diagram crosses the triangle or when a triangle with a predefined size is reached.

Indeed the algorithm above will compute the Voronoi diagram. But given the Voronoi diagram of a domain, the MAT can be computed by pruning the Voronoi edges defined by a segment–endpoint of the segment pair (See Fig. 2); that is, by pruning the Voronoi edges associated with every reflex vertex in the domain boundary. These Voronoi edges can be easely pruned on-the-fly. Let $\{e, v\}$ be a segment–endpoint of the segment pair. Note that the vertices of the triangles crossed only by the Voronoi edge associated with the pair $\{e, v\}$ are either in $IR(e)$ or in $IR(v)$. See Fig. 7. Then, these Voronoi edges are pruned just by stopping the recursion each time a triangle holding this property is found.

Several strategies to subdivide a triangle can be devised. The strategy currently applied splits each triangle into four triangles each of them defined by one vertex of the initial triangle and the two midpoints of the edges sharing that vertex. Labeling the sides of the triangles resulting from the subdivision is easely performed; sides can be labeled just taking into account the closest active boundary elements to the edge segments where they lay on.

Examples

Fig. 8 shows a simple E-shaped polygonal domain and a compatible Delaunay triangulation. Fig. 9 shows the partition of the internal edges of the

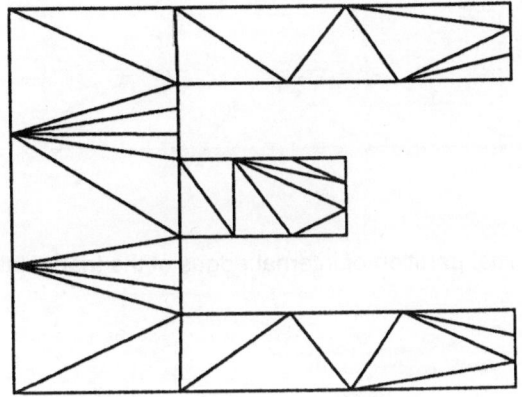

Fig. 8: Domain boundary and compatible Delaunay triangulation.

triangulation in Fig. 8. This partition is the initial MAT. Pseudo code of the algorithm to compute the initial MAT is given in Appendix A. Fig. 10 shows the MAT after a few refinement steps performed by the refinement algorithm given in Appendix B. Finally, Fig. 11 shows the refined MAT resulting from the subdivision process for a given minimum size of the triangles.

A polygonal domain with holes and complex shape, and the results generated by the algorithm are shown in Fig. 12 to 14.

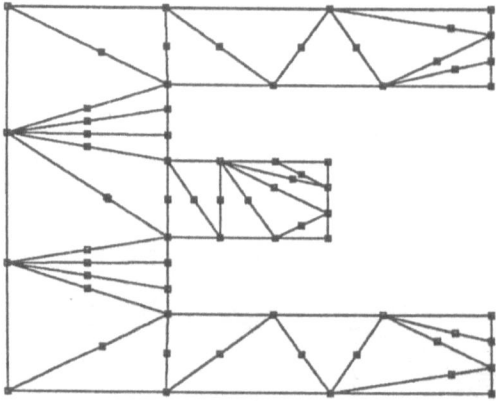

Fig. 9: Initial partition of internal edges of the triangulation.

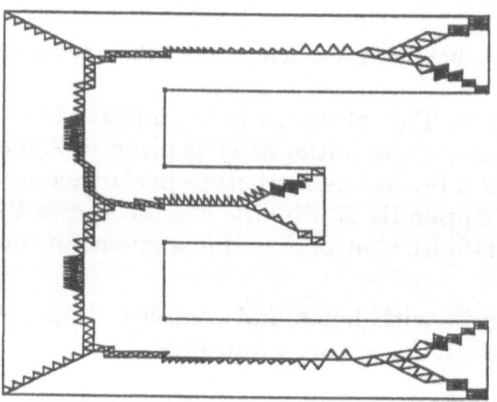

Fig. 10: MAT at an intermediate step.

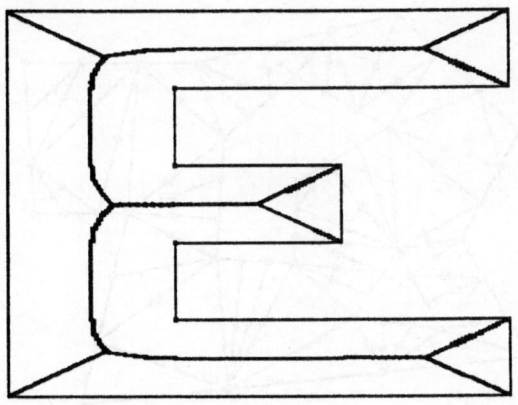

Fig. 11: Refined MAT.

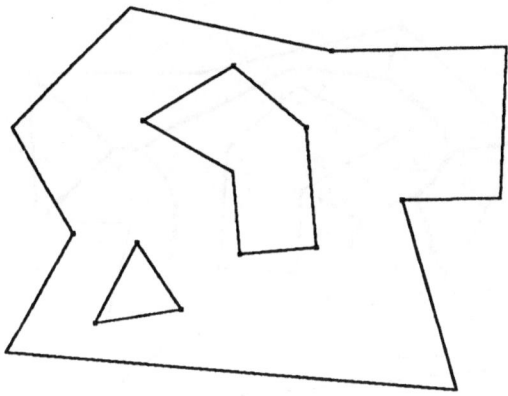

Fig. 12: Complex shape. Domain boundary.

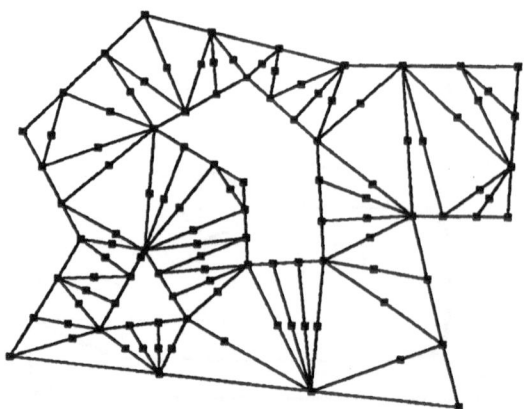

Fig. 13: Complex shape. Compatible Delaunay triangulation and initial partition of internal edges.

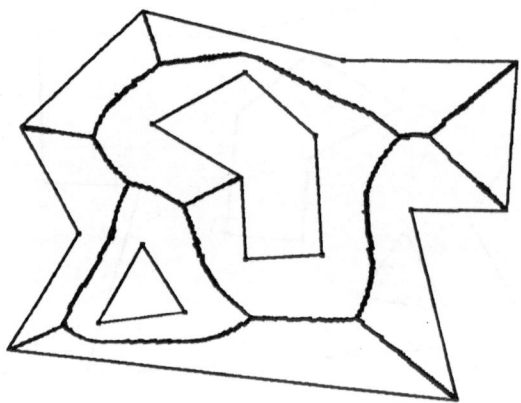

Fig. 14: Complex shape. Refined MAT.

Conclusions

An algorithm to compute the MAT of polygonal domains in a 2-D Euclidean space has been introduced. The algorithm is based on the refinement of an initial coarse MAT by subdividing the domain adaptively. The resulting algorithm is conceptually simple and easy to implement.

The same general ideas presented in this work would lead to an algorithm for computing the MAT of polyhedra in 3-D where the Delaunay triangulation compatible with the domain boundary is replaced by the equivalent domain tetrahedrization in 3-D.

Acknowledgements

R. Joan-Arinyo was partially supported by a CIRIT fellowship of the Government of Catalonia under grant 1995BEAI400071.

References

[Aur91]   F. Aurenhammer. Voronoi diagrams – a survey of fundamental geometric data structure. *ACM Computing Surveys*, 23(3):345–405, September 1991.

[Blu67]   H. Blum. A transformation for extracting new descriptors of shape. In W. Whaten-Dunn, editor, *Models for the Perception of Speech and Visual Form*, pages 362–380. MIT Press, Cambridge, MA, 1967.

[FP92]   L. De Floriani and E. Puppo. An on-line algorithm for constrained Delaunay triangulation. *CVGIP: Graphical Models and Image Processing*, 54(3):290–300, July 1992.

[GYKD91] J. A. Goldak, X. YU, A. Knight, and L. Dong. Constructing discrete medial axis of 3D objects. *Int. Journal of Computational Geometry and Applications*, 1(3):327–339, 1991.

[Kir79]   D.G. Kirpatrick. Efficient computation of continuous skele-
           tons. In *Proocedings of the 20th Annual Symposium of Foun-
           dations of Computer Science*, pages 18–27, October 1979.

[LBD+92]   D. Lavender, A. Bowyer, J. Davenport, A. Wallis, and J. Wood-
           wark. Voronoi diagrams of set-theoretic solid models. *IEEE
           Computer Graphics and Applications*, 12(5):69–77, September
           1992.

[PS85]   F. Preparata and M. Shamos. *Computational Geometry*.
           Springer Verlag, New York, 1985.

[SAR95]   D.J. Sheehy, C.G. Amstrong, and D.J. Robinson. Computing
           the medial surface of a solid from a domain Delaunay trian-
           gulation. In *Proc. ACM Symp. Solid Modeling Found. and
           CAD/CAM Applic.*, pages 210–212, Salt lake City, UT, 1995.

[SPB95]   E.C. Sherbrooke, N.M. Patrikalakis, and E. Brisson. Com-
           putation of the medial axis transform of 3-D polyhedra. In
           C.M. Hoffmann and J. Rossignac, editors, *Third Symposium
           on Solid Modeling and Applications*, pages 187–199, Salt Lake
           City, Utah, 17-19 May 1995. ACM Press.

[Vig95]   M. Vigo. An incremental algorithm to construct restricted
           Delaunay triangulations. Technical Report LSI-95-43-R, Uni-
           versitat Politècnica de Catalunya, Department LiSI, 1995.

[Wol92]   F.-E. Wolter. Cut locus and medial axis transform in global
           shape interrogation and representation. Memorandum 92-2,
           MIT Ocean Engineering Design Laboratory, January 1992.

Appendix A: Pseudo Code to Compute the Initial MAT

Assume that the boolean function OutRegion(s, b) returns true if segment s is totally outside $IR(b)$ and returns false otherwise. Similarly,
boolean function InRegion(s, b) returns true whenever s is totally inside $IR(b)$ and returns false otherwise.

```
      procedure UpdateSegmentLabel (t_segment       s,
                                     t_activeb        b,
                                     t_listofsegments l )
           l := EMPTY
```

```
    if not OutRegion (s, b) then
      if InRegion (s, b) then
        UpdateInRegionSegment (s, b, 1)
      else
        SplitSegment (s, b, 1, in)
        UpdateInRegionSegment (1.in, b, 1_aux)
        ReplaceSegmentByList (1, in, 1_aux)
      endif
    endif
  endprocedure

  procedure UpdateInRegionSegment (t_segment       s,
                                   t_activeb        b,
                                   t_listofsegments 1 )
    if TotallyCloserToB (s, b) then
      LabelSegment (s, b)
      AddSegment (1, s)
    else
      if PartiallyCloserToB (s, b) then
        BisectSegment (s, b, 1, in)
        LabelSegment (1.in, b)
      endif
    endif
  endprocedure
```

Now, interior edges can be partitioned and labeled according to their closest active boundary element as follows.

```
  procedure InitialMat ()
    FirstInteriorEdge (T, e, ok)
    while ok do
      LabelSegment (e, INFINITY)
      UpdateEdgeLabels (e, P)
      NextInteriorEdge (T, e, ok)
    endwhile
    CompactEdgesPartitioning ()
  endprocedure

  procedure UpdateEdgeLabels (t_segment e, t_polygon P)
    ListOfSegments := e
    FirstActiveBoundaryElement (P, b, ok)
    while ok do
      NewListOfSegments := EMPTY
      FirstSegment (ListOfSegments, s, ok1)
```

```
  while (ok1) do
    UpdateSegmentLabel (s, b, AuxList)
    NewListOfSegments := NewListOfSegements + AuxList
    NextSegment (ListOfSegments, s, ok1)
  endwhile
  ListOfSegments := NewListOfSegments
  NextActiveBoundaryElement (P, b, ok)
    endwhile
  endprocedure
```

Appendix B: Pseudo Code to Refine the Initial MAT

Let WhiteTriangle(t) be a boolean function that returns true whenever
the three vertices of triangle t have the same closest active boundary
element and false otherwise. Boolean function ConcaveVertexBranch(t)
returns true if and only if triangle t is crossed by one Voronoi edge corresponding to a segment-endpoint of a segment pair. Assume that the final
MAT will be stored in the static variable mat. The pseudo code for the
algorithm that refines the intial coarse MAT follows.

```
procedure MatRefinement (t_triangulation T)
  mat := EMPTY
  for each triangle t in T do
    RefineTriangle (t)
  endfor
endprocedure

procedure RefineTriangle (t_triangle t)
  if (WhiteTriangle (t) or
      ConcaveVertexBranch (t)) then return
  if (MinimumSize (t)) then
    AddTriangle (mat, t)
  else
    SubdivideTriangle (t, fourts)
    for each t in fourts do
      LabelSides (t)
      RefineTriangle (t)
    endfor
  endif
endprocedure
```

Tools for Mechanical Analysis and Simulation

Alejandro M. García-Alonso[1] and Luis M. Matey[2]

A broad range of CAD-CAE problems related to multibody systems can be simulated in real time with realistic feedback, i. e., simultaneously computing the motion of the parts and displaying them by means of 3D images. This has led to two new areas of research interest within the field of the interactive analysis of mechanisms and vehicles: taking advantage of computer networks, and solving geometric problems related to the motion of parts. Two network tools are described: a Computer Supported Cooperative Work environment for engineers and a Distributed Simulation prototype. New tools are needed to assist designers to solve some geometric problems related to mechanism design, assembly paths, and maintenance problems.

New trends for multibody mechanical CAD-CAE

Computer Graphics has played a key role in the last decade in most areas of computing, especially in CAD applications. It has changed the way in which computers are used. Two main achievements can be considered here: Graphical User Interfaces and interactive three dimensional visualization, also called Engineering Animation.

Currently we are witnessing the introduction of interactive analysis of multibody systems into mechanical CAD programs (see Figure 1). This event follows a decade of research work, which has been inspired by several factors, particularly the development of Computer Graphics.

---

[1] Universidad del País Vasco, San Sebastián, Spain
(research done while working at C.E.I.T.)
[2] C.E.I.T. , San sebastián, Spain

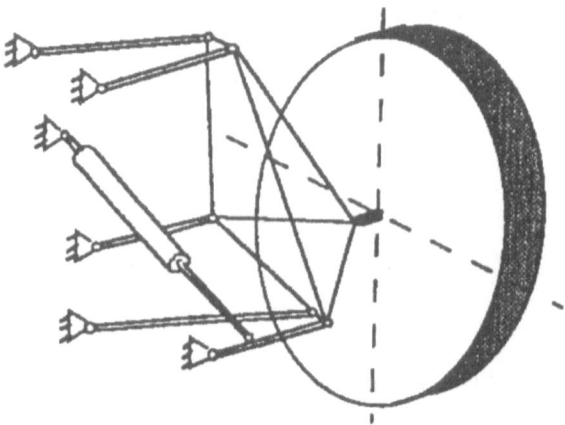

Fig. 1: Car suspension with 8 bodies, 12 linkages
among bodies and 3 degrees of freedom.

We can expect that two other research areas will play a leading role in the development of mechanical CAD in the coming years, although Computer Graphics will keep a leading position. Both networks and geometric relations among moving parts will emerge as significant areas of interest. The following facts show that this expectation may be correct and that it is possible that a new CAD era will be based on the research that is being made within these two areas.

A new revolution has just started, triggered by computer networking [Wri93]. **Networks**, like computer graphics, have been in use for a long time but there are two indicators that show they will be the key stone at the turn of the century:

- service providers and end users -both individuals and corporations- are very enthusiastic about international computer networks as the exponential growth of the internet shows [Lei94],
- broadband networks promise to provide the bandwidth required to support the large amounts of data that will be traveling along the networks [Wri93], like interactive TV [FKR95].

Moreover, CAD users in large corporations, as is the case of the aerospace industry, are very interested in the new tools and in the new ways to work offered by networks. Projects like Airbus or Ariane require that several companies must work together in the design, production, assembly and maintenance of large systems. Corporations that have offices or assembly plants in different places have also expressed their interest in getting the best from network based CAD tools. The same interest will appear in small industries that work in a close collaboration with their clients.

From the CAD research point of view, networking is an external technology. However, new network tools and capabilities affect how CAD software must be used and so designed, because they affect CAD developments in many different aspects: databases, data transfer, user interface, software structure, etc. On the other hand it can be seen bellow that **geometric relations among moving parts** follow traditional CAD research areas.

Most CAD research problems deal with geometrical relations: many constructive algorithms require the computation of intersections between surfaces; plotting has to solve the hidden line-surface problem; designs have to be checked to detect if there are objects that penetrate one another; robotics have to find free motion paths, etc. Here we will consider two problems that are fuelling research in the CAD area: geometric problems related to the motion of multibody systems (mechanisms, vehicles, etc.), and assembly and maintenance problems.

Collision detection among moving objects is a sub-area within the area of geometric interference among objects. It is a design problem that has been studied by several people [UOT83], [Mo Wi 88], [Dai89]. Special interest has been shown to integrate the tools that solve this problem with other tools that allow the real time analysis and visualisation of mechanisms [GSF 94]. Currently design engineers are interested in two new goals. In the first place it is necessary to improve interference algorithms because engineers need to use geometric descriptions that define shapes with a higher geometrical precision without increasing the time required to solve the collision detection problem. The second goal in seeking more than a simple answer of collision, yes or no (and where), tries to deliver a measure of the proximity among moving parts, which here onwards will be called the clearance problem.

Assembly and Maintenance problems have two approaches: an interactive check of possible problems, and automatic study of the current design. Nowadays interactive checking is becoming very popular due to the spread of 3-D interactive visualisation, stereo visualisation and virtual reality. However, it is out of our present scope to make a detailed comparison between both approaches. What we would like to stress is that both approaches to the A&M problem, and also the clearance algorithms, place an strong research demand on the area of geometric relations among moving parts.

Network tools and techniques

Computational mechanics for the analysis of vehicles and mechanisms has entered the communication networks. This event makes a broad set of new tools feasible, because now computers and people placed in different offices, urban areas or even countries can work together. For instance: mechanical analysis and mechanical simulation programs can distribute their tasks among different host computers; any user at any site can control a common analysis; engineers can show and discuss real time analysis and visualization with other people; remote operators can train together on a common environment, etc.

Among the new possibilities offered by networks, we shall consider two: computer supported cooperative work and distributed simulation.

A discussion of a particular analysis among several people is often needed. When all of them sit around the same monitor watching the motion of a vehicle or subsystem displayed with 3-D images, anyone can easily point out one problem and express an opinion that can be understood by the other colleagues. When engineers are scattered in their respective offices most of the existing mechanical analysis environments will make this sort of discussion unfeasible. **Computer supported cooperative work (CSCW)** techniques which help to overcome this problem, are based on computer networks.

A computer analysis can be carried out either by a large supercomputer or by a set of smaller computers that work concurrently using a network that connects them. **Distributed simulation** has a lot of appeal now that computers are everywhere.

COMPAMM (COMPuter Analysis of Machines and Mechanisms) [JAG90] has been used both to establish a CSCW environment for engineers and to test a Distributed Simulation prototype. These two network research activities are based in different environments. The CSCW is based on the use of the X window system within a LAN, whilst the distributed simulation prototype links several simulators connected to the European pilot ATM network. Data sent by means of the ATM network include: synchronization messages; analysis data shared by the simulators; and compressed video images or drawing commands that show the unique scene of where all the simulators work.

The CSCW prototype was built into ADAMS/Animation -a mechanical engineering visualization tool [Pot95]- and Distributed Simulation tests were carried out with DIVISAR -an experiment within ADONNIS (A Demonstration of New Networking Integrated Services)- [Ale95]. Both developments derive from COMPAMM object oriented classes and are currently used by both the automobile and the aerospace industries [GGS94].

Computer supported cooperative work

Currently there are some general purpose CSCW (computer supported cooperative work) tools. For instance, video-conferencing capabilities through the LAN that link workstations are becoming popular. Another CSCW tool allows copying of part of the screen onto a "blackboard". The blackboard is replicated on all the connected computers. While the users speak they can draw over the captured image. What one user draws appears in all the computers simultaneously, so it is easy to signal something or suggest a change.

However, these features are very limited in a dynamic environment like mechanical analysis. For this reason we have had to explore other alternatives.

Presently we are testing a new prototype for near real time kinematic and dynamic simulation with its own CSCW tool. In this version the user interface can be spread among several workstations. So users at different locations linked by a network can work on the same simulation. The control of any individual robot, mechanism, or vehicle can be assigned to any of the operators. Each operator can also receive as many 3D-windows as desired.

Any user is free to select how he or she wants to visualize the scene. However, it is possible that two users can choose to select the same camera. In that case any change in the camera ordered by either of them is presented to the other user. This feature is very useful when two users want to talk about a certain aspect of the analysis. All the users are active at the same time,so users do not switch between master and slave states, as most other systems require.

Figure 2 presents a simple example where two people operate on the same simulation. Each one has one 3D-window (full screen size) and the control for one of the robots.

The operative limitations are the computing power in the computer that hosts the program and, in simulations with many elements, network bandwidth. Another possible bottle-neck is the generation of views in 3D-windows, because the program must generate at least 5 frames per second to allow a good feedback in the camera control user interface.

Fig. 2: Two workstations placed in different rooms. Two
different users act over the same scene.

The views on the 3D-windows can be created by specialized 3D hardware that is used through software libraries that belong to a certain workstation vendor. They can also be created in the computer that hosts the program using Xlib functions which generate lines or polygons through the network in the remote 3D-windows. Provided homogeneous workstations are used the remote workstations should not create bottle necks. When there are heterogeneous workstations or Xlib graphics, the remote workstations actualy create bottle necks.

The network capabilities have been constructed as an overlay to the X window system and SGI GL (Silicon Graphics Inc. Graphic Language). The software has been built using C++.

Distributed simulation

ADONNIS, "A Demonstration Of New Networking Integrated Services", is an ESPRIT project that encompasses three types of experiments:

- tools which allow a collaborative design of a satellite, using the network to connect companies and allowing them to share the virtual mock-up of the satellite,
- interactive use of distant supercomputers where large numerical simulations are carried out,
- Distributed Simulation for Visualization of Space Activities in Near-Real Time (DIVISAR).

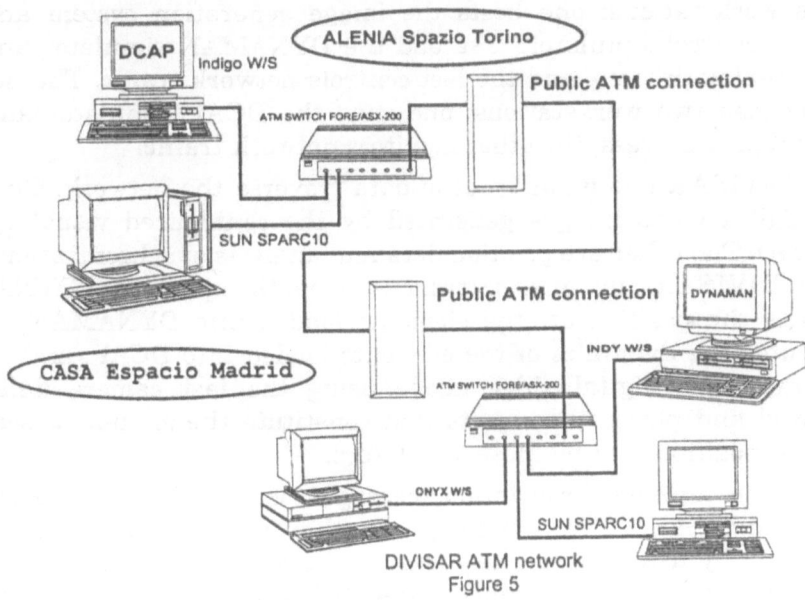

DIVISAR ATM network
Figure 5

Fig. 3: DIVISAR experimental network.

DIVISAR [GMS95] applies the high speed network to investigate the applicability of distributed simulation (different simulators controlling different actors) using a common high performing visual system able to compute the integrated scene and distribute the adequate video signals to each simulator. DIVISAR has been designed both for synchronous and asynchronous operation. Any pair of simulators can work synchronously. There is also a grasp operation mode.

Pre-existing software make the leaves of the global system: DCAP a collection of programs that model and analyze multibody rigid/flexible structures and associated control systems; DYNAMAN an interactive real time kinematic simulator specialized in ergonomical studies; and VISTA an animation and visualization software. This software has been developed by Alenia Spazio, CEIT and CASA respectively. Another software developed at Alenia, A-IPC, connects the leaves.

DIVISAR scheme applies to several mechanical analysis simulators connected among them. The initial experiments make use of two European ATM nodes, one in Madrid, the other one in Torino, which expand locally to connect five worksations (see Figure 3). In the node placed in Madrid an ATM switch provides communication amongst three workstations: one hosts the image generation system and the camera control simulator; a second the DYNAMAN simulator and one video replay process, and the last controls network traffic. The node in Torino has two workstations: one runs the DCAP simulator and one video replay process, the other monitors network traffic.

In DIVISAR two main types of data traverse the network. One type are digital video images generated by the centralized visual system (VISTA). The other are position data and analysis synchronization data. When DIVISAR runs in asynchronous mode: the operator of DYNAMAN controls the position of the elements loaded into DYNAMAN; DCAP computes the dynamics of the elements loaded into DCAP, and VISTA generates the digital video image using the last camera definition received and places the objects that constitute the simulated scene in the last position sent by those simulators.

Position and synchronization messages between the simulators are managed by A-IPC. We are doing tests that involve video images being sent directly using ATM cells, because there is a lot of data to be sent and sending ATM cells is much faster than using TCP-IP over the ATM network.

Geometric relations among moving parts

As has already been mentioned, computing efficiently geometric relations among moving parts is the key to solving new design problems associated with: mechanisms motion, assembly process, maintenance problems, etc.

Current CAD tools choose between two types of object descriptions in order to generate models with a high degree of accuracy: either trimmed parametric surfaces or models with a very large number of polygons.

We will study the characteristics and possible approaches to the clearance problem using polygonal models. Although, at CEIT, surface models are also been analyzed, results which compare both approaches are not yet available. The polygonal approach has been developed faster because it was supported by a contract with Mechanical Dynamics Inc. The tool built under that project, the **Clearance Module**, is being used in the design of car suspensions by Ford Motor Company and in the design of other vehicle and machinery elements (see Figure 4 and 5).

The starting point for Clearance was the knowledge gathered solving the collision problem among moving elements in real time in COMPAMM. The European Space Agency has made use of the collision detection tools in the DYNAMAN project. Other applications have also used the tool. The description: algorithms, characteristics and performance have been already published [GSF94].

Computing clearance data demands much more computing power than testing only for geometric interference. The end users wanted to use polygons to describe the geometry of the objects. Their argument for that decision was that the Clearance Module should support several CAD packages and that polygon descriptions have two advantages that parametric surfaces do not: all CAD systems can easily convert geometry to polygons and the interface between the CAD model and the Clearance Module requires very little human effort.

Another requirement made the problem even more difficult: the results should have a maximum error of 0.1 mm. This assertion has two consequences. In first place the polygonal description must be very detailed and it is not unusual that elements in the suspension of a car are described by tens of thousands of polygons. The second consequence affects the algorithms required to solve the problem. Since the error tolerance required by the application makes the use of approximations or pure hierarchical methods, like octrees [MMS89], unfeasible the software must always make use of polygons.

The algorithms developed by most people working in this area are restricted to convex objects [Bob89] [LiCa91]. Most mechanical objects have regions that have a great degree of convexity, so breaking down concave objects into convex ones is not possible. Published methods have two limitations: their scope of application are objects described by a few tens of polygons and they present a linear growth of the computing time as the function of the number of polygons. Linear growth can be enough for their applications, but not in the case now considered with objects three orders of magnitude more complex.

There are some key ideas that prove to be very practical. The first one is what can be called the current minimum distance. The program using frame coherence makes a guess and computes a value that is as small as possible but bigger than the minimum distance between the two objects considered. The program then loops in an effort to find the two nearest points of both objects. In each loop the current minimum distance is reduced and at the same time the 3-D volume and the polygons where the nearest points are searched for is reduced.

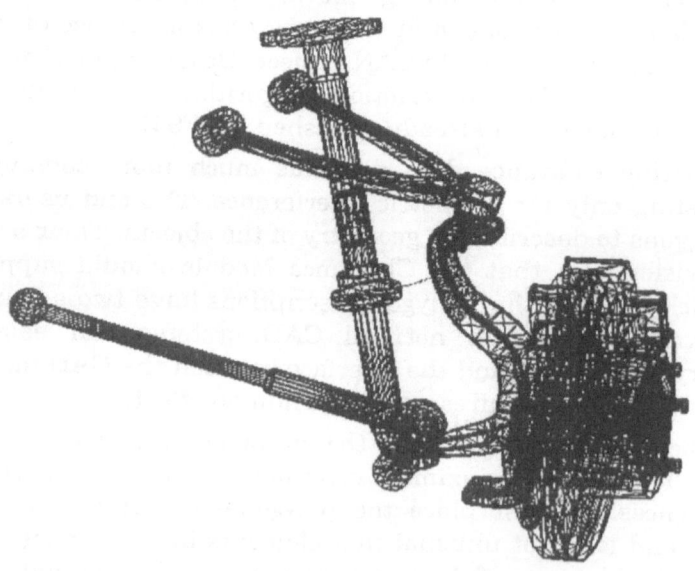

Fig. 4: Model of a car suspension

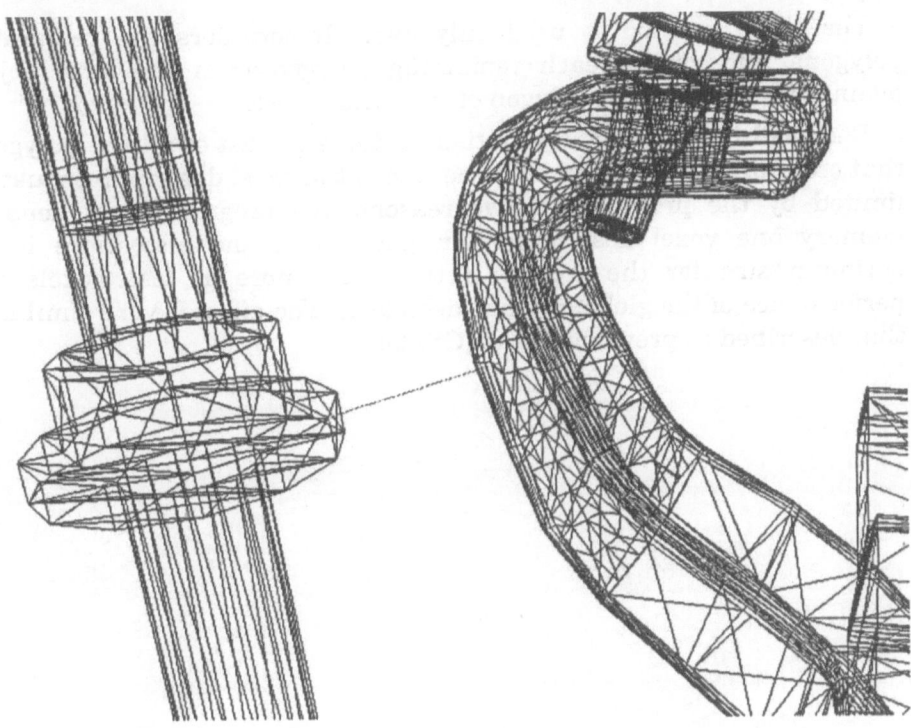

Fig. 5: Suspension detail. The two nearest points are
linked by a short line

The loop uses three types of search method. The first one consist of a matrix of voxels similar to the one described in a previous work [GSF94]. The matrix is computed only once when the program reads the description of the objects and is used at each motion step (frame) combined with the frame to frame coherence property. As a result the volume and the polygons that will be considered in the following loops is reduced.

The second search method is based on octree decomposition. This search method is used in several loops. In each loop the remaining volume is split following the octree method and part of the cells are discarded. As a consequence the number of polygons where the nearest points may be in is also reduced. We are currently testing different criteria that will be used to decide when the loop will stop the splitting process and will start the third search method. This octree has some similarities with that proposed by Brunet and Navazo [BrNa85] that also mixes volumetric information with boundary data.

The third method is used only once. It considers the remaining polygons and checks each remaining polygon from the first object against each remaining polygon of the third object.

Each cell in the voxel description contains the list of all the polygons that cross its volume. Note that the size of the voxel description must be limited by the program for two reasons: the program must keep in memory one voxel description for each object and also there is an optimum size for the voxels. If there are more or less voxels the performance of the global method decreases. The effect is very similar to that described in previous works [GSF94].

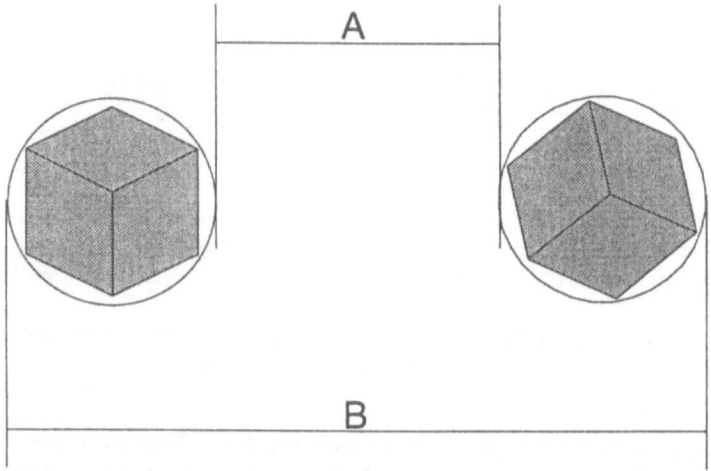

Fig. 6: Distance comparison criteria

Figure 6 shows the comparison criteria that is used to check if two cells from the voxels or the octree must be kept. If the value "A" is bigger than the current minimum value, then that pair of cells can be discarded, since they cannot contain the nearest points. If the value "B" is smaller than the current minimum value, "B" is taken as the new current minimum.

Many operations can be saved by taking into account that the center of each voxel is computed at each frame and stored and that A and B can be easily computed as the function of the center and the radius of the spheres. Computing square roots should also be avoided.

References

[Ale95]   Alenia Spazio S.p.A., ADONNIS Workshop, Torino, May 1996.

[Bob89]   J.E. Bobrow, "A Direct Minimization Approach for Obtaining the Distance between Convex Polyhedra", The Int. J. of Robotics Research, Vol. 8, No. 3, June 1989, pp 65-76.

[BrNa85] P. Brunet, I. Navazo, "Geometric Modelling Using Exact Octree Representation of Polyhedral Objects," Proc. EUROGRAPHICS 85, North Holland, 1985, pp. 159-169.

[Dai89]   F. Dai, "Collision-Free Motion of an Articulated Kinematic Chain in a Dynamic Environment," IEEE Comp. Graph. and App., Vol. 9, No. 1, 1989, pp 70-79.

[FKR95]   B. Furht, D. Kalra, A.A. Rodrigez, W.E. Wall, "Design Issues for Interactive Television Systems", Computer, Vol. 28, N. 5, May 1995, pp 25-39.

[GGS93]   J. García de Jalón, A. García-Alonso, N. Serrano, "Interactive Simulation of Complex Mechanical Systems", in G. Faconti, F. Serón, EG'93 State of the Art Reports, Barcelona 1993.

[GMS95]   V. Gómez-Molinero, J. Marczyk, L. Sarlo, M. Dumontel, A. García-Alonso, "Distributed Simulation for Visualization of Space Activities in Near-real-time (DIVISAR)", European Space Agency 3rd Workshop on "Simulators for European Space Programs", Noordwijk, The Netherlands, November 1995.

[GSF94]   A. García-Alonso, N. Serrano, J. Flaquer, "Real Time Geometric Interference Detection for Collision Problems", IEEE Computer Graphics and Applications, Vol. 14, No. 3, May 1994, pp 36-43.

[JAG90]   J. M. Jiménez, A. Avello, A. García-Alonso and J. García de Jalón, "COMPAMM - A Simple and Efficient Code for Kinematic and Dynamic Numerical Simulation of 3-D Multibody Systems with Realistic Graphics", in Multibody Systems Handbook, ed. by W. Schiehlen. Springer Verlag, 1990, pp 285-304.

[Lei94]   B.M. Leiner, "Internet Technology", Communications of the ACM, Vol. 37, N. 8, 1994, p 32.

[LiCa91]   Ming C. Lin, J. F. Canny, "A Fast Algorithm for Incremental Distance Calculation". IEEE Int. Conf. on Robotics and Automation, Sacramento CA 1991, CH2969-4/91/0000/1008-1014.

[MMS89]   F. Major, J. Malenfant, N.-F. Stewart, "Distance Between Objects represented by octrees Defined in Different Coordinate Systems", Computers & Graphics, Vol. 13, No. 4, 1989, pp497-503.

[MoWi88]   M. Moore, J. Wilhelms, "Collision Detection and Response for Computer Animation," ACM Comp. Graph., Vol. 22, No. 4, 1988, pp 289-298.

[Pot95]   C. D. Potter, "Animation for Engineers", Computer Graphics World, January 1995, pp 54-59.

[UOT83]   T. Uchiki, T. Ohashi, M. Tokoro, "Collision Detection in Motion Simulation," Com1p. & Graph., Vol. 7, No. 3-4, 1983, pp 285-293.

[Wri93]   D. Wright, "Broadband: Business Services, Technologies, and Strategic Impact", Artech House, London, 1993.

Construction Of The Constrained Delauna Triangulation Of A Polygonal Domain

Reinhard Klein [1]

A fast and easy to implement divide-and-conquer algorithm is presented for the construction of the Constrained Delaunay triangulation of a polygonal domain. The algorithm simplifies the complicated merging step inherent to divide-and-conquer algorithms for the computation of triangulations. Furthermore, no triangles are computed outside the valid region of the domain. A grid structure accelerates the computation of the visibility among vertices with respect to the boundary polygons as well as the computation of Constrained Delaunay triangles.

Introduction and previous work

This algorithm was motivated by the development of an adaptive triangulation algorithm for trimmed parametric surface patches [Kle94], [Ke95]. In the first step of this algorithm an initial Constrained Delaunay triangulation of the polygonal domain of the trimmed parametric surface has to be computed. Later on further vertices are inserted into this triangulation until the corresponding triangulation of the surface approximates the surface itself with sufficient precision. This is not the only application of the algorithm. Further examples are terrain modeling [DFP85], surface interpolation [Rip92] and finite element analysis [HL88].

Polygonal domains in two dimensions can also be considered as planar straight line graphs (PSLG). Many algorithms have been developed to compute the Constrained Delaunay triangulation of PSLGs. Lee and Lin [LL86] published in 1986 a divide-and-conquer algorithm based on a cutting theorem of Chazelle. They proofed a worst case time complexity for their algorithm of $O(nlogn)$ for polygons, where n is the number of vertices of the polygons. De Floriani and Puppo developed in 1988 an incremental algorithm with a worst case complexity $O(mn^2)$ for PSLGs, where m is the number of constrained edges and n is the number of vertices.

---

[1] Wilhelm-Schickard-Institut, GRIS, Universität Tübingen, Germany

In 1989 Chew [Che89] showed that using a divide-and-conquer algorithm the Constrained Delaunay triangulation of a PSLG can be computed in $O(n \log n)$ time. In 1993 Piegl and Richard [PR93] used a shelling technique and a uniform grid as acceleration structure to compute the Constrained Delaunay triangulation of polygonal domains. Excess triangles generated during the triangulation process contained in the convex hull of the polygonal domain but not in the domain itself are detected by a special labeling procedure and removed from the output.

Examples of algorithms specialized to compute the Constrained Delaunay triangulation of polygons are described in [AGSS89], [Cha91], [KKT90], [CTV89]. All these algorithms take advantage of the special structure of polygons and are therefore even more efficient than the algorithms described above, which also handle the general case of a PSLG.

The general idea of the algorithm presented here is also to exploit the special structure of polygonal domains. The computation of Constrained Delaunay triangles contained in the convex hull of the domain but not in the domain itself is avoided. Further a divide and conquer paradigma in combination with a uniform grid data structure accelerates the computation of Delaunay triangles and reduces the number of visibility tests between vertices as well as the number of tests to determine if an edge is contained in the domain or not. Instead of performing the test against all edges of the bounding polygons, the tests have to be performed only for the edges of the subpolygons due to the divide and conquer approach. The algorithm is very fast and easy to implement.

Basic definitions

Definition 1 (Planar domain) *A planar domain $\Omega \subset \mathbb{R}^2$ is defined by a set $B = \{b_0, \cdots, b_N\}$ of boundary polygons. The set B includes an exterior boundary b_0 and interior boundaries (holes) $b_1, \cdots b_N$. Each boundary b_i consists of a finite number (≥ 3) of oriented line segments, the* domain edges $e_{i0}, \cdots, e_{in_i}$ *and is defined by a set of* boundary nodes $V \supset V_i = \{v_{i0}, \cdots, v_{in_i}\}$. *Every boundary polygon b_i defines a region Ω_i. The interior of these regions $\overset{\circ}{\Omega}_i$ is located on the left side of the oriented boundary polygons. In order for Ω to be a well-defined finite domain, the following conditions must hold true (by $\mathsf{C}\,\overset{\circ}{\Omega}_i$ we denote the complement of $\overset{\circ}{\Omega}_i$):*

$$\mathsf{C}\,\overset{\circ}{\Omega}_i \subset \overset{\circ}{\Omega}_0, \ 1 \leq i \leq N,$$

$$\mathsf{C}\,\overset{\circ}{\Omega}_i \ \cap \ \mathsf{C}\,\overset{\circ}{\Omega}_j = \emptyset, \ 1 \leq i, j \leq N, \ i \neq j,$$

$$b_i \ \cap \ b_j \subset V, \ 0 \leq i, j \leq N, \ i \neq j.$$

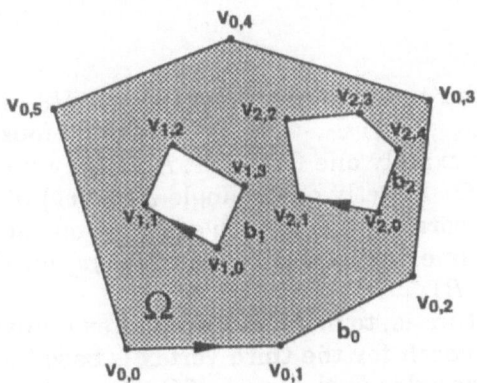

Figure 1: A simple planar domain Ω, described by the outer boundary b_0 and two inner boundaries b_1 and b_2. The edges of the boundaries are oriented in such a way, that the interior of the domain is located on their left.

Remark 2 *A planar domain is a planar straight line graph (PSLG) $G =$ (V, E), where V is the set of boundary vertices and E is the set of boundary edges.*

Definition 3 (Triangulation of a planar straight line graph) *For any PSLG $G = (V, E)$, a triangulation $T(G)$ of G is a PSLG $G' = (V, E')$, where $E \subset E'$, such that no edges can be added to E' without intersecting an existing edge $e \in E$.*

Definition 4 (Constrained Delaunay triangulation) *For any PSLG $G = (V, E)$ the Constrained Delaunay triangulation (CDT) of G, denoted by $CDT(G)$ is a triangulation $T(G) = (V, E')$, where $E \subset E'$, in which the circumcircle of each face or triangle $\Delta(v_i v_j v_k)$ denoted by $C(v_i, v_j, v_k)$ does not contain in its interior any other vertex of V which is visible from the vertices v_i, v_j, v_k of the triangle. The vertices u and v, $u, v \in V$ are visible from each other with respect to E if the line segment uv does not intersect an edge of E. The edges of the set $E' - E$ are called Delaunay edges.*

Definition 5 (Local Delaunay property) *Two triangles $\Delta(v_0, v_1, v_2)$ and $\Delta(v_1, v_3, v_2)$ adjacent along the nonconstrained edge (v_1, v_2) are locally Delaunay, iff the circumcircle $C(v_0, v_1, v_2)$ does not contain the vertex v_3. This is aquivalent to the condition that the circumcircle $C(v_1, v_2, v_3)$ does not contain the vertex v_0. If all pairs of adjacent triangles of a triangulation T are locally Delaunay, the triangulation is said to be locally Delaunay.*

Theorem 6 *A constrained triangulation $T(G)$ of a PSLG $G = (V, E)$ is a Constrained Delaunay triangulation if it is locally Delaunay.*

The algorithm

Given a planar domain Ω with border polygons $B = \{b_0, \cdots, b_N\}$ and vertices $V = \{v_{00}, \cdots, v_{0n_0}, \cdots, v_{N0}, \cdots v_{Nn_N}\}$, where no four vertices lie on a circle, then there is exactly one CDT $\mathcal{T}(V, B)$ of the inner of Ω. Look at this triangulation of Ω: Exactly one triangle $\Delta(v_i v_j v_k)$ of this triangulation in the inner of Ω corresponds to each edge $v_i v_j$ on the border. Therefore, there is exactly one vertex v_k to each edge $v_i v_j$ on the border such that $\Delta(v_i v_j v_k) \in \mathcal{T}(V, B)$.

The idea of the algorithm is, to find this third vertex for every edge on the boundary of Ω. The search for the third vertex is based on the following characterization of triangles in the inner of Ω.

Lemma 7 *Let Ω be a polygonal domain with border polygons $B = \{b_0, \cdots, b_N\}$ and vertices $V = \{v_{00}, \cdots, v_{0n_0}, \cdots, v_{N0}, \cdots v_{Nn_N}\}$ on the border and let $v_i v_j$ be an edge of some of the border polygons. Assume that no four vertices lie on a common circle. In this situation a triangle $\Delta(v_i, v_j, v_k) \subset \Omega$, $v_i, v_j, v_k \in V$ belongs to the Constrained Delaunay triangulation $\mathcal{T}(V, B)$ if and only if*

(i) $v_k \in V_{ij}$, where $V_{ij} := \{v \in V \mid v_i v \subset \Omega, \ v_j v \subset \Omega\}$,

(ii) $\overset{\circ}{C}(v_i, v_j, v_k) \cap V_{ij} = \emptyset$, i. e. in the inner of the circumcircle $\overset{\circ}{C}(v_i, v_j, v_k)$ there is no vertex $v_l \in V_{ij}$.

Remark: Let H^l_{ij} be the left halfspace defined by the edge $v_i v_j$. Then $V_{ij} = W_i \cap W_j \cap H^l_{ij}$, where W_i, W_j are the set of vertices $v \in V$ that are visible from v_i, v_j respectively with respect to the border B.

Proof: Let $\Delta(v_i, v_j, v_k) \in \mathcal{T}(B, V)$. We show the properties (i) and (ii). Because of $\Delta(v_i, v_j, v_k) \subset \Omega$ property (i) follows directly.

According to definition 4 we have $\overset{\circ}{C}(v_i, v_j, v_k) \cap W_i \cap W_j \cap W_k = \emptyset$. We show property (ii) by contradiction.

Suppose that $\overset{\circ}{C}(v_i, v_j, v_k) \cap V_{ij} = \overset{\circ}{C}(v_i, v_j, v_k) \cap W_i \cap W_j \cap H^l_{ij} \neq \emptyset$. Then there are vertices that either belong to one of the subsets C_α or C_β of $\overset{\circ}{C}(v_i, v_j, v_k)$, see figure 2. Let us suppose that the vertices belong to C_β. The other case can be handled similarly. Let $w \in V_{ij} \cap \overset{\circ}{C}_\beta$ be the vertex with smallest distance to the edge $v_i v_k$, that is $d(w, v_i v_k) \leq d(v, v_i v_k) \ \forall v \in V_{ij} \cap \overset{\circ}{C}_\beta$. Then w is visible from v_k w. r. t. B and therefore $W_i \cap W_j \cap W_k \cap \overset{\circ}{C}$. This is a contradiction to the assumption, that $\Delta(v_i, v_j, v_k) \in \mathcal{T}(V, B)$.

The other direction of the proof can be obtained as follows. From $v \in V_{ij}$ it follows that $\Delta(v_i, v_j, v_k) \in \Omega$. It remains to show that $\overset{\circ}{C}(v_i, v_j, v_k) \cap W_i \cap$

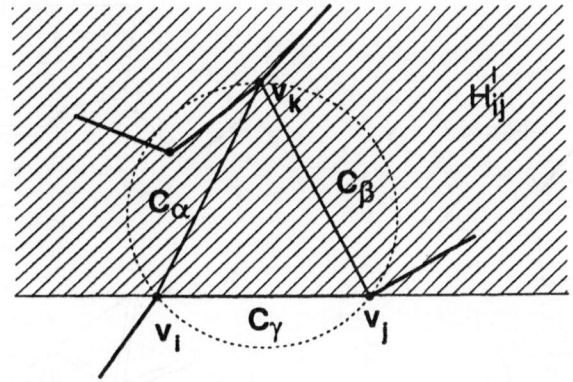

Figure 2: In triangle $\Delta(v_i, v_j, v_k)$ there are no vertices of V. Therefore, if there are vertices in the inner $\overset{\circ}{C}$ (v_i, v_j, v_k) of the circumcircle $C(v_i, v_j, v_k)$ on the left side of the oriented edge $v_i v_j$, these vertices belong either to C_α or to C_β.

$W_j \cap W_k = \emptyset$. Because of $\overset{\circ}{C}$ $(v_i, v_j, v_k) \cap V_{ij} = \emptyset$ all vertices belonging to $\overset{\circ}{C}$ $(v_i, v_j, v_k) \cap W_i \cap W_j \cap W_k$ must be contained in C_γ, see figure 2. But $C_\gamma \cap W_k = \emptyset$ and therefore, the assertion follows. ∎

Description of the algorithm

To describe the algorithm we suppose first, that the border of the domain consist of one single polygon P and discuss the general case later on.
The algorithm works recursively. While the polygon P contains more than three vertices, we choose an edge of P and search the corresponding third vertex with the properties (i) and (ii) of lemma 7.
According to the characterization of the lemma the triangle $\Delta(v_i, v_j, v_k)$ is a Constrained Delaunay triangle and subdivides the actual polygon P into two subpolygons P_1 and P_2. These subpolygons can be subdivided further independently.
In detail the following steps are performed:

1. Choose a starting edge $v_i v_j$.

2. Find the third vertex v_k with the following properties:

    (i) $v_i v_k \subset \Omega$ and $v_j v_k \subset \Omega$

    (ii) $\overset{\circ}{C}$ $(v_i, v_j, v_k) \cap V_{ij} = \emptyset$.

3. Subdivide the actual polygon P into two subpolygons
    $P_1 = (v_i, v_k, v_{k+1}, \cdots, v_{i-1}, v_i)$ and $P_2 = (v_j, v_{j+1}, \cdots, v_k, v_j)$. (The vertices are indexed modulo the number of vertices of polygon P.)

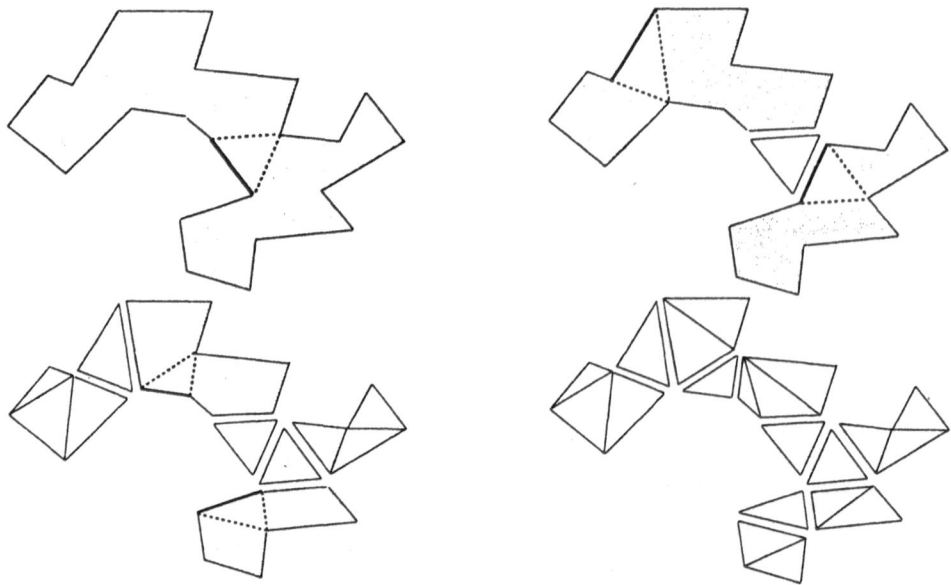

Figure 3: Functioning of the algorithm for a simple polygon.

4. Choose new starting edges in the subpolygons and repeat steps 2-4
   until the actual polygon consists of only one triangle.

Remark 8 *The merging steps consist only in the unification of the triangulations of the subpolygons.*

The correctness of the algorithm for polygons follows from the following
theorem.

Theorem 9 *Let P_1 and P_2 be the subpolygons of one recursion step of the
algorithm and T_1, T_2 the corresponding CDTs of the inner of P_1 and P_2. Let
$\Delta(v_i, v_j, v_k)$ be the triangle determined in this recursion step dividing the
polygons P_1 and P_2. Then the Constrained Delaunay triangulation consists of the union $T_1 \cup T_2 \cup \Delta(v_i, v_j, v_k)$.*

Proof: For every inner edge of T_1 and T_2 the local Delaunay property is
fulfilled. Therefore, we have to show the local Delaunay property only for
the edges $v_i v_k$ and $v_j v_k$. But for both of these edges the local Delaunay
property follows directly from Lemma 7.   ∎

Data structures

Given a polygon P and an edge $v_i v_j$ for the search for the third vertex the following three steps are repeated until the correct vertex is found:

- Choose a vertex v_k of P on the left side of the edge $v_i v_j$.

- Determine the visibility between v_i, v_j and v_k.

- Verify that in $\overset{\circ}{C}(v_i, v_j, v_k)$ there are no further vertices on the left side of the edge $v_i v_j$ which are visible from v_i, v_j, respectively, w. r. t. the border B.

Note that only for a valid third vertex all three steps are performed. These steps are accelerated by the use of a uniform grid data structure, see [PR93].

Maintainance of the grid-structure

All vertices and edges of the polygon are sorted into the corresponding grid cells. The vertices in the grid cells are administrated by double linked lists. Because of the divide and conquer approach we have to deal with several independent polygons during the algorithm. Therefore each grid cell contains a list of several linked lists of vertices, one for each subpolygon whose vertices belong to the grid cell itself, see for example figure 4. In addition each polygon holds a pointer to its linked list and each vertex of the polygon contains a pointer to its element in the corresponding linked list. Because of the number of vertices remains constant during the algorithm no more storage is neccessary to store the vertices in several lists instead of one list. The grid structure accelerates the search for the third vertex. Given an edge $v_i v_j$ the grid cells intersecting with the bounding box of $v_i v_j$ are determined. These cells defines a search area for the third vertex, which is increased stepwise until the third vertex is found, see [PR93]. A similar procedure using the uniform grid is performed to verify that for a choosen vertex $v_k \in V$ there are no vertices $v \in \overset{\circ}{C}(v_i, v_j, v_k) \cap V_{ij}$. The same is done for each edge of the polygon. Every grid cell contains a list of linked lists of edges, one for each subpolygon whose edges intersect the grid cell. To store the edges in their corresponding linked lists of the grid cells we use a modification of the algorithm of Amanatides and Woo [AW87]. The algorithm determines all grid cells intersected by a given edge. To determine the visibility between two vertices v_i and v_k the grid cells intersected by the edge $v_i v_k$ are computed with the same algorithm and the intersections of the edge $v_i v_k$ with all edges contained in the linked lists of these grid cells are computed.

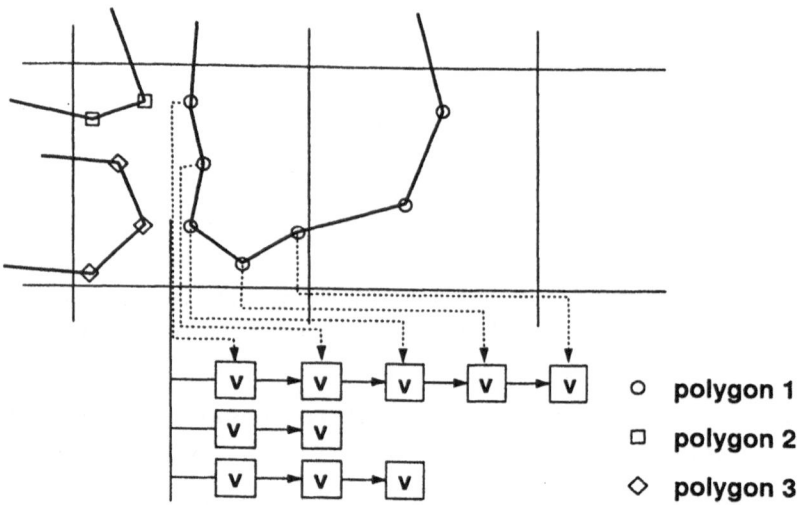

Figure 4: All vertices are sorted into grid cells. The administration of the vertices in the cells is done by linked lists. Providing that a grid cell contains vertices of a polygon, it has a vertex list in the cell.

The update of the linked lists is performed as follows. After a polygon $P = (v_0, \cdots, v_n)$ is divided by a triangle $\Delta(v_i, v_j, v_k)$ into two subpolygons $P_1 = (v_0, v_k, \cdots, v_n)$, $P_2 = (v_j, \cdots, v_k)$ the elements of the first polygon in the linked list corresponding to polygon P are copied into a new linked list and removed from the original one. The pointer of the second polygon is set to the original linked list, see for example figure 5.

Choosing a starting edge

The algorithm has optimal performance only if the polygon considered in the actual recursion step is divided in two subpolygons of about the same size. This can only be achieved by the correct choice of the starting edge, but in general this cannot be done in constant time. In the worst case a polygon with k vertices is divided into one triangle and a restpolygon with $k-1$ vertices. This leeds to a recursion depth of $O(n)$, where in the optimal case we obtain a recursion depth of $O(log n)$, i.e only $O(n)$ different starting edges are considered. A simple but efficient possibility to choose an starting edge is to consider the angles between consecutive edges of the polygons. If two consecutive angles in the polygon are both greater than 180° we can be sure that non of the neighbouring vertices of the corresponding edge is the third vertex to that edge. Choosing such an edge the worst case is avoided. In the algorithm for every edge $v_i v_j$ a functional $f(v_i v_j)$ is evaluated and the edge with maximum functional value is choosen as

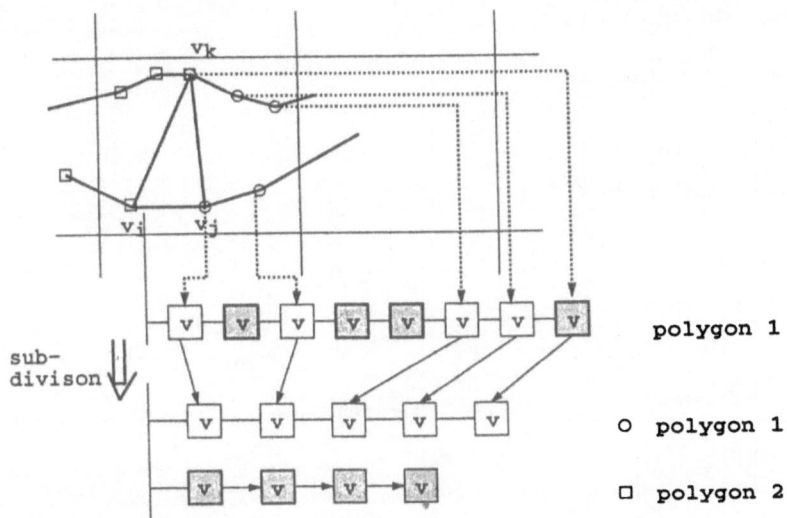

Figure 5: After the subdivision of a polygon the list in the grid cells are updated. If the polygon contains n vertices this can be done in $O(n)$ time using the pointers of the vertices to their list elements.

starting edge. We used different functionals which are motivated geometrically and constructed in such a way that the worst case is avoided:

$$f_1(v_i v_{i+1}) \;=\; \alpha_i + \alpha_{i+1}$$
$$f_2(v_i v_{i+1}) \;=\; \max(\alpha_i, 180°) + \max(\alpha_{i+1}, 180°)$$
$$f_3(v_i v_{i+1}) \;=\; (1-w)(\alpha_i + \alpha_{i+1}) + w(\alpha_{i-1} + \alpha_{i+2})$$
$$f_4(v_i v_{i+1}) \;=\; \max(\max(\alpha_i, 180°), \max(\alpha_{i+1}, 180°))$$
$$f_5(v_i v_{i+1}) \;=\; (1-w)(\max(\alpha_i, 180°) + \max(\alpha_{i+1}, 180°))$$
$$+w(\max(\alpha_{i-1}, 180°) + \max(\alpha_{i+2}, 180°)),$$

where $0 \le w \le 1$ is a weight factor. The indices are calculated modulo the size of the polygon.

At the beginning of the algorithm all angles between consecutive edges are computed. In each subdivision step we get four new angles and the functional must be updated accordingly. This can be done in constant time.

The different functionals were tested for various randomly generated polygons. An example of such a polygon is shown in figure 9. The results for different polygon sizes are shown in figure 6. In the functionals f_3 and f_5 we choose a weight factor $w = 2/3$. The functionals f_1 and f_2 delivered the best results for all example polygons. As in the optimal case the sum of the sizes of the subpolygons depends linearly of the size of the starting polygon. The functionals f_3 and f_5 shows that the consideration of more than two adjacent angles of an edge does not result in better subdivisions

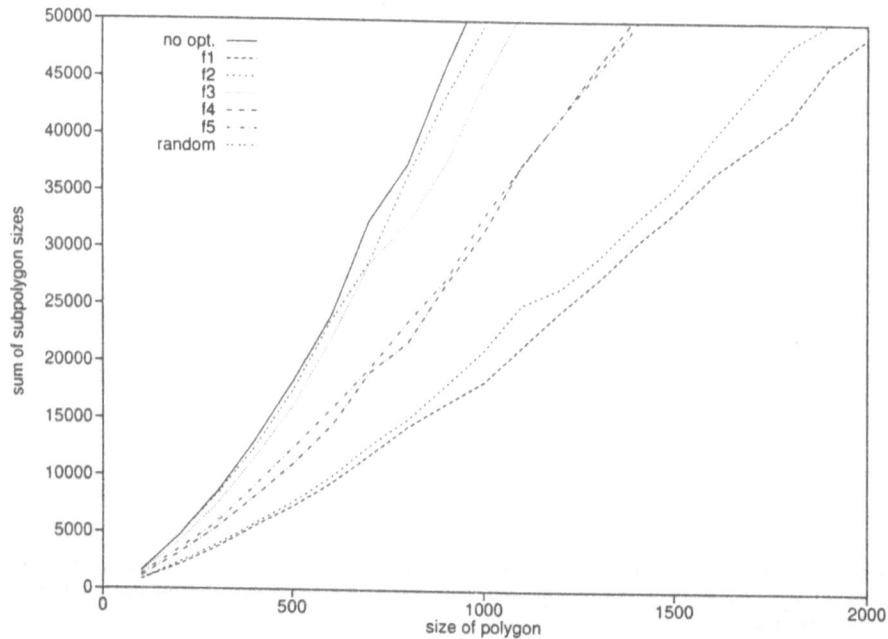

Figure 6: The sum of the sizes of all subpolygons generated during the algorithm dependent on the size of the starting polygon is shown without optimization, for different functionals $f_1, \cdots, f_5$ and for a random choice of the starting edge. If we choose the functionals f_1 and f_2 we obtain a much better dependence between the size of the starting polygon and this sum than $O(n^2)$, i.e. the polygons are subdivided in a nearly optimal way. In the optimal case we would get a dependence of $O(n \log n)$.

of the polygons. Both, choosing the edges randomly or without optimization leeds to nearly the same results and are not optimal.

Domains with more than one border polygon.

If the border B of the domain Ω consists of more than one polygon, inner polygons are processed first. In most cases the corresponding third vertex to an edge belongs to another polygon. To find the third vertex, we have to consider the edges of all other polygons. If the starting egde and the third vertex belong to different border polygons these polygons are joined, see figure 7.

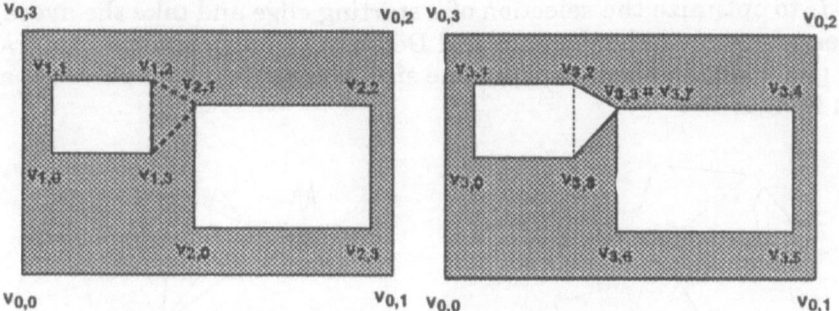

Figure 7: The corresponding vertex $v_{2,1}$ to edge $v_{1,2}v_{1,3}$ of polygon b_1 belong to an other polygon b_2. The polygons b_1 and b_2 are joined and we get polygon $v_{3,0}, \dots, v_{3,8}$.

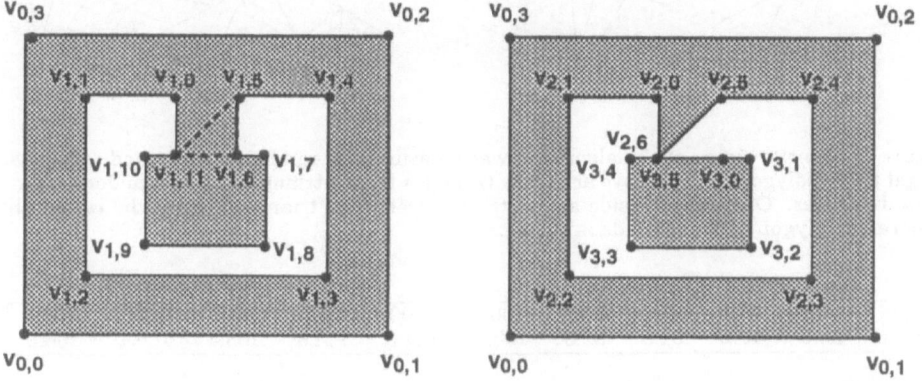

Figure 8: The triangle $\triangle(v_{1,5}, v_{1,11}, v_{1,6})$ subdivides the inner polygon $b_1 (v_{1,0}, \dots, v_{1,11})$ into two border polygons $b_2 = (v_{2,0} \dots v_{2,6})$ and $b_3 = v_{3,0} \dots v_{3,5}$. Remark that $v_{2,6} = v_{3,5}$. The Polygon b_3 lies outside the polygon b_2 and therefore b_3 can be triangulated without taking care of the other border polygons.

If the corresponding third vertex belongs to the same inner polygon, one of the two subpolygons belongs to the outer area of the other subpolygon, see figure 8. To triangulate this subpolygon the edges of the other border polygons must not be considered. If no inner border polygons are left, we are in the situation of one border polygon and can proceed as described above.

Results

The subdivision of the polygon together with the grid data structure leeds to a nearly linear dependence between time and size of the polygon in practical examples. This is shown in table 1. To get these results we use functional f_1 to optimize the selection of a starting edge and take the average of times to compute the Constrained Delaunay triangulation of 100 randomly generated polygons of the same size. Examples of test polygons are shown in figure 9.

 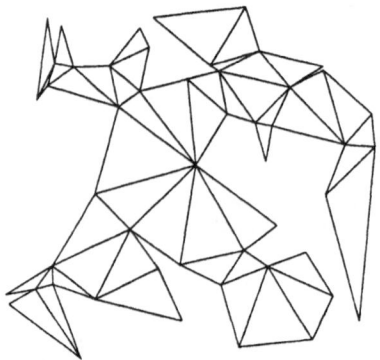

Figure 9: The run times of the algorithm was measured for randomly generated polygons. To get these polygons, we remove arbitrary triangles from a triangulation of randomly generated vertices. On the right side a Constrained Delaunay triangulation of the randomly generated polygon of the left side is shown.

size	200	400	600	800	1000	1200	1400	1600	1800	2000
time	20.6	41.2	61.9	82.5	103.2	124.0	144.6	165.4	186.1	206.9

Table 1: The run time of the algorithm for randomly generated polygons of different size. For every size the run time is averaged over 100 random generated test polygons.

Conclusions

A fast and easy to implement divide-and-conquer algorithm for the calculation of a Constrained Delaunay triangulation of planar domains was described. The algorithm combines the divide and conquer paradigma with a uniform grid as acceleration structure. In contrast to existing algorithms calculations of triangles not contained in the inner of the domain are avoided. For randomly generated polygons the run time of the algorithm depends nearly linear from the size of the border polygons of the domain.

Acknowledgement

I would like to thank J. Krämer for his efforts on all of the major implementation issues and the fruitful discussions that led to the realization of this algorithm.

References

[AGSS89] A. Aggarwal, L. J. Guibas, J. Saxe, and P. Shor. A linear-time algorithm for computing the voronoi diagram of a convex polygon. *Discrete Computational Geometry*, 4:591, 1989.

[AW87]   John Amanatides and Andrew Woo. A fast voxel traversal algorithm for ray tracing. In G. Marechal, editor, *Eurographics '87*, pages 3–10. North-Holland, August 1987.

[Boi88]   J. D. Boissonnat. Shape reconstruction from planar cross sections. *Computer Vision, Graphics and Image Processing*, 44, 1988.

[Cha91]   B. Chazelle. Triangulating a simple polygon in linear time. *Discrete Comput. Geom.*, 6:485–524, 1991.

[Che89]   L. P. Chew. Constrained Delaunay triangulations. *Algorithmica*, 4:97–108, 1989.

[CTV89]   K. Clarkson, R. E. Tarjan, and C. J. Van Wyk. A fast Las Vegas algorithm for triangulating a simple polygon. *Discrete Comput. Geom.*, 4:423–432, 1989.

[DFP85]   L. DeFloriani, B. Falcidieno, and C. Pienovi. Delaunay-based representation of surfaces defined over arbitrarily shaped domains. *Computer Vision, Graphics and Image Processing*, 32:127–140, 1985.

[FS91]   D.A. Field and W.D. Smith. Graded tetrahedral finite element meshes. *International Journal for Numerical Methods in Engineering*, 31(3):413–425, 1991.

[HL88]   K. Ho-Le. Finite element mesh generation methods: a review and classification. *Computer Aided Design*, 20:27–38, 1988.

[Ke95]   R. Klein and W. Straßer. Mesh generation from boundary models. In C. Hoffmann and J. Rossignac, editors, *Third Symposium on Solid Modeling and Applications*, pages 431–440. ACM Press, May 1995.

[KKT90]   D. G. Kirkpatrick, M. M. Klawe, and R. E. Tarjan. Polygon triangulation in $O(n \log \log n)$ time with simple data structures. In *Proc. 6th Annu. ACM Sympos. Comput. Geom.*, pages 34–43, 1990.

[Kle94]   Reinhard Klein. Linear approximation of trimmed surfaces. In R.R. Martin, editor, *The Mathematics Of Surfaces VI*, 1994.

[LL86]   D. T. Lee and A. K. Lin. Generalized Delaunay triangulations for planar graphs. *Discrete Comput. Geom.*, 1:201–217, 1986.

[PR93]   L. A. Piegl and A. M. Richard. Algorithm and data structure for triangulating multiply connected polygonal domains. *Computer & Graphics*, 17(5):563–574, 1993.

[Rip92]   S. Rippa. Adaptive approximation by piecewise linear polynomials on triangulations of subsets of scatterd data. *SIAM Journal Sci. Stat. Comput.*, 13(5):1123–1141, September 1992.

[Wat81]   D. F. Watson. Computing the n-dimensional delaunay t, tessela-tion with application to voronoi polytopes. *Comput. J.*, 24:167–172, 1981.

Multiresolution Approximation of Polyhedral Solids

D. Ayala, P. Brunet, R. Joan-Arinyo, I. Navazo [1]

Multiresolution models with different levels of detail are a basic tool for handling very large and complex systems in computer aided design applications such as ship design. In this work, we discuss several automatic simplification algorithms that generate a multiresolution family of solid models that approximate with different levels of detail the boundary representation of a given polyhedral solid. Methods based on the simplification of triangular meshes are discussed together with octree based algorithms. Comparison criteria include the possibility of geometry and topology simplification, the availability of approximation bounds and feature preservation.

Introduction

Classical geometrical models used in present CAD systems present important limitations when used for modelling very large and geometrically complex systems. Integrated applications - in the automotive and aeronautic industries for instance - are asking for almost interactive rates in the modelling and visualization of very complex assemblies. Multiple level of detail (LOD) representations or multiresolution models are becoming a powerful tool for handling and modelling these systems, [HG94], as they can automatically support different simultaneous approximations in different modelled parts of the system, depending on the relative importance of the parts. A tipical example is virtual reality navigation. In very complex systems, distant objects and parts have small projections and allow coarse approximations. An efficient virtual reality navigator must automatically switch among different LOD representations of the individ-

---

[1]Departament de Llenguatges i Sistemes Informàtics. Universitat Politècnica de Catalunya. 08028 Barcelona

ual objects, depending on their distance and visual relevance, [FS93]. A complementary technique to multiple LOD representations is the precomputation of visibility graphs of the polygon databases in order to reduce the complexity of the visibility computations, [TH93], [NV96].

Working with multiple LOD representations requires handling multiple representation databases and generating the family of the approximate representations from the geometric model of every modelled object. Of course, automatic data simplification is fundamental in these multiresolution representation approaches. Automatic data simplification deals with algorithms for obtaining a complete multiresolution (LOD) family of different approximating representations of an initial object. The need for a family of decreasing complexity representations for the same object was already stated by Clark in [Cla76]. Although multiresolution models are sometimes obtained interactively [HG94], extensive research is being performed in algorithms for the automatic generation of multiresolution models.

This Section presents several automatic simplification algorithms in the case of polyhedral models. Next section reviews several recent algorithms based on remeshing triangular meshes together with specific algorithms for - polyhedral - solids. The relevant aspects of the algorithms and their relative performances are presented and discussed. The rest of the chapter is devoted to octree-based simplification algorithms. A comparative analysis with respect to the schemes based on triangular meshes is included.

Previous Work

In this section, several proposed simplification algorithms are presented and discussed. We start by briefly describing several schemes that have been derived for piecewise triangular smooth surfaces, although they can be used for triangular-faced polyhedra.

Hamann's method [Ham94] simplifies a triangular mesh by eliminating triangles and re-triangulating the resulting region. First, the method computes principal curvature estimates for all vertices in the given triangulation [Ham93]. After that, a weight is assigned to each triangle based on the curvature at the vertices and used in such a way that triangles with low weight are first removed. Finally, each removed triangle is replaced by a point and the region affected by the removal of triangles is triangu-

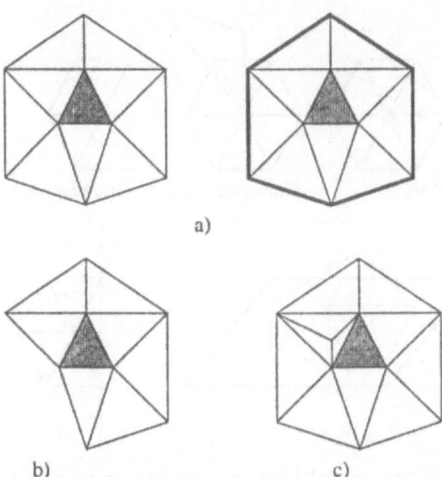

a)

b)   c)

Figure 1: a) Triangle with its triangle platelet and its connected acyclic corona. The boundary polygon is also showed. b) A disconnected corona. c) A cyclic corona.

lated again. Only triangles surrounded by a connected and acyclic corona and satisfying the halfspace test can be removed. A *triangle platelet* P_i associated with a triangle T_i is the set of all triangles sharing at least one of T_i vertices. The *corona* C_i of P_i is the set of all triangles of P_i except T_i. A corona is *connected* if all its triangles are connected and is *cyclic* if there exists, at least, one cycle of three neighboring triangles. The *boundary polygon* is the external 3D contour defined by P_i (see Figure 1). The *halfspace test* guarantees that the centroid of the triangle T_i lies within the projection of the boundary polygon on the supporting plane of the triangle T_i. The weight assigned to a triangle is $\omega = \sigma\rho$. The angle weight σ is computed as $\sigma = 2(\sum cos(\alpha_j) - 1)$, where $j \in \{1, 2, 3\}$ are the triangle interior angles, and the curvature weight ρ is given by the sum of the absolute curvatures at the triangle vertices.

Removing a triangle implies substituting its associated platelet by the corresponding boundary polygon and a new point which is computed considering the local surface geometry. Finally the re- triangulating is done by joining the new point with each vertex of the triangle platelet followed by an iterative edge swapping algorithm in order to optimize the angle weight. In this algorithm the degree of reduction can be specified either by a percentage or by an error tolerance.

The method proposed by Schroeder *et al.*, [SZL92], simplifies a triangular mesh by removing vertices and re- triangulizing the resulting region.

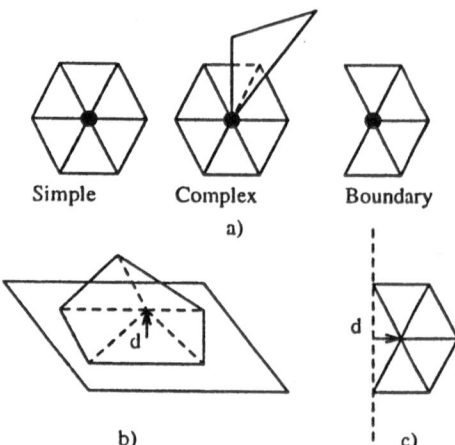

Figure 2: a) Vertex classification. b) Distance to plane criterion. c) Distance to edge criterion.

Vertices are classified into simple, boundary and complex (non-manifold). Figure 2a) shows this classification. Complex vertices cannot be removed and simple and boundary vertices are removed if they satisfy a specified criterion. Simple vertices use the distance-to-plane criterion. The distance between this vertex and an average plane, constructed using triangle normals, centers and areas of all triangles sharing this vertex, is computed and compared with a specified tolerance. Boundary vertices use the distance-to-edge criterion. In this case the distance between the vertex and the line defined by its two neighbor boundary vertices is computed and tested (see Figures 2b and c). After deleting a vertex and all its associated triangles, the resulting region is re-triangulated. The removal of a simple or boundary vertex reduces the mesh by two or one triangles respectively. This algorithm preserves the original topology of the mesh and can treat non-manifold forms. The degree of reduction can be specified either by a percentage or by an error tolerance.

Hoppe et al., [HDD+93], present a method to solve an optimization problem in which a set of points, X, and an initial triangular mesh, M_0, near them are the given input and a new reduced mesh M, that fits the set X well, is found. A mesh M is represented by its topology, K, and its geometry, V. Then the optimization problem can be solved by minimizing the following energy function:

$$E(K, V) = E_{dist}(K, V) + E_{rep}(K) + E_{spring}(K, V)$$

The first term is the sum of squared distances from the points of X to

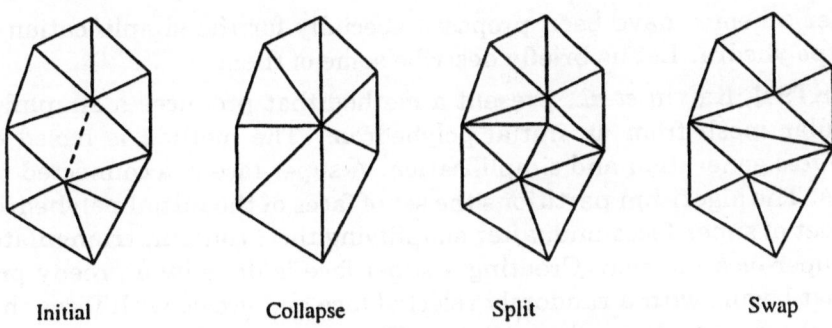

Figure 3: Legal moves: collapse, split and swap.

the mesh, the second term is proportional to the number of vertices of M and the third term is a spring energy. This minimization problem is partitioned into two subproblems: an inner minimization over V for a fixed K and an outer minimization over K. The inner minimization is a continuous optimization solved by a conjugate gradient method whereas the outer minimization is a discrete optimization based on the application of legal moves which are the three elemental transformations of edge collapse, split or swap between two neighboring triangles (see Figure 3). This method produces good results although it does not guarantee that a global minimum is found. It works as well for smooth surfaces as for surfaces with sharp edges so it preserves the initial model features.

Turk reported in [Tur92] a method that obtains a triangular mesh with a given number of vertices from an initial polyhedron. The algorithm consists of three steps. First, new points are distributed on the polyhedron's surface. These points are placed randomly and, after applying a neighbor repelling process, they become uniformly distributed. These new points will be the vertices of the final triangular mesh. In the second step a *mutual tessellation* surface is constructed that contains vertices of the initial polyhedron and the mentioned new points. This surface is obtained by triangulating each face of the initial polyhedron incorporating the new points lying on it. The third step removes old vertices. Each vertex to be deleted must fulfill the following condition. Let T be the boundary polygon of all the triangles sharing the vertex and let π be the average plane of these triangles. Then, only old vertices for which the projection of T on π does not self-intersect may be deleted. In practice, nearly all old vertices can be removed and a failing of this condition indicates that the vertex needs to be retained in order to preserve the topology of the initial object. The method is well suited for models with smooth shapes but is poorly suited for models with well-defined corners and sharp edges.

Other schemes have been proposed specially for the simplification of closed polyhedra. Let us briefly describe some of them.

In [KT94], Kalvin *et al.* present a method that produces a simplified triangular mesh from an initial polyhedron. The method is based on *super-faces* generation and simplification. A super-face is a connected set of faces. The algorithm partitions the set of faces of the initial polyhedron into a set of super-faces and, after simplifying their contour, triangulates each super-face interior. Creating a super-face is done by a greedy process that begins with a randomly selected face and grows with faces that satisfy the specified merging criteria. These criteria check the location and orientation of the candidate face with respect to the super-face faces and also prevent super-faces from becoming too long or thin. Simplifying super-face contours (which are 3D polygons) is done by polygon simplification methods and taking into account the neighbouring super-faces. Finally the resulting simplified contours are triangulated. It is possible for two triangles from different super-faces to intersect. The method is based on a bounded approximation criterion and preserves the topology of the initial object. A serious drawback of this method is that it may produce a simplified polyhedron that self-intersects.

The algorithm from Rossignac and Borrel, [RB93], ensures an increasingly smaller number of faces and vertices in the sequence of 3D approximations to the original polyhedron. The scheme works in three steps: triangulation of faces, grading of vertices and clustering of vertices. In the first step, each face is decomposed into triangles supported by its original vertices. Then, the second step computes a weight for each vertex of the initial model, related to its relative perceptual - visual - importance. Priority is given to vertices bounding large faces and to vertices that are most likely to be on the object silhouette. The clustering of vertices embeds the initial object in a regular 3D rectangular mesh and computes a representative vertex for each group of vertices - cluster - in a particular cell of the mesh. The size of the mesh controls the approximation degree of the simplified object. Once vertices have been clustered and substituted by their representative, triangular faces are simplified. They can degenerate into edges or single points. A specific data structure supporting triangles, isolated edges and isolated points receives the geometry of the simplified objects. The authors claim that significant graphics performance improvements can be obtained by a postprocess that removes duplicates from the data structure. The algorithm is time efficient and does not require the complete BRep of the initial object, but a simple array of vertices and triangles. The approximation tolerance based on the Hausdorff distance between the original and simplified model is increased during the simplification process while reducing the number of triangles. On the other hand, the method can simplify the topology of the object besides its geometry, and even merge an arbitrary number of small neighboring objects into a single point. The overall size of the object is approximately invariant during the simplification. The main drawback of the method is however that the output simplified objects are no longer polyhedra: the algorithm may produce non-regularized models with dangling faces and isolated edges and points.

The work from Gross, Gatti and Staad [GGS95] presents a remeshing algorithm for triangular meshes which controls the local level-of-detail of the surface approximation using local spectral estimates. It is presented as a 2D remeshing method, but it can be extended to 3D isosurface meshes. In the algorithm, the initial regular surface data grid is first transformed into a quadtree structure, and the remeshing algorithm works by iteratively removing vertices of the mesh and performing a local retriangulation of the neigborhood of the removed vertex. The main contribution of the paper is in the way it is decided whether a particular vertex can be removed. The algorithm starts by performing a wavelet transform of the data and, at every iteration, the detail signal is reconstructed by means of an inverse wavelet transform. The amplitude of this detail signal is used as a criterion for deciding on the removal of points. Local retriangulations are based on direct access to look-up tables. Approximation bounds can be derived, based on the properties of the wavelet transforms. The method is however limited to regular grid topologies in its present form, and should be extended to general triangulations in order to be usable for 3D simplification applications.

The method by Eck *et al.*, [EDD+95], extends the previous work of Lounsbery on surface wavelets to the problem of approximating an arbitrary mesh by a simpler mesh with subdivision connectivity, and gets an algorithm for the automatic multiresolution approximation of arbitrary meshes. The key idea in the remeshing procedure is the construction of a continuous parametrization of an arbitrary mesh over a simple domain mesh. This is obtained through the generation of a Voronoi diagram on the arbitrary surface of the initial object. One of the main advantages of this scheme is the existance of a tolerance that bounds the approximation in the resampling process. The method is however unable to simplify the topology of the object: only a multiresolution geometry simplification of the triangular mesh is obtained.

The algorithm from He *et al.*, [HHK+95], is based on first sampling and low-pass filtering the object into a voxel model. In a second step, the

	Output Model	Topology Simplification	Error Bounds	Feature Preservation
Hamann'94	N	N		N
Schroeder'92	N	N	N	
Hoppe'93		N	N	Y
Turk'92		N	N	N
Kalvin'93		N	Y	N
Rossignac'93	—	Y	Y	Y
Gross'95		N	Y	N
Eck'95		N	Y	N
He'95	MC	Y	Y	N

Table 1: Comparison of several simplification algorithms performances.

marching cubes algorithm is applied to a hierarchy of voxel volume representations in order to generate a multiresolution triangle-mesh family of approximate models of the initial object. The hierarchy of volume buffers is created by convolving the original object with a low-pass filter with a suitable spatial support. Different parametric filters can be considered, depending on the requirements of simplification speed and accuracy. In the second step, an approximate object isosurface is generated through a standard marching cubes algorithm, using up to five triangles to approximate the surface within a voxel. In addition to the multiresolution simplification algorithm, the authors also propose an antialiased rendering algorithm based on a multilayered marching cubes and on a translucency of the inner layers.

Table 1 presents a comparative analysis of the algorithms that have been discussed in this section. In all cases, the whole multiresolution set of simplified representations must be generated prior to their use. All algorithms presented in Table 1 require triangular meshes or triangular faced polyhedra as input. Concerning the output model, they usually generate conform meshes of triangular, planar faces. This is a limitation in cases with large flat faces, a triangulation being mandatory. The basic exception is Rossignac and Borrel's method, where a set of triangles, edges and points can be obtained. The scheme by He *et al.* generates triangulated objects as a result of using a marching cubes algorithm.

Concerning topology simplification, all algorithms based on remeshing techniques, except Rossignac's and He's, do not support topology simplification. This is an important requirement in practical applications, because otherwise, it will be impossible to get high simplification rates in objects of complex topologies.

The existence of error bounds or tolerances for the approximations is also a basic user requirement. Approximating tolerances can be used for instance to detect, in a visualization application, the optimal approximate representation for a distant object. Algorithms that compute approximate models by sequential remeshing of the previous triangular mesh (the first four rows in Table 1) cannot guarantee an error bound with respect to the surface of the initial polyhedron. Finally, Table 1 shows that some of the proposed schemes preserve features - as sharp edges - in the initial object. This is also an interesting property that helps in having smooth transitions between succesive objects of the approximating family.

Next section presents an octree-based algorithm for the automatic simplification of polyhedral objects. The algorithm is based on the generation of an intermediate octree representation that is subsequently used to generate the resulting multiresolution family. When compared to the schemes presented in this section, the new algorithm obtains two-manifold polyhedra as output models, it simplifies both the geometry and the topology -genus - of the initial polyhedron, an error bound for the approximation error can be derived, relevant features of the initial object such as sharp edges are preserved as much as possible during the simplification, and flat regions of the initial polyhedron are approximated by large, planar faces whenever possible.

Octrees Based Approach

The octree-based approach, [AAB$^+$96], uses an intermediate octree structure which is pruned to different levels in order to obtain a multiresolution family P_1, P_2, ..., P_m of two-manifold polyhedra approximating the initial polyhedral object P as illustrated in Figure 4. The algorithm consists on the following three steps, [AAB$^+$96],

1. The maximal division classical octree (MDCO) representation O_m of the initial polyhedron P is obtained. See Figure 4. This conversion from P to O_m is based on a simultaneous space subdivision and clipping of the boundary faces of P. O_m stands for a m-level octree. The surface of P is completely contained in the Terminal Grey (TG) nodes of the octree O_m, TG nodes being the grey nodes without descendents, at the deepest level of the tree.

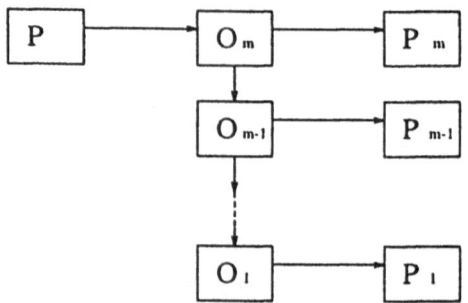

Figure 4: Multiresolution family of polyhedra.

2. A multiresolution family of octree representations $O_1, O_2, ..., O_m$ of P is obtained. Every O_k is the result of a simple prunning operation on the deepest level of O_{k+1}, Grey nodes at the k-level of O_{k+1} become the new TG nodes of O_k containing the whole boundary surface of P.

3. A feasible polyhedron P_k is reconstructed from every intermediate MDCO O_k. A polyhedron P_k is said to be feasible with respect to an octree O_k if the k-level MDCO representation of P_k is O_k. This is equivalent to the requirement of the boundary of P_k being completely contained in the space region corresponding to the TG nodes of O_k.

An immediate consequence of this approach is that a monotonically decreasing degree of approximation is automatically obtained, [AAB+96]

$$dist(surf(P), surf(P_k)) \leq \varepsilon_k = 2^{m-k}\varepsilon$$

On the other hand, the number of faces of the polyhedra P_k is monotonically decreasing from the best approximation P_m to the coarser P_1, $n_f(P_{k-1}) \leq n_f(P_k)$.

Steps 1 and 2 in the simplification algorithm are straightforward. Concerning step 3, and besides the possible use of the marching cubes algorithm, [HHK+95], that will be discussed in the next section, several octree based reconstruction algorithms can be considered. They are briefly introduced in the next paragraphs.

In the particular case of orthogonal polyhedra with all planar faces parallel to one of the coordinate planes, a simple non-iterative algorithm for the reconstruction of a feasible polyhedron P_k from O_k can be derived, [AAB95]. The algorithm works by reconstructing the vertices of P_k which are located in specific TG node classes of O_k.

In the case of general polyhedra P, the face octree-based approach [AAB$^+$96], [JAS95] first generates a set of non planar quadrilaterals that covers the set of TG nodes in O_k. The set of quadrilaterals is computed in the form of a geometrically deformed model, GDM [MBL$^+$91]. Then, a face octree [BNV93] is computed from the GDM in such a way that its tolerance ε is equal to the length of the main diagonal of TG nodes; the face octree represents the local planarity of the approximated surface. In the final step, a valid boundary representation of P_k is derived from the set of quadrilaterals with the support of the face octree.

The TG map-based approach, [AAB$^+$96] is also valid for general polyhedra P. It is based on an initial estimation and further refinement of the P_k topology. This topology is captured in the TG map data structure, with a first estimation from O_k and P_{k+1}, and is represented through TG node sets - or regions - of 6-connected nodes that are associated to the P_k faces. The TG map is afterwards refined and simplified by collapsing neighbour regions in planar zones, while being feasible. A feasible TG map is a TG map that defines a polyhedron P_k contained in the corresponding MDCO O_k. Figure 5 presents a polyhedron used as a test object and Figure 6 shows two feasible TG maps defined on its octree representations O_4 and O_6. The above octree-based algorithms guarantee a bounded approximation based on the maximum surface-to-surface distance, and a decreasing degree of approximation in the multiresolution set. An automatic simplification of both the geometry and the topology is obtained, the coarser approximation being a simple 0-genus prism in most cases. The algorithms preserve relevant features such as sharp edges, and approximate flat regions by single large, non triangular faces. Their performance is discussed in the next section, based on the simplification of the object presented in Figure 5. Possible disconnected components within the approximation tolerances can be produced in some cases, however (see Figure 6).

Results and Discussion

It has been already mentioned in the discussion of results in Table 1, the interest of having topology simplification and error bounds for the approximations. Some of the basic requirements in many applications are not guaranteed by most of the existing automatic simplification algorithms but can be ring octree based schemes or similar methods.

Figure 5: Polyhedron used as test object.

Some results obtained for polyhedra with their faces oriented in three orthogonal directions, [AAB95], are presented in Figure 7. This figure shows a building modeled from documents of the 19-century architect Ildefons Cerdà, who designed the modern Barcelona urban planning. The approximate simplifications P_{10}, P_8 and P_7 are presented. The number of faces of these approximating polyhedra is 2311, 809 and 433 respectively. The approximation error in P_k is bounded by 2^{13-k} times the main diagonal of the elementary voxel cubes of the 4096 spatial decomposition of the initial universe volume. For a detailed discussion, see [AAB95]. It can be observed that polyhedra P_1 to P_5 are simply rectangular prisms with six faces.

The results of several algorithms in the simplification of the test object shown in Figure 5 which has 1856 faces, are presented in Table 2. Results obtained by approximating the initial object with MDCOs of 4, 5 and 6 levels are shown. The table includes the total number of nodes of the in-

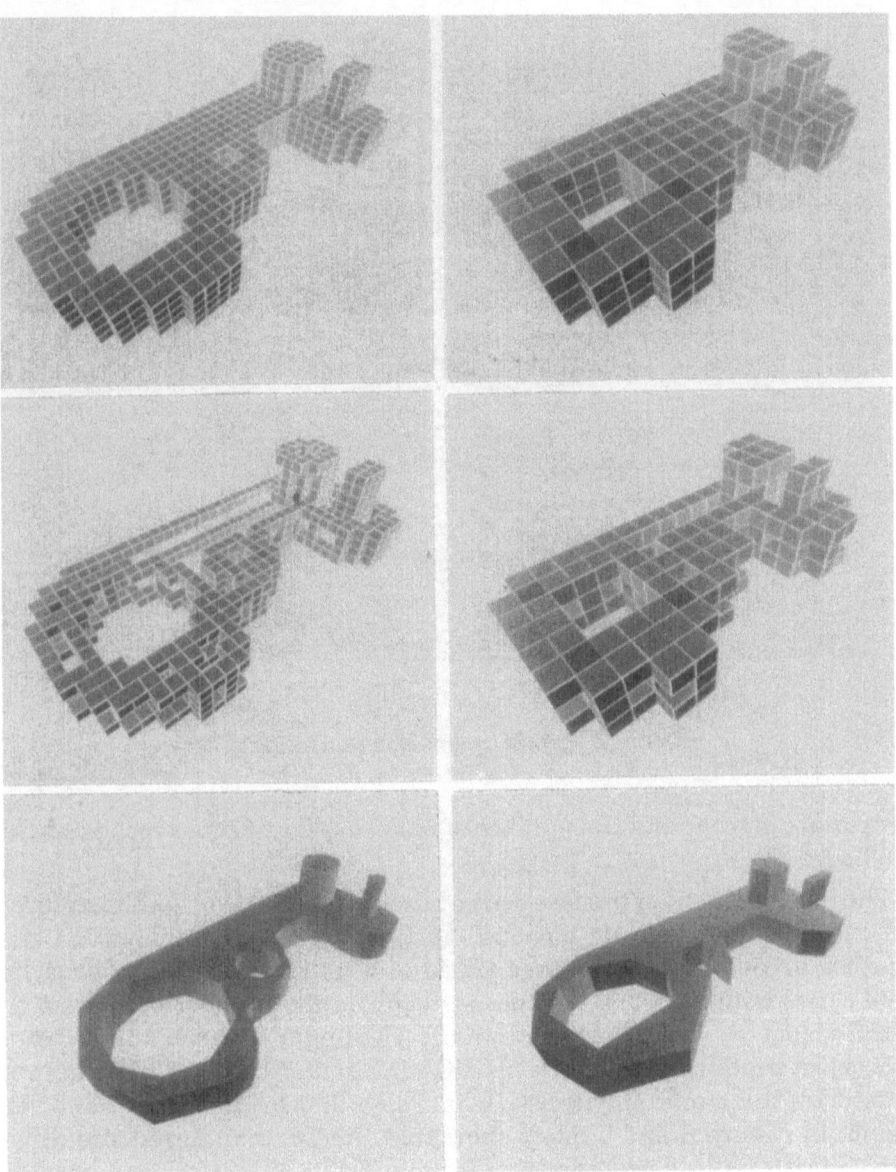

Figure 6: Left: A feasible TG map defined on the octree O_6 (the top picture shows *in*, *on* and *join* nodes whereas the center picture shows only the wireframe of *on* and *join* nodes) and the resulting simplified polyhedron (bottom picture, 65 faces). Right: The corresponding TG map and simplified polyhedron (39 faces) obtained from O_4.

Figure 7: Simplifications of a real building.

termediate octrees and the number of resulting faces in the reconstructed polyhedra P_k.

The improvement of the face octree based simplification over the marching cubes results is quite obvious. It must be observed, however, that whether or not both face octree based and marching cubes approaches yield a real simplification depends strongly on the number of faces of the initial object P, the larger the number yielding a higher simplification. Any object producing the same MDCO representation O_m will be approximated by the same polyhedra P_k in Table 2. On the other hand, the results in Figure 6 and Table 2 show that the TG map based simplification algorithm is a very promising technique.

Future work will include the design of more accurate algorithm for the TG map based scheme, specially focusing the derivation of improved fea-

MDCO	Number of nodes of the MDCO	Faces of P_k Marching Cubes	Faces of P_k Face Octree	Faces of P_k TG map
O_4	266	484	218	33
O_5	962	1904	433	48
O_6	4216	8379	852	65

Table 2: Number of nodes of the MDCO and number of faces of the resulting P_k using different approximation algorithms to the object in Figure 5.

sible functions. The use of a finite set of discrete candidate planes for the generation of the geometry of P_k will also be investigated, in order to reduce visualization artifacts produced by changes in the normal vector of the faces between subsequent approximations P_i and P_{i-1}. Alternative algorithms for the MDCO to boundary reconstruction must also be considered; seed algorithms similar to that reported in [EDD+95] may be specially interesting.

Acknowledgements

The authors would like to thank C. Andújar, Imma Boada and J. Solé for their help in programming the algorithms.

This work has been supported in part by the Comisión Interministerial de Ciencia y Tecnología (CICYT), under the project TIC-95-0630.

References

[AAB95] D. Ayala, C. Andújar, and P. Brunet. Automatic simplification of orthogonal polyhedra. In D.W. Fellner, editor, *Modelling Virtual Worlds Distribuited Graphics*, pages 137–147. Internationallen Workshop MVD'95, Infix, 1995.

[AAB+96] C. Andújar, D. Ayala, P. Brunet, R. Joan-Arinyo, and J. Solé. Automatic generation of multiresolution boundary representations. *Computer Graphics Forum*, 1996. To appear.

[BNV93] P. Brunet, I. Navazo, and A. Vinacua. A modelling scheme for the approximate representation of closed surfaces. *Computing*, 8:75–90, 1993.

[Cla76]   J. H. Clark. Hierarchical geometric models for visible surface algorithms. *Communications of the ACM*, 19(10):547–554, 1976.

[EDD⁺95]   M. Eck, T. DeRose, T. Duchamp, H. Hoppe, M. Lounsbery, and W. Stuetzle. Multiresolution analysis of arbitrary meshes. In R. Cook, editor, *Computer Graphics ACM SIGGRAPH 95*, pages 173–182, Los Angeles, August 1995.

[FS93]   T.A. Funkhouser and C.H. Sequin. Adaptive display algorithm for interactive frame rates during visualization of complex virtual environments. In *Computer Graphics ACM SIGGRAPH 93*, pages 247–254, 1993.

[GGS95]   M.H. Gross, R. Gatti, and O. Staad. Fast multiresolution surface meshing. In G.M. Nielson and D. Silver, editors, *Visualization'95*, pages 135–142. Atlanta, GA, October 29 – November 3 1995.

[Ham93]   B. Hamann. Curvature approximation for triangulated surfaces. In G. Farin, H. Hagen, H. Noltemeier, and W. Knödel, editors, *Geometric Modelling*, pages 139–153. Springer, 1993.

[Ham94]   B. Hamann. A data reduction scheme for triangulated surfaces. *Computer Aided Geometric Design*, 11:197–214, 1994.

[HDD⁺93]   H. Hoppe, T. DeRose, T. Duchamp, J. McDonald, and W. Stuetzle. Mesh optimization. In *SIGGRAPH'93, Computer Graphics Proceedings, Annual Conference Series*, pages 19 – 26, 1993.

[HG94]   P.S. Heckbert and M. Garland. Multiresolution modeling for fast rendering. In *Graphics Interface'94*, pages 43 – 50, 1994.

[HHK⁺95]   T. He, L. Hong, A. Kaufman, A. Varshney, and S. Wang. Voxel based object simplification. In G.M. Nielson and D. Silver, editors, *Visualization'95*, pages 296–303, Atlanta, GA, October 29 – November 3 1995.

[JAS95]   R. Juan-Arinyo and J. Solé. Constructing face octrees from voxel-based volume representations. *Computer-Aided Design*, 27(10):783–791, 1995.

[KT94]   A.D. Kalvin and R.H. Taylor. Superfaces: Polyhedral approx-
            imation with bounded error. In Yongmin Kim, editor, *Medi-
            cal Imaging 1994: Image Capture, Formatting, and Display*,
            pages 12 – 13, Newport Beach, CA, 1994. Proceedings SPIE
            2164.

[MBL+91] J.V. Miller, D.E. Breen, W.E. Lorensen, R.M. O'Bara, and M.J.
            Wozny. Geometrically deformed models: A method for ex-
            tracting closed geometric models from volume data. *Computer
            Graphics*, 25, 4:217–226, 1991.

[NV96]   I. Navazo and S. Vila. Handling very complex environments
            using a discrete visibility graph. *This issue*, 1996.

[RB93]   J. Rossignac and P. Borrel. Multiresolution 3D aproximations
            for rendering complex scenes. In B. Falcidieno and T.L. Kunii,
            editors, *Modeling in Computer Graphics*, pages 455 – 465.
            Springer-Verlag, 1993.

[SZL92]   W. J. Schroeder, J. A. Zarge, and W. E. Lorensen. Decimation
            of triangle meshes. *Computer graphics*, 26(2):65 – 70, 1992.

[TH93]   S. Teller and P. Hanrahan. Global visibility algorithms for
            illumination computations. *Computer Graphics Annual Con-
            ference Series*, pages 239 – 246, 1993.

[Tur92]   G. Turk. Re-tiling polygonal surfaces. *Computer Graphics*,
            26(2):55 – 64, 1992.

Handling Very Complex Environments Using a Discrete Visibility Graph

Isabel Navazo, Sebastià Vila[1]

When scenes with a large number of elements have to be used, it is difficult to do a real time walk-through. An algorithm to compute a weak visibility graph of a large data set based on its discretization by means of a regular uniform grid is introduced. The algorithm computes the visibility graph using a new approach for the cell to cell visibility test and an auxiliary quad-tree to speed up.

Introduction

In the last years, the growing power of graphic hardware is going in parallel with the growing size of the data that graphic applications are working on. Therefore, new problems arise due to the handling of big data models. Typical problems appear when we want to store and retrieve those models, when we want to query the model or when an operation is requested between two data sets.

A big amount of work is being carried out by researchers on speeding-up the rendering of these complex scenes. This is an important problem, related mainly to the interactive walk-through inside a virtual reality scene. Two main approaches have been proposed to increase the speed when rendering a scene during a walk-through. Both are briefly sketched next.

The first one copes with the complexity by using a simplified model of the scene objects. That is, instead of rendering a complex model of an object a simpler one is used that produces approximately the same image when rendered. Several interesting topics arise when using simplification. Among them: how to produce good simplified models or which

---

[1]Departament de Llenguatges i Sistemes Informàtics. Universitat Politècnica de Catalunya. Spain.

criteria should be used to choose a level of detail for a given object. The papers [RB92], [FS93] and [AAB+96] offer more thorough presentation of these techniques.

The second one is related to the precomputation of the visibility relationships. The central idea is to precede the walk-through phase by a preprocess in which the visibility relationships between scene regions are computed. Later, when we are doing the walk-through, this information can be used to read the set of potentially visible objects to be rendered, depending on the observer's position.

Computing the exact visibility between space regions can be a very hard task [PD86]. Nevertheless this is not required if we are using fast polygon-rendering hardware. In fact, the set of visible polygons can be overestimated without significantly increasing the expected rendering time. Thus we propose a simpler algorithmic treatment relying on the concept of weak visibility.

The two problems to tackle for visibility precomputation are how to partition space and how and how to compute the visibility relationships between regions.

Several authors have worked on these problems and presented solutions to them. Teller et altri ([TS91], [TH93], [Tel92]) use information of the wall structure on architectural models to break the scene into cells. Other partitioning methods have been proposed for related problems. Specially close to our approach are the octree and other spatial subdivision methods usually applied to ray tracing and radiosity rendering algorithms ([Gla84], [CDP95]).

We consider a given scene discretized by means of a regular uniform grid (i.e. a voxel model[1]). We use an octree as an auxiliary structure for computing the visibility relationships between the regions associated to the cells. At the end of the process, the octree nodes give the visibility graph between cells. As this visibility graph is related to the discretization of the space, we dub it discrete visibility graph. The graph is used during the walk-through phase to fetch a reduced set of objects from the scene to be rendered in order to accelerate the rendering process. Because of the independence between the breaking method used to obtain the discrete scene and the octree procedure employed to compute the visibility graph, we expect to achieve significant gains on a broad spectrum of scenes. Moreover, due to the hierarchical structure of the octree, a kind of multi-resolution visibility scheme is obtained. At present, all the analisys is being done in the two dimensional space.

---

[1] We want to note that discretizing the scene and labeling its nodes (cells) is an interesting problem in its own but it is out of the scope of this chapter

The next section describes the method while introducing some useful definitions. Then, methods for computing the visibility relationships between cells are explained and their properties discussed. After that the quad-tree hierarchical technique to compute the Discrete Visibility Graph is proposed. Finally, some conclusions and future work are presented.

Description of the Method

Given an n-dimensional scene S, we partition it with a superimposed regular uniform grid. Hereafter, the scene is handled as a discrete scene DS, namely a collection of grid cells, of each of which we only case whether they are empty (white or transparent) or not (black or opaque). After this, an auxiliary complete octree structure is built based on the DS. The visibility relationships between transparent and opaque octree will be computed. We name the result *Discrete Visibility Graph, DVG*. This data encodes the inter-cell visibility properties thus allowing to answer queries about which is the set of cells visible from a given cell. Finally, this querying capability will be used during the walk-through phase. For a given viewpoint position, the transparent cell where it lays is computed and the set of candidate visible cells is computed. Those cells, or the data inside them, could be clipped through the frustrum of vision and only the remaining data rendered.

Note that, increasing to the maximum level of subdivision admissible in the octree, the size of the region associated with a cell decreases and better visibility accuracy for a given viewpoint will be obtained.

The process scheme can be seen in figure 1, where the auxiliary quad-tree structure is not drawn in order to improve the comprehension of the picture.

Computing Cell to Cell Visibility

We say that two points p and q from a discrete scene are *visible* iff there is a sight line between them intersecting no opaque cell. This fact is expressed by using the notation $p \sim q$. We say that two cells u and v

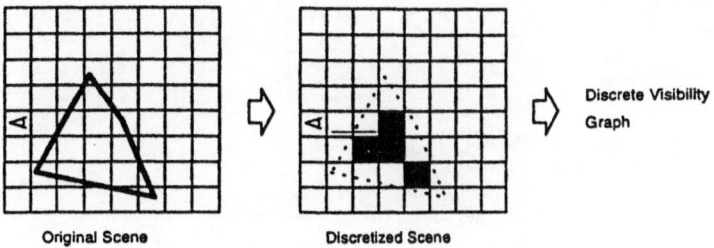

Original Scene   Discretized Scene

Figure 1: Overall process scheme

are *visible* (in a weak sense) iff there are two points, the first in u and the second in v, that are visible. We denote this by $u \sim v$. The set of segments going from u points to v points is named *corridor* between u and v (see figure 4a) and is denoted by $C(u, v)$. Because we work on a discrete scene, it makes sense to define the *discrete corridor* as the set of cells intersecting the corridor. Any opaque cell belonging to the discrete corridor is an *occluder*.

The cell to cell visibility problem can be stated as the problem of computing the predicate $CC(u, v)$ defined to be true iff cells u and v are mutually visible. This problem has a hard connection with classical visibility problems of computational geometry and with shadow generation algorithms. Three distinct approaches have been studied to solve the problem. We now review them briefly.

The first approach uses the results obtained from shadow generation algorithms ([BP93], [NON85], [Tel92], [DF94]) to compute the visibility predicate $CC(u, v)$. The chief idea is to consider the u cell as an area light emitter and let the opaque cells to act like obstacles producing umbra and penumbra areas. Therefore, if the v cell is totally inside the umbra region, u and v are not mutually visible (see figure 2). The method's worst case complexity is $O(n)$ being n the number of occluders. More about the method can be read in [Nav95], which shows how to take advantage of a uniform isothetic cell distribution to compute the umbra and penumbra areas.

The second approach is strongly connected to the computational geometry study of visibility inside a polygon ([LP79], [She92], [SS90]). The key idea (see figure 3) is to study the corridor between u and v to determine if the convex hull of the lower occluders L and the convex hull of the upper occluders U have a null intersection. The lower convex hull L is the convex hull of the lower corridor edge and the occluders that it intersects. The upper convex hull U is defined in a similar way. Then we can make

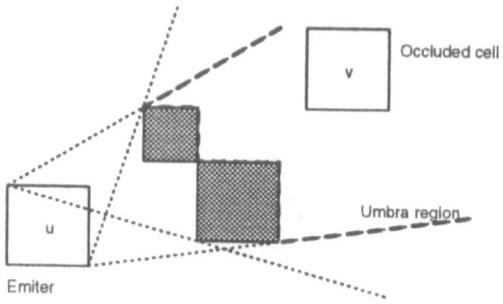

Figure 2: Computing Visibility via Shadow Generation

use of the following result: u and v are mutually visible iff there is a null intersection between L and U. There is a proof of this fact in [VN95]. This method has an $O(n)$ complexity in the worst case, being n the number of occluders, and it is only useful for equal sized cells.

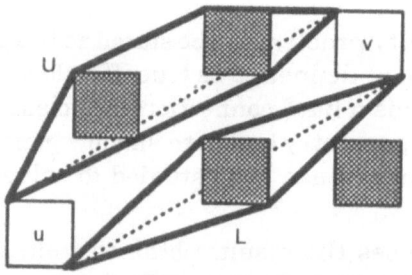

Figure 3: Computing Visibility via Convex Hull Analysis

The third approach uses the well known method of moving the problem to a dual space. We choose a transformation that maps lines to points and vice versa liki in [HT92]. The x and y dual space axes are chosen according to the relative position of the u and v cells in such a way that they contain two vertices of the profile of the cell u (or v) as seen from the other. In figure 4a, those axes contain the $[u_1 u_2]$ and $[v_1 v_2]$ segments respectively. Each feasible sight line is parameterized by its intersection with the two axes. This means that the l line in the original space is converted into a point $L = (L_x, L_y)$ where L_x (L_y) is the distance between the l intersection with the x (y) axis and its origin (see figure 4).

Some other interesting properties of this parameterization are the following:

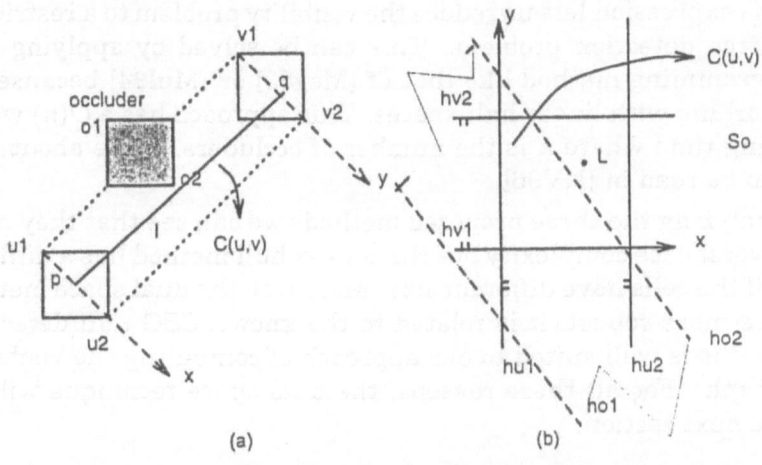

Figure 4: Mapping to Dual Space

- The set of lines through a point R are mapped to a line r.

- The set of lines $\{l\}$ such that $l(R) \geq 0$ ($l(R) \leq 0$) are mapped to an oriented linear half-space h_r.

Thus, it is easy to see that all lines $\{l\}$ inside the corridor fulfills

$$l(u_1) \geq 0 \wedge l(u_2) \leq 0 \wedge l(v_1) \geq 0 \wedge l(v_2) \leq 0 \qquad (1)$$

so the corridor between two cells is mapped to the set of points inside a rectangle as shown in figure 4b. This set can be expressed as the CSG tree:

$$C(u, v) = h_{u_1} \cap \bar{h}_{u_2} \cap h_{v_1} \cap \bar{h}_{v_2}$$

Moreover, the set of feasible sight lines which stab an opaque cell o is such that equation 1 and $l(o_1) \geq 0 \wedge l(o_2) \leq 0$ are satisfied and it could also be expressed as the CSG tree:

$$S_o = h_{o_1} \cap \bar{h}_{o_2} \cap C(u, v)$$

Therefore, two cells u and v are visible iff:

$$CC(u, v) \equiv C(u, v) - \bigcup_{\forall o \in O} S_0 \neq \emptyset \qquad (2)$$

This CSG expression lets us reduce the visibility problem to a restricted CSG null tree detection problem. This can be solved by applying any linear programming method like that of [Meg83] or [Mul94] because we are only working with linear half-spaces. This approach has a $O(n)$ worst case running time where n is the number of occluders. More about this method can be read in [NV96].

After analyzing the three proposed methods we can see that they have the same worst case complexity but the convex hull method has a difficult extension if the cells have different size. Moreover, the dual space method seems to be more robust, it is related to the known CSG null detection problem and it is well suited to our approach of computing the visibility discrete graph. For all these reasons, the dual space technique will be used in the next section.

Quad-tree Approach to Compute the Discrete Visibility Graph

Imagine a regular uniform grid discretization like that in figure 1. The brute-force algorithm to compute the DVG by visibility computation between each pair of cells has a worst case computational cost that could be bound above by $O(n^5)$, where the grid has an $n \times n$ resolution.

In order to reduce this complexity in the average case, an algorithm is proposed that uses coherent visibility. That means to take advantage of the $CC(u, v)$ computation to evaluate $CC(u, v')$ where v' is a neighbour of the v cell.

From the uniform grid partition, a top-down quad-tree is built by means of doing a grid traversal [Sam90]. According to the type of the grid cells inside a quad-tree node, this will be labeled as a *white/transparent* cell when all grid cells inside are transparent ones, *black/opaque* cell when all cells inside are black ones or a *grey* cell otherwise. The last one have to be subdivided.

The procedure ComputeDVG computes the visibility between the first level quad-tree nodes. Figure 5 presents a conceptual algorithm. The actual implementation takes advantage of several optimization that would obscure the the description here. As the main application related to this paper is the walk-through, only the visibility between white cells, the regions where the viewpoint could be, and black cells need to be computed. This is done by the procedure ComputeVisibility. Nevertheless, the visi-

```
procedure ComputeDVG (quad)
    Subdivide(quad, cell)
    for i := 1,4 do
        if cell[i]=G then
            ComputeDVG(cell[i])
        end if
        for j := 1,4 do
            if i ≠ j then
                ComputeVisibility(cell[i], cell[j])
            end if
        end for
    end for
end procedure
```

Figure 5: DVG computing algorithm

bility between white and grey nodes will also be computed in order to use this result in the visibility analysis between the white node and the descendents of the grey one. Moreover, if the visibility between a grey and a white node has to be checked, the procedure ComputeDVG is recursively called in order to compute the visibility between the grey descendents.

The procedure ComputeVisibility($cell_i$, $cell_j$) uses the dual space method, analyzed in the previous section, to check the visibility from $cell_i$ to $cell_j$. Therefore, it has to compute the CSG tree of the corridor $C(cell_i, cell_j)$ and the CSG tree of the occluders USo in order to verify the equation 2. In fact, if $cell_i$ and $cell_j$ are neighbor cells, the computation of the two CSG trees and their visibility is straightforward [NV96].

After analyzing the type of the nodes, the ComputeVisibility procedure goes on according to the table 1 criteria:

		i		
		W	B	G
j	W	–	–	–
	B	~	–	~↓
	G	~↓	–	~↓

Table 1: Criteria used for computing visibility. Symbol ~ means compute visibility and ↓ subdivide if CC predicate is true.

- If the CC predicate is true and $cell_i$ is white and $cell_j$ is black then $cell_i$ stores $cell_j$ as a visible region. Notice that $cell_j$ could include several cells of the uniform grid.

- If CC predicate is true and $cell_i$ is white and $cell_j$ is grey then a traversal of the grey node is done and the ComputeVisibility procedure is executed recursively between $cell_i$ and the descendants of the $cell_j$ according to the table 1 criteria. Notice that because the location of the $cell_j$ descendants are known, the new corridors could easily be computed from the previous one and the CSG of the occluders must be updated including the descendant black nodes of $cell_j$ and pruning the tree respect to the node location. Therefore *coherence visibility* is used to speed up the computation of the CSG trees needed to verify the CC predicate.

- If CC predicate is true and $cell_i$ is grey and $cell_j$ is black or grey then a traversal of the grey node is done and the ComputeVisibility procedure is executed recursively from descendants of the $cell_i$ to $cell_j$ according to the table 1 criteria. Moreover, it is possible to apply a coherence visibility principle similar to that exposed in the previous paragraph.

- If the CC predicate is false, it means that $cell_i$ and $cell_j$ are not visible, so it is not necessary to store this result in the graph and it is not necessary to traverse nor the descendants of the $cell_i$ (if it is grey) nor the descendants of $cell_j$ (if it is grey). As $cell_i$ and/or $cell_j$ could include several cells of the uniform grid, it will be necessary to evaluate less times the CC predicate than when it is considered a uniform grid, so a reduction of the complexity of the DVG would be expected.

When the ComputeDVG finishes, inside each white node of the quadtree there is a list of black nodes (regions) it can see, so the DVG has been obtained.

White nodes in the quadtree may be very large and thus induce very unprecise visibility computations for viewers within them. To overcome this, one may choose a certain level of the quad-tree up to which all white nodes are subdivided, only for the purpose of a more precise location of the viewer. The increased complexity causes the need to evaluate more CC predicates, but does not impact the cost of computing each of them, since this is always done with the coarse quadtree. In this sense we speak of a *Multi-Resolution Discrete Visibility Graph*, as more precise location may be used to futher reduce the list of candidates.

Conclusions and Future Work

A method for computing the visibility graph of scenes is given, using a uniform space subdivision scheme. As a consequence, different algorithms for computing the CC predicate are studied concluding that the one involving the dual space is better suited for cell to cell visibility computation. By using an auxiliary quad-tree the computing time of the visibility graph is reduced because one takes advantage of the scene coherence. Moreover, due to the hierarchical nature of the quad-tree, a multi-resolution graph is obtained. At present, we are working on simulating the visibility graph computation algorithm. The obtained so far results allow us to expect good improvements over the non hierarchical algorithm. Nonetheless, more tests should be done to confirm it. On the other hand, using the graph information while doing the walk-through considerably improves the rendering time, as shown in the figure 6, obtained by simulation.

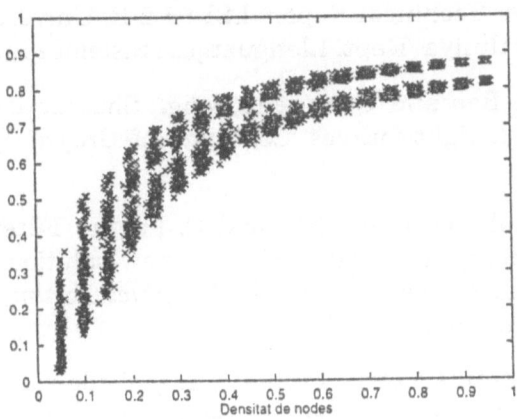

Figure 6: Rendering time improvement depending on the scene density. The x axis represents the scene node density and the y axis the rendering improvement.

All the work has been developed on two dimensional space. It has applications in architectural walk-throughs and traffic simulations, for instance. Future work will include the extension of the algorithms to three dimensional space. Structure will remain the same but computing cell to cell visibility becomes more difficult due to the appearance of quadric surfaces defining the corridor boundary. On the other hand, different algorithms for discretizing the scene will be analyzed.

Acknowledgements

Isabel Navazo thanks Jarek Rossignac, Paul Borrel and the other members of the 3D Graphics and Interactions Department of the I.B.M T.J. Watson Reasearch Center for their ideas, comments and help. This research was funded in part by the Comision Interministerial de Ciencia y Tecnologia (CICYT), under the project TIC-95-0630, and by the DGICYT for supporting the Isabel Navazo stay in the I.B.M. T.J. Watson Research Center in 1994.

References

[AAB+96] C. Andújar, D. Ayala, P. Brunet, R. Joan-Arinyo, and J. Solé. Automatic generation of multiresolution boundary representations. Technical Report LSI-96-2-R, Universitat Politècnica de Catalunya. Dept. Llenguatges i Sistemes Informàtics, 1996.

[BP93]   Hujun Bao and Qunsheng Peng. Shading models for linear and area light sources. *Computers & Graphics*, 17(2):137–146, 1993.

[CDP95]   F. Cazals, G. Drettakis, and C. Puech. Filtering, clustering and hierarchy construction: a new solution for ray-tracing complex scenes. *Computer Graphics Forum*, 14(3):371–382, August 1995.

[DF94]   G. Drettakis and E. Fiume. A fast shadow algorithm for area light sources using backprojection. *Computer Graphics*, pages 223–230, July 1994.

[FS93]   Thomas A. Funkhouser and Carlo H. Séquin. Adaptative display algorithm for interactive frame rates during visualization of complex virtual environments. *Computer Graphics*, pages 247–254, August 1993.

[Gla84]   Andrew S. Glassner. Space subdivision for fast ray tracing. *IEEE Computer Graphics and Applications*, 4(10):15–22, October 1984.

[HT92] Michael E. Hohmeyer and Seth J. Teller. Stabbing isothetic boxes and rectangles in $o(n \log n)$ time. *Computational Geometry: Theory and Applications*, 2(4):201–207, December 1992. COMGEO 133.

[LP79] D.T. Lee and F.P. Preparata. An optimal algorithm for finding the kernel of a polygon. *Journal of the ACM*, 26(3):415–421, July 1979.

[Meg83] Nimrod Megiddo. Linear-time algorithms for linear programming in R^3 and related problems. *SIAM Journal of Computing*, 12(4):759–776, November 1983.

[Mul94] Ketan Mulmuley. *Computational Geometry. An introduction through randomized algorithms*. Prentice-Hall, 1994.

[Nav95] Isabel Navazo. Computing visibility between cells by means of shadow generation. Research report, Departament de Llenguatges i Sistemes Informàtics, 1995.

[NON85] Tomoyuki Nishita, Isao Okamura, and Eihachiro Nakamae. Shading models for point and linear sources. *ACM Transactions on Graphics*, 4(2):124–146, April 1985.

[NV96] Isabel Navazo and Sebastià Vila. Computing visibility by csg null tree detection. Technical report, Departament de Llenguatges i Sistemes Informàtics, 1996.

[PD86] W. H. Plantinga and C. R. Dyer. An algorithm for constructing the aspect graph. In *Proc 6th. ACM Symposium on Foundations of Computer Science*, pages 123–131. 1986.

[RB92] Jarek R. Rossignac and Paul Borrel. Multi-resolution 3d approximations for rendering complex scenes. Technical Report RC 17697 (#77951), IBM Research Division, T.J. Watson Research Center. Yorktown Heights, NY 10598. U.S.A., 1992.

[Sam90] H. Samet. *The Design and Analisys of Spatial Data Structures*. Addison-Wesley, 1990.

[She92] Thomas C. Shermer. Recent results in art galleries. *Proceedings of the IEEE*, 80(9):1384–1399, september 1992.

[SS90] Jörg-Rüdiger Sack and Subhash Suri. An optimal algorithm for detecting weak visibility of a polygon. *IEEE Transactions on Computers*, 39(10):1213–1219, October 1990.

[Tel92]   Sethy J. Teller. Computing the antipenumbra of an area light source. *Computer Graphics*, 26(2):139–148, July 1992.

[TH93]   Seth J. Teller and Pat Hanrahan. Global visibility algorithms for illumination computations. *Computer Graphics*, pages 239–246, August 1993.

[TS91]   Seth J. Teller and Carlo H. Séquin. Visibility preprocessing for interactive walkthroughs. *Computer Graphics*, 25(4):61–69, July 1991.

[VN95]   Sebastià Vila and Isabel Navazo. On the relation between the cell visibility problem and the visibility inside a simple polygon. Research report, Departament de Llenguatges i Sistemes Informatics, 1995.

Index

Springer
and the
environment

At Springer we firmly believe that an international science publisher has a special obligation to the environment, and our corporate policies consistently reflect this conviction.

We also expect our business partners – paper mills, printers, packaging manufacturers, etc. – to commit themselves to using materials and production processes that do not harm the environment. The paper in this book is made from low- or no-chlorine pulp and is acid free, in conformance with international standards for paper permanency.

 Springer